Sophocles, one of the three great tragic playwrights of ancient Athens, was probably born in 496 B.C., in Colonus Hippius. His life intersected with two other greats, Aeschylus and Euripides, and a popular anecdote has Sophocles' first victory in a dramatic competition as one in which he upsets the favorite, the prominent and older Aeschylus. Sophocles continued to rise in popularity and stature, writing more than one hundred plays, only seven of which are now extant. Although of rather humble background and not particularly political, Sophocles was several times elected to high political and military positions. He died in 406 B.C.

Paul Roche, a distinguished English poet and translator, is the author of *The Bible's Greatest Stories*. His other translations include *Aristophanes: The Complete Plays, Euripides: Ten Plays*, *Oedipus Plays of Sophocles*, and *The Orestes Plays of Aeschylus*.

Matthew S. Santirocco is Professor of Classics and Seryl Kushner Dean of the College of Arts and Science at NYU. He has written on Greek and Roman literature and edits the journal *Classical World*.

THE COMPLETE PLAYS

SOPHOCLES

Translated by Paul Roche

With a New Afterword
by Matthew S. Santirocco

SIGNET CLASSICS

SIGNET CLASSICS
Published by New American Library, a division of
Penguin Group (USA) Inc., 375 Hudson Street,
New York, New York 10014, USA
Penguin Group (Canada), 90 Eglinton Avenue East, Suite 700, Toronto,
Ontario M4P 2Y3, Canada (a division of Pearson Penguin Canada Inc.)
Penguin Books Ltd., 80 Strand, London WC2R 0RL, England
Penguin Ireland, 25 St. Stephen's Green, Dublin 2,
Ireland (a division of Penguin Books Ltd.)
Penguin Group (Australia), 250 Camberwell Road, Camberwell, Victoria 3124,
Australia (a division of Pearson Australia Group Pty. Ltd.)
Penguin Books India Pvt. Ltd., 11 Community Centre, Panchsheel Park,
New Delhi - 110 017, India
Penguin Group (NZ), 67 Apollo Drive, Rosedale, North Shore 0632,
New Zealand (a division of Pearson New Zealand Ltd.)
Penguin Books (South Africa) (Pty.) Ltd., 24 Sturdee Avenue,
Rosebank, Johannesburg 2196, South Africa

Penguin Books Ltd., Registered Offices:
80 Strand, London WC2R 0RL, England

Published by Signet Classics, an imprint of New American Library,
a division of Penguin Group (USA) Inc.

First Signet Classics Printing, March 2001
First Signet Classics Printing (Santirocco Afterword), May 2010
10 9 8 7 6 5

Copyright © Paul Roche, 2001
Afterword copyright © Matthew S. Santirocco, 2010
All rights reserved

(Performance rights and permissions can be found on page 441.)

 REGISTERED TRADEMARK—MARCA REGISTRADA

Printed in the United States of America

for
Mitey
(*Cordelia Virginia Clare*)

Contents

Acknowledgments

First of all, to the late Sir Richard Claverhouse Jebb, whose painstaking and responsible prose translations of all Sophocles' plays, though nearly a hundred years old, retain their efficacy. I owe him an enormous debt, but—surprise, surprise—on multiple occasions I found that I was much closer to the Greek.

Next, to Dr. Hugh Lloyd-Jones, whose Greek text in the Loeb Classics I have used for many of the plays. His scrupulously faithful prose translation has steadied me throughout, and if I have made any blunders the fault is entirely mine.

And last, to my editor at Penguin Putnam, Mr. Hugh Rawson, who watched over my endeavors with all the patience and enlightenment of a perspicacious editor.

Introduction

Every generation tends to think of itself as the last and the worst and the best. Meanwhile the disasters of the past and the present, the wars and rumors of wars, the torturings and murders, the ineluctable decimation of the rain forests, keep pace with our fears and our greed. History seems to repeat itself with unflagging zeal, as if to hammer home the lessons we are so reluctant to learn. Indeed, the once popular song "Where Have All the Flowers Gone?" says it all with its plangent refrain: "When will they ever learn? When will they ever learn?"

And yet, and yet, with the dawn of the twenty-first century, perhaps we are learning something. A new consciousness is in the air, a new hope, and a more comprehensive soul is becoming aware that we are all one and that what we do to another we do to ourselves.

How does all this relate to Sophocles and Greek tragedy? It relates because these create the metaphors by which we understand ourselves. Sophocles lived some 2,500 years ago, yet the metaphors he was inspired to invent in his plays—especially *Oedipus*—tell us dramatically what it is like to be a human being, and though the times and the settings are different, these plays are about ourselves.

Knowing this and being made to feel it through the harrowing vicissitudes of Sophocles' heroes and victims is to glimpse the full mortal scene and to find that the mere events of our lives are thereby turned into real experiences. Memory, association, and contrast create the resonances that echo through the halls of the imagination and make tragedy tolerable, sadness sweetened, the ugly beautiful, and whatever happens to us significant. Herein lies the salvific necessity of poetry and the arts, of which one of the most powerful and sublime movers is the works of Sophocles.

PORTRAIT OF SOPHOCLES

We have very little to go on, so the portrait must be drawn from a mélange of provable fact and plausible legend—in any case, a portrait worth trawling for.

He was born at Colonus, a deme just outside Athens, from well-to-do upper-class parents, the date being 496 or 495 B.C., and he died in 406, having lived almost all his life in his beloved Athens.

As a youth he was graced with a comely and athletic body, and he won crowns in both wrestling and music—which assuredly also meant dancing, for he danced naked to the strains of the lyre in the victory procession celebrating the defeat of the Persians in the naval battle of Salamis. Balance and harmony were as much the hallmarks of his soul as they were of his physique. Aristophanes describes him in *The Frogs* as: "A charmer here and a charmer down there."* But he was not simply an elegant and pleasing personage. Several times in his life he held important executive positions either as a military commander or as an arm of the government.

As a playwright he learned much from the illustrious Aeschylus, who was about sixteen years older and whom he defeated at the City Dionysia in Athens in 468 when he was only about twenty-seven. Thereafter he won first prize twenty times and came in second on many occasions. He wrote in all 123 plays, of which we have only 7. His chief rival for the applause of the Athenians was Euripides, younger than he was but never as popular in his lifetime, though more so after the time of Alexander the Great.

It has been said that Sophocles wrote about humanity as it ought to be and Euripides, as it was: the one excelling in the sublime and the majestic, the other in the tender and the pathetic. The story has it that when Soph-

---

*ὁ δ' εὔκολος μὲν ἐνθάδε εὔκολος δ' ἐκεῖ.

ocles heard of the death of Euripides, rivals though they were, he brought on his chorus dressed in mourning.

The language of Sophocles is concentrated, vivid, spirited, and powerful. Cardinal Newman calls it "the sweet composure, the melodious fullness, the majesty and grace of Sophocles." But it was also free, molten, fusile with elements from the lofty poetry of the epic, the strains of the lyre, and the lowly commonplace of the marketplace. He wrote in a Greek never quite heard before, and though it would be too much to say that he remade the language, he certainly revitalized it: taking risks, coining words, inventing grammatical and syntactical constructions, condensing, eliding, twisting figures of speech inside out, and sometimes stretching the elasticity of Greek—that most lively language—to the breaking point. What is magical is that when all is said and done he makes everything sound moderate, simple, and natural.

Translator's Preface

Greek is swift, much faster than English, which is bogged down by consonants, and with its syllabic richness, its athletic grammatical inflections, which free the word order for emphasis and euphony, its shifting affixes of prepositions that can change the whole nuance of a word in the twinkling of an eye, its directness and precision, it achieves the miracle of being simultaneously formal and fluid.

Many years ago in my first attempts to translate Greek drama, I wondered how I could transcribe the iambic trimeter of the Greek, which is a twelve-syllable line set out in two sets of three with a caesura. If read naturally and not with the theoretical quantities imposed on it by grammarians, the line reads with six basic stresses. I saw the pitfall into which translators were stumbling, slapping this into hexameters even though the English hexameter is too slow and not the equivalent.

This made me cast my early translations in the shorter line of iambic pentameter; but I came to realize that pentameter was too much of a straitjacket for the fluidity of the Greek, so I adopted a line I called Compensated Pentameter. In this, the length of the line could vary, so long as the overall count was the same. For instance, if I went into a hexameter I would compensate by making the next line a tetrameter.

This worked fairly well, but though I sprinkled around a goodly smattering of dactyls, anapests, trochees, and spondees, I found the line still too rigid to reflect the limpid fluidity of the Greek. Then I thought: different though English is from Greek, both tongues love iambs. Indeed, iambs are natural to English in verse and prose, though in prose one should not strive for a musical line unless the emotion requires it.

The upshot of all this was that I alighted on what I christened the Freewheeling Iambic, and that is what I use now. The Freewheeling Iambic reads very easily, and I have arranged the lines exactly as they should be spoken.

The meters of the choral parts are another matter. In the *Ajax, Electra, Philoctetes,* and *The Women of Trachis,* I try to get as near as I can to the meters of the original, taking care to make the strophes and antistrophes strictly correspond. When I first approached the Oedipus plays, some forty years ago, I did not attempt this, considering myself too inexperienced. Though the three Oedipus plays were first published in 1958, I have recently revised all three. As to the other four plays, they were translated between 1997 and 1999. The final revision of all seven plays in *Sophocles: The Complete Plays* was concluded in the late summer of the year 2000.

Perhaps I should also say again that my main endeavor in translating is to find out as nearly as possible what the great playwright said and how he said it. This is very different from adapting or paraphrasing in the manner of Robinson Jeffers, Jean Anouilh, Ted Hughes, and Christopher Logue. Such "imitations" have their value and can be masterpieces in their own right (vide Dryden's *Virgil* and Pope's *Homer*), but as scholarly transcriptions of what was actually said and meant, they are virtually useless.

One last point: in some of the newer translations the text is set out like a modern play. This has many advantages, not least of which is that it reads more familiarly to the contemporary eye and ear. It has, however, one drawback: it does away with the formality of the Greek, which is half the reason why these plays are so compelling. The ritual of the various balances—prologue against parados, first episode against first choral lyric, choral dialogue against stichomythia (line by line), the iambic trimeter against the complicated meters of the choral parts—all these balances are abolished.

Even some of the best of the newer translations succumb to these aberrations. Brilliantly idiomatic, they reduce the line-by-line crescendo of feeling in the stichomythia to a shorthand of chatty information, thereby losing the cumulative thrust of lines that appear to be prose but are in fact strictly metrical and stuffed with every prosodic device.

Take for example lines 105 and 106 in the Loeb Classics, where Ajax is answering Athena's question of whether he has captured his hated adversary Odysseus among his victims:

"Yes, the sweetest, sitting inside, dear goddess, neatly trussed up. But I don't want him to die just yet."

Here it is in the Greek.

ἥδιστος, ὦ δέσποινα, δεσμώτης ἔσω
θακεῖ. θανεῖν γὰρ αὐτὸν οὔ τί πω θέλω.

haydistos o despoina desmotays eso
thakay thanayn gar outon oo tee po thelo.

My count in just two lines is nine alliterations, nine assonances, five rhymes.

One may cut through all this, ignore rhythm, cadence, and tone, and write a modern play, but it is not Greek tragedy and it is not Sophocles. It may entertain, but to engender feeling it will have to have this pumped into it by the actor—as Ms. Diana Rigg did a few years ago in a virtuosa performance of the *Medea* in London and New York.

In the Bantam edition of Sophocles containing Sir Richard Jebb's prose translations, the late Moses Hadas—that wisest of scholars—has this to say: "The prose must not be commonplace, as it may be for Euripides; it must communicate the stately remoteness of the original . . . maintaining the high formalism and dignity appropriate to Sophocles."

Failing this, we may indeed be given, as I implied, a brilliant modern play, but it has about as much to do with Greek tragedy as Punch and Judy has to do with Shakespeare.

Dates of Production

Ajax	450–430
Antigone	c. 442
The Women of Trachis	450–430
Oedipus the King	429–425
Electra	420–410
Philoctetes	409
Oedipus at Colonus	401

ΩΤΟΥΣΤΡΑΤΗΓΗΣΑΝΤΟΣΕΝΤΡΟΙΑΠΟΤΕ
ΑΓΑΜΕΜΝΟΝΟΣΠΑΙΝΥΝΕΚΕΙΝΕΞΕΣΤΙΣΟΙ
ΠΑΡΟΝΤΙΛΕΥΣΣΕΙΝΩΝΠΡΟΘΥΜΟΣΗΣΘΑΕΙ
ΤΟΓΑΡΠΑΛΑΙΟΝΑΡΓΟΣΟΥΠΟΘΕΙΣΤΟΔΕ
ΤΗΣΟΙΣΤΡΟΠΛΗΓΟΣΑΛΣΟΣΙΝΑΧΟΥΚΟΡΗΣ
ΑΥΤΗΔΟΡΕΣΤΑΤΟΥΛΥΚΟΚΤΟΝΟΥΘΕΟΥ
ΑΓΟΡΑΛΥΚΕΙΟΣΟΥΞΑΡΙΣΤΕΡΑΣΔΟΔΕ
ΗΡΑΣΟΚΛΕΙΝΟΣΝΑΟΣΟΙΔΙΚΑΝΟΜΕΝ
ΦΑΣΚΕΙΝΜΥΚΗΝΑΣΤΑΣΠΟΛΥΧΡΥΣΟΥΣΟΡΑΝ
ΠΟΛΥΦΘΟΡΟΝΤΕΔΩΜΑΠΕΛΟΠΙΔΩΝΤΟΔΕ
ΟΘΕΝΣΕΠΑΤΡΟΣΕΚΦΟΝΩΝΕΓΩΠΟΤΕ
ΠΡΟΣΣΗΣΟΜΑΙΜΟΥΚΑΙΚΑΣΙΓΝΗΤΗΣΛΑΒΩΝ

What the first twelve lines of the *Electra* would look like
in an early manuscript.

SOPHOCLES

The Complete Plays

AJAX

ΑΙΑΣ

In Greek drama it is not so much the intervention of a god or goddess that is important—which to us seems arbitrary—as the way the protagonists respond to it. And the way that Ajax responds to Athena's darkening of his mind so that in his rage at not being awarded the arms of Achilles he slaughters the camp's cattle reveals a character that surely must have been Leo: swift to act, courageous, impatient, but careless of the effect his words and actions have on others and suicidally proud.

Ajax was second only to Achilles among the Greek leaders at Troy for manliness, bravery, and, I daresay, good looks. He was also selfish, brutish, and stupidly headstrong. Yet the beautiful valedictory speech he gives vent to as he walks towards his own dismissal could almost have been spoken by a Messiah. His very disillusion with himself and the agonizing discovery of his failure as a man make him pathetically forgivable. Indeed, he is forgiven by Sophocles, who grants him final burial—for a Greek, tantamount to the Last Sacraments or a sanctified passage to Hades. That is why the prolonged struggle over his huge dead body is so important.

As for Odysseus, who does not always have a good press—especially in Euripides—he comes across as a balanced and considerate human being who deals wisely and firmly with the predictably inflated Menelaus and his brother Agamemnon.

Tecmessa, the captive Phrygian princess whom Ajax has made his "wife," shows with touching and unwavering loyalty that she loves and cares for him and is filled with a desperate pity.

The goddess Athena, though Sophocles never goes as far as Euripides in showing contempt for the Olympians, manifests a rather callous magnanimity, and the unpleasant way she enjoys watching Ajax make a disastrous fool of himself (which she herself contrived) is hardly calculated to make us like her. Perhaps there is also an element of inverted sexism in her makeup: the thrill of the intransigent and professional virgin bringing down a strapping young male.

Teucer, son of the island king of Salamis and half brother of Ajax, to whom he is devoted, is a pitiably clear-sighted youth who knows he is going to have to face his father's wrath and be accused not only of not having saved his brother but also of having failed to do so with the sinister intention of stealing his inheritance.

As always with Sophocles, the dramatic hero is the vehicle for an alchemy that changes the dross of arrogance and ineptitude into the gold of compassion and self-knowledge. The sadness of the story cannot be abrogated, but it can be overlaid with a message of hope, acceptance, and harmony.

The play was produced between 450 and 430 B.C. at the City Dionysia in Athens, which would place Sophocles squarely in his robust middle age and also belies the belief once held by scholars that the *Ajax* was one of his earliest plays. It is clearly a mature masterpiece.

CHARACTERS

ATHENA, the goddess
ODYSSEUS, king of Ithaca
AJAX, son of Telamon, king of Salamis
CHORUS, of sailors from Salamis
TECMESSA, "wife" of Ajax
SOLDIER, a messenger
TEUCER, half brother of Ajax
MENELAUS, son of Atreus and king of Sparta
AGAMEMNON, son of Atreus and king of Mycenae

MUTES

EURYSACES, young son of Ajax and Tecmessa
ATTENDANTS, including a nurse for Eurysaces
SOLDIERS

TIME AND SETTING

It is morning on the plains of Troy outside the Greek camp. Ajax has just learned that the armor of Achilles (fashioned by Hephaestus) is not to be awarded to him as he expected but to Odysseus. The decision was made by the two commanders, Agamemnon and Menelaus. He is filled with fury and determines to do away with all three, but Athena has mystified his mind into believing that these are the camp's cattle, which he rounds up and slaughters. Odysseus suspects him of the outrage but wants proof. Athena watches him scrutinizing the ground for tracks.

PROLOGUE

ATHENA: There you are, son of Laertes,
   ready as always to grasp a chance of worsting a foe!
So now I see you by the ships
   where Ajax has his camp in the last row,
   lurking near his tent and scanning his fresh footprints
   to see if they show whether he's at home or not.
You have the nose of a Spartan bloodhound
   hot for the trail.
Well, the man this minute has gone inside,
   his face and sword-butchering hands lathered in sweat.
So you won't have to go on prying.
But what makes you so intent?
Tell me, I can enlighten you . . . I know.
ODYSSEUS: Athena, my fondest immortal,
   I do not see you, but your voice rings true,
   as clear as a bronze-throated bugle call,
   right into my soul.
You have guessed correctly.
I am scouting around the tracks of a man I dislike:
   Ajax with his great shield.
He's the suspect I've been trailing and none other,
   because last night he did something shocking beyond
                              belief . . .

if it was indeed he . . . we can't be sure . . . we're
                                                wondering;
and I have volunteered to find out.
We've just discovered all the cattle we took from Troy
    hacked to pieces by some human hand
    together with their herdsmen.
This criminal act, all say, was his.
One of our scouts saw him bounding over the plain
                                                alone,
    his sword reeking, and reported to me—describing
                                                everything.
I raced off on his trail at once.
Some of the tracks are clearly his;
    others I find baffling.
I am so glad you're here.
As in the past, so now,
    I need your guiding hand.
ATHENA: I knew it, Odysseus,
    and set out at once to help you in your hunt.
ODYSSEUS: Dear lady, is there any point in my labors?
ATHENA: Yes . . . he was the man that did it.
ODYSSEUS: Whatever drove such frenzy into his hands?
ATHENA: Rage at not being given Achilles' armor.
ODYSSEUS: But why should that make him lash out at
                                                sheep?
ATHENA: He fancied it was your blood he was dipping
                                                into.
ODYSSEUS: And imagined he was killing Greeks?
ATHENA: Which he would have done had I not been
                                                alert.
ODYSSEUS: How could he be so ruthless and so reckless?
ATHENA: Alone against you and cloaked in darkness.
ODYSSEUS: Did he come anywhere near succeeding?
ATHENA: He was already at the tents of the two
                                                commanders.
ODYSSEUS: So what stopped his brisk hand from murder?
ATHENA: I did.
    I infused his eyes with a criminal fancy
    and switched his frenzy onto the livestock and animals
    with their keepers and not yet distributed.
He hacked the horny tribe to death,

cleaving spines in all directions.
Here it was the two Atreidae
    he thought he'd got in his hands and was killing,
    there, some other general, there that.
As he roved to and fro in these obsessions,
    I fueled his paroxysms, and baited the trap.
Then, exhausted with his efforts,
    he roped the surviving cattle and sheep together
    and paraded them home.
He thought he was leading a batch of men,
    not just animals with horns.
Now they're all bound up in his tent,
    and he's torturing them.
I'll show you openly his insanity,
    and you can describe the sight to all the Greeks.

[*Seeing the look of alarm on* ODYSSEUS' *face*]*

Bear up! Meet the man! Nothing is going to happen.
I'll bamboozle his gaze and he'll not notice you.

[*Turning towards* AJAX' *tent*]

You, there,
    pinning your prisoners' arms behind their backs,
    come on out. I'm calling *you*—yes, you, Ajax,
    come on out before the tent.
ODYSSEUS: What are you doing, Athena? For God's sake
                        don't call him out.
ATHENA: Be quiet. And don't be such a coward.
ODYSSEUS: By all the gods, let him stay inside!
ATHENA: What are you afraid of? He's still only a man.
ODYSSEUS: And still my worst enemy.
ATHENA: Aren't the nicest jokes jokes against one's
                        enemies?
ODYSSEUS: All the same, I'd rather he stayed inside.
ATHENA: Are you afraid of a manifest madman?
ODYSSEUS: I'd face him all right if he were sane.
ATHENA: He won't even see you anywhere near.

---

*Italics within brackets signify stage directions.

ODYSSEUS: He still has the same eyes.

ATHENA: I'll make them dim, be they ever so open.

ODYSSEUS: Well, with gods all is possible.

ATHENA: Keep quiet, then, and stand where you are.

ODYSSEUS: All right, I'll stay, but I'd much rather not.

ATHENA: You there, Ajax, I'm calling you again.
Is this the way to treat a friend?

AJAX: [*coming out of his tent*] Welcome, Athena! Welcome, daughter of Zeus!
You've been so good to me,
and to thank you for this catch
I shall load you with golden spoils.

ATHENA: That's good of you, but tell me this:
have you well and truly dipped your sword
in the Argive army's blood?

AJAX: Nothing less is my boast. I shall not deny it.

ATHENA: And the two sons of Atreus? Get them, too?

AJAX: Never again will they make a fool of Ajax.

ATHENA: The two of them are dead? Am I correct?

AJAX: Dead. Let them cheat me of my armor now.

ATHENA: Well done! . . . Laertes' son? What of him?
Did he give you the slip?

AJAX: Ah, the crafty fox! Do you mean him?

ATHENA: I do: Odysseus, your adversary.

AJAX: Yes, the sweetest: sitting inside, dear lady, neatly
trussed up. But I don't want him to die just yet.

ATHENA: Until you have done . . . ? What's your
pleasure?

AJAX: Until I have lashed him to a post inside my tent
and . . .

ATHENA: Done something horrible to the poor man?

AJAX: Blooded his back with my whip. Then he dies.

ATHENA: You shouldn't torture the wretched man.

AJAX: Please yourself, Athena, in everything else, but
not this:
he has to take what's coming to him.

ATHENA: If that's your pleasure, get on with it.
Don't leave out a single item.

AJAX: And so to work! But remember this:
be at my side always as now you are.

[AJAX *goes into his tent as* ODYSSEUS *steps forward*]

ATHENA: Do you note. Odysseus, the power of the gods?
   Was there ever a more resourceful man once than
                                              this?
   One equal to any occasion?
ODYSSEUS: I know of none. And yet I pity him,
   against me though he is.
For he is shackled to a dreadful end.
His fate makes me think of my own.
I see that our lives are nothing but illusion:
   fugitive shades.
ATHENA: Seeing this is so,
   let no haughty word against the gods escape your lips,
   nor be puffed up if you excel another
   in prowess or material gain.
A single day can level down or level up
   every human enterprise.
Heaven loves the wise of heart
   and with the arrogant will have no part.
   [ATHENA *fades from view and* ODYSSEUS *leaves*]

PARADOS OR ENTRY MARCH

[*The* CHORUS *of* AJAX' *sailors from Salamis enters in a
slow march, chanting. They show sympathy with their
master, reluctant to believe he could have perpetrated
the rumored outrage. If he did, some god must have
stolen his wits. They beg* AJAX *to come out in the open
and prove himself.*]

Son of Telamon, Ajax,
   from the sea-splashed pedestal
Of Salamis, when you do well
   I celebrate, but not
When you are hit by Zeus
   and the gossipy tongues of the Greeks
Let hideous rumors fly;
   then I am anxious, alarmed:
   Like a dove with frightened eye.

As to last night, there are startling
  reports that disgrace us, saying
You entered the animals' paddocks
  and slaughtered the beasts, the booty
Won by the Grecian spear
  but not yet shared among all,
Butchering them with a flashing sword.
Such are the calumnies whispered
  by Odysseus, breathing them into
All-too-willing ears.
  A plausible tale he tells,
And everyone who hears it
  enjoys the hearing more
Than the teller of the tale,
  crowing over you.
That's the way it is:
  if you aim your arrows
At a noble spirit, you won't
  miss, but if at me
Anyone aimed such slanders
  he wouldn't be believed.
It is the one who has
  that envy stalks. And yet
Little men without
  the great, do not suffice
To guard the walls; it needs
  little and great together
  The great being helped out by the little.

The shallow refuse to listen,
  like those inveighing against you.
Without you, our king,
  we have no way to stop
The things they charge against you:
  unchallenged by your eye
They go twittering
  like a flock of birds.
But should you suddenly show
  they would huddle petrified:
  Mute before the glorious eagle.

[*At this point the meter and music change, and the prosody goes into strophe strictly balanced by antistrophe.*] [see below*]

STROPHE

Was it Taurópola Artemis, Zeus's daughter
  (Oh, ineluctable rumor
  mothering my discomfort)
That impelled him against our army's cattle?
In revenge perhaps for not having offered her tribute
  For some military triumph,
Thus dispossessing her of some substantial booty?
Or was it for not giving a gift after shooting a deer?
Or was mail-clad Mars in a temper for not being
                            thanked,
Who so concocted the outrage?

ANTISTROPHE

You would have been out of your mind, O Telamon's
                            son,
  To wander so far astray
  As to pounce upon the flocks.
It must have been some giddiness sent from heaven.
May Zeus and Phoebus Apollo undo this Argive rumor,
  And if the two mighty kings,
With that despicable Ulysses, are trumping up charges
And broadcasting fraudulent nonsense, please do not,
Do not, my king, stay closeted in your tent by the sea
  Earning a scandalous name.

EPODE

Get up from where you are sitting
In the long respite from battle,
Letting a bonfire of destruction flare to heaven
And the insolence of your foes go blazing
Unchecked through the windy glades;
And the babble of tongues runs riot

---

*In English usage single syllable words ending in s double the s for the possessive case. Hence St. James's Park, not St. James' Park.

In a nasty way, leaving me
In constant pain.

[TECMESSA *emerges from* AJAX' *tent, distraught*]

CHORAL DIALOGUE

TECMESSA: Sailors of Ajax' ship and descended
From that Eretheus who sprang from the earth,
We are swamped with grief for a faraway house
For Ajax our mighty and awesome lord
With all his rugged strength lies shaken
With a storm in his soul.
CHORUS: What disastrous change since yesterday
Happened last night?
Child of Phrygian Teleutas, tell us:
You the war-won bride that valiant Ajax
Has embraced and cares for,
Give us a hint of what has happened.
TECMESSA: A tale too awful to tell—how can I tell it?
Worse than death is what you will hear.
During the night our wonderful Ajax
Was hit with madness and went berserk.
You will see the proof of it in the tent:
Holocausts dripping with gore by his hand.
A sinister omen of what is to follow.

STROPHE

CHORUS: What is this news you have of this man, this
hero:
Untellable news with no outlet from telling,
Which the miserable Greeks have reported and fanned
into rumor?
I tremble at what is to come.
The public disgrace is enough to kill him:
The somber sword in his frenzied hand
Slaughtering the herds
And grooms with their horses.
TECMESSA: [*pointing to the meadows*] From there, from
there he hurried in
Ushering the flocks all roped, then some

He felled straightaway right on the floor
Then the remainder he sundered apart
Hacking their flanks. Two white-footed rams:
He sliced off the head of one, then its protruding
Tongue, and tossed these away; but the other
He bound, standing it upright against a pillar
And with a hefty strap for tethering horses
Flogged it and flogged it with whistling lashes
All the time screaming such obscenities
As no mortal, only a god,
Could ever have taught him.

ANTISTROPHE

CHORUS: The moment has come to hide my face and
slink
    Away, or squat on the bench of oars and swiftly row
    Heading the ship out to sea, because of the threats
    The two kingly sons
    Of Atreus are now hurling against us.
I want no part in the horror and pain
    Of stoning beside this man who is gripped
    By an inexorable fate.
TECMESSA: Not any longer, for
    like a breeze from the south
    When the searing lightning ceases
    his fury abates,
    But in his right mind a new
    torment hits him:
    To gaze on the harm he has done and to know
    That no one but he
    had a hand in it.
This pierces his soul with the bitterest spasm.

FIRST EPISODE

CHORUS: If the fury has left him, there is surely hope
    that all may yet be well.
The horror of events has dwindled.
TECMESSA: If you had the choice, which would you prefer:

to pain your friends but yourself be happy,
or take their pain upon yourself?

CHORUS: A double unhappiness, my lady, is the greater
curse.

TECMESSA: So now, his sickness is over but not our pain.

CHORUS: By which you mean? . . . I do not follow.

TECMESSA: At the height of his frenzy
he enjoyed the crises of his obsessions,
though to us who were sane his very presence was an
ordeal.

But now in the respite
when his malady has lifted,
he is racked with every kind of remorse,
and we are equally in pain, no less than before.

Is this not a double
in place of a single agony?

CHORUS: I agree, and I cannot help but think a god has
struck him;
otherwise why, when the plague is over,
is he no happier than when it lasted?

TECMESSA: Things being as they are, you need to be told
why.

CHORUS: Yes, how did the trouble start?
Tell us who share your distress what happened.

TECMESSA: You shall know the whole thing,
for you are part of it.

At the dead of night, with the night lights out,
he took his two-edged sword
and made as if to go on some unknown errand.

When I protested, saying:
"What are you doing, Ajax?
No herald has summoned you, no bugle sounded.
What is the point of this unasked sally?"

His answer was curt—the usual put-down:
"Wife, women are beautiful when they keep their
mouths shut."

Schooled so, I held my tongue, and he charged off alone.
What happened outside, I cannot tell you,
but he came back with a pack of bulls, sheepdogs,
captive sheep
all roped together.

Some he beheaded,
    others he stood upside down and cut their throats or
                            smashed their spines.
Still others he tied up and tortured.
He attacked the animals as if they were men.
Finally he dashed through the door
    barking out remarks to a shadow
    and reviling sometimes the Sons of Atreus, sometimes
                            Odysseus,
    laughing wildly at the thought of the damage he had
                         done in his raid.
Then he bundled back into the tent,
    where gradually and painfully he came to his senses.
Casting his eyes at the shambles in the tent,
    he battered his head and uttered a horrible shout,
    then collapsed among the prostrate carcasses of butch-
                       ered sheep.
There he squatted, clenching his fists and tearing his
                       hair.
He sat for a long time without saying a word,
    then he began to threaten me
    unless I recounted the whole grisly affair,
    demanding to know exactly where he stood.*
I was terrified, my friends,
    and told him all that had happened, as best I could.
Immediately he broke down in loud sobs
    such as I had never heard from him before;
    for he always used to say that no real man,
    only the craven and cowardly, cried.
But his crying was a deep bellow like a wounded bull.
Floored by the disaster,
    without food or drink, he now sits where he collapsed
    in a welter of sword-slashed beasts.
He is obviously contemplating some terrible act,
    which his words of remorse prefigure.*
Dear friends, go inside and help me if you can.
People in his condition can be swayed by the words of
                       friends.

CHORUS: Tecmessa, daughter of Teleutas,

*A line bracketed as dubious by some scholars.

the anguish you describe that besets this man
is truly terrible.

AJAX: [*from within the tent*] A . . . h!

TECMESSA: Soon he's likely to be worse.
You heard that shattering cry? It was Ajax.

AJAX: It's the end!

CHORUS: It seems the man is either sick
or sickened by his recent conduct.

AJAX: My son! My son!

TECMESSA: Dear God! He's calling for you, Eurysaces.
What does he intend . . . Where are you? . . . I'm at a
loss.

AJAX: It's Teucer I'm calling. Where is Teucer?
Is that raid of his going on forever—while I'm dying?

CHORUS: The man's come to his senses, it seems.
Hullo there, open up!
Perhaps the sight of me will sober him.

TECMESSA: Look, I'm opening.
You can see what he's done and the state he's in.

[TECMESSA *opens the entrance to the tent, revealing*
AJAX *sitting motionless among the slaughtered animals*]

CHORAL DIALOGUE

STROPHE I

AJAX: Good sailors, you my only friends, the only ones
Still loyal to me,
See what giant wave a deadly swell
has thrown swirling around me!

CHORUS: [*to* TECMESSA] What you described is all too
true.
It clearly shows an unhinged mind.

ANTISTROPHE I

AJAX: You tribe of skillful seamen who embarked with
me
To row the main,
You are my only helpers left.
Come, fell me with the cattle.

CHORUS: Mind what you say. Do not heal hurt with hurt
or make the remedy worse than the disease.

STROPHE II

AJAX: But I the bold, the stalwart, the fearless
   In battle, have excelled myself—do you see?—
Grappling with innocent beasts. Oh the shame!
A laughingstock! What a disgrace I have suffered!

TECMESSA: Ajax, my lord, I beg you, do not say these
                                                things.

AJAX: Away with you, go! The shame! The shame!

TECMESSA: For the love of the gods, listen and be
                                          reasonable!

AJAX: What a wretch I am, letting damnable people
   Slip through my grasp and smiting instead
   Horned oxen and goodly herds,
   Spilling black blood!

CHORUS: What use is regret for what can't be undone?
Nothing can be what it is not.

ANTISTROPHE II

AJAX: And you who miss not a thing, you tool
   Of every crime, yes, you Laertes' son,
   Foulest rascal in the army,
   How you must be laughing in your cups!

CHORUS: To laugh or cry is at the gods' disposal.

AJAX: If I could only see him, shattered though I am . . .
                                          A . . . h!

CHORUS: What presumption! Don't you see the state you
                                          are in?

AJAX: O Zeus, source of my fathers,
   If only death could wreck that most designing
   Cheat of them all whom I detest,
   As well as the two brother kings . . .
   Then die myself!

TECMESSA: When you make that prayer, pray that I die
                                                too.

Why should I live when you are dead?

STROPHE III

AJAX: Darkness that is my light,

Hell's gloom that I find bright,
Take me, take me to live with you,
I am no longer fit to behold the gods
Nor mortal men with any grace.
The daughter of Zeus, that strong goddess,
Is torturing me to death.
Where can I flee,
Where find shelter?
If the fame of my past is gone, my friends,
As gone as these slaughtered beasts
And I have chosen
A foolish quarry to hunt,
Let the whole army with lifted swords
Strike me dead.

TECMESSA: What a tragedy to hear a strong man say such
things:

words that never passed his lips before!

ANTISTROPHE III

AJAX: Good-bye, you tracts of sea
Surging by coves on the shore:
The endless, endless days you kept me
In the purlieus of Troy; but now no longer,
No longer shall I deign to breathe . . .
Of that let everyone be assured.
Scamander, nearby river,
So kind to Greeks,
You'll never see
In the whole army that came to Troy from Hellas
(If I may make a mighty boast)
Another man
Who compares with me
Yet here I lie disgraced
Prostrate in shame.

SECOND EPISODE

CHORUS: Whether to let you speak or keep quiet—I'm
at a loss—
so great is your ideal.

AJAX: Ah, who would have guessed my name should shape
my doom?*
How fitting, then, that I should cry "Aias, Aias, Aias,"
a triple time to match my doom!
I whose father came home
back from the land of Ida full of glory,
with the army's greatest prize for valor,
but I his son
coming to the same Troy with no less a force
and showing no less magnificence in action,
languish here, a disgrace to the Greeks.
Yet this I think I know:
if Achilles were alive and awarded the prize for valor
in a contest for his armor,
nobody but I would win it.
As it is, the Sons of Atreus
have willed them to a criminal
and set at naught this man's mighty deeds.
Had these eyes of mine and this twisted mind
not bolted from my senses,
they would never have voted to cheat another man.
But as things stand,
Zeus's intractable fire-eyed daughter
has undermined me and cast a spell of madness on me
just as I was about to challenge them,
and I have besmirched my hand with the blood of
these pathetic beasts.
Meanwhile, the gloating villains have gone scot-free,
though I am not to blame.
If a god is out to hurt
even a coward can outdo a man of courage.

So what am I to do:
manifestly hated by the gods,
loathed by the whole Greek armada,
hateful too to Troy and these very plains?
Shall I cross the Aegean Sea,
abandon the ships and harbor,
leave the Atreidae in the lurch and go home:

Aiai in Greek means "Alas!" and *Aias* means Ajax.

there to face my father, Telamon—but how?
How will he bear to look at me,
    empty-handed, devoid of the glory
    that won him a crown of fame?
It is unthinkable.
Well, then, shall I stand beneath the walls of Troy,
    challenge the lot of them to duels,
    distinguish myself, and perish in the action?
Not that:
    it would please the Atreidae.
I must think of some doughty deed
    that proves to my father his son was not a coward.
When a man finds no respite from sorrows,
    it is beneath his dignity to cling to life.
What joy is there, from day to day,
    taking one step forward and one step back—from
                                                dying?
I despise a man fueled by inflated hopes.
To live and die well is the only way . . .
You have heard all I have to say.
CHORUS: Nobody, Ajax, can assert
    that these words of yours are not your own—
    spoken from the heart.
But yield for once and let the ones who love you
    guide your judgment.
Let go these thoughts.
TECMESSA: There is no greater hardship for mankind
    than a fate imposed on them by force.
I was the daughter of a freeborn father,
    richer than the richest Phrygian,
    and now I am a slave:
    such by the will of the gods and your strong arm.
Therefore, since I have come to share your bed,
    your welfare is mine.
So by the Zeus of our hearth I beg you, and by our bed,
    do not condemn me to the incriminations of those
                                                who hate you;
    do not toss me aside for one of them.
For make no mistake,
    the day you are no more and desert me by dying,
    I shall be seized by the Argives with your son

and suffer the indignity of a slave.
Then one or other of my owners
   will scoff at me:
"Look at Ajax' concubine,
   the army's mightiest man.
Observe her servitude,
   she who was so elite."
So will he jeer,
   And I, I shall be anchored to my fate.
   You too and your family will be shamed.
Think of your father,
   whom in his dismal old age you will desert,
   and of your mother—whose years are lengthening,
   and who often prays to the gods
   that you'll come home alive.
And, my king, pity your son.
Think of the rending sadness you will bequeath to him
                                    and me by dying.

Losing you,
   he will be cheated of your cherishing care
   and live under the thumb of loveless guardians.
There is nobody I can look to but you.
You raped my land by the spear.
Another destiny took my mother and father down to
                                             Hades.
What country, what resources can there be for me but
                                             you?
My whole well-being rests on you.
Think of me, too, in this:
   a man should cherish any act that gave him pleasure.
Kindness engenders kindness still,
   which if a man forgets
   he is no longer honorable.
CHORUS: Ajax, would that pity touched your heart as it
                                        touches mine,
   you would then appreciate her words.
AJAX: Appreciation she shall have,
   if she will be brave enough to do what I say.
TECMESSA: Ajax, my beloved, I shall obey in all things.
AJAX: Then bring me my son. I wish to see him.
TECMESSA: Why? . . . I was afraid and sent him away.

AJAX: The danger from my insanity, you mean?

TECMESSA: Yes, in case the poor boy met you and was killed.

AJAX: That would have been quite in keeping with my fate.

TECMESSA: At least I guarded him from that catastrophe.

AJAX: I applaud your action and the foresight you showed.

TECMESSA: And now how can I serve you as things stand?

AJAX: Let me speak to him and see him face-to-face.

TECMESSA: Why, yes, he's near, in the charge of servants.

AJAX: Then I need not be waiting for him, need I?

TECMESSA: [calling] Son, your father's asking for you. . . . Servants, whoever is looking after him, bring him here.

AJAX: [impatiently] Well, is the man coming, or hasn't he heard?

TECMESSA: He's on his way, bringing him.

[A servant ushers in EURYSACES, a boy of about three]

AJAX: [opening his arms] Lift him up, lift him here: he won't be frightened at the sight of fresh blood if he's a true son of mine.

[Turning to TECMESSA]

You must begin to break him in to the toughness of his father
and mold his character to mine.

[Holding EURYSACES in his arms]

Dear boy, may you prove luckier than your father
but be like him in all else.
You'll be no milksop then.
I envy your innocence—
oblivious of our tragedy.
Ah, life is at its sweetest
before one has to grapple with pleasure or pain!
When you come to that you must show your enemies

the mettle of the father's son you are.
Till then, let gentle breezes nourish you
and nurture your young life:
so may you be a comfort to your mother.
I am sure no Greek,
even without me by your side, will dare molest you;
for I shall leave a fearless bodyguard to ward you as
you grow—
Teucer, though at the moment he is out raiding.

[*Turning to the* SOLDIERS *and* SAILORS]

You warriors and you men of the sea,
with my gratitude I lay on you this charge:
to let Teucer know my will—
that he conduct this boy to my home
and deliver him to Telamon and my mother, Eriboea:
to be a lasting consolation to them in old age
till their time to go to Hades comes.
As to my armor,
there is to be no contest for it set up by the Greeks,
and certainly not by the one who ruined me.*

[*He beckons to a* SERVANT *to bring his shield*]

No, my boy.
Take this thing, the thing that gives you your name
Eurysaces.†
You hold and wield it by its strong leather thong—
my spear-proof shield made from seven hides.
The rest of my armor shall be buried in my grave.

[*He hands* EURYSACES *to* TECMESSA]

There's to be no lingering.
Just take the boy and bar the doors . . .
No tears either outside my tent

---

*Odysseus, who accepted the arms of Achilles from Agamemnon
and Menelaus when Ajax expected them.
†*Eurysakēs* means broad-shield.

—what weepers you women are!—
Go, shut the entrances at once . . .*
No physician is so naif
  as to chant over injuries that need the knife.
CHORUS: This eagerness alarms me.
Your sharp injunctions do not reassure me.
TECMESSA: My lord, Ajax, what do you have in mind?
AJAX: Do not ask. Do not probe.
Discretion is a virtue.
TECMESSA: My heart is breaking.
By all the gods, I beg you for your own son's sake
  do not desert us.
AJAX: You vex me.
Don't you understand that my service to the gods is
                      done?
TECMESSA: Do not say such things!
AJAX: Go, sound off to those who'll listen.
TECMESSA: And you're not one of them?
AJAX: You've said too much already.
TECMESSA: Because, my king, I am terrified.
AJAX: [*turning to attendants*] Why aren't the entrances
                      closed off at once?
TECMESSA: [*falling on her knees*] For the gods' sakes,
                      please!
AJAX: A bit late in the day to change my character now!

[AJAX *strides into the tent.* TECMESSA *hands* EURYSACES
to a nurse and limply follows]

CHORAL ODE

[*The sailors of the* CHORUS *review* AJAX' *condition and
lament his mysterious deterioration*]

STROPHE I

Famous Salamis lapped by the sea
  Blessed by the gods, forever a vision,
  I'm the unlucky one lingering here,

*It seems likely that Ajax' first intention was to commit suicide
inside his tent.

Camping out month after month
In the grassy prairies of Ida and worn out
By the passage of time
Which only the bleak
End in view of descending down to sinister Hades.

ANTISTROPHE I

And I must cope with the difficult task
   Of living with Ajax—possessed by a god.
Mighty once he sallied forth
   Strong as a warrior, but now changed.
He nurses his solitary thoughts till we his friends
   Grieve for him
   And his brilliant past.
He is not liked by the most unlikable sons of Atreus.

STROPHE II

Surely his mother in her old age
   White with the years, when she hears he is sick
   With the collapse of his senses
   Will hardly refrain from
   Raising her voice in deep lamentation
   Like that piteous bird the nightingale
   Shrill in the plangent trill
   Of a dirge, with the thud of her hands
   Beating her breast and tearing her hair.

ANTISTROPHE II

Surely it's better when hopelessly sick
   To be buried in Hades, for he the noblest
   Of the battle-tested Greeks
   Is no longer true
   To his nature but lost in alien fancies.
Desolate father—to bear the wreck of your son—
   Something you still have to hear—
   A spell that none of the scions
   Of Aeacus has ever engendered.

THIRD EPISODE

[AJAX *comes out of his tent with drawn sword, followed by* TECMESSA]

AJAX: The long uncountable years drag truth from the
                                                darkness,
  then bury it from vision.
Nothing is a surprise—nothing:
  the unbreakable oath is broken,
  so too the obstinate will.
Look at me:
  once hard as smelted steel,
  now melted by this woman,
  and filled with regrets at leaving her a widow.
  with an orphaned boy a prey to enemies.

I shall go to the meadows by the shore and wash,
  to purge away my taint
  and escape the crippling anger of the goddess.
Then I shall look for some untrodden spot
  and bury this sword of mine—the cruelest of weapons—
  in a hole I'll dig that none shall see.
There let night and Hades keep it buried.
For since I took this gift from Hector,
  my deadliest enemy, nothing good among the Argives
  has happened to me.
How true the saying is:
  gifts from enemies are no gifts at all and profit
                                                nothing.
From now onwards let us yield to the gods
  and learn to respect the Sons of Atreus.
They are in command, so we must bow to them. How
                                                otherwise?
Why even the strongest and most indomitable of things
  have a season for bowing.
Winter's snow and blizzards
  give way to fruitful summer
  and the taut sphere of intransigent night
  dissolves before the white coursers of day bring in the
                                                light;
  and the wild blasts of wind-bursts dwindle
  over an encalming sea.
Even Sleep the all-powerful
  lets go and unlooses those he has bound
  and does not keep them imprisoned forever.

Surely, then, we must learn to show some balance.
I for one shall, having lately learned
    that the enemy we hate today will be our friend
        tomorrow,
    just as the one we help today
    may one day be our friend no longer:
    because for most mortals friendship is elusive.

[*Turning to* TECMESSA]

For the rest, all shall be well.
Now go inside, my wife,
    and pray to the gods to fulfill my heart's desires.

[TECMESSA *leaves and* AJAX *addresses the* CHORUS *of sailors*]

You my comrades,
    respect my commands as truly as she does,
    and tell Teucer when he comes
    to concern himself with my affairs and be loyal to you.
For I must go to where I must and you must do my
        bidding.
Perhaps you'll come to know
    that though I'm unlucky now, I have come through.

CHORAL ODE

[*The sailors of the* CHORUS *prepare to celebrate* AJAX' *change of heart, unaware of what he really intends*]

STROPHE

I'm thrilling with ecstasy shot with love:
    Yahoo! Yahoo! O Pan, Pan!
Yes, Pan, over the sea
    Come to us from the craggy peaks
    Of Cyllene drifted in snow, you
    Choreographer of the deities' dances.
Trip with me to the measures
    You taught yourself from Gnossus and Nysa.
I'm longing to dance; and may Apollo,

Lord of Delos, come over the sea—
The Icarian Sea—and be with me
As kind as ever.

ANTISTROPHE

The war-god has lifted the dread
    From my eyes—Yahoo!—and now once more
O Zeus, yes, now, let glittering day
Shine on the swift seagoing ships,
Now that Ajax has turned his back
On his ordeal and means to follow
The laws of the gods and fulfill them
With reverence, rite, and sacrifice.
In Time, the majestic, all things fade:
    Nothing's beyond belief, I'd say:
    Like Ajax forgetting his anger
    Against the Atreidae.

FOURTH EPISODE

[A SOLDIER *hurries in with news*]

SOLDIER: Men, friends, my main news is that Teucer's
                                                    here
    back from the hills of Mysia.
When he had reached headquarters in midcamp
    he was immediately reviled by all the Argives in one
                                                    body.
They saw him coming from a long way off
    and thronged around him in a circle,
    jeering at him from every direction.
"You're the brother of that maniac," they called,
    "that underminer of the Greek armada,"
    whom they swore they would not be satisfied with till
                                        he was dead—
    pounded to pulp with stones.
It came to swords being drawn and swung,
    till at the height of the squabble the elders had to cool
                                        things down.
But tell me where Ajax is so I can let him know.
My news is vital

and he's the one it most concerns.

CHORUS: He's not inside; he's just gone off
with a new purpose matching a new mind.

SOLDIER: Great heavens! Then the one who sent me on
this mission
sent me too late, or else I must have been too slow.

CHORUS: Too late for what? . . . What's going on?

SOLDIER: Teucer said that Ajax mustn't leave his quarters
till he himself arrived.

CHORUS: Well, he's gone: resolved on a wiser course,
to make his peace with the gods he was so angry with.

SOLDIER: Arrant folly! if Calchas' prophecy is sound.

CHORUS: What prophecy? What details do you bring?

SOLDIER: This much I know, for I was there.
Leaving the circle of the generals,
Calchas moved away from the Atreidae
and taking Teucer warmly by the hand
charged him at all costs to keep Ajax in his tent
for that entire day and not to let him stir—
if he ever wished to see him alive again.
"The anger of divine Athena," Calchas said,
will pursue him only for today."
He went on to explain
that when men's lives are swollen with hubris
they are toppled down by some disaster sent from
heaven:
so much for human nature devoid of humane thought!
"Ajax, even before he first left home
gave an inkling of his foolishness when his father wisely
said:
'My son, court success in war,
but success only with the help of heaven.'
To which he boastfully and stupidly replied:
'Father, a mere nobody can triumph with the help of
heaven,
but I expect to achieve that glory even without.'
Yes, that was his arrogant pretension.
Then later, when divine Athena was urging him on
and encouraging him in his bloody stand against the
enemy,
he came out with something unspeakably impudent:

'Queen, go and help the other Argives,
    I don't need propping up in battle!'
This sally earned him
    the unremitting anger of the goddess:
    all because of his superhuman pride.
If he can outlive this day, however,
    perhaps with the gods' help we can save him."

Such was the gist of the seer's speech,
    and Teucer rose at once
    to dispatch me with these orders.
If we are too late,
    that man no longer lives or Calchas is no prophet.
CHORUS: [*calling into the tent*] Unhappy Tecmessa, born
                                          to tragedy,
    come and hear the news this fellow brings . . .
The razor shaves too close for comfort!
TECMESSA: [*emerging from the tent, carrying* EURYSACES]
Why have you got me up
    just when I was having some respite from horror?
CHORUS: Hear this man: he's come with news of Ajax—
                                          most disturbing!
TECMESSA: Oh, no! What is it, my man? . . . Something
                                          shattering?
SOLDIER: As to its being "news," madam, I couldn't
                                          rightly say.
It's just that if Ajax is abroad, I'm sorely worried.
TECMESSA: He *is* abroad. I'm shaken by what you may
                                          imply.
SOLDIER: Teucer's injunctions were explicit:
    to keep him in the haven of his tent
    and not let him out alone.
TECMESSA: Where is Teucer? What makes him say this?
SOLDIER: He's just come back.
He's worried Ajax' sortie may spell his end.
TECMESSA: Dear God! . . . From whom did he get this
                                          news?
SOLDIER: From the seer, Thestor's son.
Today's a matter of life or death for Ajax.
TECMESSA: Dear friends, defend me from the danger that
                                          threatens.

Some of you go and fetch Teucer quickly here.
Others go to the western and the eastern bays
  and find out which way the doomed man went.
I see he has tricked me:
  expelled me from the confidence I once enjoyed.
I'm at a loss . . . What shall I do, child? . . .
We can't just sit here.
I'm going, too—as far as I can.
This is no time for dawdling
  if we are to save a man intent on dying.
CHORUS: I am ready, and not just with words.
Swift action is the thing.

[TECMESSA *hands* EURYSACES *to a nurse and hurries off
with one half of the* CHORUS. *The other half goes in a
different direction towards the coast. There is a pause
while the scene changes to a remote spot on the shore,
where* AJAX *is seen fixing his sword in the ground with
the blade pointing upwards.*]

FIFTH EPISODE

AJAX: The killer sword is sharply tilted for his work—
  if one had but the leisure to admire it!
It was a gift from Hector,
  though I hated him, the very sight of him.
Now it's fixed in this alien earth of Troy,
  all newly honed to a biting edge.
I have planted it with maximum precision,
  so let it treat me to a quick demise.

[*He stands looking at the sword*]

Well, I've done my part.
The next is yours, great Zeus, as is right and proper.
  Do me a favor—it's not too much to ask—
  send a messenger with the sad news to Teucer
  so that he'll be the first to raise me from the dripping
                                                        sword

where I have fallen, and I not be discovered
by some enemy who'll throw me to the dogs and
vultures.
This much, O Zeus, I beg of you.
And I call on you, Hermes, too,
who escorts men to the underworld,
to lull me to a gentle sleep and with no writhing:
just one quick leap as I drive the sword into my side.
And you everlasting maidens, I ask your help,
you who never cease to overseer the woes of mortals,
you awesome and long-striding Furies.
Please bear witness that my life was wrecked
by the Sons of Atreus.
[Grab the two of them
and requite them with destruction equal to their own:
swamp them with ruin when they see my death by my
own hand
and let them die by *their* own hands
through their darling children.]*
Go to it, you speedy avenging Furies;
don't stint your appetite—glut it on the whole armada.
And you, the sun-god,
who drive your chariot through high heaven:
when you gaze down on my native land,
rein in your golden reins
and announce my tragedy and death to my old father
and the unhappy one who nurtured me . . .
Poor mother, when she hears the news!
Her wail of lamentation will echo through the city.
But how useless mourning is!
Now for the final act, as quickly as I can.
[Death, Death, cast your eyes on me—
we'll have converse when we meet.
Meanwhile, light of this bright day
and you high-riding sun,
I address you for the last time and never again]*
Sweet daylight and holy soil of my own Salamis,
pedestal of my natal hearth,
and you, resplendent Athens with your race,

*Bracketed as doubtful.

and springs and rivers here on the plains of Troy,
I salute you all, you have sustained me.
These are the last words of Ajax to you;
the rest will be to those in Hades down below.

[AJAX *falls on his sword. Meanwhile the sailors of the* CHORUS *in two groups are seen approaching the strand.*]

CHORAL COLLOQUY

CHORUS GROUP I: Toil and trouble! Toil and trouble!
Where, where,
Where have I not yet been?
There is no spot where I have not
Been drawn to search . . .
Listen! Look! I hear a bang.
GROUP II: It's your fellow sailors.
GROUP I: How goes it, comrades?
GROUP II: We've ransacked the whole western side of the
fleet.
GROUP I: And you have found . . . ?
GROUP II: Absolutely nothing but trouble.
GROUP I: And there's no sign, either, of the man
along the path hit by the morning sun.

STROPHE
WHOLE CHORUS: Oh, for a clue from some sedulous
fisherman
Toiling sleeplessly for a catch,
Or a nymph from the Olympian heights
Or even a Bosporus river
To spot the maniac
Wherever he's rambling and summon us there!
It's hard that I, professional wanderer,
Cannot come on his tracks and fail to discover
Where the sick man is.

[*A wail of anguish is heard from the direction in which* AJAX *killed himself*]

TECMESSA: A . . . h!

CHORUS: Whose cry was that coming from the depths of
thickets?

TECMESSA: [*reeling into vision*] I am destroyed.

CHORUS: Look, the desperate war-won bride, Tecmessa,
steeped in the agony of that cry.

TECMESSA: I am no more, lost, my friends, I am finished.

CHORUS: What is it?

TECMESSA: Our Ajax lies just now slain:
his body a sheath for the sword that lies buried in him.

CHORUS: Oh, then there's no return?
No coming home for me, my king:
You have killed your seaman fellow.
Poor brokenhearted lady!

TECMESSA: So it is with him and the grief is ours.

CHORUS: Unhappy man! By whose hand was it done?

TECMESSA: By his own, for one can tell:
the sword planted in the ground is proof.

CHORUS: Curse my purblind shallowness:
Bereft of friends, alone,
You fell in your blood while I
Was deaf to it all—a clueless dunce.
But where, where does Ajax lie—
That intractable man of ominous name?

TECMESSA: No eye shall look on him, none.
In this shroud I shall wrap him.
No one who loved him could endure the sight
of blood oozing from his nostrils and the black gore
from the deadly gash of his self-slaughter.
A . . . h! What shall I do?
Who, what friend shall raise you? . . . Where is Teucer?
If only he would be here
to dress the body of his brother!
Most tragic Ajax:
What a man and what an end!
Mourning becomes him even by enemies.

ANTISTROPHE

CHORUS: You were hopelessly set, yes, hopelessly set
On driving yourself on to a tragical doom,

Foreshadowed even in the recriminations
Uttered with anger and venom
In the dark and sometimes the light
Against the Atreidae. That was the time
This disastrous outcome was hatched
When the golden armor of Achilles
Became a contest of wills.

TECMESSA: The pain of it!

CHORUS: I know the pangs that pierce a loyal heart.

TECMESSA: A . . . h!

CHORUS: Your double anguish, my lady, does not surprise me.

TECMESSA: You can imagine it, but I suffer it.

CHORUS: I know.

TECMESSA: My poor child, what a yoke of slavery is coming
with the sort that will be our masters now!

CHORUS: Unspeakable, yes,
The sufferings you have just envisaged
From the two merciless Sons of Atreus.
But may a god avert it!

TECMESSA: The gods? But for them none of this would
have happened.

CHORUS: They've laid on us an insupportable burden.

TECMESSA: One that the daughter of Zeus, dreadful Athena,
for Odysseus' sake has fomented.

CHORUS: That most tenacious of men must be gloating
In his tenebrous soul:
Howling with laughter at our terrible anguish.
And with him will laugh those two
Royal Sons of Atreus.

TECMESSA: Let them jeer and gloat over this man's
downfall.
If they did not miss him while he lived
they will in the grim struggle of battle miss him dead.
Hollow men never know the good in their hands
until they lose it.
And though his death is bitter for me and sweet for
them,
it was his pleasure, the fulfillment of his will,
the death he longed for.

What triumph then is that for them?
It was the gods, not they, that killed him—absolutely
not.

So let Odysseus vaunt his vacuous taunts at our bereave-
ment.

They do not possess Ajax anymore—he has gone,
though leaving me in tears and pain.

SIXTH EPISODE

[TEUCER *is heard approaching*]

TEUCER: Oh, the tragedy!
CHORUS: Silence! I think I heard the voice of Teucer.
It sounds to me as if he knows.
TEUCER: [*staggering in*] Oh, Ajax, my beloved brother,
the apple of my eyes,
have you really done what rumor says?
CHORUS: He's gone, Teucer, be sure of that.
TEUCER: No, I cannot bear it!
CHORUS: But it is a fact.
TEUCER: I am devastated, utterly.
CHORUS: All we can do is mourn.
TEUCER: An irreparable blow!
CHORUS: Beyond all, Teucer.
TEUCER: The sorrow of it! But what of his son?
Where in the land of Troy can I find him?
CHORUS: All by himself, near the tent.
TEUCER: Then fetch him at once
before some ruffian seizes him
like a forlorn lioness's pup.
Quick. Go. Get help . . .
People like to kick the fallen.

[TECMESSA, *with* ATTENDANTS, *hurries away*]

CHORUS: You are right, Teucer: Ajax when he was alive
asked you to look after the boy, and you do.
TEUCER: [*at first sight of* AJAX' *body*] Oh, the spectacle
I see is the worst vision of my life!
The trail I followed, dearest Ajax, to find you

and have found it leading to where you died
is the most agonizing pathway I have trod.
A winged rumor as if from heaven that you were dead
sped through the Achaean lines, dear fellow.
I had the horror of hearing it while still far off,
and I groaned, struck dumb,
but now I see it I am reduced to nothing.
Come, lift the shroud; let me see the worst.

[ATTENDANTS *uncover the body of* AJAX]

Oh, shattering sight
and form that harbored such relentless courage,
what sufferings you have sown for me by dying!
Where can I go? What people receive me,
who have been so useless to you in your crisis?
I hardly think that Telamon, father of us both,
will welcome me with sunny smiles
when I come home without you—
and he's a man who smiles but little at the best of
times.

What blame will he hold back,
what condemnation not pronounce on me
the bastard son from a war-won woman,
the weak coward who failed you, dearest Ajax,
or the crafty one who, with you dead,
would usurp your name and heritage?
That is the line Telamon will take:
a man of passion, peevish in old age,
who loses his temper over nothing.
Finally, I shall be banished from the realm,
branded as a slave, a man no longer free.
That is what I may expect at home,
while at Troy I face a host of enemies
with little in my favor
and even that has vanished with you gone.

[*Gazing at* AJAX' *corpse with pity and revulsion*]

And now what am I to do?
How bring myself to pry you from the polished point

of this ruthless steel?
Extraordinary the assassin, my poor victim,
    that put an end to your life:
How Hector in the end, though dead, has killed you!
[Contrast, if you will,
    the destiny of these two men:
    Hector was tied to chariot rails*
    by the very belt Ajax had given him
    and dragged till he was a mangled corpse,
    while Ajax fell on the very sword Hector gave him
    and died on it.
Surely it was a Fury who forged that sword
    and Hades the grim artisan who fashioned that belt.
I can only conclude that this and everything always
    is arranged for us mortals by heaven.
If anyone thinks that this is my opinion,
    that is his right, but it is also mine.]†
CHORUS: Stop wasting time in talk
    and think of how you're going to bury him,
    and what you're going to say in a moment,
    for I see some blackguard coming
    who is probably going to make fun of our misery—
    the way they do.
TEUCER: A man from the army, is it? Who?
CHORUS: Menelaus, for whom we made this voyage here.

[*Heralded by trumpets,* MENELAUS, *clad in the panoply
of a commander in chief and escorted by a contingent
of soldiers, swaggers in*]

MENELAUS: You—don't you dare touch that corpse.
Leave it where it lies.
TEUCER: Do you really enjoy wasting breath?
MENELAUS: It's my decree—a commander in chief's
                                            decree.
TEUCER: And will you deign to give a reason for it?
MENELAUS: The reason is we thought we'd brought an
                                            ally here from home,

---

*By Achilles.
†Within the brackets almost certainly a later interpolation.

a friend to the Greeks, but when it came to the test
we found him a more vicious foe than the Trojans
even:
a man who planned to annihilate the army,
putting us to the spear in a night attack.
If a god hadn't scotched his plan
our fate would have been just what his is
and we'd be lying there dishonored and dead
and he'd be still alive.
A god, however, switched his violence to sheep and
cattle.

This is the reason that no man here has authority enough
to bury this body.
It shall be tossed onto the pallid sands
as fodder for the birds along the shore.
Therefore quieten down your fiery retorts.
If we could not govern him while he lived,
at least we'll govern him when dead—
whether you like it or not . . . He is in our hands.
He never listened to me when alive,
the hallmark of an inferior being,
a subordinate who won't take orders.
Without law and order no city functions,
and without fear and respect
no army can be governed.
Even a man of massive physique should remember
that he can be toppled at a touch.
A man who has some fear in him, therefore respect,
can be certain of his safety,
but where insolence and willfulness are rife
a city that seems to be sailing along quite well
will plummet to the bottom.
A certain appropriate awe is in order.
Let us not imagine we can do whatever we please
and pay no price for our pains.
Reality is turn and turn about.
This man had his turn at being hot and insolent,
now it's my turn to be arrogant.
So I warn you not to bury him
unless you want a grave yourself.

CHORUS: Menelaus, after laying down such balanced
principles,
don't flout them by a sacrilege against a corpse.
Even if true, words can sting.
TEUCER: Men, I'll never again be surprised if a man
who is a nothing does something wrong,
when those supposed to be nobly born
utter such persiflage as this.
Come, repeat it for my ears:
you say it was you
who brought this man out here to help the Greeks.
Didn't he sail here on his own account?
How are you his superior?
What claim have you to command those he brought
from home?
You came as king of Sparta, not as our commander.
You have no more jurisdiction over him than he has
over you.
You sailed here subordinate to others,
not as our commander.
So lord it over those whose lord you are
and scold them with your pompous diatribes.
This man, though you forbid it and the other generals,
I mean to give a decent burial.
I'm not in awe of all your verbiage.
It was not for your wife's sake that he went to war,
as did those two worn-out incompetents,
but to keep a promise. It was not for you:
he was not concerned with nonentities.
Next time you show yourself
bring the Big Chief with you—and more trumpets.
For the sake of a man like you with all your bite
I'll not bother to turn my head from left to right.
CHORUS: I can't say I like
letting the tongue loose like this when things are
difficult.
Even if true, hard words can bite.
MENELAUS: It seems this marksman has rather elevated
sights.
TEUCER: Naturally! It's a noble skill and I'm an expert.

MENELAUS: And you'd be even more "expert" if you had a shield.

TEUCER: Even without a shield I could take you on fully armed.

MENELAUS: Your tongue is fueled by such marvelous courage.

TEUCER: No, confidence at having justice on my side.

MENELAUS: Justice? For my assassin to be applauded?

TEUCER: Assassinated, were you? Congratulations on being still alive!

MENELAUS: Alive because saved by a god—not thanks to *him*.

TEUCER: Saved by a god? Then why are you dishonoring the gods?

MENELAUS: Dishonoring the laws of heaven? Why should I?

TEUCER: You do, by standing there and blocking burial of the dead.

MENELAUS: Burying my country's enemies is wrong.

TEUCER: Was Ajax ever your antagonist?

MENELAUS: You know very well: we hated one another.

TEUCER: Naturally, when in the voting you were proved a cheat.

MENELAUS: His rejection was decided by the judges, not by me.

TEUCER: You could make the most underhand dealings fair.

MENELAUS: And you could be clobbered for that remark.

TEUCER: No less than you could.

MENELAUS: I'll cut this short: that man shall not be buried.

TEUCER: And in short, my answer is: buried he *shall* be.

MENELAUS: I once knew a man, a bombastic man
who incited sailors to set sail in a storm,
but when the storm raged at its height,
he doubled up under his duffel
and let any sailor trample over him at will.
So will a puny cloud
turn into a tearing squall
that blasts you and your loud mouth to nothing
and stoppers up your clamor.

TEUCER: I too once knew a man,
   a man chockful of foolishness,
   who harassed others when they were down;
   and seeing him, a man like me said this:
"Fellow, do no evil to the dead,
   for if you do you can be sure you'll come to a bad
                                              end."
Such was his warning to this misguided wretch,
   and now that I see that man,
   I think he is no one else but you.
Do I speak in riddles?
MENELAUS: I am going. I would be ashamed to have it
                                              known
   that I was scolding when I had the power to squash.
TEUCER: Off with you, then. I, too, should be ashamed
   to have put up with a fool spouting folly.

[MENELAUS *turns on his heel and stomps off*]

CHORUS: A struggle is going to ensue
   from this quarrel.
Teucer, ready yourself
   and quickly hollow
A trench for this man
   where he will lie
In a dank grave that shall be
   remembered by mortals.

[TECMESSA *enters, leading* EURYSACES *by the hand*]

TEUCER: Here come the man's son and his wife in the
                                              nick of time
   to dress the grave of this poor corpse.
Come over here, my boy, stand by him
   and take your father's hand in prayer.
Now sit by him and ask his help
   with snippets of hair in your hand:
   mine, hers, and yours—offerings for the grave.
If anyone from the army
   tries to tear you from this body,
   let him be cursed to perdition with no burial,

a fit disaster for a disastrous man.
Let his whole race be cut off root and branch
  even as I now snip off this lock of hair.
Hold him, boy, and keep him.
Throw yourself on him and cling
  if someone tries to move you.

[*Turning to the sailors*]

You men, don't stand around like women.
Come and help at what I'm at.
I'm going to dig a grave, no matter what.

[TEUCER *departs with a contingent of sailors while the*
CHORUS *chants a dismal litany of regrets*]

STROPHE I
CHORUS: When shall these interminable years
  Come to an end, these restless years:
  The barren ordeal of ceaseless battle
  On the prairies of Troy
  To the horror and shame of Greece?

ANTISTROPHE I
That man who first instructed the Greeks
  How to make war with horrible tools,
  Should have been snatched up to the sky
  Or buried in Hades. What sorrows
  He spawned for the ruin of man!

STROPHE II
Yes, he's the one who has forfeited my
  Garlands and drinking and fluting of pipes,
  Beautiful sleep at night—and all for sorrow.
And he's cut me off from love, wonderful love.
Here uncared for I make my bed
  Drenched by heavy dews
  Thinking of miserable Troy.

ANTISTROPHE II
Once I had the all-omnipotent Ajax

To screen me from the arrows and night,
But now he's gone to the malignant god of fate.
Not a single joy shall bless me again—not one.
I wish I were on the wave-lashed cape
Of wooded lofty Sunium
In sight of holy Athens.

SEVENTH EPISODE

[TEUCER *reenters the strand, spade in hand, ready to bury the body of* AJAX]

TEUCER: I'm in a hurry because I see Agamemnon, the
commander,
marching towards us.

[AGAMEMNON, *accoutred in a general's regalia and coming from the direction of the camp, strides into view*]

AGAMEMNON: You there,
who I'm told frothed at the mouth against us
and are still at large—
you, the bastard brother-in-law of a captive woman,
I'm talking to you.
If you'd been born of a decent woman, I do believe,
you'd be walking on air,
though in fact you're a nobody championing a nobody.
You had the nerve to make a deposition
that we did not come here either as commanders of
you
or admirals of the Greek fleet,
maintaining that Ajax sailed as his own captain.
Is it not outrageous
to hear such pretensions from a slave?
Who is this man you boost with such presumption?
Did he go anywhere, stand anywhere, where I did not?
Do the Greeks have no men else but him?
It almost makes me regret the day
we announced the contest for the arms of Achilles:
yes, if we are to be denigrated by one Teucer,

who even when defeated refuses to bow
to the decision of the judges
and now heaps us with abuse—
stabs us in the back all on his own.
If this sort of behavior is countenanced,
all order is annulled,
and we are expected to push aside the winners
and bring forward those who came in at the tail end.
No, this has to be stopped.
When it comes to the crunch,
it's not the broad-backed bruiser one relies on,
it's the one with common sense—he scores.
A big-boned bull is steered along the road
by a small prod:
that's the answer, I would say, for you
if you fail to come to your senses soon.
You are so full of bravado and free with your tongue
that you insult us even though the man is dead
and already a shade.
Can you not learn some sense?
Can you not remember who you are?
Go and get a freeborn man to speak in your stead.
When you do the speaking, I don't understand:
I don't know Barbarian.
CHORUS: If only you two could be reasonable!
I don't know what else to say.
TEUCER: [*ignoring* AGAMEMNON *and addressing the
corpse*] So much for gratitude to the dead!
How soon and traitorously it betrays!
This man, Ajax, has no thought of you—not the
slightest;
and he's the one you protected and risked your life
for.
It's all dismissed, tossed aside.

[*Turning to* AGAMEMNON]

You, you mouther of platitudes,
have you no memory of the times you were boxed up
in your lines,

a lost man in the turning tide of battle,
and this man all on his own came and saved you?
And the time the bonfires licked around the sterns of
the ships
and Hector was leaping over the trenches towards the
hulls . . .
Who stopped this? Wasn't it he,
the one you said went nowhere where you did not?
Was this the conduct of a criminal?
Then again, when he faced Hector man to man,
not because he was ordered to
but because when he cast his token into the crested
helmet
—his pebble, mark you, no mere lump of clay—
it was the first to come leaping out* . . .
These acts were his, and I was there with him:
I "the slave, the brat of the barbarian mother."
You miserable man,
whom did you think you were looking at when you
said that?
Don't you know that Pelops, your father's father,
was a Phrygian, a barbarian,
and that your own father, Atreus,
made an obscene banquet of his brother's children for
his brother?
Or that you yourself are the son of a Cretan mother,
whom your father surprised in the arms of a lover
and dispatched to be gobbled up by fishes?
With such a pedigree
how dare you criticize my own!
My father was Telamon,
awarded the army's greatest prize for valor
my mother for his bed—
a princess, daughter of Laomedon
and given to Telamon by Alcmena's son.†
Do you imagine that I,

---

*This was a mode of selection in which the various contenders threw
their tokens into a helmet, which was then shaken till a token flew
out: which signified the winner.
†Heracles.

born noble from two noble parents,
  would dishonor my brother in his misfortune
  by shamelessly letting you throw him out unburied?
You can be sure of this:
  if you do toss him away
  you'll have three others to toss away as well.*
Yes, I am proud, in the view of all,
  to die in his defense . . .
  and not for that woman of yours—
  or should I say your brother's?
Be careful, then,
  not for my position but for your own.
For if you do me any harm
  you'll wish you'd played the coward
  in dealing with me, and been less forward.

[ODYSSEUS *enters from the direction of the harbor*]

CHORUS: Odysseus, my lord, you've come just in time,
  not to embroil, I hope, but mediate.
ODYSSEUS: Good sirs, what is it?
A long way off I heard a noisy altercation
  from the Atreidae over this brave man's body.
AGAMEMNON: [*pointing to* TEUCER] With good cause, lord
  Odysseus:
  were we not subjected to insults from this fellow?
ODYSSEUS: Insults? I can forgive a man who insults when
  insulted.
AGAMEMNON: I insulted him because of what he was
  doing.
ODYSSEUS: And what was he doing that so upset you?
AGAMEMNON: He insists on not leaving that corpse
  unburied
  and intends to bury it against my will.
ODYSSEUS: May a friend be frank with a friend
  and be no less his friend than before?
AGAMEMNON: Speak, I'd be a fool not to let you.
I number you my greatest friend among the Argives.

*Ajax' wife, son, and brother.

ODYSSEUS: Hear me, then. I ask you by the gods
  not mercilessly to cast out this man unburied.
Never let brute force take over
  and trample humanity underfoot.
He, too, in the whole army was my worst enemy
  the moment I became possessor of Achilles' armor.
Even so, I cannot fail to respect him
  or deny that except for Achilles
  he was the bravest of all the Argives that came to
                                 Troy.
Therefore I cannot dishonor him without injustice.
That would be destructive not just of him but the laws
                            of heaven.
When a brave man dies
  it is wrong to injure him even if you loathe him.
AGAMEMNON: So, Odysseus, you are taking his side
                    rather than mine?
ODYSSEUS: Son of Atreus, you should not take pleasure
                    in something ugly.
AGAMEMNON: It's no easy thing for a ruler to submit to
                    reverence.
ODYSSEUS: But such should submit to a friend's good
                    advice.
AGAMEMNON: And a good man should submit to authority.
ODYSSEUS: So be it! And to submit to friends is to be a
                    winner.
AGAMEMNON: Recall, however, the kind of man you're
                    being kind to.
ODYSSEUS: Yes, an enemy but a worthy one.
AGAMEMNON: So what do you mean to do? Reverence
                    this alien corpse?
ODYSSEUS: Alien, no doubt, but I value his excellence
                    more.
AGAMEMNON: Typical of an inconsistent man!
ODYSSEUS: Inconsistent, yes: friends one day, all hostile
                    the next.
AGAMEMNON: Is this the kind of man that you approve
                    of?
ODYSSEUS: What I don't approve of is a rigid mind.
AGAMEMNON: So today you'll make us all look like
                  cowards.

ODYSSEUS: Not at all: but men who are humane in the
　　　　　　　　　　　　sight of all the Greeks.
AGAMEMNON: You are telling me to allow this body to
　　　　　　　　　　　　be buried?
ODYSSEUS: I am. And one day I shall need the same.
AGAMEMNON: A universal truth! . . . that every man is
　　　　　　　　　　　　out for himself.
ODYSSEUS: If not out for oneself, then out for whom?
AGAMEMNON: Very well, but let it be seen as your deci-
　　　　　　　　　　　　sion, not mine.
ODYSSEUS: Let it be seen as an act of your generosity.
AGAMEMNON: Know that I would grant you an even
　　　　　　　　　　　　greater favor.
Meanwhile that man has my hatred
　both on the earth and in the shades.
So do what you will.

[AGAMEMNON *leaves for the camp*]

CHORUS: Odysseus, anyone who says you're not a clever
　　　　　　　　　　　　man
　when it comes to things like this is a perfect fool.
ODYSSEUS: [*turning to* TEUCER]
And now, Teucer, I want to make it clear
　that from now on I am as much your friend
　as once I was your enemy.
I am anxious to join you in burying the dead man
　and leaving no service undone in helping you
　with this the best of mortals.
TEUCER: Most generous Odysseus,
　I have no words to thank you,
　you have gone far beyond anything I dreamed of.
You were this man's most deadly antagonist among the
　　　　　　　　　　　　Greeks,
　yet you alone have supported him with all the help
　　　　　　　　　　　　you could
　and not simply stood by jeering
　because he was dead and you alive,

when that lunatic commander and his brother
wanted to discard him sacrilegiously without burial.
For that may the Father, supreme on Olympus,
    and the recording Furies
    and the unrelenting god of justice
    destroy them as ruthlessly as they ruthlessly planned
    to jettison this man in the most disgraceful fashion.
Nevertheless, scion of Laertes,
    I hesitate to let you help me in this burial
    lest it hurt the feelings of the dead.
In all else be our fellow-worker;
    and no matter whom you bring in from the forces,
    that will not offend me.
I shall see to all the rest,
    but I want you to know that in all your dealings with
                                                    us
    you have been most generous.
ODYSSEUS: It was my wish to help
    but if you do not think it right
    I respect your decision, and now depart.

[ODYSSEUS *salutes and moves off in the direction of
the camp*]

TEUCER: So be it! We have lingered long enough.
Let some of you hasten to hollow his grave,
    And others set up the tripod over the fire
    For the requisite rubrics of ablution.
Some of you men
    Fetch from the tent the armor he wore.

[*Turning to* EURYSACES]

You my boy, with what strength you have,
    Lay a loving hand upon your father
    And help me lift his body,
    Whose hot black blood is oozing still.
Come, everyone here who claims the name of friend,
    Hasten to serve this man, the perfect hero:

Never before have you served a nobler man.
CHORUS: Mortals learn so many things by seeing,
  Yet no man can
  See the future of his being.

ELECTRA

ΗΛΕΚΤΡΑ

The *Electra* of Sophocles is a cruel play: its theme revenge, its action pursuit of victims—a far cry from any tremor of pre-Christian forgiveness, as Electra and Orestes hound their mother and her paramour to their deaths. And there is much to forgive: Clytemnestra could forgive her husband for having sacrificed their daughter, Iphigenia (albeit against his will); Electra could forgive her mother for murdering her father; Clytemnestra, her daughter for almost twenty years of doting on a defunct father; and Orestes, Aegisthus for daring to cohabit and to collaborate with his mother.

If at first one is tempted to regard Electra as a professional complainer seething with self-pity, one soon discovers that there is much to complain about. She is hated by her mother, treated like a slave and condemned to live under the same roof as the two who murdered her father. Yet her stamina and strength of purpose thrust her inexorably towards a sinister fulfillment: an ominous apprehension of triumphant doom.

It is difficult not to entertain a certain sympathy for Clytemnestra, who gives a convincing apologia for having killed her rather disreputable husband. But in the end her exodus is pathetic rather than tragic—hurried and undignified. She moves towards her dissolution with none of the Lady Macbeth–like intransigence that she manifests in Aeschylus' portrayal (in *Agamemnon*), nor for that matter in the way she dies in Euripides' *Electra*, arriving in a horse-drawn carriage with all the aplomb of a grande dame coming to open a garden fête.

The characters of the two young men, Orestes and Pylades, are only lightly drawn. Pylades, as usual, is silent as a dummy and never utters a syllable. Orestes, whom his sister welcomes home as the linchpin of the plot to avenge their father, does not go weak at the knees (as he does in Euripides' play) at the enormity of killing his mother, but addresses himself to the deed with the dispatch of a schoolboy scoring a goal at soccer.

Aegisthus, for his part, appears somewhat less despicable than is usually depicted, and when finally trapped accepts his dismissal with an inevitability that, if not exalting, is at least full of pathos.

As to Chrysothemis, Electra's sister, she seems. to be a run-of-the-mill sensible girl out to avoid unnecessary trouble and is appalled by her sister's murderous intentions.

It is the old tutor in this gory story who seems to come off best. Straightforwardly cunning and sharp, his language sometimes borders on the witty and his whole invention of Orestes' disastrous chariot race is a masterpiece of fiction.

The play was produced in Athens between 420 and 410 B.C., which would put Sophocles somewhere in his early eighties.

CHARACTERS

TUTOR, of Orestes
ORESTES, son of Agamemnon and Clytemnestra
ELECTRA, sister of Orestes
CHORUS, young women of Mycenae in Argos
CHRYSOTHEMIS, sister of Electra
CLYTEMNESTRA, mother of Electra, Chrysothemis, and Orestes
AEGISTHUS, paramour of Clytemnestra

MUTES

PYLADES, friend of Orestes
SERVANT GIRL
ATTENDANTS

TIME AND SETTING

It is dawn before the royal palace at Mycenae in the central Peloponnese. An old man, erstwhile tutor of the young prince Orestes, stealthily conducts him and Pylades to a lookout from which they can see laid out before them the ancient city over which Orestes' father, Agamemnon, once ruled as king. Twenty years have passed since Agamemnon came back triumphant from Troy and was murdered by his wife and her paramour, Aegisthus. Now Orestes, obeying an oracle of the god Apollo, is on a mission to avenge his father. The Tutor, after pointing out various landmarks, urges him to begin.

PROLOGUE

TUTOR: Son of Agamemnon,
  commander once of our forces at Troy,
  now you can look out with your own eyes
  over all that you have so craved to see.
There lies Argos,
  that ancient city for which you pined,
  and the arena from which the gadfly drove poor Ino
  daughter of Inachus.
Over there, Orestes,
  is the Lycean marketplace of the wolf-killing god,*
  and left of it, the famous temple of Hera.
Just tell yourself we've actually arrived,
  can see Mycenae—so laden with gold—
  and the palace of the Sons of Atreus—so laden with
                                              death!
It was from here, after your father's murder,
  that I once took you from your sister's arms
  and carried you to safety.
I rescued you and brought you up
  to be a fine young man—ready to avenge his mur-
                                       dered father.
And so, Orestes,
  and you too, Pylades—dearest of friends—

*Apollo.

you must quickly decide what you will do,
for already the bright beams of the sun
trigger the dawn chorus of the birds
and black night with its stars has gone.
So before anyone comes out of his house
you must plot your course.
This is not a place for dithering,
but action perforce.
ORESTES: My beloved and loyal servant of our house,
you are like an old horse of stalwart pedigree
that never is dismayed by danger
but pricks up his ears.
So it is with you:
urging us on and in the forefront of support.

Well, let me tell you what I have decided.
Listen carefully and correct me
if in anything I have missed the mark.
On my visit to the Pythian oracle
to find out how to take revenge on my father's
murderers,
the answer Apollo gave me was this:
"Alone and secretly,
without armed support and without an army,
you must snatch by cunning
the vengeance that is yours by right."
Now since this is what the oracle enjoined,
I want you to go into the palace when you get the
chance
and find out everything that is going on in there
and bring us back an exact report.
They will not know you:
your age, the lapse of time, your silvered hair . . .
they will never suspect.
This is your story:
you are a stranger and have just come from Phanoteus
the Phocian,
the greatest of their allies.
And then tell them—swear it on oath—
that Orestes has been killed in a fatal accident:

flung from his flying chariot at the Pythian games.
That is your story.

But the first thing now is to honor my father's tomb,
    as the god commanded,
    with drink offerings and a thick lock of my hair.
Later we shall come again
    bearing in our hands the bronze urn,
    hidden in the undergrowth—as I think you know—
    to celebrate with the false and happy news
    that my body has been burned to cinders.
How can this hurt me:
    a fictional death and a live reality
    all poised for success.
A fib that does you good cannot be bad!
I have known many a wise man to be reported dead,
    but not dead at all; and they come back home
    with double the fame.
The same with me:
    I shall emerge from this rumor alive, like a radiant
                       star,
    blazing down on my enemies.

[*Moving with outstretched hands towards the altar of Dionysus*]

But you, land of my fathers, and you gods of this place,
    bless me with good fortune in this enterprise;
    and you too my father's house, for I have come to
                      cleanse you,
    sped on my way here by heaven.
Do not dismiss me from this land disgraced
    but grant that I may reign over my possessions
    and restore my house.

Enough for the present.
Now it is for you, old man, to carry out your part.
The two of us will now go off. The time is apt,
    and men must seize the opportune for every act.

[*The voice of* ELECTRA *is heard from within*]

ELECTRA: Ah ... Unbearable!

TUTOR: My son, I thought I heard a groan coming from
indoors:
some handmaid, perhaps.

ORESTES: Or perhaps Electra, unhappy creature.
Shall we stay here and listen?

TUTOR: I think not!
Before we do anything we must listen to the injunctions
of Apollo,
and begin by pouring out those drink offerings for
your father.
I'm convinced that our success and triumph lie in that.

[TUTOR, ORESTES, *and* PYLADES *move away as* ELECTRA
enters. She is drably dressed and has shorn hair]

LYRIC APOSTROPHE

ELECTRA: [*standing with outstretched arms*] O holy light
That shares with the air the mantling of earth,
How many times have you heard me lament?
How many times have you heard me beating
My breast till it bled in the falling dark?
And my miserable bed in this house of regrets
Has long been aware of my sleepless nights
Sobbing the loss of my stricken father,
Whom the bloody god of war released from Troy
That alien country, just for my mother
And Aegisthus her bed companion
To cleave his head with a murderous axe—
Like a woodman felling an oak.
Only from me, Father, has a burst of pity
Mourned your pitiable and dreadful death.
And I shall not cease my cries of sorrow,
No, not at all,
So long as I look upon the light,
Upon the luminous and throbbing stars.
I'll be like the nightingale bereft of her young,
Singing my sorrow loud to the world—
Singing at the portals of my father's house.

O home of Hades and Persephone!
O Hermes, conductor of the shades below!
O you virulent goddess of curses,
   And you awesome daughters of heaven, the Furies,
   Witnesses when a life is wrongfully severed,
   Who see when a marriage bed is fouled—
   Come to my help!
Avenge the murder of our father
   And send to me my brother;
   For I have not the stamina alone
   To bear the grief that weighs me down.

[*The* CHORUS *of* YOUNG WOMEN OF MYCENAE *march
and sway into view*]

PARADOS OR ENTRY ODE
CHORAL DIALOGUE

STROPHE I

CHORUS: Child, child, sorrowful daughter,
   Electra, of a degraded mother,
   Must go on pining forever
   Over Agamemnon brutally felled
   So long ago by a trick of your mother:
   Dispatched to his doom by a ruthless hand?
If I am allowed to speak outright:
   Perdition take the one who did it.
ELECTRA: O good-hearted, generous ones
   Who have come to console me in my sorrow,
   I understand, I am completely aware,
   Nothing escapes me, but I'll never give up
   Mourning for my overthrown father.
And you who lavish your friendship upon me,
   Allow me my raving.

ANTISTROPHE I

CHORUS: But, but no lamentation,
   No amount of earnestly praying
   Will raise your father from the marsh of Hades,
   Which all must go through. To abandon reason,
   To drown in irreparable sorrow,

Is grief run wild, grief destroying,
Nor will it ever annul the hurt;
So why are you so devoted to anguish?

ELECTRA: Shallow is one who forgets a parent's
Pitiless end. Give me instead
The sorrowful nightingale, she who sings*
Itys Itys—forever distraught:
Emissary of Zeus. And Niobe, you,
Mistress of sorrows, overwhelmed
In your rocky tomb.

STROPHE II

CHORUS: My daughter, you are not
The only mortal sorrow has stricken
Yet you suffer it far less calmly than your sisters do,
Chrysothemis and Iphianassa ... One,
Exuding youth and sheltered from pain,
Will one day be welcomed home and come
To that famous land of Mycenae
So rich in tradition:
One brought by the kindly hand of Zeus—Orestes.

ELECTRA: Yes, him I await unwearingly, lost,
Childless, unwedded, bathed in tears
With unstaunchable grief, whilst he forgets†
All that he suffered, all that he has heard.
Is there a single word from him not canceled?
Yearn though he may, he does not deign to appear.

ANTISTROPHE II

CHORUS: Bear up, my child, bear up!
Zeus still is great in his heaven
Overseeing and ordering all; commit to him
Your excessive rage. Do not be angry
Beyond all sense against the ones that hate you.
Nor yet forget. Time is a god that heals.
Agamemnon's son who dwells
By the pastures of Crisa

---

*Greek ornithology was sorely awry. It is only the cock bird who sings.
†Orestes was only an infant when his father was murdered.

Has not forgotten; nor has the god who reigns in
Acheron.*

ELECTRA: So much of my life has passed frustrated,
My strength is failing, I have no children nor
A protecting husband, but like a common slave
I serve in the halls of my father, depressingly clad
In these rags, stationed at impoverished tables.

STROPHE III

CHORUS: Shattering was his cry for help,
Shattering, his coming home,
Strewn by the blow he lay—
Your father—cut down by the axe.
Deceit was the plotter, lust the assassin:
Monstrosity spawning a monstrous thing,
Whether begotten by a god or man.
Whichever the doer.
ELECTRA: The appalling horror of that day!
The most revolting day of my life!
And that bitterest of nights!
The obscene banquet
At which my father clearly saw
The deadly death stroke dealt by the hands of two
That has cheated me of life
And given me over to desolation.
May the absolute god of Olympus
Pay them with punishment put in their path.†
May their glory be joyless and they never enjoy it:
They who could perpetrate such goings-on.

ANTISTROPHE III

CHORUS: Be careful! Utter no more!
Don't you see that self-pity
Is fueling your suffering
And piling up more and more?
You fabricate wars for your sorrowful soul.
Bear with it. You cannot contend

---

*Pluto, also called Hades. Acheron is the netherworld.
†A splendid example of alliteration in the Greek: ποινιμα παθεα
παθειν ποροι (*poinima pathea pathein poroi*).

With these in control.
ELECTRA: But a horrible life
  Impels horrible ways, I know,
  I am well aware of intolerant frenzy,
  But damaging though this be, I'll not
  Curb my laments,
  Be the results what they may,
  Never, so long as I live. Who could imagine,
  Who with a balanced mind,
  That I could listen to a word of comfort?
No, you generous friends! So leave me,
  You comforters, leave me my unhealable malady.
I cannot abate my legion of sorrows,
  So cannot abate my laments.

EPODE

CHORUS: At least it is my love that prompts me
  Like a mother you can trust;
  So stop adding grief to grief.
ELECTRA: All very well, but where is the limit
  To what I am suffering? Do you imply
  That it is good to neglect the dead?
  Is that a valid human piety?
I'll have no part with those who think so.
And in my life I'll never be happy
  If I've clipped the wings of loud lament
  Disgracefully for my dear father.
Why, if the fallen victim
  Is left lying in oblivious dust
  Most wretchedly
  While the culprits
  Are never made to pay with blood for blood,
  That is the end on earth
  Of reverence and good.

FIRST EPISODE

CHORUS: I came here, my daughter,
  as anxious for your welfare as my own,
  but if you cannot agree with me, so be it!
We shall still support you.

ELECTRA: Good women, I am embarrassed
   that you think I overdo my pourings out of grief,
   but this grief is ineluctable,
   so bear with me.
How could any woman of generous spirit
   behave otherwise, given the torments that I face:
Which are not waning
   but flush in the springtide of their virulence.
To begin with,
   I have to cope with my mother's enmity—
   the woman who gave me birth.
Next, in my own home,
   I have to live cheek by jowl with my father's murderers.
They are my masters,
   and it rests with them whether to give or to withhold.
On top of that,
   can you imagine what it is like
   to see Aegisthus seated on my father's throne?
To see him sporting the same regalia
   and pouring out libations on the very hearth
   at which he murdered him?
And the crowning outrage:
   to see the assassin in my father's bed
   alongside my despicable mother . . .
   if indeed that concubine can be called a mother!
But so hardened is she,
   she couples with the polluter blissfully
   without fear of Furies.
On the contrary, she gloats on it:
   fixes the day she tricked my father into death
   as a monthly celebration with dance and sacrifice,
   in thanksgiving to the gods for her salvation.

When I see all this,
   I, unhappy creature under the same roof,
   weep and pine and bewail
   the unholy festivities in my father's name,
   but alone, for I may not give my grief full rein.
Yes, this woman, professedly so well bred,
   shouts at me with a fishwife's tongue:
"Sanctimonious and horrid girl,

are you the only one who has lost a father?
Is there no other mourner in the world?
Pestilation take you!
And may the gods of hell
    never rid you of your present gloom!"

Thus she abuses me,
    but when she hears some rumor of Orestes' return,
    she goes berserk
    and stands over me and screams:
"You are to blame for all this:
    aren't you the one who stole Orestes from my arms
    and sneaked him away?
Well, you're going to pay for it,
    be sure of that!"
So she froths at the mouth
    while that coward, that piece of nothing—
    her so illustrious consort—
    stands by and cheers her on.

Meanwhile, here I am waiting still,
    in the depths of misery,
    for Orestes to come and put an end to this.
His vacillation has destroyed every hope I had,
    every hope I could have had.
So, my friends, as things stand,
    moderation makes no sense.
The situation is intolerable
    and makes intolerable behavior abominable.
CHORUS: Tell me, is Aegisthus at home or away,
    that you can let go your feelings with such freedom?
ELECTRA: Away, of course!
You don't imagine I'd be allowed to roam at will
    if he were here. . . . No, he is in the country.
CHORUS: Which makes it easier for me to talk.
ELECTRA: He's away just now, be sure of that.
Feel quite free to ask your questions.
CHORUS: About your brother—will he come
    or will he put it off? I'd like to know.
ELECTRA: He says he'll come,
    but what he says and what he does are very different.

CHORUS: Well, a big decision demands a big deliberation.
ELECTRA: Really? There was no big deliberation when I
saved *him*.
CHORUS: Be patient! He's too noble-hearted
not to help the ones he loves.
ELECTRA: I believe that, or I'd not go on with life.
CHORUS: Shh! Say no more,
for I see your sister coming from the palace,
Chrysothemis, born of the same father and same mother.
She's carrying funeral offerings in her hands,
ritual gifts for the shades below.

[CHRYSOTHEMIS *enters, a girl much younger than* ELEC-
TRA. *She bears a tray on which are incense, locks of
hair, grains of barley, bowls of milk, wine, and honey*]

CHRYSOTHEMIS: Sister, what have you been saying
to these people outside the palace?
Will you never learn
to give up these inept exhibitions of useless anger?
Speaking for myself, I can only say
that I am so upset by the way things are
that had I the nerve I would show them
what my feelings really were.
But in this time of turbid waters
I think it best to shorten sail
and give the impression of acquiescence—
it does no harm.
I wish you would do the same.
I know that the truth lies with you and not with me,
but if I am to live in peace
I must submit in everything to those in power.
ELECTRA: How strange it is that you,
the daughter of such a father,
should forget him and think only of your mother!
All the strictures that you level at me
are inspired by your mother:
not a syllable is your own.
Make your choice, then:
be a fool or put safety first and forget your friends.
You said just now that if you had the strength

you would demonstrate your loathing for them,
yet when I am doing all I can to revere my father
you not only give no help but try to stop me.
Is this not capping misery with cowardice?
For tell me—or let me tell you—
 how would it help me if I ceased from my laments?
Am I not alive?
Miserably, to be sure, but it will do.
And I annoy them by respecting the dead,
 if indeed the dead get any pleasure from it.
But you, you say you hate—you form the words—
 yet in your conduct go along with your father's killers.
Never shall I give in to them,
 not even if someone offers me the privileges you revel
 in:
 the groaning table, the luxurious life.
Well, enjoy it!
My sustenance is to be true to myself;
 I do not want your perquisites.
Neither would you if you had any sense.
So now, when you could be known
 as the daughter of the best of fathers,
 be known as your mother's daughter;
 so let your pusillanimity be evident
 and the betrayal of your father and your friends your
 monument.
CHORUS: Please, for the gods' sake, no bitterness!
There is something in both your declarations.
If only each of you could take something from the other!
CHRYSOTHEMIS: Good women, I am not exactly ignorant
 of her claims,
 and I would never have said a word had I not heard
 of a serious threat to muzzle her unending moaning.
ELECTRA: Out with it, then, this "serious threat"!
If you can tell me anything worse than what I suffer
 now,
 I shall not argue with you.
CHRYSOTHEMIS: All right, I'll tell you everything.
 If you do not stop these lamentations
 they intend to send you to where you'll never see the
 sun:

you'll be buried in a dungeon outside this land,
buried alive to chant your dismal monody.

Take note of that
and don't blame me later for what you have to go
through.

Now you have the chance to show some sense.

ELECTRA: So that is what they have in mind?

CHRYSOTHEMIS: Yes, as soon as Aegisthus comes home.

ELECTRA: The sooner the better, then, so far as I'm
concerned.

CHRYSOTHEMIS: You poor misguided creature, must you
condemn yourself?

ELECTRA: If he is going to come and carry out his threat,
I wish he would.

CHRYSOTHEMIS: Just to make you suffer? Are you insane?

ELECTRA: Just to get away from you all—as far as
possible.

CHRYSOTHEMIS: Getting away from the life you live at
present?

ELECTRA: Oh, yes, my present life is marvelous!

CHRYSOTHEMIS: It could be, if only you would show some
sense.

ELECTRA: Don't give me lessons on how to betray my
friends!

CHRYSOTHEMIS: I'm not trying to teach you that,
but simply to bend before the strong.

ELECTRA: That kind of bending is for you. It's not my
way.

CHRYSOTHEMIS: But mere self-esteem demands that we
avoid catastrophe.

ELECTRA: Then let's have catastrophe,
if that means being loyal to my father.

CHRYSOTHEMIS: But I am sure our father would understand.

ELECTRA: Such are the consolations of a coward.

CHRYSOTHEMIS: So you will not listen—not follow my
advice?

ELECTRA: Of course not! May I never be so vacuous!

CHRYSOTHEMIS: So be it! I am off on the errand I was
given.

ELECTRA: Where are you off to?

Whom are you carrying these offerings for?

CHRYSOTHEMIS: Mother told me to offer them on our
                              father's tomb.

ELECTRA: You don't mean it? Offerings for the one she
                              most hates?

CHRYSOTHEMIS: For the man she killed, is what you
                              meant to say.

ELECTRA: Who of her friends persuaded her, and with
                              what intent?

CHRYSOTHEMIS: I think she had a nightmare.

ELECTRA: Gods of my fathers, be with me at last!

CHRYSOTHEMIS: Does this fright of hers give you hope?

ELECTRA: Explain the dream and I can tell you.

CHRYSOTHEMIS: I can't tell you much. I know very little.

ELECTRA: Then tell me that.
    Sometimes the tiniest trifle can make or mar.

CHRYSOTHEMIS: The story is that she saw our father,
                              yours and mine,
    once again in the world of light.
He took the scepter he used to carry,
    held by Aegisthus now, and thrust it in the hearth.
From it sprouted a luxuriant tree
    that cast its shade over all Mycenae.
That is the story I heard from someone who was there
    when she proclaimed her dream to the Sun.
I know no more than this,
    except that fear made her send me on this mission.
[I beseech you by the family gods
    to listen to me and not be wrecked by your pigheadedness.
If you oppose me now,
    later you'll be running for my help.]*

ELECTRA: Dear one,
    let none of what you carry touch his tomb.
It would be a sacrilege
    in the eyes of heaven and of men
    to offer our father ritual gifts from a wife who hated
                              him.
Toss them to the winds,
    or bury them in a deep hole

---

*Bracketed as doubtful. And rightly so! These lines are a quite
unnecessary interpolation.

for her to find when she dies herself.
They must not disturb his place of rest.
It takes a shameless woman like her
    to load these disgraceful offerings
    on the tomb of the man she murdered.
Is it likely, do you think, that the deceased in his grave
    would welcome these honors from the hands of one
                                who cut him down
    like an enemy alien, destroyed his dignity,
    mutilated* his corpse,
    and wiped off the bloodstains on his head?
Do you think for a moment
    that these tokens will absolve her?
Of course not!
Throw them away and instead
    snip locks from your hair and from mine—
    unhappy creature, it's all I have!—
    and give these to him . . . my hair, a symbol of petition,
    and this plain, undecorated girdle.
Fall on your knees and beg him
    to come himself from the world below
    and help us against the ones we hate.
Ask that his son Orestes
    may live to trample down his enemies,
    so that ever afterwards we may deck our father's tomb
    with more opulent hands than those that deck it now.
I believe, I really do believe
    he took some part in sending her those ugly dreams.
In any case, my sister,
    do this service to help yourself and me—and him, of
                                        course—
    that dearest of men,
    resting now in Hades: your father and mine.
CHORUS: What the young woman says is sensible,
    and you, my dear, would be wise to follow it.

---

*The word in the Greek is μασχαλιζω (*maschalizo*), which came
to mean *to mutilate* a corpse but originally meant to cut off the
extremities and lodge them under the armpits. This was a talisman
to avert vengeance. It is not clear whether Clytemnestra went to
such lengths.

CHRYSOTHEMIS: I shall.
When an obligation is quite clear
  it is absurd to let two voices argue it,
  and we must hurry.
But if I proceed in this, my friends,
  I must ask you for the gods' sake to keep quiet.
                        If my mother gets to hear of it,
  I think I'll be very sorry for my defiance.

[CHRYSOTHEMIS *leaves, but* ELECTRA *stays to hear the
comments of the* CHORUS, *which sings an optimistic ode
of support, ending, however, in a sinister observation
on the curse-bound house of Pelops*]

STROPHE
CHORUS: If I am not a secondrate prophet with no com-
                                    mon sense
  I'd prophesy that justice is coming:
Justly triumphant. Yes,
  My child, coming very soon, I am sure
  Now that I have heard
  The bad dream that breathes
  A breath of fresh air.
The one who was your sire, the king
  Of the Greeks, will not forget;
  Neither will the axe of bronze,
  The ancient axe with double edge
  That savagely felled him.

ANTISTROPHE
The brazen-clawed Fury with multiple hands and multi-
                                    ple feet
  That lurks in ambush is about to pounce.
Fired by lust, the wicked
  Hurried to a forbidden bed, a foul
  Coupling. I am sure
  The message of the dream
  Does not favor them,
  The wicked partners of the act.
No one will ever tell
  The future in dreams and oracles

If the nightmare portent of the dream
Is not fulfilled.

Epode

That race of the Pelops* ages ago,
   That chariot race, source of sorrows,
   Has been calamitous for this land.
For ever since
   Myrtilus was pitched into
   The sleep of death and was hurled
   From his golden chariot
   In the direst accident,
   Never has
   A plethora of dire mishaps
   Gone lacking from this house.

SECOND EPISODE

[CLYTEMNESTRA *enters, bristling when she catches sight
of* ELECTRA]

CLYTEMNESTRA: Ranging at large again, I see,
   with Aegisthus out of the way!
He always took good care
   to keep you from making a fool of yourself outside
   in front of our friends.
But with him gone, you ignore me:
   tell people over and over again
   how overbearing I am,
   an unprincipled bully
   riding roughshod over you and yours.
I am not rough,
   and if I abuse you it's because
   you so often abuse me.

---

*Pelops was the grandfather of Agamemnon, Menelaus, and Aegisthus.
He won his bride, Hippodameia, by defeating her father, Oenomaus,
in a chariot race, having bribed the charioteer, Myrtilus, to loose
the linchpins. When Myrtilus claimed his reward (Hippodameia,
whom he was going to share with Pelops), Pelops killed him. Thus
began the curse on the House of Pelops.

It's your father, always your father:
    yes, I killed him—I know that,
    no need to deny it!—I and Justice
    were the killers . . . the goddess Justice,
    and you would agree with her if you could think.
This father of yours you are forever whining about
    decided all on his own out of all the Greeks
    to sacrifice your sister to the gods.*
He wasn't the one to go through agony
    when I gave her birth. . . . So tell me,
    whom did he sacrifice her for?
For the Greeks, you say?
But who gave them the right to kill what was mine?
Did he kill what was mine to help his brother Menelaus?
Then Menelaus should pay the price.
Menelaus had two children, did he not?
Surely they are the ones who should have been the victims,
    not my daughter?
It was for the sake of their father and mother
    that the whole voyage took place.
Or did Hades for his dinner
    prefer my children to hers?
Or did your useless father
    have feelings for Menelaus' brats
    but none for his own?
Wouldn't that be the mark of a father who was a fool,
    devoid of common sense?
I think so,
    though no doubt you would not;
    and so would the murdered child if she could speak.
I review the past without remorse,
    and if you think I am a senseless mother,
    think again before you judge another.
ELECTRA: For once you must admit
    it was not I that prompted this diatribe of yours;
    so with your permission I would like to speak

---

*Agamemnon, yielding to the prophecy of the seer Calchas and to
prevent a mutiny of the Greek fleet (becalmed in the bay of Aulis),
sacrificed Iphigenia to get a fair wind for the armada to Troy.

for the dead man and my sister.
CLYTEMNESTRA: You have my permission;
    and if only you had always addressed me so politely
    you would have been listened to without unpleasantness.
ELECTRA: Then speak I will.
You admit you killed my father.
Isn't that, right or wrong, the most disgraceful confession?
In any case, let me tell you, it was wrong.
You were pushed to do it by that evil man
    with whom you are now cohabiting.
Ask Artemis, goddess of the hunt,
    whom she was punishing when she held back
    every wind in Aulis.
No, let *me* tell *you*,
    because you won't find out from her.
My father—from what I have heard—
    was out hunting in the goddess' sacred grove,
    and when his footsteps startled a dappled antlered stag
    he shot it—and he boasted.
Artemis was so angry
    that she held back the Greek armada,
    exacting in requital for the slaughtered beast
    my father's slaughtering his own daughter.
That was why she was sacrificed.
It was the only way of releasing the Greek army
    either for home or for Troy.
He did it for this,
    and he did it against his will,
    with utmost reluctance—
    and not for the sake of Menelaus.
But even if it had been—to take your point—
    even if it was to help him,
    is that sufficient reason for you to murder him?
By what law?
If you start inventing laws to suit humanity
    take care you don't invent for yourself
    pain and remorse.
Because if we were swapping life for life,
    and you got what you deserved,
    you'd be the first to die.

*   *   *

Just consider the falsity of your position
    and tell me, if you will,
    what makes you commit the most disgraceful sin of all:
    sleeping with the criminal
    after first murdering my father with his help
    and then producing children
    while casting out the ones you have:
    decent children from a decent marriage?
How can I applaud this?
Will you assert that this, too,
    is to pay him back for Iphigenia?
If you do it's a disgraceful plea:
    one does not mate with an enemy for a daughter's
                sake.
But what is the good of talking to you
    when at every turn you scream
    that I vilify my mother?
My mother! No, more like a domineering jailer
    I would say: I who live this miserable life,
    tormented incessantly by you and by your mate.
And what of that other, the luckless Orestes,
    wearing out his unhappy days in exile—
    who only just escaped your clutches?
You have often accused me of nurturing him to punish you,
    and I would have done so—be sure of that—
    had I had the power.
So go ahead and call me what you like:
    denounce me to all as thoroughly bad—
    a loudmouthed traitor, chockful of insolence.
If this conduct proves me an adept too,
    it only shows how amply I take after you.
CHORUS: My word, she breathes out fire!
But whether justly or not she seems not to care.
CLYTEMNESTRA: Nor do I, for how could I even consider
                          one
    so rude to her mother, and old enough to know better?
Can you think of any single thing
    she would not do without shame?
ELECTRA: Shame? I am full of it, if you only knew.
I'm all too conscious that my conduct ill fits my age

and is out of character,
  but your antagonism and behavior
  make me act against my nature.
Bad example teaches bad behavior.
CLYTEMNESTRA: Impertinent hussy!
Whatever I say or do is fuel for your excesses.
ELECTRA: You are the one who says and does, not I.
What you do determines what you say.
CLYTEMNESTRA: By our lady Artemis,
  you'll pay for this when Aegisthus comes.
ELECTRA: You see? You tell me I am free to speak,
  then fly into a rage when I do.
You don't know how to listen.
CLYTEMNESTRA: Oh, do be quiet
  and let me get on with my sacrifice!
I've allowed you to say whatever you wanted.
ELECTRA: I'm not stopping you. Get on with your sacrifice,
  and don't blame me—I'll say no more.
CLYTEMNESTRA: [*beckoning a maidservant who carries a tray of offerings*] Lift up this cornucopia, my girl, with
                                                                    me
  while I lift up my prayers to the lord Apollo
  to free me from the fears that press me.

[*Together they move towards a statue of Apollo, and* CLYTEMNESTRA *stretches out her hands*]

O Phoebus our protector,
  lend an ear to my petition,
  whispered in the dark,
  because I dare not divulge it to the light of day
  with her standing near,
  ready with her hatred and her loudness
  to broadcast every kind of rumor through the town.
So listen thus to my muted prayer,
  for so it must be.
Grant, great Apollo,
  that if the double visions that I saw last night
  are favorable, they may be fulfilled,
  but if they are negative, that they redound
  on those who hate me.

And if there are any plotting to rob me
   of my present riches, stop them,
   and grant that I continue to live unharmed,
   reigning over the House of Atreus and this realm,
   sharing my prosperity with those I love,
   who share it now, and with my children:
   those untainted with hatred and bitterness.
Lord Apollo, graciously hear me
   and answer the prayers of us all.
For the rest, I need not spell it out.
As a god you know everything
   even if I do not say a thing;
   for the children of Zeus must see everything.

[*The* TUTOR *approaches, as if just entering Mycenae*]

TUTOR: Good ladies, am I right in thinking
   this is the palace of King Aegisthus?
CHORUS: It is. You are quite correct.
TUTOR: And am I also right in thinking
   this lady is his wife?
She has the bearing of a queen.
CHORUS: Right again, and here she comes!
TUTOR: Greetings, my queen!
I bring good news from a friend for you and Aegisthus.
CLYTEMNESTRA: I'm pleased to hear it, but tell me first
                                       who sent you.
TUTOR: Phanoteus the Phocian, on a matter of some
                                            import.
CLYTEMNESTRA: What is it, sir? Don't hesitate to tell me.
It will be a friendly message, coming from a friend.
TUTOR: Orestes is dead. . . . You know the worst!
ELECTRA: O . . . h! I am dead this day!
CLYTEMNESTRA: What? What, sir? Go on—don't listen
                                            to *her*!
TUTOR: As I said, and say again: Orestes is dead.
ELECTRA: This is the end. I am no more.
CLYTEMNESTRA: [*turning viciously on* ELECTRA] You
   mind your own concerns! . . . Now, sir,
   tell me exactly how he died.
TUTOR: That is why I was sent here:

I shall tell you everything.
He went to the famous games at Delphi,
　　the glory of Greece:
　　where they compete for prizes.
And when he heard the resounding announcement of
　　　　　　　　　　　　　　　　　the first race
　　he entered the lists—a magnificent figure,
　　which he matched with his victory in that race
　　and flourished the coveted prize.
How can I be brief when there is so much to tell?
Let me say only this:
　　never have I seen a man of such prowess and strength.
But one thing you must know:
　　in every contest the judges announced,
　　he carried off the prize,
　　and everyone roared their applause when he was
　　　　　　　　　　　　　　　　　announced:
"Orestes, from Argos, son of Agamemnon,
　　who once mustered the glorious Greek armada."

So far, so good,
　　but when a god sends trials
　　not even a strong man can escape.
On a subsequent day at sunrise,
　　he entered the lists of the chariot races,
　　competing with many charioteers.
One from Achaea, one from Sparta,
　　two Libyans—professional charioteers—
　　another with Thessalonian mares, the fifth;
　　the sixth from Aetolia with chestnut colts;
　　the seventh from Magnesia;
　　the eighth an Aenian with white horses;
　　the ninth from Athens—that heaven-built city;
　　the last a Boetian in the tenth chariot.

They took up their positions by lot,
　　sorted by the umpires,
　　reining-in their chariots till the trumpets sounded.
Then they were off,
　　shouting to their horses,
　　slapping the reins in their grip,

till the whole stadium rang with the din of clashing
                                                chariots
  as the dust flew up and they pressed together.
They did not spare their whips
  as each man tried to propel his wheels and his snorting
                                                horses
  past his rivals.
They were so close that the froth of horse breath
  lathered the horses' rumps
  and even the wheels with foam.

Orestes, driving near the pillar
  and almost grazing the post at each turn,
  gave rein to his right trace-horse
  and tried to block off the man behind.
Up till then there'd been no mishap
  but suddenly on the sixth lap
  the hard-mouthed colts of the Aenian began to bolt
  and swerving into the seventh
  careened headlong into the Barcaean team.
A pileup of crashes followed, smash on smash,
  till the whole arena of Crisa
  was a mishmash of wrecked chariots.
Seeing this, the smart charioteer from Athens
  pulled into the side
  and let the shamble of chariots roar past him in mid-
                                                course.
Orestes was behind, keeping his chariot back,
  confident of the final goal.
But when he saw that only the Athenian was left
  he let out a yell in the ears of his horses and gave
                                                chase.
Neck and neck they drove their chariots together,
  one man, then the other, pulling ahead.
Up till then he'd safely managed every lap,
  keeping himself and his chariot intact.
Then, rounding the corner,
  he let out his left rein and struck the edge of the pillar,
  smashing his axle in two.
He was pitched over the rail but caught in the reins,

and as he fell his colts plunged into the middle of the
course.

When the crowd saw him fall from his chariot,
    a wail of distress went up for the young man
    who had so distinguished himself
    and was now being so mercilessly
    tossed to the sky or dragged along.
Finally the grooms managed to stay the bolting horses
    and unloose him.
He was so covered in blood that none of his friends
    would have recognized his mangled body.
A deputy of men from Phocia
    consumed it on a pyre, and now bring home in a small
                                                    bronze urn
    the ashes of that magnificent physique,
    to be buried in the land of his fathers.

Such is my story, terrible to tell,
    and for those who saw it—as I did—
    the greatest disaster I have ever beheld.
CHORUS: Dear gods! Dear gods!
The whole ancestral line, it seems, wiped out—extinct!
CLYTEMNESTRA: [*to herself*] Great Zeus, what can I
                                                    make of this?
Am I to call it a lucky break or terrible?
Saving self by damning self—what irony!
TUTOR: What is it, madam, that is troubling you?
CLYTEMNESTRA: How strange the power of motherhood!
Even when they treat one badly
    one cannot hate one's children.
TUTOR: It seems, then, that we have come in vain.
CLYTEMNESTRA: No, not in vain; how can you say "in
                                                    vain"
    when you have brought me undeniable proof of his
                                                    death?
Though my son, sprung from my own life,
    he turned away from my nurture and my breast
    and became an exile and an alien.
He never saw me again after he left this land.
He charged me with his father's murder

and threatened me with such dire reprisals
that neither by night nor by day
could I let the sweet consolation of sleep close my eyes.
I lived from minute to minute like a condemned criminal.
But now, on this day of days,
I have been released from the menace
of this woman here and him.
She was the greater plague,
living with me and sucking my lifeblood.
Now perhaps we can spend our days
safe from her threats.

ELECTRA: O what a tragedy, Orestes!
Your mother crows over you. Is this right?

CLYTEMNESTRA: Not for you exactly, but in his case, yes.

ELECTRA: Just listen to that! She invokes Nemesis,* god-
                                    dess of ruin,
on the lately dead.

CLYTEMNESTRA: Nemesis has heard what she needed to
                                    hear
and has acted.

ELECTRA: Go on with your taunts! This is the time of
                                    your triumph.

CLYTEMNESTRA: And neither you nor Orestes can put a
                                    stop to it.

ELECTRA: Now, *we* have been stopped: far from our stop-
                                    ping you.

CLYTEMNESTRA: [*turning to the* TUTOR] You, sir, deserve
                                    a great reward
if you have stoppered her clamorous tongue.

TUTOR: Then with your permission I'll go, if all is well.

CLYTEMNESTRA: Unthinkable!
That would be ungrateful to you and the friend who sent
                                    you.
Come inside and leave her here
moaning out her dirges for herself and those she loves.

[CLYTEMNESTRA *leads the* TUTOR *into the palace*]

ELECTRA: Can you imagine?

*Nemesis saw to it that all received their just deserts.

Did the callous woman cry and mourn for her dead son?
Was there an ounce of grief or pain?
Not a bit of it. She left us laughing.
O my poor dearest Orestes,
    you have snuffed my life out by your death.
You have wrenched away and wrung from my heart
    the last vestige of hope I had
    that you would come one day
    and avenge your father and me—miserable me.
Where shall I turn to now:
    alone, stripped of you and of my father?
Now I must go back to being a slave again
    among the people I hate most: my father's murderers.
Is this the best I can do? No!
I'll not go back in there to live with them.
I'll drop down by this gate
    and wither away without a friend.
Their annoyance and my death would be a pleasure.
To go on living is unbearable and I wish no future.

CHORAL DIALOGUE

STROPHE I

CHORUS: Where are the thunderbolts of Zeus
    And where is the blazing sun if they
    Look on this and are dumb?
ELECTRA: Aiai! Aiai!
CHORUS: Daughter, do not weep.
ELECTRA: I do.
CHORUS: No loud cries!
ELECTRA: You'll be my death.
CHORUS: How?
ELECTRA: If you hint at an inkling of help
    From those who have visible gone to Hades,
    You will trample me down harder than ever.

ANTISTROPHE I

CHORUS: Remember what happened to Amphiareus,*

---

*Amphiareus was tricked by his wife, Eriphyle (who had been bribed with a golden necklace), into going to the Trojan War, where he knew he would be killed. He arranged for his son, Alcmaeon, to murder his mother as soon as this happened.

Wrecked by a woman's golden chain
And now below the earth.

ELECTRA: So what?

CHORUS: He is a king with power..

ELECTRA: Aiai!

CHORUS: Aiai, but at least . . .

ELECTRA: The culprit was killed.

CHORUS: Yes.

ELECTRA: I know all this, I know it well:
A champion arose to avenge the dead.
But the champion I had has been snatched away.

STROPHE II

CHORUS: Struck you are by a stricken fate.

ELECTRA: Well do I know it, all too well:
My life is a rolling cascade of sorrow
Month by month without cease.

CHORUS: Yes, we understand.

ELECTRA: Please do not direct me to where . . .

CHORUS: Where what?

ELECTRA: To where
There are no longer any hopes of help
From the son of a noble sire.

ANTISTROPHE II

CHORUS: All mortals must face an end.

ELECTRA: But an end beneath the bolting hooves
Of horses, the way my brother died
All entangled in the reins?

CHORUS: Unbelievably cruel!

ELECTRA: It was, and on foreign soil
Without my aid.

CHORUS: I know!

ELECTRA: Buried with no obsequies, and I
Not there to mourn him.

THIRD EPISODE

[CHRYSOTHEMIS *enters from the palace, breathless*]

CHRYSOTHEMIS: Dearest sister, the most wonderful news

has propelled me here in undignified haste.
I bring you relief
   from your long unhappiness and sorrow.
ELECTRA: Where would you find relief for what I suffer?
It is incurable.
CHRYSOTHEMIS: Orestes is with us—O do believe me!—
   as real as you see me here.
ELECTRA: Are you out of your mind, poor girl?
Are you turning our desolation into a joke?
CHRYSOTHEMIS: No, I swear it on our father's heart,
   no joke. I tell you he is really here.
ELECTRA: Don't be so silly!
Where, pray, on this earth do you get such nonsense
   that you believe?
CHRYSOTHEMIS: Yes, I believe, and not on hearsay:
   with my own eyes I've seen the living proof.
ELECTRA: What have you seen, you little fool?
What was the vision that has got you all fired up?
CHRYSOTHEMIS: Listen, please for God's sake, and I'll
                        tell you.
Then see if I'm a fool or not.
ELECTRA: Go ahead, then, if it makes you feel good!
CHRYSOTHEMIS: I'll tell you everything I saw.
When I went to our father's ancient tomb,
   I noticed that a fresh stream of milk
   had trickled down from the top of the tomb
   and that my father's urn was wreathed
   with every kind of flower.
I was puzzled and gazed about
   to see if anyone was near.
After I had calmly surveyed the place,
   I approached the tomb
   and saw on the top of it a lock of hair,
   obviously just cut.
The moment I saw it—O what a moment!—
   I was flooded with the certainty
   that what I saw was no less than the exhibit
   of him I love most on earth—Orestes.
I took it in my hands,
   said nothing to break the spell
   as my eyes welled with tears of joy.

I know now, as I knew at once,
　　that this token came from nobody but him,
　　for you and I are the only others.
I know that I didn't do it,
　　neither did you.
How could you
　　when you can't even leave the house to pray at the
　　　　　　　　　　　　　　　　　　　　shrines
　　without getting into trouble?
Our mother could not have done it either
　　without our knowing. And it's not in her character.
No, these offerings at the tomb come from Orestes.
Bear up, dear heart!
Human life is not saddled by a single fortune.
Ours has been full of awfulness,
　　but today perhaps is the harbinger of happiness.

ELECTRA: You've no idea what nonsense you've been
　　　　　　　　　　　　　　　　　　　　talking!
I'm sorry for you.

CHRYSOTHEMIS: What? Don't you believe me?

ELECTRA: You do not have a clue
　　of where your feet and thoughts are taking you.

CHRYSOTHEMIS: How can I not know what I saw with
　　　　　　　　　　　　　　　　　　my own eyes?

ELECTRA: My poor dear sister, he is dead.
All chance of being saved by him is over.
Do not look to him.

CHRYSOTHEMIS: No, no! . . . From whom did you hear
　　　　　　　　　　　　　　　　　　　　this?

ELECTRA: From the man who was present at his death.

CHRYSOTHEMIS: Where is he? I am in a daze.

ELECTRA: He is in the house. Mother's not unwelcome
　　　　　　　　　　　　　　　　　　　guest.

CHRYSOTHEMIS: Too bad! But who could have left all
　　　　　　　　　　　　those offerings on Father's tomb?

ELECTRA: They were probably put there in memory of
　　　　　　　　　　　　　　　　Orestes, so lately dead.

CHRYSOTHEMIS: I am shattered!
I ran here so excited by the news,
　　with no inkling of disaster,
　　only to be plunged back in our miseries,

with new ones added.
ELECTRA: So matters stand,
    but if you will listen to me
    you can lighten the load of our present troubles.
CHRYSOTHEMIS: I cannot raise the dead.
ELECTRA: That is not what I was getting at:
    I am not so insane.
CHRYSOTHEMIS: What are you suggesting, then, that I can
                                                        do?
ELECTRA: Have the courage to do what I tell you.
CHRYSOTHEMIS: If it helps, of course I'll not say no.
ELECTRA: Bear in mind: there's no success without a
                                                struggle.
CHRYSOTHEMIS: I know, and I'll do everything in my
                                                    power.
ELECTRA: Here is what I propose to do,
    and remember that we have no friends to help us:
    Hades has taken them and we are on our own.
So long as I knew that my brother was alive and well
    I had hopes that he would come at last to avenge his
                                                        father.
But now that he is no more I look to you.
You must not flinch in helping me your sister
    to kill our father's murderer, Aegisthus.
I must hide nothing from you anymore.

[After a shocked pause]

What are you waiting for? It's been long enough.
What possible hope can you still entertain?
All you can do is bewail being bereft of your father's
                                                    wealth
    and regret growing older every day
    with no wedding, no nuptials in sight.
Aegisthus is not such a fool
    as to let any children from you or me come into being
    and threaten him.
But if you will go along with me,
    your filiality will first of all earn your dead father's
                                                        praise,
    and your dead brother's too,

then you will ensure a future that is free,
which is yours by nature and by right,
and you will win a worthwhile marriage:
for nobility of spirit does attract.
As to your reputation in the eyes of men,
surely you see the glory that will be yours and mine
if you do what I suggest?
What citizen or foreigner will not salute us
admiringly at sight?
"Just look, friends, at these two sisters
who saved their father's house!
They took their lives in their hands
though their enemies were entrenched
and bravely stood to avenge a murder.
All should love them.
All should respect them.
All should pay them homage at festivals and meetings
for their courage."
That is the kind of thing all will say of us.
Our esteem in life and death will never fade.

Come, dear heart, be persuaded!
Work with your father; support your brother;
save yourself and rescue me from all my pain.
A shameful life, remember, is for the wellborn shame.
CHORUS: Clear thinking in such cases
benefits those who speak and those who listen.
CHRYSOTHEMIS: And she should have thought, my friends,
before she opened her mouth if she had any sense.
But she has none.

[*Turning on* ELECTRA]

How can you possibly be so reckless
and ask me to second you?
Don't you understand that you are a woman, not a man,
and certainly no match for your adversaries?
Their star rises day by day,
ours declines and dwindles into nothing.
Who could ever aim at demolishing such a powerful foe
and come off unscathed, not annihilated?

Be careful!
Even if a hint of this plan leaks out
  our crisis and misfortune double.
And what is the good of fame after an infamous death?
Dying is not the worst,
  but not being able to die when one longs to.
So please, I beg you, curb your anger
  before we're all destroyed and our race wiped out.
I shall be careful not to let your dangerous secret out,
  and you must finally learn to yield to power
    when you are quite without.
CHORUS: [*to* ELECTRA] Listen!
Caution and prudence are mortals' greatest safeguard.
ELECTRA: You have said nothing I did not expect.
I knew well enough that you would refuse what I pro-
                                                 posed.

Well, I must do it alone—single-handed.
I am not going to give it up.
CHRYSOTHEMIS: Too bad!
A pity you didn't show such determination
  when our father died!
You would have carried all before you.
ELECTRA: My feelings were the same; my resolution less.
CHRYSOTHEMIS: Endeavor to keep that resolution all
                                              your life!
ELECTRA: An admonition that surely means you will not
                                              help me.
CHRYSOTHEMIS: No. The very attempt courts disaster!
ELECTRA: I admire your prudence but hate your lack of
                                              courage.
CHRYSOTHEMIS: I shall accept both from you, praise and
                                              blame.
ELECTRA: Praise from me? No fear of that!
CHRYSOTHEMIS: Time will tell!
ELECTRA: Go, you're no good to me!
CHRYSOTHEMIS: I am, if only you were ready to accept!
ELECTRA: Go and tell all this to your mother.
CHRYSOTHEMIS: No, I'd have to hate you to do that!
ELECTRA: May be, but know the disappointment that you
                                              cause me!

CHRYSOTHEMIS: Disappointment? I am only thinking of
your good.

ELECTRA: So I'm expected to follow your idea of good?

CHRYSOTHEMIS: When you can think straight, I am ready
to follow you.

ELECTRA: What a pity that one so lucid goes so wrong!

CHRYSOTHEMIS: A perfect description of your own mistake!

ELECTRA: So you don't think that I speak the truth?

CHRYSOTHEMIS: The truth's not always nice: it can hurt.

ELECTRA: I am not prepared to live by such a law.

CHRYSOTHEMIS: If you carry out your plan
you will come to see that I am right.

ELECTRA: Carry it out I will, no matter how much you
disparage me.

CHRYSOTHEMIS: You really mean to? Can you not change
your mind?

ELECTRA: No. There is nothing worse than muddled
thinking.

CHRYSOTHEMIS: You seem not to understand a single
thing I say.

ELECTRA: I made my decision long ago, not just now.

CHRYSOTHEMIS: Then I'll be off,
since you don't approve of what I say
nor I of what you do.

ELECTRA: By all means go inside!
I shall never follow you
no matter how much you want me to.
Your enticements are a waste of time.

CHRYSOTHEMIS: Well, go on thinking that,
if you imagine it makes sense.
But when you run into trouble you'll remember what I
said.

[CHRYSOTHEMIS *walks into the palace as the women of
the* CHORUS *begin an ode in which after expatiating on
the anomalies of life they focus on the dissension within the
House of Atreus but finally approve of* ELECTRA's
action]

STROPHE I

CHORUS: When we observe how the birds of the air

Unwaveringly sustain and care
For those that give them life and joy,
Why do we not do the same?*
Meanwhile, preparing to strike
Is Zeus' lightning and Justice on high.
O you voice that reaches the dead
Under the earth, make a clarion call
To the Sons of Atreus below
With a dismal message of shame.

ANTISTROPHE I

Say that their house is mortally sick,
That the children quarrel, all harmony shattered.
Daughter Electra braves the storm:
Betrayed and alone, lamenting forever,
Like the incessant nightingale,
Her father's sorrowful fate, she scorns
The thought of dying—as if she wished
To renounce the light—and to entice
The Fury twins to come and avenge.
Could anyone be so loyal to a father?

STROPHE II

No one nobly-hearted
Succumbs to a cowardly inglorious fame:
No, daughter, my daughter!
And you in spite of your tears have chosen
To make a splendid decision:
To arm your remedy and win
By a single act a double renown
To be called a daughter wise and perfect.

ANTISTROPHE II

May I yet see your life
Exalted as much above your hates
In power and prosperity
As now it is beneath them. I
Have found you living a life

---

*A strange observation! The birds of the air do not sustain their parents, whereas we do.

You cannot enjoy, though you have won
The highest prize in the greatest laws:
Your filial loyalty to Zeus.

THIRD EPISODE

[*From the direction of the country* ORESTES *arrives carrying an urn. With him are* PYLADES *and two* ATTENDANTS. ELECTRA *lurks in the background*]

ORESTES: Ladies, could you tell us
  if the directions we were given were correct—
  is this the right way to . . . ?
CHORUS: Where? It depends on what you want.
What have you come for?
ORESTES: I've been asking for where Aegisthus lives.
CHORUS: You have found it. Your directions were correct.
ORESTES: Will one of you, then, please, tell the house
  that at long last we've both arrived?
CHORUS: This girl here is ready to announce it.
ORESTES: Will you go in, Miss, and tell them
  that a party of Phocians are looking for Aegisthus?
ELECTRA: [*glancing at the urn and stepping forward*]
Dear God, I hope you are not bringing proof
  of the terrible rumor.
ORESTES: I know nothing of any rumor,
  but old Strophius instructed me to give you tidings of
                                        Orestes.
ELECTRA: Tidings, sir? . . . How a pang goes through me!
ORESTES: He is dead. And in this small urn we carry
                                        home
  his little heap of ashes.
ELECTRA: Ah, the pain of it! All apprehension gone
  with that burden in your hands.
ORESTES: It may be a consolation for you to know,
  if your tears are for Orestes,
  that this vessel holds his body.
ELECTRA: Please, sir, I beg you,
  if this urn indeed contains him,
  to let me hold it,
  that I may wail and mourn over these ashes

for myself and my whole family.

ORESTES: [*to an* ATTENDANT] Take it and give it to her,
    whoever she may be.
She clearly means no harm and is obviously
a friend or relative.

ELECTRA: [*taking the urn in her hands*] You last remnant
                  and memorial
    of the man I most loved on earth,
    how far from the hopes with which I sent you forth
    is the way I now receive you back!
Now you are nothing
    and I hold you in my hands,
    but you were radiant, my boy, when I sent you hence.
I wish I had breathed my last
    and never stolen you away in these hands of mine
    to rescue you from murder and sent you to a foreign
                  land.

You could have died that very day
    and lain beside your father in his tomb.
Instead, you have perished miserably
    in exile, far from home and from your sister.
What is so sad is that I never bathed you
    with my loving hands,
    or retrieved your body, as I should have,
    from the flaming pyre.
These rites you had from strangers' hands, you poor
                  dear one,
    and now come home to us as a little heap in a little
                  urn.

Wasted, wasted, gone in vain,
    all my nursing of you long ago, the labor I delighted
                  in!

You were never your mother's pet so much as mine,
    nor was anyone in the house your nurse but me,
    whom you always addressed as "sister."
With your death all this has vanished in a day,
    all with you in a whirlwind swept away:
    My father is gone, me you have killed, and you your-
                 self dead.

The ones that hate us laugh,
    and your non-mother mother is mad with joy.

You promised in secret messages
   to come and punish her,
   but your sad destiny, yours and mine, has not allowed
                                                       it
   and sends instead of your sweet form
   the ashes of an aimless shade.

[*Breaking down in tears as she hugs the urn*]

Sad! Sad!
Your pitiable body unbearably sad!
Ah, my darling brother, how your tragic exodus destroys
                                                    me—
   yes, has destroyed me!
Receive me in your present home,
   a nothing into nothing
   that I may live with you below forever.
For when you were above
   we shared our fate together;
   so now I want to die and share your tomb:
   Those who die—I do not see them suffer.
CHORUS: Electra, remember this:
   you are the child of a mortal father
   and Orestes was mortal too;
   therefore do not overdo your grief.
This is a debt we all must pay.
ORESTES: Dear God, what can I say? What line to take?
How shall I break the news? I cannot hold my tongue.
ELECTRA: What is the matter? And why this outburst?
ORESTES: Is the figure before me that of the noble
                                              Electra?
ELECTRA: This is she—a most unhappy woman.
ORESTES: The pity of it! The pain of this whole thing!
ELECTRA: Surely it is not for me, sir, that you are so
                                                 upset?
ORESTES: The abuse and wreckage of a person!
ELECTRA: Exactly that! Your description, sir, is apt.
ORESTES: I cannot bear to think of your wretched un-
                                              wedded life.
ELECTRA: Sir, what makes you so sorrowfully stare at
                                                   me?
ORESTES: My troubles were nothing. I had no idea.

ELECTRA: What have I said that makes you say such
things?

ORESTES: The evidence in you of untold suffering.

ELECTRA: What you see is hardly even half.

ORESTES: Half! What could be more unbearable to see?

ELECTRA: Because I live with murderers?

ORESTES: Murderers of whom? What crime are you hinting at?

ELECTRA: Murderers of my father, while I am forced to
be a slave.

ORESTES: Who is it, then, that forces you?

ELECTRA: A so-called mother, who is far from motherly.

ORESTES: What does she do? Is she violent and oppressive?

ELECTRA: Violent and oppressive in every kind of way.

ORESTES: Is there nobody to help you and put a stop to
it?

ELECTRA: Nobody! There was once and you have shown
me his ashes.

ORESTES: Poor unhappy one, I am brooding on your
misery!

ELECTRA: Then you are the only one, be sure of that.

ORESTES: Yes, the only one to come and show you
sympathy.

ELECTRA: Could you be, I wonder, some unknown
relative?

ORESTES: I could answer that if these women can be
trusted.

ELECTRA: They are loyal and can be trusted, so speak
quite freely.

ORESTES: [*moving to take the urn*] Then let go that urn
and I'll tell you everything.

ELECTRA: No, no, sir, by all the gods, do not be so
heartless!

ORESTES: Do what I say and you will not be sorry!

ELECTRA: [*looking down at the urn*] Ah, not to bury you,
Orestes; I cannot bear the thought!

ORESTES: Say nothing so sinister. There is no cause for
regret.

ELECTRA: No cause for regret for my dead brother?

ORESTES: It is not correct to call him that.

ELECTRA: Not correct? Am I worth so little to my dead
                                                         brother?
ORESTES: No, not worth so little but not appropriate.
ELECTRA: It is, if in this urn I hold Orestes' dust?
ORESTES: It is not Orestes, except in fiction.
ELECTRA: Then where is the tomb of this unlucky man?
ORESTES: There is no tomb. The living do not need one.
ELECTRA: What, boy, are you saying?
ORESTES: I am telling the truth.
ELECTRA: Do you mean the man is alive?
ORESTES: If I am alive, yes.
ELECTRA: What? Are you he?
ORESTES: See this signet ring? It was my father's,
    and tell me if I am telling the truth.
ELECTRA: [*putting down the urn*] O day of bliss!
ORESTES: Pure bliss indeed!
ELECTRA: Really your voice at last?
ORESTES: None other can reply.
ELECTRA: [*flinging herself into his arms*] Do I really hold
                                                   you in my arms?
ORESTES: You can hold me there forever.
ELECTRA: Beloved women and fellow citizens,
    look on Orestes here, who pretended to be dead
    and now by pretense has come to life.
CHORUS: We see him, daughter, and the very sight
    pricks our eyes with tears of joy.

CHORAL DIALOGUE

STROPHE

ELECTRA: You blessed son:
    Son of the one that I loved most
    At last you have come:
    You are here, you have seen her you loved.
ORESTES: Yes, I am here, but keep it quiet and wait.
ELECTRA: Whatever for?
ORESTES: It is best to keep quiet so those inside won't
                                                      hear.
ELECTRA: By Artemis ever a virgin, I refuse to cower
    Before those females within who pollute the earth.
ORESTES: But remember that women can be martial too,

As I think you know from bitter experience.

ELECTRA: Ah, the horror, the horror!

Our terrible past never to be ridded or hidden or forgotten.

ORESTES: I know and wait for the time when we can
undo the damage.

ANTISTROPHE

ELECTRA: Yes, every moment,
Every day of that time you recall,
Which only just now
Are my lips set free to speak of.

ORESTES: Yes, and I say the same, but guard that freedom.

ELECTRA: Guard it how?

ORESTES: By being careful in speech till the time is ripe.

ELECTRA: Would you prefer silence to speech when you
Have just reappeared and I have seen your face?
Something I hardly hoped or ever dreamed of.

ORESTES: You see it . . . The gods have prompted me to
come.

ELECTRA: A grace beyond all joy!
It must indeed have been a god that brought you home.

ORESTES: I must not stop your joy, but too much makes
me nervous.

EPODE

ELECTRA: O welcome:
You who have made this happiest journey here
After so many years
And appeared before me!

But since you have seen my sorrows now you must
not . . .

ORESTES: Must not what?

ELECTRA: Cheat me of the sweet
Vision and consolation of your face.

ORESTES: If anyone tried to do that I would be furious.

ELECTRA: So you consent?

ORESTES: Of course I consent!

ELECTRA: O you beloved!
The voice I never expected to hear
And yet managed to curb my excitement,

Make myself go dumb when I heard it.
But I have you now with your dear face
  Which even in my darkest hours I never forgot.

FOURTH EPISODE

ORESTES: Enough of talk:
  no need to explain to me
  what a criminal our mother is,
  and how Aegisthus with mindless extravagance
  leaches away the wealth of our father's house.
The recital would filch from you the time to act.
So tell me what we need to do:
Should we come out in the open or be hidden
  in our design to stopper our enemies' laughter?
Meanwhile, when we enter the palace
  we must beware because of your radiant face
  that our mother does not become suspicious.
We must continue to mourn as though
  the fiction told were really the truth.
After our success will be the time
  to celebrate and laugh.
ELECTRA: Brother, I'll suit my conduct to your wishes.
All my happiness is a gift from you, not from myself.
I would never let myself inflict on you the smallest pain
  even to give myself the greatest gain.
That would overturn the providence that befriends us
                                                now.
I think you understand how things are here,
  how could you not?
You must have heard that Aegisthus is not here,
  but Mother is at home.
Do not be afraid that she'll see my face
  lit up with smiles;
  long hatred of her has seeped into my heart,
  and my seeing you will keep tears flowing for joy.
How could they cease, when on this day
  I see you back—first dead and then alive?
So amazing is the change you have wrought on me
  that were my father to return alive
  it would not seem a greater miracle and I'd believe it.

After such a reappearance as this,
   command me any way you like.
Had I continued on my own
   I should have chosen from a double path:
   either a courageous freedom or courageous death.
ORESTES: Quiet! I hear someone coming out.
ELECTRA: [*to* ORESTES *and* PYLADES, *who now carries the
               urn*] Good sirs, go inside.
You carry something no one would refuse and no one
                              want.

[*The* TUTOR *hurries out of the palace*]

TUTOR: You total fools, you mindless children,
   are you tired of life, completely witless?
Have you no idea
   that you are not just cheek by jowl with danger
   but in the very center of it?
Had I not been on my guard at these doors all this time
   your plans would have entered the place long before
                              you.
But I've taken care of that;
   so stop all your persiflage and cries of joy,
   which you cannot get enough of, and come with me.
Delay is dangerous and must cease.
ORESTES: Once inside what may I expect?
TUTOR: Nothing bad, for no one knows you.
ORESTES: I presume you have reported me as dead?
TUTOR: Yes, you are now among the shades in Hades.
ORESTES: Is there rejoicing? What are they saying?
TUTOR: I'll tell you later.
Meanwhile all goes well in there—and all does not.
ELECTRA: [*pointing to the* TUTOR] Brother, who is he?
                        Please tell me.
ORESTES: Can't you guess?
ELECTRA: I've never seen him before.
ORESTES: Don't you recognize the man
   into whose hands you put me once?
ELECTRA: What man was that? I don't follow you.
ORESTES: The man who through your providence
   sneaked me out to the plain of Phocis.

ELECTRA: Is he the man who proved my only friend
   when my father was assassinated?
ORESTES: He is. No more questions, please!
ELECTRA: O happy day! You single savior of Agamem-
                                          non's house,
   how are you here?
Are you really the one who rescued my brother and me
   from so many horrors?

[*She begins to shower him with kisses*]

Bless your dear hands and your gentle feet!
How could you be with me so long unrecognized?
You were the death of me in your report,
   and then the sweetest remedy in act.
I salute you, father,
   for I see in you a father. Bless you!
Strange that I have hated and loved you in a single day!
Yes, more than any other mortal.
TUTOR: Enough, I think!
Let the story of the time between
   like the spiral of the nights and days,
   unfold all this to you, Electra.
But to you standing here, let me insist:
   now is the time to strike.
Now Clytemnestra is alone,
   now no man is with her.
If you wait you will have to fight
   not just the inmates but a numerous and more experi-
                                          enced crew.
ORESTES: Pylades, our mission needs no further speeches.
We must go inside at once
   after paying homage to the deities
   who preside at my father's portals.

[ORESTES, PYLADES, *and the* TUTOR *enter the palace.*
ELECTRA *turns to the statue of Apollo and opens her
                                          arms in prayer*]

ELECTRA: O King Apollo, graciously support them
   and me as well.

So many times I have approached your shrine in prayer
  with such offerings that I had.
And now, Lycian Apollo, with what offerings I can
                                  promise,
  I fall on my knees before you,
  I beg you and implore you
  to give us your most generous help
  and show the world how the gods requite the wicked.
[ELECTRA *follows the others into the palace*]

STROPHE

CHORUS: See how Ares advances
  With blood in his breath for vengeance.
Into the house already have gone the hounds
  That no one can flee from, the hounds that hunt
  The guilty wicked.
And I foresee the deed that follows.

ANTISTROPHE

The champion of the departed
  Is stealthily entering the palace:
  The ancestral home of his father with all its wealth.
  He carries a weapon newly honed for blood
  And Hermes has cloaked
  The act in darkness soon to happen.

FOURTH EPISODE

[ELECTRA *comes out of the palace*]

CHORAL TRIALOGUE

ELECTRA: [*darting out of the palace*] Dearest women, the
                    men will soon have done the deed
  But wait in silence.
CHORUS: How is it going? What are they doing?
ELECTRA: She's on her way to bury the urn. Those two
                    are with her.
CHORUS: But what has made you hurry out?
ELECTRA: I must watch
  In case we miss Aegisthus when he enters in.

[*A cry is heard from within the palace*]

CLYTEMNESTRA: O gods! The house is empty of friends
but full of killers.

ELECTRA: Women, did you hear that cry coming from
inside?

CHORUS: Yes, a desperate cry
Enough to make me shudder.

CLYTEMNESTRA: [*from within*] Help, help, Aegisthus!
Where are you? O help!

ELECTRA: There again, another shriek!

CLYTEMNESTRA: [*within*] My son, my son,
Have pity on your mother.

ELECTRA: You had no pity
On him or his father.

CHORUS: O you fated city!
You unlucky line! Destiny and death
Have been creeping up on you from day to day.

CLYTEMNESTRA: [*within*] Ah, I am struck!

ELECTRA: Strike again if you have the power.

CLYTEMNESTRA: [*within*] And struck again!

ELECTRA: I wish it were Aegisthus too.

CHORUS: The spells are working, the buried live.
Now is the turn for the killer's blood:
Blood for the blood that was spilled from those so
long ago.

[ORESTES *and* PYLADES *emerge from the palace with
dripping swords*]

ANTISTROPHE*

CHORUS: Look, here they come from Ares with reeking
hands:
I cannot blame the act.

ELECTRA: Orestes, how did you do?

ORESTES: It all went well in the palace.
The prophecy Apollo made has been fulfilled.

ELECTRA: Is the cursed woman dead?

ORESTES: Never again

*Since five lines are missing from the antistrophe, there cannot be
a correspondence.

Will your overpowering mother ever hurt you.
CHORUS: Hold! I see Aegisthus in the distance.
ELECTRA: Boys,
   Get back!
ORESTES: Where do you see the man?
ELECTRA: He comes
   Towards us from the edge of town with a smile on his
                                                        face.
CHORUS: Tell him something reassuring
   Inducing him to hurtle blindfold
   Into the hidden trap and tussle with his doom.

                    FIFTH EPISODE

[AEGISTHUS *dressed in traveling clothes halts before
the palace*]

AEGISTHUS: Which of you can tell me
   where the Phocian visitors are who brought us news
   that Orestes lost his life in a chariot accident?

[*Turning on* ELECTRA]

You, you there—yes, I'm talking to *you,*
   so forward usually; this affects you most
   you must have most to tell.
ELECTRA: Certainly I know!
I could hardly be a stranger to what happens
   to those I love.
AEGISTHUS: Then where are those visitors? Out with it!
ELECTRA: Inside . . . They have a way to their hostess'
                                                        heart.
AEGISTHUS: Did they really say that he was dead?
ELECTRA: Not just say but produce the evidence.
AEGISTHUS: Is one able to see it with one's own eyes?
ELECTRA: One can, but it's not a pleasant sight.
AEGISTHUS: Delightful information! Not usual from you!
ELECTRA: You are welcome to it, so enjoy it.
AEGISTHUS: I order the doors open for all to see—
   every Argive and Mycenaean,
   so that anyone who cherished empty hopes in this man

may now see him dead.
This saves me of the need to teach you sense by force.
ELECTRA: I am carrying out my orders,
    for I've learned to be subservient to superior force.

[*The palace gates open, disclosing a shrouded corpse,
at the side of which stand* ORESTES *and* PYLADES]

AEGISTHUS: [*expecting to see the corpse of* ORESTES] I
                look on that which heaven has allowed,
    and rightly so—if that is not presumptuous.
Remove everything that hides his face—those eyes.
Let me, yes, even me, lament my relative.
ORESTES: [*whom, of course,* AEGISTHUS *does not recognize*] Lift the shroud yourself.
It's not for me but you to look upon
    and murmur tender words.
AEGISTHUS: Good advice, and I shall follow it,
    but call Clytemnestra out, if she is in the house.
ORESTES: She is very near. Look no further.

[ORESTES *lifts the covering over the corpse*]

AEGISTHUS: My God, the shock! What am I looking at?
ORESTES: Shock from what? . . . Someone you know?
AEGISTHUS: A trap! Caught in a trap!
Who are the men behind it?
ORESTES: Do you not realize that you, still living,
    have been parleying with the dead?
AEGISTHUS: How monstrous, you make it all too clear:
    you are Orestes!
ORESTES: Such a clever seer and wrong so long!
AEGISTHUS: Done for and destroyed! . . . Let me say a
                          word!
ELECTRA: For the gods' sake, brother,
    do not let him talk.*
Kill him at once, and offer his body

---

*I have omitted the following bracketed sentence, which seems to
me an obvious interpolation: "When mortals are overtaken by disaster what good is a short reprieve from death?"

to the creatures who will give it the burial it deserves—
out of our sight.
Only this will compensate for all that I endured.
ORESTES: Go inside at once.
It's not words I want from you, but your life.
AEGISTHUS: Must you push me into the palace?
If killing me is a handsome thing to do,
    kill me here, not in the dark.
ORESTES: Stop dictating, and go where you killed my
                                                father—
    to die in the selfsame spot.
AEGISTHUS: Is this house doomed to see
    the full demise of the Pelopian line
    present and to come?
ORESTES: Yours at least I can predict with certainty.
AEGISTHUS: A pity your father did not have that skill!
ORESTES: Your repartee is delaying us. Get inside!
AEGISTHUS: Lead the way!
ORESTES: No, you go first.
AEGISTHUS: So I won't escape?
ORESTES: So you won't die just wherever you choose.
I want the experience to be bitter.
Swift justice should overtake every criminal act:
    Death to all who decide to flout the law,
    then the prevalence of crime would be no more.

[ORESTES and PYLADES, *at the point of the sword, hustle*
AEGISTHUS *into the palace*]

CHORUS: House of Atreus, how many sorrows have you
                                                endured,
    But finally freed this day and finally cured?

PHILOCTETES

ΦΙΛΟΚΤΗΤΗΣ

Philoctetes—the name means Lover of the Bow and is pronounced Philoctétes, not Philóctetes—is a genuinely pathetic and even disarming character. Deserted on the lonely island of Lemnos because of his stinking foot by the higher-ups of the Greek expeditionary force to Troy, he is abominably treated by them. Essentially an honest human being, he finds himself pitted against the powerful and unscrupulous, in which conflict he shows himself honest to the point of naïveté, and in the last section of the play his rhythmical altercation with the sailors of the Chorus comes perilously close to being comic, as his dogged recalcitrance tumbles over itself in a litany of desperations.

As to Neoptolemus, he is a likable enough youth, but he is torn between the dishonesty of cheating Philoctetes out of the magic bow given to him by Heracles and a decent behavior, which, however, lets the Greeks down. The purpose of the story is to highlight the claims of truth and right action against those of expediency. Confronted with this quandary, Neoptolemus is no match for the clever and ruthless Odysseus, who trips him into a series of pretenses and lies.

Heracles makes a timely and fairly credible deus ex machina. He was a mortal who, because of his services to mankind, was granted immortality and later worshiped. He gave Philoctetes his magic bow that was fashioned by Hephaestus in reward for a deathbed service. When Heracles mounted his funeral pyre it was Philoctetes that lit it. As the flames consumed the hero's mortal parts, his astral body was freed to mount to heaven.

The play was produced in 409 B.C. at the City Dionysia in Athens when Sophocles was in his eighty-seventh or eighty-eighth year. Long before, in 468, he won first prize with his first play, the lost *Triptolemus,* when he was only twenty-seven; and now with almost his last play, *Philoctetes,* he wins it again.

Incidentally, if I am not mistaken, this is the only play in the whole canon of Greek drama in which—if one excepts nymphs—no female plays a part or is even mentioned.

CHARACTERS

ODYSSEUS, king of Ithaca and one of the Greek chiefs at Troy
NEOPTOLEMUS, prince and son of Achilles
CHORUS, sailors under the command of Neoptolemus
PHILOCTETES, Greek warrior
MERCHANT, disguised as a sailor
HERACLES, deified Greek hero
SCOUT, sailor from one of the ships (nonspeaking)
ATTENDANTS, sailors attending Neoptolemus and Odysseus

TIME AND SETTING

The war against Troy has been dragging on for almost ten years and seems to have reached a stalemate. Meanwhile, many years ago, Philoctetes was forced to eke out a Robinson Crusoe kind of existence on the uninhabited island of Lemnos, where he was marooned by the Greeks because of the stinking wound in his foot, induced by a snakebite. Now the Greeks, under Odysseus, have come back for him because an oracle has revealed that Troy will never be overthrown without Philoctetes and the magic bow of Heracles that is in his possession— the bow that never misses. The scene is Philoctetes' cave in the side of a cliff on the island of Lemnos. Odysseus and Neoptolemus accompanied by a scout come from the direction of the harbor.

PROLOGUE

ODYSSEUS: So here we are on the sea-girt island of Lemnos!

What a godforsaken spot!
No tread of human feet . . . quite uninhabited!
Yet it was here, Neoptolemus,
    you son of Achilles, the most illustrious of the Greeks,
    that long ago I landed Philoctetes the Malian, son of
                                 Poeas,
    because I was told to do so by those in command.
His foot was a rotting mass of pus
    that left us no peace to sacrifice or pour libations
    because the whole camp was curdled by his screams
    and sinister bellowing.
But I won't go on:
    this is not the time for explanations,
    in case he finds out that I am here
    and upsets my plan for capturing him.
Come, we have work to do and I need your help.
We have to find a cave somewhere here
    with two entrances:
    one with a sunny aspect for cold weather,
    the other letting in sleepy breezes in the summer:
    in other words, an opening at each end.
A little below this, on the left,
    there ought to be a spring of drinkable water—
    unless it has given up.
Move quietly, and give me a sign if he's still living there;
    otherwise we'll have to search elsewhere
    and I must discuss with you what course we ought to
                                     take
    and you and I can pool conclusions.
NEOPTOLEMUS: [*gazing upwards*] Odysseus, my lord, our
                          objective is not far off:
    I think I see exactly the cave that you describe.
ODYSSEUS: Up or down? . . . I'm not clear.
NEOPTOLEMUS: It's above, and I hear no footsteps.
ODYSSEUS: Careful! He could be curled up in sleep.
NEOPTOLEMUS: I see a sort of room with no one in it.
ODYSSEUS: And no sign of someone's living there?
NEOPTOLEMUS: Yes, a mattress of leaves that looks used.
ODYSSEUS: Nothing else? Nothing under the roof?
NEOPTOLEMUS: Only a wooden cup, crudely made, and
                            some kindling.

ODYSSEUS: What you describe are his treasures.

NEOPTOLEMUS: Aha! There's something else: some rags
drying in the sun.

They're blotched with sort of pus stains from a sore.

ODYSSEUS: This is obviously where the man lives,
and he must be somewhere near.

A man crippled with a gangrenous foot
cannot travel very far, can he?

I expect he's gone looking for food,
or perhaps some medicinal herb he knows of.

Tell the man with you to keep a sharp lookout
in case I'm ambushed.

He'd give anything to get hold of me,
more than anyone in the Argive army.

NEOPTOLEMUS: The man is on his way to watch the path.
Is there anything else? Let me know.

ODYSSEUS: Son of Achilles,
the mission you're on will test your worth,
and not just with your body.

I've given you a strange task, something new to you,
but you must do it. You are here to help me.

NEOPTOLEMUS: What are your orders?

ODYSSEUS: You have to spin a yarn to Philoctetes.

When he asks you who you are and where you're from,
say "the son of Achilles"—
no need to lie about that—and you're sailing home.

You can't stand the Greeks anymore
and have left the armada in a rage.

They lied to you about leaving home,
their only hope of taking Ilium,
but when you did,
instead of handing over to you the arms of Achilles—
yours by rights—they gave them to Odysseus.

Say whatever you like about me:
heap me with abuse . . .
it won't hurt me in the least,
but anything less will spell disaster for the Greeks;
for unless this man's bow is taken
you'll never conquer the land of Troy.

Let me explain to you
why it is safe for you to deal with this man

but not for me, and without risk.
When you set sail you'd pledged yourself to none,
  you were not compelled,
  nor part of the earlier expedition;
  but none of these conditions apply to me.
If he comes on me with bow in hand,
  I'm a dead man;
  and you, my friend, because of me will be dead as
                                                  well.

So what we have to plan
  is a way for you to steal the magic bow.
I know, my boy, it's not your character
  to lie or injure others;
  but success is always sweet
  if we get something that we want.
Just do it, and we'll be proved right.
Lend yourself to me
  and be a rascal just for a day.
Afterwards, you'll have all the time in the world
  to be the most upright man alive.
NEOPTOLEMUS: Son of Laertes, it distresses me
  to carry out a program I find shocking.
It's not in my nature to deceive.
That's just the way I am. So was my father.
I am ready to take the man by force but not by fraud.
With only one foot
  he can't be a match for the rest of us.
I was sent to help you
  and the last thing I want is to seem disloyal,
  but I'd rather make an honest blunder, my lord,
  than triumph through a lie.
ODYSSEUS: Son of a princely father,
  I too when I was a lad
  kept a ready arm but a careful tongue,
  but now when it comes to the test
  I see that for us mortals
  it's the tongue rather than activity that directs events.
NEOPTOLEMUS: So what do you want? Anything but
                                                  lying.
ODYSSEUS: To take Philoctetes by a trick.
NEOPTOLEMUS: Why trickery rather than persuasion?

ODYSSEUS: He'll never be persuaded, nor you capture
                  him by force.

NEOPTOLEMUS: Is he as formidable as all that?

ODYSSEUS: Yes, his lethal arrows cannot miss.

NEOPTOLEMUS: So he's unapproachable?

ODYSSEUS: Except by trickery, as I am telling you.

NEOPTOLEMUS: But telling lies is shameful, don't you
                  think?

ODYSSEUS: Not if the lie brings salvation.

NEOPTOLEMUS: How can one face oneself as a liar?

ODYSSEUS: You're a loser if you hesitate.

NEOPTOLEMUS: But what do I gain if he comes to Troy?

ODYSSEUS: Troy. His bow is the only thing that takes it.

NEOPTOLEMUS: I thought you said that I was the one to
                  take it?

ODYSSEUS: You can't without the bow, and the bow can't
                  without you.

NEOPTOLEMUS: In that case it's worth trying to get it.

ODYSSEUS: If you do, you'll be a double winner.

NEOPTOLEMUS: Winner of what? Tell me and I'll do it.

ODYSSEUS: You'll have the reputation of being both in-
                  telligent and brave.

NEOPTOLEMUS: Fine! I'll do it, scruples and all.

ODYSSEUS: Then do you remember my instructions?

NEOPTOLEMUS: Of course! Especially as I now agree.

ODYSSEUS: Very well, stay here and wait for him.
I'll disappear and not be seen
    and send the scout back to the ship.
If you seem to be taking too long
    I'll send the same man back here again
    disguised as a sea captain. . . . He won't be known.
Then, my boy,
    listen carefully to the yarn he spins
    and pick up the clues.
Now I'm off to the ship.
Everything's in your hands.
May Hermes, god of cunning, guide us,
    and Athena, goddess of victory, too—
    who never lets me down.

[ODYSSEUS *goes off in the direction of the harbor, to-*
gether with the SCOUT, *as the* CHORUS *of sailors enters*]

PARADOS OR ENTRY MARCH

[*The* SAILORS, *nervous of having to deal with someone as tricky as* ODYSSEUS, *ask the advice of their commander,* NEOPTOLEMUS, *in a choral dialogue, expressing their pity for the miserable* PHILOCTETES]

STROPHE I

CHORUS: An alien in an alien land, good master,
　　What do I say to this wary man?
Please, will you tell me.
Your skill and cleverness excel
　　Others, and in your hands the scepter divine
　　Of Zeus is held. To you has descended
　　The ancestral power. So tell me, my son,
　　How must I serve you?
NEOPTOLEMUS: It is safe for the moment to look for his
　　　　　　　　　　　　　　　　　　　　den
　　Deep in the woods, but when he returns
　　To his lair, this ominous vagabond, then
　　Be ready to answer my signals in time
　　And render assistance as required.

ANTISTROPHE I*

CHORUS: Long have I taken care of your cares, my Lord,
　　With an eye on the lookout for what you need,
So tell me now
　　The kind of retreat he makes his home.
Where is it? I need to know, lest suddenly
　　He drops on me from somewhere. Where
　　Does he rest and where does he roam
　　When not at home?
NEOPTOLEMUS: Over there is his rocky cell. Can you see
　　The double openings?
CHORUS: But the wretched inmate—where has he gone?
NEOPTOLEMUS: Probably dragging his pain-stricken foot
　　Somewhere near, searching for food.
Such is the rumored life he leads:
　　Shooting beasts with his flying shafts,

*In the extant texts strophe and antistrophe do not always match.

Tortured in his torturing hurt,
And no one, they say,
Ever comes near to heal his pain.

STROPHE II

CHORUS: I feel for him, for nobody cares,
He has no comrade he can look to:
Miserable man, always alone,
Savaged by a savaging sickness,
At a loss, in constant lack.
How does this sad man keep going?
What devious decisions of heaven!
What a blighted race is man—
And life unkind!

ANTISTROPHE II

Perhaps no less a scion than any
Of great families, this fellow
Lies bereft of everything,
Famished and alone among
The spotted furry animals:
Uncared for, incurable, and in pain,
While Echo with unstoppered mouth
Seemingly so far away
Repeats his cries.

EPODE

NEOPTOLEMUS: Nothing of this is new to me,
And if *I* am allowed to judge
I'd say his sufferings had their source
From cruel Chryse,* allowed by heaven.
And now his life without companions,
The gods have willed, to stop him bending
His magic bow against Troy
Until such time as by their shafts
Troy is doomed to fall.

---

*It was on the island of Tenedos at the shrine of Athena Chryse that Philoctetes presumed to approach too near the altar of the goddess and was bitten in the heel by a water snake, the guardian of the sanctuary.

CHORUS: Quiet, my boy!
NEOPTOLEMUS: What now?

STROPHE III
CHORUS: A sound rang out
  Like from a man in desperate pain.
It came from over there, I think,
  Or here—a booming booming sound:
  A cripple's voice fumbling his way.
I can't mistake
  The tortured cry of human pain.
Even from afar it is too clear.
And so, my son . . .
NEOPTOLEMUS: Yes, what?

ANTISTROPHE III
CHORUS: We must be alert.
  The man is not far off, he's here:
  Not piping music on a flute
  Like a shepherd in the meadows,
  No, but stumbling along, I think,
  With rending cries that travel far;
  Or perhaps because of the shock
  Of seeing the anchored ship. His cry
    Is something awful.

FIRST EPISODE*
PHILOCTETES: [*bedraggled and uncouth, limping in*] Good
strangers, who may you be
  putting into this shoreless harbor,
  this uninhabited domain.
Might I guess what country and what race you're from?
You are dressed like Greeks—my most beloved land.
But let me hear you speak.
Do not shrink from me
  in revulsion at my savage aspect
  but befriend an unhappy, lonely wretch

---

*"Episode" means literally "In addition to the Ode," or after it.

crushed by this malady, without companion or mate.
Speak if you come as friends.
Oh, answer, please.
It would be a sin
    not to talk to me as I do to you.
NEOPTOLEMUS: Understand first, good sir, that we are
                                              Greeks—
    which you are so anxious to be told.
PHILOCTETES: Oh blessed sound!
The joy of being greeted so after all this time!
But what was the reason, my son, that brought you here?
What impelled you to come?
Which of the winds, I wonder, was so kind?
Tell me everything . . . I must know who you are.
NEOPTOLEMUS: I was born on the island of Scyros
    and now am sailing home.
I am known as the son of Achilles
    and my name is Neoptolemus.
Now you know all.
PHILOCTETES: Then you are son of a most loved father
    from a well-loved land;
    and your grandfather was Lycomedes.
What is your purpose in lighting on these shores,
    and from where have you sailed?
NEOPTOLEMUS: I am on a present course from Ilium.
PHILOCTETES: How so? You were assuredly not one of
                                              our team
    on the first voyage to Ilium.
NEOPTOLEMUS: Do you mean to say you were involved
                                              in that?
PHILOCTETES: Then can you guess, my son, whom you
                                              are looking at?
NEOPTOLEMUS: [*hedging*] How could I know a man I've
                                              never seen?
PHILOCTETES: Then you've never even heard my name
    or heard the story of the miseries that torture me?
NEOPTOLEMUS: Believe me, I know nothing of what you
                                              ask.
PHILOCTETES: Then what an abomination in the sight of
                                              heaven I must be,

to think that nothing of my plight
has reached my home or anywhere in Greece;
while the men who cast me adrift so callously
keep it dark and laugh, and my disease
waxes in virulence.
My son, my boy, whose father was Achilles,
I am the one you may have heard of
as master of the bow of Heracles.
I am the son of Poeas, I am Philoctetes,
whom the two commanders and Odysseus, lord of
Cephallus,
disgracefully deserted in this solitude,
though I was withering away with a savage sore
struck by the bite of a deadly snake.
Yes, my son,
they put in here, after the island of Chryse, with their
ships
and left me desolate with my disease.
After all the tossing of the voyage
I was sleeping in a cavern on the shore.
They took advantage of that and slipped away,
setting out as for a beggar
a few rags and a pittance of provisions.
May heaven reward them with the same!
Can you imagine, my son,
the awakening that was mine when they were gone?
The tears I shed, the desperation that I felt
when I saw that all the ships with which I'd sailed
were gone?
There was nobody there: not a soul to help
or soften the course of my disease.
When I looked around me
anguish was all I saw—a plentitude of that, my son.

The seasons passed one by one
and I was left to provide for myself in my shoddy home.
My belly's needs, this bow provided,
bringing down wild pigeons on the wing.
To retrieve the quarry that my shaft brought down,
I would drag my foot to it in dismal loneliness.
Or if water needed to be fetched

and firewood collected when the first frosts struck,
as they do in winter here,
I would crawl out in misery and cope with it.
There was no fire
until I learned to strike two flints together
and laboriously coax the buried spark to action.
That has been my salvation.
And so you see,
a roof over my head and a fire
give me all I need except a cure for my corruption.

And now, my son, a word about the island.
No seaman chooses to come here:
there is no proper anchorage,
no outlet for commerce or hospitality.
This is no place for any man in his right mind.
Nevertheless, on those occasions when someone is
forced to put in here,
(which happens at times in man's long history),
such visitors are filled with compassion for me,
and out of pity sometimes give me a little food or
clothing,
but one thing nobody will do when I mention it:
take me home.
For nine years now I have been withering away,
miserable in my hunger yet feeding my disease.
That is how the Sons of Atreus and the selfishly propelled
Odysseus have treated me, my boy.
May the gods of Olympus deign
to do the same to them one day!

CHORUS: I am sure I feel the same pity for you, son of
Poeas,
as those strangers did who came here.

NEOPTOLEMUS: And I too recognize the truth of what
you say,
having found like you that the Sons of Atreus
and the selfishly propelled Odysseus are evil men.

PHILOCTETES: So you too have a grievance against the
benighted Sons of Atreus and are angry?

NEOPTOLEMUS: Yes, I'd give anything one day to show
my loathing

and teach Mycenae, and Sparta too,
that Scyros also can mother stalwart sons.
PHILOCTETES: Well said, my boy!
Now tell me what it was that sparked your rage against
them?
NEOPTOLEMUS: Son of Poeas, let me tell you,
painful though it is to speak of it,
the abuse I suffered at their hands when I went to
them.
For when it was Achilles' destiny to die . . .
PHILOCTETES: Oh no? . . . Say no more until you tell me:
Is the son of Peleus dead?
NEOPTOLEMUS: Dead, and by no mortal hand but by a
god's,
downed, they say, by an arrow from Apollo.
PHILOCTETES: Illustrious, then, the slayer and the slain!
Which leaves me wondering which I should do first, my
son:
ask about your wrongs or mourn for him.
NEOPTOLEMUS: Your own sufferings are enough, poor
man, I think,
without your taking on the grief of others.
PHILOCTETES: You are right!
So go back to your story of how you were abused.
NEOPTOLEMUS: They came for me in a decorated ship,
"noble" Odysseus and my father's tutor,
saying—whether true or not I do not know—
that now my father was dead
no other but me would take the towers of Troy.
Saying which, they did not let me linger,
and I sailed at once.
I longed to see my dead father before his burial,
for never once had I beheld him.
But there was this too,
the fascinating promise that if I went
I would topple the towers of Troy.
The second day of the voyage
oar and wind brought me already to nasty Sigeum.
The army immediately thronged around me

with congratulations, declaring
that they saw in me Achilles alive again.
But of course he was dead. Laid out.
Unhappy me! I wept for him,
then went to the Sons of Atreus, supposing they were
                                    friends,
to claim my father's arms and all that belonged to him.
I could hardly believe their disgraceful answer.
"Seed of Achilles,
you can have everything that was your father's,
but his arms already belong to Odysseus, son of Laertes."
Tears pricked my eyes
and I leapt up in a passion,
biting out the words:
"Rascal, have you had the effrontery
to give my arms to someone else without my leave?"
Odysseus, who was standing by, said:
"Yes, boy, it was a right decision,
for I was there and rescued them and him."
In my rage at being cheated of my armor,
I flung every kind of abuse at him bar none.
At which point,
nettled by my taunts but without anger, he replied:
"You were not here with us
but somewhere where you should not have been;
and because of your impudent tongue
you shall never sail to Scyros with those arms."

Thus scolded and insulted I am sailing home,
robbed of what was mine
by that meanest of the mean—Odysseus.
Nevertheless, I lay the blame
not so much on him as on the commanders:
the whole state and army are under their control
and undisciplined men become criminals because of
                                    them.
That is everything I have to say.
My blessing and the gods' as well
on all who hate the Atreidae.

STROPHE

CHORUS: Mother of mountains, Earth,
Mother even of Zeus:
Who churn up the gold in the Pactolus river,
I called for your help, my lady Mother
When the Sons of Atreus
In all their insolence
Came up against this man and handed over
His father's arms to Laertes' son . . .
O you who sit behind
Bull-butchering lions—
O blessed one!

SECOND EPISODE

PHILOCTETES: I am in full sympathy with you, my friends,
who have sailed here with a grievance so like mine.
I recognize exactly
the machinations of the Atreidae and Odysseus,
whose tongue spews every kind of villainy and mischief,
all to gain the most sordid of ends.
This does not surprise me;
what does is that Ajax the Big* was there and endured it.
NEOPTOLEMUS: No, my friend, he was no longer alive:
if he'd been living I'd never have lost my arms.
PHILOCTETES: You don't say? Is he too dead and gone?
NEOPTOLEMUS: Think of him no longer in the world of
light.
PHILOCTETES: How sad! . . . What an irony
that the son of Tydeus,† and Odysseus (who is really
the son of Sisyphus),
never manage to die when they ought never to have
lived!
NEOPTOLEMUS: How right you are!
They are flourishing now in the Argive army.
PHILOCTETES: Worst luck! . . . But what of Nestor,
my courageous old friend—is he alive?
He might have stopped their foul play by his alertness.

*There were two Ajaxes, Big and Little.
†Diomedes, a prominent Greek hero at Troy.

NEOPTOLEMUS: He's in a bad way:
  He's just lost his son Antilochus,
  the one who was with him.
PHILOCTETES: How very sad!
The death of these two is the last thing I should wish to
                        hear.
It's too bad! But what can one expect
  when they are dead and Odysseus is alive,
  who most certainly should be dead instead of them?
NEOPTOLEMUS: A clever wrestler that one, Philoctetes,
  but even cleverness sometimes is brought down.
PHILOCTETES: Do tell me where Patroclus was:
  the greatest favorite of your father?
NEOPTOLEMUS: Dead too. And let me say in short:
  death picks off the good, not the second-rate.
PHILOCTETES: How I agree! . . . Which makes me ask:
  what about a second-rate but clever man
  with a marvelous tongue?
NEOPTOLEMUS: Of course, you have to mean Odysseus?
PHILOCTETES: Actually, I meant one Thyrsites,
  who was incapable of being brief and bored us all.
Is he still alive?
NEOPTOLEMUS: I did not see him but heard he was.
PHILOCTETES: Naturally!
Nothing disreputable is known to perish.
The gods take precious care of that.
They seem to delight
  in keeping perverts and criminals out of Hades
  while dispatching the righteous and noble there.
How can we explain this?
How can we possibly applaud
  when we look to the divine and find it devilish?
NEOPTOLEMUS: For my part, you son of a father from
                        Oeta,
  I shall keep my distance both from Ilium
  and the Sons of Atreus and be wary of them.
When the inferior man flourishes over his better,
  when goodness wilts and the coward is in power,
  I refuse to countenance such people, and from now on
  my craggy Scyros is good enough for me
  and I'll be content to stay at home.

Now to my ship,
    so farewell to you, son of Poeas, a most sincere fare-
                                well!

May the gods cure your malady
    as completely as you could wish.

    [*Signaling to the* SCOUT]

We must be off,
    ready to set sail the moment the god allows.
PHILOCTETES: Must you really go, my son?
NEOPTOLEMUS: We have to seize the chance,
    be ready on the spot and not too far away.
PHILOCTETES: I beg you, my boy,
    by your father and your mother,
    by all at home that you find dear . . .
I solemnly beseech you:
    do not abandon me like this,
    alone and helpless, stranded
    in the deplorable state you see
    and of which you have heard.
Let me be a stowaway.
I know what a nuisance it would be to take me,
    but put up with it.
A generous spirit shrinks from meanness
    and glories in good works.
If you turn your back on this good work
    you tarnish your good name;
    but if you do it, my boy,
    and I reach the land of Oeta still alive
    your reward will be a leap in fame.
Look, it won't cost you more than a single day.
Take the trouble,
    stow me anywhere you like:
    in the hold, the prow, the stern;
    wherever I will be least trouble to your crew.
By Zeus, the god of suppliants, my son, be persuaded.
Crippled though I am, helpless and disheartened,
    I fall on my knees before you.
Do not leave me in this dreadful state
    far from humanity.

Take me either to your home
  or establish me in Chalcodon's* in Euboea.
From there, along the hills of Trachis
  and past the river Sperchius,
  it is a short voyage to Oeta,
  where you can present me to my dear father,
  though I have often brooded on the possibility he is
                                              no more,
  for I've sent many messages by those who came here,
  earnestly begging him to sail here himself
  and bring me home.
Either he is dead, or more likely,
  the messengers took little notice of me
  (as was natural) and hurried homewards.

But now that I have come to you,
  you can carry home both my message and myself;
  so please, please, take pity on me, save me.
The fortunes of mortals are fraught with anxiety
  and the constant risk that success is followed by
                                              disaster.
[It behooves us when free from trouble†
  to anticipate the fearful,
  and when we are all safe and sound
  then most of all we must be on guard
  against the creeping of disaster underground.]

                    ANTISTROPHE‡
CHORUS: Take pity on him, Prince:
  He has told you how hard
  His manifold ordeals have been. May none
  Of my friends ever experience the like!
And if you hate the Sons
  Of Atreus, my Prince,
  Turn their criminal acts to this man's gain
  And take him home where he longs to be
  In your good swift ship

*Father of one of the Greek warriors at Troy.
†Bracketed as doubtful.
‡Answering the strophe on pages 122–23.

And you will elude the just
Anger of the gods.

NEOPTOLEMUS: Take care that though you are now so
clement,
you are not a different person later on
when thrown together with his disease.

CHORUS: Not at all!
You'll never have reason to charge me with that.

NEOPTOLEMUS: And I'd be ashamed to prove less ready
to help him than you are.
So if you are ready let us set sail and him embark at
once.
The ship will not refuse to carry him.
It remains to the gods
to see us safely out of this land
and onwards to wherever we decide to sail.

PHILOCTETES: What a day of joy! What a lovely man!
And those adorable sailors!
I wish I could show you the friend you have made in me!
Let us be off, my boy, when I have said good-bye
to the innards of my homeless home
and you have seen how I managed to keep alive
and the effort that this took.
I do believe that the very sight of it
would have finished any man but me,
but patience made me learn to put up with necessity.

[PHILOCTETES *heads for the cave and* NEOPTOLEMUS *is
about to follow him*]

CHORUS: Wait! Stand where we are! Two men approach:
one a seaman from your ship, the other a foreigner.
Let us hear what they have to say, before we enter.

[*Two men enter from the direction of the port: a* MER-
CHANT *disguised as a sailor and a sailor*-SCOUT]

THIRD EPISODE

MERCHANT: Son of Achilles,
I asked my shipmate, the sailor here,

who was guarding your ship with two others
    to tell me where you were.
I ran into them by chance,
    never expecting to anchor off the same shore.
I am captain of a ship sailing with a few passengers
    from Ilium to Peparethus,* with its vineyards,
    and when I learned that all the sailors
    were members of your crew,
I decided not to continue my voyage
    without speaking to you and, for a consideration,
    giving you a warning.
I don't suppose you know how you stand
    since the new decisions the Argives have made con-
                     cerning you,
    and not just decisions but already put in motion.
NEOPTOLEMUS: Sir, I sincerely thank you for your kind-
                     ness
    and shall remember it.
Please explain the situation you have mentioned
    so's I can consider this new decision of the Argives.
MERCHANT: In pursuit of you a party has set sail:
    the aged Phoenix† and the sons of Theseus.
NEOPTOLEMUS: To force me to come back or tempt me?
MERCHANT: That I do not know, but have come to tell
                     you what I heard.
NEOPTOLEMUS: What makes Phoenix and his lot so keen
                     to please the Sons of Atreus?
MERCHANT: The mission is real, I assure you—not in the
                     future.
NEOPTOLEMUS: Why wasn't Odysseus ready to sail him-
                     self and be his own messenger?
Did some fear stop him?
MERCHANT: Just as I was setting out, he and the son of
                     Tydeus‡
    were busy in pursuit of someone else.
NEOPTOLEMUS: Who was this someone else that Odys-
                     seus went sailing after?

*A small island off the coast of Macedonia, northeast of Scyros,
famous for its wine.
†Once the tutor of Achilles.
‡Diomedes.

MERCHANT: [*in a whisper as he eyes* PHILOCTETES] It was
  someone who . . . but tell me first
who that man is . . . and keep your voice down.

NEOPTOLEMUS: [*whispering back*] Sir, you are looking at
  the notorious Philoctetes.

PHILOCTETES: What is he saying, my boy—the captain?
And why such undercover carrying on?

NEOPTOLEMUS: I am not yet sure myself, but whatever
  he has to say
he must say it openly before you and these other men.

MERCHANT: Child of Achilles, do not denounce me to
  the army
if I tell you what I shouldn't.
I'm a poor man, and they pay me for my services.

NEOPTOLEMUS: And I am out of favor with them,
  but this man is my greatest friend
  because he loathes the Sons of Atreus.
Since you have come to me in friendship
  you must conceal nothing from us of what you may
    have heard.

MERCHANT: Be careful what you're up to, son!

NEOPTOLEMUS: I've been careful all along.

MERCHANT: I'll hold you accountable.

NEOPTOLEMUS: Fine—but speak!

MERCHANT: [*pointing to* PHILOCTETES] Very well! . . . It's
  for this man
that the two men I told you of—
  the son of Tydeus and great Odysseus—
  are sailing here.
They have sworn to bring him back
  either by inducement or sheer force.
Every single Achaean heard Odysseus say this clearly:
  he was more confident than the others of bringing this
    off.

NEOPTOLEMUS: But what made the Atreidae after such a
  lapse of time
bother to capture someone they had jettisoned so long
    ago?
What is this sudden craving for him?
Is it fear of some divine necessity—
  the retribution of past crimes?

MERCHANT: Let me explain. You seem not to have heard.
The crafty Odysseus—well known for shameful and
                                        criminal acts—
    went out on his own one night and ambushed
    the illustrious prophet called Helenus, a son of Priam.
He paraded him in the midst of the Achaeans
    like a captured beast.
Helenus proceeded to prophesy,
    and among other things predicted
    that they would never topple the towers of Troy
    unless they enticed Philoctetes away and brought him
    from the island where he lived.
When the son of Laertes heard the prophet saying this
    he immediately promised the Achaeans
    that he would fetch the man and put him on display
                                        before them.
He reckoned he could get him by his own free will,
    but if he refused he would get him willy-nilly.
If he failed in this,
    anyone who wanted could chop off his head.
So now you've heard it all, my boy,
    and I recommend that you and anyone you care for
    act at once.
PHILOCTETES: I am aghast!
Did that man, that total pest,
    really swear that he would abduct me to the
                                        Achaeans?
I would as soon be persuaded
    to come back from Hades to the world of light—like
                                        his father.*
MERCHANT: I know nothing of this and am off to the
                                        ship.
May the gods help the rest of you!

[*The* MERCHANT *gathers himself together and departs*]

PHILOCTETES: It really is shocking, my boy, don't you
                                        think,

*Odysseus' father was possibly not Laertes but the cunning Sisyphus,
who escaped from Hades by a trick (to return there later).

the way Laertes imagines he can blandish me
into being shipped off for display among the Argives?
I'd sooner take notice of that most hateful thing,
    the snake that turned me into a cripple.
He is a man that will say anything,
    fly in the face of anything,
    and I am quite certain he will come.
So let us hurry away, my son,
    and put an expanse of sea between us and Odysseus'
                                             ship.

Let's go!
Speed when needed can be followed
    by sleep and rest when the task is done.

NEOPTOLEMUS: Yes, as soon as the breeze is abaft we'll
                                             set sail;
    at the moment it is against us.

PHILOCTETES: There is always a following wind
    when one is flying from trouble.

NEOPTOLEMUS: I know, and the wind is against them too.

PHILOCTETES: Against pirates out to rob and kidnap
    there's no such thing as an adverse wind.

NEOPTOLEMUS: All right, if you want, let's go!
Take from the cave whatever you need or most want.

PHILOCTETES: There *are* some things I need, but not
                                             many.

NEOPTOLEMUS: What might you need that's not on board
                                             my ship?

PHILOCTETES: There is an herb, a palliative,
    I use from time to time to ease my pain.

NEOPTOLEMUS: Then bring it! What else do you want to
                                             take?

PHILOCTETES: Any arrows left around.
I don't want anyone to get hold of them.

NEOPTOLEMUS: And is that the famous bow that you are
                                             holding?

PHILOCTETES: Yes, the one in my hands. I have no other.

NEOPTOLEMUS: May I take a closer look at it,
    hold it in my hands and kiss it, as if it were divine?

PHILOCTETES: For you, dear boy, of course!
And anything else that's in my power to give.

NEOPTOLEMUS: I'd certainly like to but only like to if

that is right for me; otherwise, forget it.
PHILOCTETES: You are a pious boy, and of course it is
right.

No one but you has made it possible for me
    to enjoy the light of the sun,
    to see the land of Oeta again,
    and my old father and my friends,
    and when I was floored by my enemies, raised me up.
So of course it's right for you to handle the bow,
    and when you've given it back you can boast
    that because of your generosity
    you are the only mortal who has touched it.
For the bow was a reward to me for an act of kindness.*
NEOPTOLEMUS: I am happy to have found you and won
your friendship.
Whoever knows how to be kind when a kindness has
been done
    is a proven friend beyond all price.
Let us go inside.
PHILOCTETES: Let me lead you in as well,
    for I need your support because of my ill.

[PHILOCTETES *leads* NEOPTOLEMUS *into the cave. The*
CHORUS, *now alone, expresses a sympathy for* PHILOC-
TETES *that is now genuine; before, it was pretended*]

STASIMON†

STROPHE I

CHORUS: I've heard it said but never seen it seen
    How Zeus the almighty
    Son of Cronus racked the body
    Of Ixion on a furious wheel
    Who came to steal
    His own wife from his bed,
    But never have I seen or heard a fate
    To compare for black despair with this man's here

---

*The act of kindness was kindling the funeral pyre of Heracles.
†The stasimon is the first choral ode after the first episode.

Who never hurt a human being,
Made no foes,
A just man to the just,
Yet left like this to decompose.
And now I am amazed:
How did he keep his hold day after day,
Desolate and alone
With the gride of the combers grounding near—
How—
On such totally tear-marked, mind-martyred years?

ANTISTROPHE I

None but his own next man with whom to walk
And none ever near him,
No neighbor with whom he could talk
His pain, so conjure some support
Against the plague
That raged and consumed
His life away, with none to hear his groans
Nor any to soothe into sleep with healing herbs
The biting curse that oozed hot pus
From his putrefying,
Maggot-crawling heel
With spasms of pain whenever he went
Grubbing for sustenance
From the life-sustaining earth, as he crawled
Backwards and forwards
Like a baby that has lost its nurse,
Searching
For fodder as the disease ate away his soul.

STROPHE II

Not in the holy soil did he seed his livelihood:
None of that provender *we* wrest from the earth with
toil.
Only his bow with its fast-feathered arrow could bring
For his body's need
Some living thing.
Poor lost soul who for ten years never touched a sip of
wine,

Casting around for puddles with his eyes bent low
To wreak his design.

ANTISTROPHE II

But blessed he emerges now from suffering.
This princely son shall cleave the seas with him
　　And after many a month shall bring him home—
　　Home at last
　　To the Malian nymphs
　　Where on Sperchius' banks under Oeta's heights
　　The man with the brazen shield, Heracles on his pyre,
　　Passed away to the gods—incandescent passed—
　　Through Zeus' fire.

FOURTH EPISODE

[NEOPTOLEMUS *and* PHILOCTETES *emerge from the cave*]

NEOPTOLEMUS: Why have you gone silent
　　and stand like one struck dumb
　　though nothing has been said?
PHILOCTETES: [*in pain*] A . . . h!
NEOPTOLEMUS: What is it?
PHILOCTETES: Nothing serious. . . . Let's go, son.
NEOPTOLEMUS: Is it pain? Your foot playing up?
PHILOCTETES: No, no, I think I am getting better . . .
　　　　　　　　　　　　　　　　　　dear gods!
NEOPTOLEMUS: Then what are the groans for and calling
　　　　　　　　　　　　　　　　　　on heaven?
PHILOCTETES: To be kind and come and help us . . .
　　　　　　　　　　　　　　　　　　A . . . h!
NEOPTOLEMUS: What's the matter with you? Why won't
　　　　　　　　　　　　　　　　　　you tell me?
Are you dumb? . . . You're obviously in trouble.
PHILOCTETES: Son, I'm desperate . . .
　　I cannot hide my agony from you—A . . . . . h!
　　　　　　　　　　　　　　　　　　A . . . . h!
　　The pangs go clean through me, through me—
　　The misery, the pain! . . . I'm a wreck, my son . . .
　　eating me away . . . A . . . . . h! A . . . . . h! A . . . . . . h!
If you have a sword handy, son, strike,

Slice off my heel . . . please, please, even my life!
On with it, boy!

NEOPTOLEMUS: What are these spasms that make you cry
out and groan?

PHILOCTETES: You know, my son.

NEOPTOLEMUS: What, then?

PHILOCTETES: My boy, you know.

NEOPTOLEMUS: No, I don't . . . What?

PHILOCTETES: How can you help knowing? A . . . . h!
A . . . . h!

NEOPTOLEMUS: Your malady? I see it is terrible.

PHILOCTETES: Terrible indeed! Indescribable! Be com-
passionate!

NEOPTOLEMUS: What can I do?

PHILOCTETES: Don't take fright and run.
The sickness gets upset if I move around—
it comes in person.

NEOPTOLEMUS: You poor stricken creature!
Stricken from all sides!
Would you like me to take hold of you?

PHILOCTETES: No, not that! But take the bow you asked
for earlier
and keep it safe until the spasms pass.
Sleep always follows the attacks,
which last till then.
So now you must let me go to sleep,
but I beseech you if those people come
not on any account to let them have it—
willingly, unwillingly, or any way whatever,
or it will be my death and yours—to whom I turn.

NEOPTOLEMUS: Have no fear! I'll take great care of it:
nobody but you or me shall touch it.
So hand it over! May it bring good luck!

PHILOCTETES: [*holding out the bow*] There, take it, boy;
and kiss it to break the spell
that haunted me and the one who had it before.

NEOPTOLEMUS: Please, you gods, grant us that, and let
our voyage
be safe and swift to wherever the gods think we ought
to go.

PHILOCTETES: [*writhing*] A . . . h! A . . . h!

I fear, my boy, your prayer will not be answered,
   for the black oozing blood from deep inside
   is seeping out again.
Which makes me suspect the worst . . . A . . . h! the
                                            worst! . . .
It's on its way, it's on its way! Foot, you foot,
   how you torture me!
I am desperate, a victim; you see it at first hand;
   please, please, do not run away . . . A . . . h!
Wretch from Cephallus, Odysseus,
   I'd like this pain to rivet your chest . . .
A . . . h, Aaah, agony again!
Agamemnon and Menelaus, you brace of chiefs,
   if only you could take my place
   as fodder for this ulcer—and for equal time!
Oh oh oh—I'm done!
Death, Death, will you never come,
   though I call you day after day?
Son, my noble boy, seize me,
   hurl me into this fire, this Lemnian fire,
   yes, generous one! As I once too
   did the same to Heracles the son of Zeus
   in exchange for those weapons now in your keep.
What do you say, boy? What do you say?
Silent? Where are you, child?
NEOPTOLEMUS: In pain . . . long lost in yours.
PHILOCTETES: Son, bear up!
   These attacks are fierce but are over fast . . .
   You won't desert me, will you? Please!
NEOPTOLEMUS: [*indicating* ATTENDANTS *and* SCOUT] Have
                              no fear! We shall stay.
PHILOCTETES: You will really stay?
NEOPTOLEMUS: Be sure of it!
PHILOCTETES: It wouldn't be right to make you swear,
                                            my son.
NEOPTOLEMUS: It wouldn't be right for me to go without
                                            you.
PHILOCTETES: Promise me . . . your hand!
NEOPTOLEMUS: [*taking the hand of* PHILOCTETES] I prom-
                              ise to stay.

PHILOCTETES: [*staring up at the sky*] Up there, up there . . .

NEOPTOLEMUS: Up where?

PHILOCTETES: Above.

NEOPTOLEMUS: Are you raving again? Staring up at the
sky?

PHILOCTETES: Let me go! Let me go!

NEOPTOLEMUS: Let you go where?

PHILOCTETES: Just let me go!

NEOPTOLEMUS: No, I will not!

PHILOCTETES: Your grip is killing me.

NEOPTOLEMUS: [*releasing his hold*] I'll let you go, then—
if you are in your right mind.

PHILOCTETES: [*limping a few steps and collapsing*] Good
Earth, let me die, receive me just as I am.
I am not able to stand for the pain.

NEOPTOLEMUS: He will soon be asleep, I think.
See how his head droops,
and his body is bathed in sweat.
There's a trickle of dark blood oozing from his heel.
Let us leave him to sleep in peace, my friends.

SEMI-CHORAL EXCHANGE

STROPHE

CHORUS: Sleep that knows no anguish, tolerant Sleep,
Come with your gentle breath and gently
Breathe gentleness all over him, my lord.
Hold his eyes against the shine of light:
Come, great Healer, come! . . .
Be alert, my son, of where you stand
And what you plan.
Right action is right before your sight.
Why do you delay to act?
The opportune moment demands execution:
Right is the victory of a prompt decision.

NEOPTOLEMUS: He may not be hearing a thing, but to
me it is clear
that we sail away in vain
if we've taken his bow but leave without him.
It is he who must crown our success.

It is him the god told us to bring.
It would be a disgrace to boast of a triumph
   founded on fraud.

ANTISTROPHE*

CHORUS: That, my son, the god will see to. Tell me
   Your plan, my son, in brief—briefly tell me.
   The unslumbering slumber of the sick has sight.
   What needs to be done must be done in secret—
Secretly done . . . You know
   Of whom I am speaking, if you and he
Still think the same.
   I see dangers ahead—pitfalls galore.

EPODE

The man lies stretched in the dark, blissfully sleeping.
He has no command at all
Of hand or foot or anything,
As if lying in Hades.
   See that your decision fits the occasion.
   A bold move, as far as I can tell,
   Is best, my boy.
NEOPTOLEMUS: Silence, please! And keep your wits about
                       you:
   the man has opened his eyes and raised his head.
PHILOCTETES: Ah, light of day that follows sleep,
   and you watchful friends beyond my dreams!
Never did I expect, my boy, that you would help me
   and wait on my affliction with such compassion.
The Sons of Atreus—Oh those so noble generals!—
   had not the nobility to endure it.
But you, my son, are truly noble—nobly bred.
You took it in your stride:
   endured my screams, endured the stench.
But now that the pangs seem to have passed
   and leave me in peace, my son,
     please will you lend yourself and lift me up
     and help me to stand;

---

*Sophocles has not made strophe and antistrophe correspond, so
neither have I.

so as soon as the sleepiness goes
we can make a move for the ship
and delay our voyage no longer.

NEOPTOLEMUS: I am delighted to see you still alive
when there seemed no hope—
still breathing and with no pain.

The terrible symptoms you were going through
looked like the end.

But now get up,
or let these men carry you if you prefer.

It would be no trouble at all,
now that you and I are at one.

PHILOCTETES: Thank you, my boy:
lift me up as you offer, but don't bother these,
lest they have to suffer the stink before they need.

Being with me on the ship will be bad enough.

NEOPTOLEMUS: So be it! Stand up and hold on to me.

PHILOCTETES: Right! The force of habit will straighten
me.

NEOPTOLEMUS: Dear gods! What do I do next?

PHILOCTETES: What is the matter, boy? Are you wandering?

NEOPTOLEMUS: I'm at a loss for words to frame my
problem.

PHILOCTETES: What problem? Don't say things like that,
son.

NEOPTOLEMUS: The fact is, I'm at the end of my tether.

PHILOCTETES: I hope it isn't that my nasty sickness has
come home to you
and now you're not going to take me on board?

NEOPTOLEMUS: Everything goes against the grain
once one acts against one's character.

PHILOCTETES: At least you are not acting against your
father's character
when you help a worthy man.

NEOPTOLEMUS: I'm a manifest fraud:
that's what's upsetting me.

PHILOCTETES: Not in your behavior . . .
you disturb me nonetheless.

NEOPTOLEMUS: Great Zeus, what am I to do:
damned if I don't speak up, and damned if I do?

PHILOCTETES: If I am right, it looks to me as if
   this man is going to sail away and leave me in the
          lurch.

NEOPTOLEMUS: No, not to leave you; but I dread the
          thought
   of launching you on a painful voyage—*that* bothers
          me.

PHILOCTETES: What do you mean, my son? I don't follow
          you.

NEOPTOLEMUS: I'll not hide it from you: you must sail to
          Troy,
   join the Achaeans and the Atreidaes' armada.

PHILOCTETES: Good heavens! What have you just said?

NEOPTOLEMUS: Save your anguish until you know . . .

PHILOCTETES: Know what? . . . What are you going to
          do to me?

NEOPTOLEMUS: First, cure you of your malady,
   then with you ravish the plains of Troy.

PHILOCTETES: Is this really what you are going to do?

NEOPTOLEMUS: On one ineluctable condition . . .
   don't be angry when you hear it.

PHILOCTETES: So, I am miserably betrayed!
Stranger, what have you done to me?
Give me back my bow, and now!

NEOPTOLEMUS: I'm afraid I cannot:
   duty and policy force me to obey those in command.

PHILOCTETES: You bonfire of monstrosity! You master-
          piece of vice!
   What have you done to me? How you have tricked
          me!
Do you not blush to look me in the eyes, you villain,
   I who turned to you in need?
By taking my bow you have robbed me of my life.
Give it back! I beg you, give it back!
My son, I beseech you!
By the gods of your fathers, do not deprive me of life:
   not poor wretched me!

[*He waits for a reply*]

And now he won't talk to me; looks away;

he will never give it up.
You harbors and headlands,
   you friendly mountain beasts,
   you rocky pinnacles:
   you are the only companions that I know
   and can now address and tell the hurt
   that Achilles' son has done to me.
He swore to take me home
   and is taking me to Troy.
He pledged his word with his right hand
   and confiscates my sacred bow—
   the bow of Heracles the son of Zeus,
   and wants to show me off among the Argives
   as if exhibiting
   some champion fighter that he took by force,
   unaware of the corpse he's killing,
   this shadow of smoke, this phantom wisp.
Yet in the days of my strength he would never have
                         taken me,
   nor even as I am—except by a trick.
I have been obscenely cheated. What shall I do?
   Oh, give it back!
Even now it is not too late: be true to yourself.

[*He waits again for a response*]

What do you say? Nothing?
I am desperately lost.

[*Glancing up at his cave*]

Cave of mine with twin entrances,
   once more I'll enter you, but stripped and destitute:
   alone in this bunker I shall pine away,
   unable to shoot a bird on the wing or beast of the
                         hills—
   never, without my bow.
I myself shall die and become a meal
   for those on whom I fed:
   the quarry of those who once were mine,
   lifeblood for blood—victim that I am—

and all because of one who seemed so innocent.
May you be damned! But not till I know
whether you'll change your mind.
If not, may you die and rot!
CHORUS: What shall we do? It's up to you, my Prince,
whether we sail away or listen to this man's plea.
NEOPTOLEMUS: I have to confess a curious compassion
for this man,
now and from the beginning.
PHILOCTETES: Then by the gods show it, my boy!
Do not allow yourself to go down forever as one who
deceived me!
NEOPTOLEMUS: I am at a loss. What am I to do?
If only I'd never left Scyros!
My dilemma is unbearable.
PHILOCTETES: You are no criminal,
but it seems you have come here primed by those that
are.
Now you have the chance of rendering to others their
due
and sailing away—after giving me back my bow.
NEOPTOLEMUS: Men, what should we do?

[ODYSSEUS *suddenly appears from the port and rounds
on* NEOPTOLEMUS]

ODYSSEUS: Rascal, what are you up to?
Away with you and give that bow to me!
PHILOCTETES: Dear gods, who is this man? Do I hear
Odysseus?
ODYSSEUS: You do indeed: Odysseus in person!
PHILOCTETES: So I am ruined, sold out!
He was the one, then, behind my capture and theft of
my bow!
ODYSSEUS: Yes, none other than me; I admit it.
PHILOCTETES: [*turning to* NEOPTOLEMUS] Give it back,
boy. Give me back my bow!
ODYSSEUS: That he shall never do, even if he wants to;
and you must come as well—even if dragged.
PHILOCTETES: Dragged by force? You lowest of the low,
you brazen bully!
ODYSSEUS: By force, if you won't come willingly.

PHILOCTETES: Oh, Lemnos, with your mighty Hephaes-
tion* forges,
can this be borne?
Can this creature wrench me away by force?
ODYSSEUS: It is Zeus, let me tell you,
Zeus the lord of this land,
Zeus whose order this is and whose servant I am.
PHILOCTETES: You loathsome thing! What will you not
invent?
Using gods as a screen and making them liars!
ODYSSEUS: Not at all: tellers of truth! Now come along!
PHILOCTETES: A flat No to that!
ODYSSEUS: But I say Yes and you have to submit!
PHILOCTETES: [*sarcastically*] I see—my sire must have
spawned a slave, no free man!
ODYSSEUS: On the contrary: equal to the chiefs
with whom you will capture Troy and reduce it to
rubble.
PHILOCTETES: Never! Even if I have to suffer the worst
from this pinnacle of cliff.

[*He steps briskly to the edge*]

ODYSSEUS: What are you doing?
PHILOCTETES: Getting ready to hurl myself from this rock
and scatter my blood on the rocks below.
ODYSSEUS: Grab him! He must not do it.

[*Two* SAILORS *take hold of* PHILOCTETES]

PHILOCTETES: Poor arms, pinned by this man's order,
how helpless you are without my beloved bow!

[*Turning to face* ODYSSEUS]

You there,
who cannot conceive a single healthy, generous
thought,
you stole up and tricked me,

---

*The god of fire and forges.

using this boy as a screen—a boy I did not know:
too good for you but good enough for me,
who knew only that he had to do your bidding
and is already full of remorse for his sin
and for my sufferings.
But your nasty mind,
　　forever on the lookout from its arse-hole,
　　soon had him trained—
　　inept and unwilling as he was—
　　to be a master criminal.
And now, you miserable man,
　　you mean to tie me up and carry me off:
　　away from these shores on which you cast me,
　　friendless, homeless, an abandoned living corpse.
To hell with you!
Something I have often prayed for,
　　but since the gods never answer my prayers,
　　you are alive and happy
　　while my life is one long pain:
　　made a fool of by you and the two commanders,
　　the Sons of Atreus—whose tool you are in all this
　　　　　　　　　　　　　　　　　　　　　　　business.
Yet you sailed with them because you were tricked and
　　　　　　　　　　　　　　　　　　　　　　　had to,
　　while I, fool that I am, sailed of my own free will
　　and with seven ships, until they, as you say,
　　but you, as they say,
　　treated me as trash and threw me out.

And now, why are you taking me?
Why are you carrying me off?
What is the point?
I am nothing to you:
　　have been dead to you long ago.
Why—you most detestable to the gods?
Why have you stopped finding me an evil-smelling
　　　　　　　　　　　　　　　　　　　　　　　cripple?
How, if I sail with you,
　　can you carry out your sacrifices, your libations
　　the very reason that you threw me out?
I sincerely hope you come to a wretched end.

And you will, for the wrongs you've done me—
                              if the gods care at all for justice.

Land of my birth and you watchful deities,
    punish them, punish them all, late but at last,
    for my pitiful life—for my life *is* pitiable,
    but if I could see them brought to naught
    it would be like seeing my malady cut short.
CHORUS: Bitter words from a bitter man, Odysseus.
He does not crumple under his woes.
ODYSSEUS: I could answer him in full if there were time,
    but now let me say just one thing.
I am a man to fit the occasion,
    and when it comes to straightforwardness and honesty
    you will find nobody more meticulous.
But I like to win, it's part of my nature,
    to win—but not over you,
    so I willingly yield.

[*Signaling a group of* SAILORS]

Take your hands off him and let him go.

[*To* PHILOCTETES, *sneeringly*]

We don't need you anymore
    now that your weapons are ours.
We have Teucer, an adept at archery,
    and I'm good too.
I think I can manage the bow no worse than you
    and aim it with a steady hand.
So why do we need you?
Wander around Lemnos and enjoy yourself.
Perhaps this treasure that you should have kept
                              will be assigned to me.
PHILOCTETES: Unutterable distress! but what can I do?
    The thought of you flaunting my weapons before the
                                                      Argives—
    how can I bear it?
ODYSSEUS: Don't bother to answer that—I must go.

PHILOCTETES: Son of Achilles, will you not even talk to
                                                     me?
Are you going to go off like this?
ODYSSEUS: [*to* NEOPTOLEMUS] Come with me!
Do not so much as look at him, kind though you are,
    or you will bring bad luck.
PHILOCTETES: [*addressing the surrounding* SAILORS]
Friends, are you going to leave me desolate too?
    Where is your compassion?
CHORUS: This boy is our captain.
    Whatever he says to you, we say too.
NEOPTOLEMUS: [*to* PHILOCTETES] Odysseus will say that I
                               am too softhearted,*
    but you'd best stay here if he approves.
Meanwhile the sailors will prepare the ship for sailing
    and we shall offer prayers to the deities.
Perhaps in time this man
    will come to think better of us.

[*To the* SAILORS]

Odysseus and I must be off.
Be ready to come when we call you!

[NEOPTOLEMUS *and* ODYSSEUS *leave for the port*]

CHORAL DIALOGUE

STROPHE I

PHILOCTETES: Dear hollow of my caverned rock
    At times so cold, at times so hot,
    Sorrowfully it seems at last
    That my unhappy destiny
    Is never to leave you until death:
Sad sad sad!
    You den haunted by my pain,
    What shall be my daily lot?
    What hope of finding provender?
    Dismal it is, dismal am I.

*In not forcing him to sail to Ilium.

You creatures frightened of me once,
I have no power to take you now.
How shall I shoot you flying above me on the breeze,
The whistling breeze?
CHORUS: It is you yourself, you poor fate-entangled man,
 Who have chosen this; from nobody else has come
 The power to enslave yourself, for when
 You could have been wise enough to choose the better
 You chose the worse.

ANTISTROPHE I

PHILOCTETES: Wretched I was, wretched I am:
 Battered by sorrows. From now on
 I must live alone with none—
 No companion in the days to come,
 And in misery I shall die—
Sad sad sad!
 No longer bringing home the catch,
 No longer springing the winged fletch
 From my strong hands. Left in the lurch
 By a cunning and deceitful man
 Whom I never suspected. I wish I could see
 The spinner of this plot undone:
 Doomed to the sufferings I have had and for as many
Horrible days!
CHORUS: It was not I that lent a treacherous hand
 Against you. It was a destiny sent from heaven,
 So aim your curses and your ire
 At others. My one concern is that you don't
 Reject me as friend.

STROPHE II

PHILOCTETES: Alas, I see down there by the shore
 Where the pallid waves are curling,
 Him, that man who jeers at me.
 He flourishes the very thing
 That was my livelihood. Ah, me!
 The thing no other hand had held.
 Beloved bow, you were wrenched away
 And if you could feel you must surely see
The sorrow of this friend

Of Heracles, who never again shall handle you.
For now you are swung by the hands
Of that cunning brute whose deceits
You have to behold, and also see
That treacherous antagonist*
Who has done me so much wrong
Hatched in shameless trickery.
CHORUS: A man has a right to argue his case, but when
He has spoken he ought to refrain
From lashing out with a stinging tongue.
Odysseus was only one
Among the armada's hordes, and he
Was under orders to do a service to all.

ANTISTROPHE II

PHILOCTETES: You my flying prey on the wing
And you my clear-eyed beasts of prey
Abundant in this mountain range,
Never again shall you be flushed
From your shy coverts, for my hands
No longer clasp the shafts that once
Showed my prowess. I am bereft,
So come and go as you please:
I am crippled.
You need no longer be afraid,
And now in revenge you can glut
Upon my trembling flesh, for I
Cannot but soon pass away,
Because how shall I find a livelihood?
Who can feed upon the breeze
When his provender is gone, his power
To live off the ever life-providing earth?
CHORUS: For the love of the gods, if you care for a visit-
ing friend†
Get close to him as he has to you.
Take note of this, oh, do take note!
You have the power to doff your plight.

---

*Neoptolemus.
†Meaning the visiting sailors.

Cruel is the thing that feeds on you,
Which while it lasts no patience can abate.

EPODE

PHILOCTETES: Again again you speak my pain.
　Why must you, kindest though you are
　Of all who have come to this place, destroy me?
What have you done to me?
CHORUS: What ever makes you say this?
PHILOCTETES: Are you trying to get me to go to the horrible land of Troy?
CHORUS: I really think that is best for you.
PHILOCTETES: Leave me at once!
CHORUS: Just what I want to do, just what I want:
　I'm only too happy to do just that.
Let's go, let's go
　Each to his post on the ship.
PHILOCTETES: No, by the Zeus of curses, no!
I beseech you.
CHORUS: Keep your calm!
PHILOCTETES: Please, my friends,
　In the gods' name stay!
CHORUS: Whatever for?
PHILOCTETES: Because, because, my fate, my fate, I am
lost.

　Foot, my foot, what shall I do with you
For the rest of my miserable life?
Friends, please, please, come back!
CHORUS: What can we do, you've changed your mind?
That's not what you said before.
PHILOCTETES: You must not be upset
　If a man in terrible pain
　Says things that are insane.
CHORUS: Very well, then, come with us.
PHILOCTETES: Never, never, not on your life!
　Not if the lord of lightning himself
　Came to consume me in blaze and thunder.
　To hell with Ilium and everyone under
　Its walls who were callous enough to leave me
With my tortured foot.
　Good visitors, grant me one ultimate wish!

CHORUS: And what might that be?

PHILOCTETES: Hand me a sword or an axe or a dart.

CHORUS: And what do you want to do with that?

PHILOCTETES: Lop off my head and every limb.
  It's death I want, immediate death.

CHORUS: Whatever for?

PHILOCTETES: To find my father.

CHORUS: Your father, where?

PHILOCTETES: Down in Hades.
  For he lives no longer in the light.
  My city, my city, my native land,
  If I could only see you now,
  Wretched creature that I am,
  I who left your sacred stream
  To go and help the Greeks! But now
  There is nothing left of me.

CHORUS: I should have been on my way long ago and
                                    on my ship,
  but now I see Odysseus coming with Achilles' son.

[ODYSSEUS *and* NEOPTOLEMUS *come from the port, as*
PHILOCTETES *retreats into his cave. The bow hangs from*
NEOPTOLEMUS' *shoulder*]

ODYSSEUS: I wish you'd tell me why you are hurrying
                            back at such a pace?

NEOPTOLEMUS: To undo a wrong I did before.

ODYSSEUS: That sounds serious. What was the wrong?

NEOPTOLEMUS: Obeying you and the whole armada.

ODYSSEUS: What exactly did you do that was so wrong?

NEOPTOLEMUS: I deceived a man by the lowest kind of
                                            trick.

ODYSSEUS: Dear me! Whom? . . . Are you planning a
                                        surprise?

NEOPTOLEMUS: No surprise but the son of Poeas.

ODYSSEUS: What are you planning to do? It makes me
                                        nervous.

NEOPTOLEMUS: The man I took this bow from, give it . . .

ODYSSEUS: Great Zeus! You don't mean—give it back?

NEOPTOLEMUS: Yes, I got it by a lie, not honestly.

ODYSSEUS: Come on . . . You're only saying this to tease

me!

NEOPTOLEMUS: Yes, if to tease is to tell the truth.

ODYSSEUS: What are you saying? What have you just said, child of Achilles?

NEOPTOLEMUS: Do you want me to repeat it twice—or thrice if necessary?

ODYSSEUS: I'd rather not have heard it at all—even once.

NEOPTOLEMUS: Well, you have . . . That's all I have to say.

ODYSSEUS: There is somebody, yes, somebody, to stop you.

NEOPTOLEMUS: Meaning what? Who is this somebody to stop me?

ODYSSEUS: The whole Achaean army—including me.

NEOPTOLEMUS: You may have been born with sense but are talking nonsense.

ODYSSEUS: You are neither talking sense nor behaving sensibly.

NEOPTOLEMUS: If talking sense makes sense, it's better than cleverness.

ODYSSEUS: How does it make sense to give up what you got through me?

NEOPTOLEMUS: The wrong I did was shameful, and I mean to right it.

ODYSSEUS: In doing which, have you no fear of the Achaean forces?

NEOPTOLEMUS: With right on my side I have no fear of your forces.

ODYSSEUS: I suggest you have some fear of force.*

NEOPTOLEMUS: Use all the force you like. I shall not yield.

ODYSSEUS: We won't be fighting Trojans, then, but you.

NEOPTOLEMUS: Go right ahead!

ODYSSEUS: Do you see my right hand on my sword hilt?

NEOPTOLEMUS: In a moment you'll see mine on mine.

ODYSSEUS: All right, I'll let you be!
But I am going to report this to the whole army:
they'll deal with you.

---

*This line is missing except for the word "fear." My conjecture is based on the following line.

NEOPTOLEMUS: Very wise of you! Keep it up!
Then perhaps in future you won't go walking into
trouble.

[ODYSSEUS *stamps off in the direction of the port.* NE-
OPTOLEMUS *calls up to the cave*]

NEOPTOLEMUS: Come on out, son of Poeas, Philoctetes:
leave the shelter of your rocky home.

[PHILOCTETES *emerges from the cave*]

PHILOCTETES: What is all this clamor outside my cave?
Why are you summoning me?
Sirs, what are you after?

[*Seeing* NEOPTOLEMUS]

I know, I know it is something bad!
You are here to pile another catastrophe
on top of what I have already.
NEOPTOLEMUS: Have no fear,
just listen to what I've come to tell you.

[PHILOCTETES *climbs down gingerly from the cave*]

PHILOCTETES: But I do fear.
Once before I listened to your reassurance,
and it led to disaster.
NEOPTOLEMUS: Is there no room for a change of heart?
PHILOCTETES: That's exactly what you said when you
filched my bow:
a deadly confidence trick!
NEOPTOLEMUS: Not this time! I only want you to tell me
whether you've decided to stay here and suffer
or sail with us.
PHILOCTETES: Stop right there! Say no more!
Speechifying will be a waste of time.
NEOPTOLEMUS: So you're staying here?
PHILOCTETES: More decidedly than ever.
NEOPTOLEMUS: Well, I only wish you'd been persuaded,

but if it's not what you want I'll say no more.
PHILOCTETES: It would be a waste of time,
for I'll never trust you again.
You sneaked up and cheated me of my livelihood—
you, you rascally offspring of a noble father!
A plague on you all,
especially the Sons of Atreus and Odysseus,
and, of course, you!
NEOPTOLEMUS: [*taking the bow from his shoulders*]
Enough of recriminations!
Just receive from my hands this bow!
PHILOCTETES: What did you say? Is this another trick?
NEOPTOLEMUS: No, by the sacred majesty of Zeus most
high! I swear!
PHILOCTETES: Oh, wonderful . . . but too good to be true!
NEOPTOLEMUS: [*holding out the bow*] The fact can speak
for itself.
Hold out your right hand
and take command of your weapon!

[ODYSSEUS *suddenly strides in*]

ODYSSEUS: I forbid it—by the gods I forbid it!—
in the name of the Sons of Atreus and the entire army.
PHILOCTETES: My son, whose voice is that? Odysseus?
ODYSSEUS: Correct! and he's right here,
ready to carry you off to the plains of Troy
whether the son of Achilles wants it or not.

[PHILOCTETES *with lightning speed fits an arrow to his
bow and levels it at* ODYSSEUS]

PHILOCTETES: Not so quick, sir, or this arrow will find its
mark.
NEOPTOLEMUS: [*rushing in between*] No, no! for the love
of the gods, don't shoot!
PHILOCTETES: For the love of the gods, dear boy, let go.
NEOPTOLEMUS: I will not let go.
PHILOCTETES: [*putting his bow down as* ODYSSEUS *slips
away*] Why on earth did you stop me from shooting
the life out of that horrid man?

NEOPTOLEMUS: It would not have been a good idea for
                                    either you or me.
PHILOCTETES: All I know is, that these commanders in
                                    chief,
these fraudulent spokesmen for the Greeks,
are bully-bombasts but battle-cowards.
NEOPTOLEMUS: Anyway, you have your bow,
so you can't be cross or blame me anymore.
PHILOCTETES: You are right, son,
and you've shown yourself worthy of your stock:
a child not of Sisyphus* but Achilles—
a man most famous in life and now among the dead.
NEOPTOLEMUS: It gives me pleasure to hear you praise
                                    my sire and me,
but there is something special I must ask you.
We mortals have to accept the fortunes the gods allot us
but self-imposed ordeals, like yours, are inexcusable
and deserve no pity.
You are running amok
and listen to nobody.
If someone tries to tell you something,
with every good intention,
you simply turn your back on him,
say he is just an enemy and against you.
So let me speak quite plainly,
and may Zeus, the god of pledges, back me up!
Mark what I say and stamp it in your heart.
You got the painful sickness heaven sent you
when you blundered into the precincts of Chryse's
                                    guardian,†
that secret snake that protects her roofless shrine.
Know that, as sure as the sun rises in the east and sets
                                    in the west,
you will never be free of this noisome disease
until you come of your own free will to the land of
                                    Troy.

*Sisyphus was the supposed father of Odysseus.
†It was on the island of Tenedos at the shrine of Athena Chryse
that Philoctetes approached too near the altar of the goddess and
was bitten in the foot by a water snake.

There you will meet the sons of Asclepius,* who are
with us,
and be cured.
And with this good bow and me
you will be revealed as toppler of the towers of Troy.

Let me tell you how I know all this.
We have a Trojan prisoner called Helenus, a noted seer,
who tells us that all this is bound to happen.
What is more: that this very summer
will see the complete overthrow of Troy,
and if it turns out that he's been talking nonsense,
we have his permission to take his life.
Now that you know all this,
graciously comply.
Besides the kudos of being the best of all the Greeks
you'll be coming into healing hands,
and secondly you'll win the highest fame by taking
Troy,
the cause of all our griefs.
PHILOCTETES: Life, life, you loathsome thing,
keeping me living above ground
when I should be down below in Hades!
I simply don't know what to do.
How can I ignore this man's advice
when he counsels me for my own good?
But if I give in,
won't I put myself on display as the spineless wretch
I am?

Who will speak to me?
And you, these very eyes of mine
who have watched the goings-on around me,
how can you tolerate my being with the Sons of
Atreus,
the cause of my ruin?
And how can I be with that hateful Odysseus,
Laertes' son?
It is not the sting of the past that pains me
but what I now see coming.

*God of medicine and healing.

Because once evil incubates in men's minds,
   it spawns more evil.
And another thing:
   your own behavior makes me wonder:
   you yourself ought not to go to Troy,
   let alone take me there.
These fellows treated you like dirt
   when they went off with your father's arms,
   and are you now going tamely to fight with them
   and make me do the same?
No, my son, absolutely not!
Instead, what you swore to do:
   take me home and ensconce yourself in Scyros,
   and let these vicious people stew in their own juice.
By doing this you will earn a double thanks:
   from my father and from myself.
And by not abetting criminals
   you will avoid being branded one yourself.

NEOPTOLEMUS: What you say makes sense; all the same,
   I wish you would put your faith in the gods and my
                                                 advice,
   and sail away from here with me as your friend.

PHILOCTETES: What, to the plains of Troy
   and the odious son of Atreus*
   with my stinking foot?

NEOPTOLEMUS: No, to those who will save you, heal you
   and stop the agony of your rotting foot.

PHILOCTETES: What nonsense you talk! Can't you talk
                                          some sense?

NEOPTOLEMUS: It *is* sense: the best thing for you and me.

PHILOCTETES: How can you say that without blushing be-
                                          fore the gods?

NEOPTOLEMUS: One does not blush for helping one's
                                             friends.

PHILOCTETES: Helping one's friends or helping the Sons
                                          of Atreus?

NEOPTOLEMUS: No, helping *you*. I say it as your friend.

PHILOCTETES: Really? When you want to hand me over
                                       to my enemies?

NEOPTOLEMUS: Sir, remember: beggars can't be choosers.

*Agamemnon, who was already at Troy.

PHILOCTETES: You'll be the end of me with talk like this.
NEOPTOLEMUS: No I won't . . . But you've got to
understand.
PHILOCTETES: Understand why the Atreidae threw me
out?
NEOPTOLEMUS: Threw you out, but perhaps now are sav-
ing you.
PHILOCTETES: It's no use. I'm not willingly going to Troy.
NEOPTOLEMUS: What are we to do, since nothing will
persuade you?
The time has come: I'll shut up
and you'll go back to living in your trammels.
PHILOCTETES: Allow me the sufferings I must suffer,
but carry out your oath to me
when you gripped my right hand
and swore that you would see me home.
Just do that, my son, without delay;
and don't mention Troy again—
I've had enough of that.
NEOPTOLEMUS: All right, let's go!
PHILOCTETES: Oh blessed words!
NEOPTOLEMUS: [taking his hand] Plant your footsteps
after mine!
PHILOCTETES: To the best of my ability.
NEOPTOLEMUS: How am I going to square this with the
Atreidae?
PHILOCTETES: Don't bother.
NEOPTOLEMUS: What if they ravage my country?
PHILOCTETES: I will be there with . . .
NEOPTOLEMUS: How can you help?
PHILOCTETES: . . . with Heracles' arrows.
NEOPTOLEMUS: What?
PHILOCTETES: I shall ward them off.
NEOPTOLEMUS: Then kiss the ground and say good-bye.

[There is a rumble of sound and HERACLES appears
above the rocks of PHILOCTETES' cave]

HERACLES: Not yet, not until you have heard
What I have to say, O son of Poeas.
It is the voice of Heracles you hear,

His form you see.
  I have left my home in heaven for you
To tell you Zeus's will
  And stop you from embarking on your voyage.
Listen carefully.

But let me first
  mention my own progression
  and how after many labors I passed to eternal glory,
  as you can see.
For you too it is ordained, be sure of that,
  to pass through your ordeals to a blessed life.
You are to go with this man* to the town of Troy,
  first to be cured of your troublesome disease,
  then to be acclaimed the champion of the army.
You shoot down Paris with my bow—
  the cause of all this struggle—and then take Troy,
  carrying home to your father, Poeas,
  high on Oeta's tableland,
  the army's richest spoils.
Some of the hoard from this enterprise
  you shall dedicate to my pyre in memory of my bow.

[*Turning to* NEOPTOLEMUS]

For you, son of Achilles,
  my counsels are the same.
You are not strong enough to take Troy
  without his help, nor he without yours:
  you are like a brace of lions that protect each other.

[*To* PHILOCTETES *again*]

To cure you of your canker
I shall dispatch Asclepius to Ilium,
  which is destined to fall a second time before my
                                       arrows.†
But be careful when you ravage the land

*Neoptolemus.
†The first time was in the legendary past when Laomedon was king
of Troy. Heracles raised an army against him and sacked the city.

to show reverence towards the gods;
because in the mind of Zeus my father
everything takes second place to this.
For piety to heaven does not expire with man the mortal:
  whether he lives or dies it is eternal.

CHORAL DIALOGUE AND EXODUS

PHILOCTETES: Oh you whose accents I have longed to
                                hear,
Manifest at last!
  I shall not disregard your orders.
NEOPTOLEMUS: And I too submit to them.
HERACLES: Now is the time for action:
The wind is astern.
PHILOCTETES: And now is the time for me to salute this
                                 land:
  Farewell home that shared all my endeavors,
  Farewell you water nymphs of the meadows,
And booming voice of seas on the cape,
  When deep in my cave my head was often
  Drenched by the beaten spume from the wind
  And the mountain of Hermes growled in echo
  As the storm raged, but now you springs
  And Lycian* drafts, we are letting you go,
  Oh, letting you go—beyond all dreams.
  Good-bye, sea-skirted isle of Lemnos:
  Breeze me away on a faultless voyage
  To whatever haven Fate will waft me,
  To whatever purlieus the wish of my friends
  And the universal god of happenings brings me.
CHORUS: Together then let us all be gone,
  With a tryst to the ocean nymphs that they
Will see us safely on our way.

*An odd allusion, because Lycia was in Asia Minor.

THE WOMEN
OF TRACHIS

———

ΤΡΑΧΙΝΙΑΙ

Deianeira is undoubtedly the tragic heroine of this powerfully nuanced play. At first sight she is a gift from the gods for the straying male and might be compared with that rarest of wives, one who knows that her husband sleeps with every secretary he engages and still forgives him. Should we then say: "Greater love than this . . ." or "You poor misguided woman!"?

But in fact she is deeply hurt by her husband's infidelity, and the whole play is the story of how she attempts to redress it. She is no weakling. Even the way she reduces the lying Lichas to near speechlessness by the volley of her slamming questions is a masterpiece of invective and dismissal.

And yet she is tenderhearted to the distressed and beautiful princess Iole, whom she knows her husband has brought back from his campaigns as a dainty morsel for his bed. The cruel and final irony of it all is that her remedy for this crisis becomes the instrument of destruction for the husband that she loves.

It is perhaps too easy to dismiss Heracles as something of an oaf, as gauche as he is strong, but one must remember that while he was embarked on his twelve labors, with all the odds against him, he did a real service to humanity, risking his life over and over.

As to his son Hyllus, one is riven with sympathy for the boy, who first of all has to discover by the most painful gradations that his mother was not perfidious after all and that his father, whom he adores, is willing to put him through tests of loyalty that are superhuman, while himself remaining serenely adamant.

The Messenger, who comes to tell Deianeira what her husband really has been doing, makes a short appearance but it is a powerful one, and the way he drags the truth out of Lichas is trenchantly effective.

The Nurse and the Old Man are fairly stock characters: purveyors and conductors of information.

The Chorus of young Tranchinian women reacts intelligently to the vicissitudes of the story and is, if anything, a degree less platitudinous than choruses often are in Greek tragedy.

The play was produced in Athens sometime between 450 and 430 B.C. We do not know what other two plays went with it.

CHARACTERS

DEIANEIRA, wife of Heracles
NURSE, old family retainer
HYLLUS, son of Heracles and Deianeira
MESSENGER, from nearby Malis
LICHAS, herald of Heracles
HERACLES, strong man and hero
OLD MAN, friend of the family
CHORUS, young women of Trachis
IOLE (mute), captured princess

TIME AND SETTING

Fifteen months have elapsed since Heracles left his family to go on campaign. Deianeira is worried because when he left he told her that if he were not back within fifteen months he was either dead or on his way home. She learns, however, that after he had sacked Oechalia* he was conducting an affair with its captured princess, Iole, whom he has sent to Trachis to await his arrival. Deianeira is desperate. Besides her worries for him she wants above everything to regain his love and preserve her home. It is midmorning in Trachis. She comes out of the house with the old nurse.

_____

*Another name for Laconia or Sparta.

PROLOGUE

DEIANEIRA: There is an illuminating old adage going
                                                        around
   that declares you cannot assess
   the quality of any human's life—whether "blighted or
                                                        blest"—
   until they are dead.
I on the contrary know only too well,
   long before I go to Hades,
   that my life is blighted—bitterly so.
While I still lived in Pleuron
   in my father Oeneus' house,
   my betrothal was a nightmare:
   something no young woman in Aetolia
   ever had to face.
My wooer was a river-god, Achelous,
   who came to ask my father for me in three disguises.
Sometimes as a bull,
   sometimes an uncoiling lurching serpent,
   and sometimes as a man with a bull's head on a
                                                        human frame,
   from whose disheveled beard
   fountains of water dribbled on everything.
The vision of such a monstrous suitor
   made me so wretched that I prayed for death
   to save me from ever coming near his bed.
To my relief, at the very last moment,
   Heracles, that wonderful son of Zeus and Alcmena,
   fought a duel with him and so redeemed me.
Anyone sitting there
   not terrified out of his wits could tell you;
But I was sitting there numb with terror:
   fear that my beauty would pitch me into disaster.
Finally, the Zeus-of-Battles
   brought matters to a happy conclusion—
   if happy it really be—
   for now I am joined to Heracles as the bride he won
   and find myself hatching one worry after another
   on his account.
They come to me at night and are gone the next.

We have children, of course,
   towards whom he behaves like a farmer
   who has taken over a derelict field:
   assiduous only at the sowing and at the reaping.
His life has been a never-ending
   leaving home and coming home—
   all in servitude to a certain master.*
But now that he has triumphed
   in his litany of "labors"
   I am more worried than ever.
We've been living here in Trachis
   ever since he slew the stalwart Iphitus:
   living as exiles, the guests of a foreign friend.
But now nobody knows where Heracles is.
   I only know how his going pierced my heart with
                         anguish.
I feel sure that he has run into some terrible trouble,
   for no short time has elapsed, but fifteen months
   since we've had news of him.
Witness the calendar he left me!
It makes me importune the gods over and over
   not to let it spell disaster.
NURSE: Deianeira, my dear mistress,
   so many times I have seen you doing this:
   pouring out tears at the absence of Heracles.
So now, if a slave may instruct the freeborn,
   let me tell you what you ought to do.
Why, when you are blessed with so many sons
   do you not send one of them to look for their father?
Hyllus especially would be suitable—
   if he cares a rap about his father's well-being . . .
But here he comes:
   almost sprinting to the house on his quick feet.
So if you think my advice makes any sense
   you can make use of it and of the man himself.

---

*Eurystheus, king of Mycenae, cousin and rival of Heracles,
whom he hoped to destroy by imposing on him a series of impossible feats (sanctioned by Zeus) known as the Twelve Labors
of Heracles.

[HYLLUS, *somewhat out of breath, halts before them*]

DEIANEIRA: Son, my boy,
  what good advice even the lowborn can sometimes
                                                give!
This woman's a slave
  but she has the common sense of a freeman.
HYLLUS: In what way? Explain it, Mother, if you can.
DEIANEIRA: She says your father has been away so long
  you ought to feel embarrassed
  not to have found out where he is.
HYLLUS: True enough, but can one depend on what peo-
                                            ple say?
DEIANEIRA: And where in the world, my son,
  do they say he is?
HYLLUS: All last year it is said
  he worked as the lackey of a Lydian woman.*
DEIANEIRA: Nothing surprises me if he put up with that!
HYLLUS: But now he is free of it, I hear.
DEIANEIRA: Where is he reported to be at present—alive
                                            or dead?
HYLLUS: They say he is in Euboea, in the town of Eurytus,
  waging, or getting ready to wage, a war.
DEIANEIRA: Are you aware, my son,
  that he left me a prediction about that enterprise
  and how we should behave?
HYLLUS: What kind of prediction, Mother? I don't follow
                                                you.
DEIANEIRA: That he is on the brink of either dying
  or coming out on top of his ordeal
  and living happily ever afterwards.
And so, my son,
  since his life hangs in the balance,
  will you not go and help him?
For we are preserved if he has saved his life
  or we are lost with him.
HYLLUS: Of course I will go, Mother.

---

*Omphale, who fell in love with Heracles, bought him, and finally
freed him. She was queen of Lydia. They produced a son.

If I had known the seriousness of this prediction
  I would have gone long ago;
  but Father's habitual buoyancy
  prevented me from being too anxious.
DEIANEIRA: Then go, my boy!
Even arriving late is its own reward
  if what we hear is what we have desired.

[As HYLLUS *hurries away, with the* NURSE *following,
the* CHORUS *of young women of Trachis enters. They
chant to the Sun-god, asking him to locate* HERACLES
and, after expressing sympathy for DEIANEIRA, *counsel
her to moderate her anxiety and grief*]

PARADOS OR ENTRY ODE

STROPHE I
CHORUS: O Sun-god of light, iridescent Night
  On her deathbed gives you birth but flares into fire
    The sleep of your setting,
      Sun, great Sun,
  Discover the whereabouts, please
  Of the son of Alcmena for us—
  You incandescent glory of light!
Is he threading the Euxine Sea?
Is he lolling between two shores?*
O tell us with your omnivident eyes.†

ANTISTROPHE I
Deianeira, I hear, ever anxious with breaking heart—
  She who was fought for and won—is like a stricken
                                                     bird
      Unable to lull
      Her yearning eyes
  To sleep without many tears.
  She feeds an insatiable fear
    That wears her away for her missing lord.
    She pines on her anxious widowed bed

*Meaning the Strait of Gibraltar: the Pillars of Hercules.
†"Omnivident"—a word I have had to coin!

Where he is not, imagining
The very worst is happening.

STROPHE II

Just as one watches wave after wave
Churned by blasts from the north or south
With wallowing billows widely following
   On the broad main,
    So is the stormy life like the sea of Crete
Fodder for Heracles born in Thebes,
Making him famously vulnerable, but
   Some god or other
Always saves him from Hades' realms.

ANTISTROPHE II

Much as I sympathize with your lot
   I cannot approve of your losing hope
   And fretting away. The son of Cronus
   Zeus himself,
Who orders everything, has not arranged
For mortals to be free from pain.
But the fixed revolving Bear
   Brings to all
Suffering and happiness in turn.

EPODE

The glitter of night
   The sufferings of men
   The trappings of wealth
   Losing or winning:
   None of it stays.
They come and go . . . My lady, think of that.
So there is always hope. For when
   Has Zeus ever forgotten his children?

FIRST EPISODE

DEIANEIRA: [*to the* CHORUS] What I am going through, I
                         believe,

   is what brought you here,
   but I hope you never have to experience

such agonies of heart as mine.
Yours are the purlieus where youth is nourished:
  untouched by the Sun-god's heat or by rain and wind,
  untroubled until the time one is called
  no longer "maiden" but "woman."
Then the worries at night begin:
  fears for one's husband, fears for one's children.
Confronting these, you would understand
  what weighs me down.
But though there has been much to make me weep,
  there is something new I have not told you
  and tell you now.
When my husband Heracles was starting out
  on his latest expedition,
  he left in the house an ancient tablet with a calendar.
In the past he had always gone
  with a certain mission in mind
  and never with instructions of what to do if he died.
But this time, as though already doomed,
  he gave me details of my dowry and how his estate
  was to be shared among his children.
He fixed a certain date,
  three months and a year, after which
  he would either be dead or coming home
  to a blissful, painless life.
Such was the future, he said,
  laid out for him by heaven—the end of Heracles'
                                          labors—
  as he had heard predicted at the ancient oak of
                                          Dodona*
  by the two priestesses called doves.
We are at the exact date now
  for all this to be fulfilled.
In the depths of the sweetest slumber
  I start awake with terror,

---

*Dodona, now called Dodoni, was the most ancient of all the Greek
oracles. Prophecies were decoded variously, and at one time by the
movement of the leaves on the famous oak trees (of which I saw
not a trace during the filming of *Oedipus the King* in the old amphi-
theater in 1967). Dodoni is in the extreme northwest corner of
Greece.

convinced I have lost the most wonderful man alive
and must live alone forever.
CHORUS: Enough for now . . . I see a man coming.
He is garlanded and must bring good news.

[*A* MESSENGER *enters. He is elderly and bows before*
DEIANEIRA]

MESSENGER: My lady Deianeira,
let me be the first to bring you reassuring news.
Your husband the son of Alcmena is triumphantly
alive.
He is on his way here with the first fruits of battle
to offer to this country's gods.
DEIANEIRA: What exactly do you have to say, old man?
MESSENGER: That very soon your admirable husband will
be home,
resplendently victorious.
DEIANEIRA: And from whom have you heard this—a citi-
zen? a stranger?
MESSENGER: In the meadow where cattle graze in sum-
mer,
I got the story from one Lichas
who was telling it to a crowd.
So I hastened here to be first with the news . . .
to be in your favor and do myself some good.
DEIANEIRA: But if he has been successful,
why is he not here himself?
MESSENGER: [*thinking she means* LICHAS] It is not that
easy, madam.
He's being swamped by the whole of Malis,
all shooting questions at him.
He can't move a step he's so pressed.
Everyone wants the full story for himself
and won't let him go.
But in a moment you will see him face-to-face.
DEIANEIRA: [*thinking he means* HERACLES] Great Zeus
who holds sway
over the upland meadows of Oeta,
which no scythe ever shears,
at long last you have made us happy.

Break out in cheers, good women:
  you inside the house and you in these courts.
This is the harbinger beyond all hope
  of a new dawn.
CHORUS: [*singing and wildly dancing*] Bellow with happiness, house and hearth!
Explode with joy for the groom coming,
  And let all the fellows as well, shout to Apollo—
      Archer and our defender;
      While we girls in unison
      Cry out Paean, a paean!*
Call up his sister, Artemis, too, the shooter of deer,
      Flaring her double torches,
      Bringing the nearby nymphs.
      Dionysus, you mind controller,
  Give me the flute, I am too excited to stay calm:
      The ivy has gone to my head.†
Just look how I whirl in a Bacchic twirl:
      Yahoo! Yahoo! Paean O Paean!
See me, dear lady,
      With wide-open eyes:
      O look!

[LICHAS *leads in a group of captive young women, including* IOLE]

SECOND EPISODE

DEIANEIRA: [*realizing that it was* LICHAS *who was delayed, not* HERACLES] I see you all right, dear women,
  and I see this new procession;
  and I welcome Lichas, you the herald,
  who have got away at last . . .
  if you have something good to tell.
LICHAS: I am pleased to be here, dear lady,
  and pleased with your welcome,
  which matches a happy outcome.

*Paean was another name for Apollo; also for a song addressed to Apollo or his sister Artemis.
†Chewing ivy leaves was reputed to induce Bacchic intoxication.

How good it is to announce success!
DEIANEIRA: You dear dear man!
  Tell me first the thing I long for:
  shall I have Heracles back alive?
LICHAS: Well, I left him hale and hearty,
  full of vigor and brimming with health.
DEIANEIRA: In what country, tell me?
  His own or on foreign soil?
LICHAS: He's been consecrating altars
  on a headland off Euboea
  and celebrating a harvest festival for Zeus at Mount
                                              Cenaeum.
DEIANEIRA: Was this something he had vowed
  . or had there been an oracle?
LICHAS: Because of a vow he made
  prior to conquering and despoiling
  the country of these women you see before you.
DEIANEIRA: Who are they, please tell me?
To whom are they attached?
LICHAS: He singled them out for himself—and for the
                                              gods—
  when he sacked the city of Eurytus.
DEIANEIRA: Was sacking that city the reason he was gone
                                              for so long—
  so very long?
LICHAS: No, most of that time he was in Lydia,
  kept there, he says, like a slave—sold.
Don't be shocked by the word, my lady,
  it was Zeus's doing . . .
Anyway, Heracles was sold to a foreign woman, Om-
                                              phale,
  and served out a year with her—as he told me.
But he felt so humbled by the experience
  that he swore on oath that one day he would enslave
  the man who had made this happen,
  together with his wife and child.
And he kept his word.
As soon as he had been purified
  he raised a mercenary army against the man
  who was uniquely to blame, he said, for that barbarity:
  Eurytus.

Eurytus, supposedly, was an old friend,
   but when Heracles visited his house and hearth
   Eurytus heaped him with insults—
   coming from a sick mind.
"You may have those inescapable arrows,"* he jeered,
   "but when it comes to archery
   my own sons outmatch you . . .
Besides, you are a slave, not a freeman at all."
And at a dinner, when Heracles was full of wine,
   Eurytus threw him out.
Simmering with resentment,
   when later Eurytus' son Iphitus came to the cliff of
                                                    Tiryns
   looking for lost horses,
   with his gaze and his mind going in different direc-
                                                    tions,
   Heracles hurled him from the battlements.
This was the reason almighty Zeus, father of all,
   sold him into slavery.
This was the first time Heracles
   had killed someone behind his back,
   and Zeus found that intolerable.
If he had tackled him openly
   Zeus would have forgiven him—
   that would have been honest dueling:
   what the gods can't stand is criminal violence.

Meanwhile, that same haughty crowd
   are now all in Hades and their city is enslaved
   and these women who have come into your presence
   have switched from prosperity to misery.
This is your husband's report,
   which I faithfully deliver.
As to himself,
   be assured that he is about to come
   as soon as he has sacrificed to Zeus his father in
                                                    thanksgiving.
After all the happy rigmarole I've just told you

---

*Heracles possessed the magic bow, fashioned for him by Hephaestus, which could not miss. Vide Sophocles' play *Philoctetes.*

this is surely the nicest titbit of the lot.
CHORUS: Queen, your delight is manifest:
  part realized and part promised.
DEIANEIRA: Yes, how right you are!
How could I not be overjoyed
  by my husband's success.
My happiness must match his triumph.
All the same, a cautious mind is always nervous
  lest success is followed by collapse.
For instance, these poor women that I see here,
  without a home, without a father,
  lost in an alien land,
    were probably once daughters of freeborn parents,
    and now they are slaves.
Great Zeus, god of conquest,
  never let me see you reduce a child of mine to this.
And if you do,
  do not let it happen while I live!
Seeing these women fills me with apprehension.

[*Turning to* IOLE]

You poor unfortunate girl, tell me who you are?
You're not married or a mother, are you?
You look quite innocent of such mysteries
  but are obviously of noble birth.
Lichas, who on earth is this foreign girl?
Who is her mother, who is her father—
  the parents that produced her?
I felt sorry for her the moment that I saw her.
  She was the only one that showed she understood.
LICHAS: [*hedging*] How should I know? Why ask me?
  I expect she comes from one of the upper classes over
                                         there.
DEIANEIRA: Is she royalty? Had Eurytus children?
LICHAS: I have no idea. I did not ask a lot of questions.
DEIANEIRA: Surely you heard her name from one of the
                                         others?
LICHAS: I did not. I worked in silence.
DEIANEIRA: Sad girl, tell me yourself:
  I'd be sorry not to know who you are.

LICHAS: If she lets out a syllable, I assure you,
  it will be a transformation.
She has done nothing but weep, poor creature
  in deep distress,
  ever since she left her windy home.
She is quite crushed and needs our sympathy.
DEIANEIRA: Very well, then,
  let her go into the house just as she pleases
  and not have me adding to her pain:
  the pain she is suffering now is quite enough.
Now we will all go into the house
  so that you can prepare for your return
  and I can make things ready.

[DEIANEIRA *is about to follow* LICHAS *and the captive
women into the house, when the* MESSENGER *detains
her*]

MESSENGER: Madam, pause for a moment before you go
  and, with them out of earshot, hear
  who exactly it is you are taking into your home.
As yet you know but little, and I know it all.
DEIANEIRA: Really? I cannot fathom what makes you
                                    keep me here.
MESSENGER: Just stand here and listen.
What I told you before was worth your hearing
  and this, I do believe, will be even more so.
DEIANEIRA: Shall we call the others back,
  or do you want to speak only to me and to these
                                        women?
MESSENGER: I can talk freely to you and to them;
  forget about the others.
DEIANEIRA: Well, they have gone, so you can begin your
                                              story.
MESSENGER: None of what this fellow told you is the
                                              truth.
He lied before and he is lying now.
DEIANEIRA: You don't mean it? . . . Tell me everything
                                        you know,
  because I don't know what you are talking about.
MESSENGER: I heard this man declare

before several witnesses,
that it was entirely because of this girl
that Heracles toppled Eurytus and the lofty towers of
Oechalia.
It was Eros alone that fueled this prowess of arms,
or for that matter, his incursions among the Lydians,
his servitude to Omphale,
and the hurling of Iphitus to his death.
Now the fellow ignores all this
and broadcasts a different story.
No, the truth is,
when he failed to persuade her father
to let him have her as his mistress,
he challenged him on some trifling pretext
and declared war against her country,
killed the king her father and raped the city.
And now, as you see,
he sends her to this house against his own coming—
all premeditated, madam,
not as a slave—don't expect that!—
but as an object of his lust.

I thought I would tell you all this, my lady,
exactly as I heard it from the lips
of that fellow Lichas.
It was common knowledge
among the Trachinians in the marketplace:
you can ask any of them,
and if this is not a pleasant piece of news, I'm sorry,
but it is the truth.

DEIANEIRA: What misery! How am I placed now?
What hidden mischief have I given shelter to?
A nameless one, he swore;
but dazzlingly beautiful in looks and person.

MESSENGER: She is the daughter of Eurytus and named
Iole.
Anything more about her history, he didn't say:
because of course he never asked.

CHORUS: A curse not just on evildoers
but especially on a sneak who broadcasts lies!

DEIANEIRA: Women, what am I to do?

What we have just heard has struck me dumb.

CHORUS: Get hold of Lichas and force him to tell the
truth.

DEIANEIRA: Good advice! I shall do just that.

MESSENGER: And the rest of us? Shall we stay here?

DEIANEIRA: Stay, because without my summoning him
the man is coming out.

[LICHAS, *dressed for travel, emerges from the house*]

LICHAS: Madam, what am I to say to Heracles?
Give me instructions because, as you see, I am leaving.

DEIANEIRA: Why the hurry?
After all the time it took you to come here!
We haven't had a chance to talk.

LICHAS: Well, here I am—at your disposal.

DEIANEIRA: And you are ready to tell the honest truth?

LICHAS: Zeus almighty!
Of course I'll tell you all I know.

DEIANEIRA: Then who is the woman that you brought?

LICHAS: She comes from Euboea.
I don't know who her parents are.

MESSENGER: Look, man, do you realize to whom you
speak?

LICHAS: What a question to ask!

MESSENGER: And if you've got any sense you'll answer it.

LICHAS: I am speaking to the reigning Deianeira,
if I can believe my eyes: the daughter of Oeneus,
wife of Heracles, and my mistress.

MESSENGER: Exactly! So you say she is your mistress?

LICHAS: Quite right!

MESSENGER: Right, you say?
Then what do you think would be the right punishment
if you are caught not being right with her?

LICHAS: What do you mean by "right"? Is this a riddle?

MESSENGER: Not at all. You are the riddle.

LICHAS: I am going. It was stupid of me to listen to you.

MESSENGER: Going you are not . . .
until you have answered a simple question.

LICHAS: Spill it out! You are not lost for words.

MESSENGER: The captive girl you led into the house—
do you know about her?

LICHAS: I do. What is your question?

MESSENGER: Did you not say that this girl,
whom you professed not to know,
was Iole the daughter of Eurytus?

LICHAS: Where on this earth and from whom
will you find anyone who heard me say that?

MESSENGER: From a number of citizens.
In the very center of the marketplace:
quite a few Trachinians heard you say it.

LICHAS: [*cornered*] Yes . . . but . . . I said I *heard* it.
That is not the same as saying one thinks it's true.

MESSENGER: "Think"? Did you not say on your word of
honor
that you had brought her as a mistress for Heracles?

LICHAS: [*turning to* DEIANEIRA] A mistress? Dear God,
madam! Who is this stranger?

MESSENGER: There was someone there who heard from
your own lips
that it was his craving for this girl
and nothing to do with the Lydian woman*
that made him sack the city.

LICHAS: Madam, send the man away.
To bandy words with someone sick in the head
is not logical.

DEIANEIRA: [*rounding on* LICHAS] For the love of Zeus,
who strikes lightning through the glens of Oeta,
do not cover up the truth.
You are talking to a woman
who is neither perverse nor ignorant
of the ways of men
and knows the inconstancy of the human heart.
Anyone who has a boxing match with Eros is a fool.
The god of love does exactly what he likes—
even with the gods.
If he rules me,
then why not another woman in the same way?
To blame my husband for succumbing to lovesickness

*Queen Omphale.

is sheer nonsense, any less than blaming her,
who hasn't shamed or harmed me in the least.
Of course not!
But if you are carrying out his instructions to lie,
then you have embarked on a dishonest course,
in which if you have made headway,
and you cannot claim to be an honest man
without being a thorough scoundrel.
Come now, tell me the truth.
No freeman wants to be labeled a liar.
Moreover, you are bound to be found out,
because you talked to a lot of people
and they will tell me.
You ought not to be afraid,
because if it is not knowing the truth that disturbs me
what is so awful about knowing it?
After all,
Heracles has slept with many women,
and never once have I reviled him,
least of all would I in this one—
even if he were eaten up with passion.
I was overwhelmed with pity when I saw her.
Her beauty had undermined her life,
and it was not her fault, poor creature:
not her fault that she had plunged her country
into ruin and slavery.
All of which is mere words in the wind,
except just this:
with others you can lie your head off if you like
but with me you must always tell the truth.
CHORUS: You had best listen to what my lady says,
and you will never come to regret it;
and you will earn our gratitude as well.
LICHAS: Very well, dear mistress,
seeing your mortal tolerance for mortality,
I shall tell you the whole truth, concealing nothing.
Yes, it is just as this fellow says.
One day an ineluctable lust for this girl
swept over Heracles, and it was for her
that he smashed down her native city of Oechalia.
To give him credit,

he never told me to deny this or hush it up.
It was I myself, mistress, who did wrong—
    if any of this is wrong—
    afraid the news would wound you to the core.
And now that you know the whole story,
    both for his sake and your own,
    show compassion for the woman
    and abide by the sentiments you expressed about her,
    because the strong man who has conquered all and
                                                sundry
        has been brought to his knees
        by his fever of desire for this girl.
DEIANEIRA: That is precisely what I think and shall act
                                                upon.
    I do not intend to succumb to the malady
    of grappling with the gods—
    that is not my character.
Let us now go into the house
    so that you can take down my messages
    and be given the exchange presents that go with them.
It would not be right
    for you to return with empty hands
    after all the toil
    of bringing so large a party here.

[DEIANEIRA, LICHAS, *and the* MESSENGER *go into the
house while the young women of the* CHORUS *sing an
ode to the power of love and describe the battle between* HERACLES *and* ACHELOUS *to win the hand of*
DEIANEIRA]

STROPHE

CHORUS: Overwhelming, the power that Aphrodite wields!
    Invariably
She conquers. But I
Shall not mention how she tricked the son of Cronus*
Or gloom-ridden Hades
And earthshaking Poseidon.

*Zeus.

But when it comes to the betrothal of this bride,
                                        Deianeira,
What mighty antagonists entered then the lists
    To claim her!
What a turmoil the contest was,
    With dust flying!

ANTISTROPHE

One claimant in the struggle, a tremendous river,
    Took the shape
Of a four-legged horned bull.
    He was Achelous from Oeniadae; and the other
Came from Bacchic Thebes
Shaking his great club
    And complete with bow and arrows: Zeus's son,
                                        Heracles.
    They clashed in combat for the bride and for her bed,
        And lovely
    Aphrodite was there in their midst,
        The only umpire.

EPODE

What a din then ensued
  · Of fists and quivers and bulls' horns all together!
    And legs twisted round waists, and lethal blows
        Raining on heads,
        And groans from both
    While she with her tender beauty sat
        On a faraway hill
    Wondering which her groom would be . . .
    A bride waiting in anguish as the prize
        To be suddenly snatched from her mother,
            Like a forlorn calf.

THIRD EPISODE

[DEIANEIRA *comes out of the house carrying a casket*]

DEIANEIRA: While the visitor is saying good-bye
    to the captive girls before he leaves,

I've slipped outside partly to tell you
what I have been busy at
and partly to have your moral support
in what I am going through.
I have taken on board the maiden—
   though I doubt she is a maiden anymore—
   rather like a captain taking on board cargo;
   but it is playing havoc with my feelings.
Here we are,
   under the same sheets for Heracles to embrace,
   a man extolled for truth and loyalty,
   and this is my reward
   for keeping his home intact for all these years.
I cannot bring myself to be enraged
   with a husband so besotted with his present malady,
Yet what woman could put up with someone
   sharing her life and her marriage with the same man?
Besides, I see her youth advancing to its bloom,
   mine fading.
The lustful male eye turns away
   from those it has deflowered.
And so you see my fears that Heracles,
   called my husband, is a younger woman's man.
But as I have implied,
   it is no use for a sensible woman to be merely angry:
   let me tell you the remedy I have devised.

Long long ago, as a girl,
   I had a present from the shaggy-chested centaur,
                                Nessus,
   as he lay dying—it was soaked in his blood—
   and I stored it in a brazen urn.
Nessus, for a fee,
   used to carry people across the broad sweep
   of the river Evenus in his arms:
   in his arms—not by sail or oar.
He was carrying me on his shoulders
   in the days when I first knew Heracles and was his
                                 bride,
   having been dispatched into the world by my father.

In midstream he began to fondle me salaciously
   and I screamed.
Heracles, son of Zeus, swung round
   and let fly a feathered arrow.
It whipped into the centaur's chest and lungs
   and the expiring creature called out this:
"Child of ancient Oeneus,
   you are the last passenger I carried
   and I can tell you something to your benefit.
Collect the clotted gore around my wound,
   blackened by the arrow tinged with poison—
   poison from the Hydra of Lake Lerna*—
   and you will have a talisman for the heart of Heracles,
   so that he'll never again fall in love with another
                                                    woman."

Well, my dears, I remembered this
   and everything the centaur told me while he lived,
   (for after his death I locked it up in a secret place),
   and now I have rubbed it into this robe
   and done everything he said.
I am not interested in reckless remedies,
   and I loathe women who go in for them,
   but I've done what I've done in the hope
   that I can work on Heracles and quell this girl
   with talismans and spells . . .
Or do you think I am being foolish,
   in which case I shall give it up.
CHORUS: If you believe there is a chance of all this
                                                    working,
   we don't think you have wasted your time.
DEIANEIRA: I believe it up to a point
   but have never put it to the test.
CHORUS: There's no way of knowing until you do:
   trial and error is the only formula.
DEIANEIRA: Well, we shall know presently,
   for here is that man Lichas at the door:

*Lake Lerna was in the Peloponnese. The Hydra had multiple heads
and if one was chopped off two more would immediately grow. One
of Heracles' labors was to overcome the monster.

he will soon be leaving.

[LICHAS *enters*]

LICHAS: Daughter of Oeneus, what are my instructions?
  We are already considerably late.
DEIANEIRA: I was attending, Lichas, to that very thing
  while you were talking to the foreign girls inside.
I want you to take this splendid garment
  as a gift to my husband from my own hand.
But when you give it to him make sure
  that no one else puts it on but he.
Moreover, it must not be exposed to the light of the sun,
  or in the temple precincts,
  or before blaze of the hearth,
  until the day he stands in the sight of all
  and shows it off to the gods
  when the bulls are slain.
For I made a vow
  that if ever I saw or heard he was safely home
  I would clothe him in this robe
  and manifest to heaven
  a new sacrificer radiant in a new attire.

[*Handing him a signet ring*]

Take this emblem,
  which he will recognize at once:
  the seal of my signet ring.
Now go, but remember
  the first rule of a messenger:
  not to be distracted from his mission.
Then you will earn his joint gratitude with mine:
  a double thanks—by no means mean.
LICHAS: [*taking the casket from a maidservant who has
been holding it*] To be sure, madam,
  if I fulfill this mission as well as Hermes* would
  you will never have a better messenger.
I shall carry the casket and deliver it intact

---

*Hermes was the god of errands on Mount Olympus.

together with your words of dedication.

DEIANEIRA: Go at once.
You know how matters stand inside the house.

LICHAS: I know and shall bear it in mind.

DEIANEIRA: And you can report as an eyewitness
how kindly I treated the foreign girl.

LICHAS: It warmed my heart to see it.

DEIANEIRA: [*moving towards the house*] There's nothing
more, then, is there
for you to say to him?
It's too early, I'm afraid, to tell him how I miss him
before I know if he misses me.

[DEIANEIRA *enters the house and* LICHAS *takes to the
road, while the* CHORUS *expresses its optimism that
there is soon going to be great rejoicing for the return
of* HERACLES]

STROPHE I

CHORUS: You who dwell by the harbor between the hot
springs*
And the heights of Oeta along the Gulf of Malis'
shores
Belonging to Artemis,
Virgin goddess with the golden shafts,
Where the Greeks gather in parliament near the fa-
mous gates,

ANTISTROPHE I

Yes, you, you are going to hear again and soon
The beautiful notes of the flute uncorroded with
sorrow,
And instead,
Melodies of the Muses' lyre;
For Alcmena's son by Zeus is hurrying home with tro-
phies of valor.

STROPHE II

Yes, he who utterly vanished from here

---

*The Straits of Thermopylae.

Leaving us all ignorant
Waiting over the main for twelve
Whole months; leaving his dearest
Wife unhappy, deeply unhappy
In her heart. But now the irritable
War-god has released her from
   Her poignant sorrow.

ANTISTROPHE II

Come, let him come, and the many-oared ship
Bringing him make not a stop until
He enters this city, leaving behind
The island altar where they say
He was offering sacrifice.
May he come full of desire
In a bond of love that the monster's blood
Has made irresistible.

FOURTH EPISODE

[DEIANEIRA *emerges from the house in obvious distress*]

DEIANEIRA: Ladies, I have a dreadful feeling
   that I've made a big mistake in what I've done.
CHORUS: What is it, Deianeira, child of Oeneus?
DEIANEIRA: I am not sure, but I have a terrible fear
   that I may have caused a tragedy
   in the attempt to do only good.
CHORUS: Surely it is not about that gift you gave to
                               Heracles?
DEIANEIRA: Exactly that . . . I shall warn people
   never to act precipitately in a risky project.
CHORUS: Describe your fear, if you will.
DEIANEIRA: Dear women,
   you will be quite astounded by what has happened.
The piece of fleece that I used from a white sheep
   for rubbing the robe my husband was to wear
   has melted into nothing, self-consumed:
   not by anything in the house.
It has simply crumbled off the stone slab.

But let me tell you the whole story of what has
                                            happened.

I neglected nothing of what the brutish centaur told me,
    with the poisoned arrow in his side.
I observed it to the detail:
    graven on my memory like letters in bronze.
His instructions were these, and I carried them out.
I was to keep the unguent in a secret place,
    away from the fire and away from the sun
    until the moment came to apply it freshly
    on what I wanted.
When the time came to do this
    I carried out the anointing secretly in a private room,
    rubbing it in with a tuft of fleece
    taken from one of our sheep.
Then I folded up the garment,
    untouched by the sun, in the casket that you saw.
On going back into the house
    I encountered something too weird for words,
    beyond all human understanding.
I had tossed the tuft of wool I had used for the rubbing
    onto the floor, which was hot from the sun,
    and immediately it melted away and shriveled to
                                            powder—
    like a sort of sawdust.
And then on the ground where it lay
    a clot of foam bubbled up: a glaucous blue-green
    like Bacchus' fermenting grape juice
    being poured on the earth.
I am deeply troubled
    and quite at a loss to know what to think,
    convinced I have done something terrible.
Surely the centaur in his death throes
    wasn't intending to do me a kindness
    when I was the cause of his death?
On the contrary, he tricked me:
    he wanted to destroy the man who had shot him.
All too late now, I realize this,
    and to no profit.
For if I am not mistaken,

I alone will be responsible for my husband's death.
I am shattered.
I know that even the centaur Chiron
    who is immortal was mortally wounded
    by one of Heracles' poisoned arrows.
They destroy any creature that they strike.
So surely that black poison oozing from the fatal wound
    will destroy my husband too . . . I think so.
Well, I have made up my mind
    that if this means his downfall,
    I shall die at the same time with him.
No woman who cares for a good name
    can go on living with an evil fame.

CHORUS: It is true that we must be wary of the worst,
    but we must not give up hope until it is a fact.

DEIANEIRA: Hope? There is no hope
    when one has acted like a fool.

CHORUS: But when one has acted foolishly unwittingly
    as have you,
    there should be no bitterness or remorse.

DEIANEIRA: It is easy to say this
    when not in the thick of trouble,
    but not for someone who has actually caused it.

CHORUS: Well, say no more about what you fear may
                                follow,
    unless you want to talk about it to your son;
    for here he is after going to find his father.

[HYLLUS *comes in from the country, obviously distraught*]

HYLLUS: Mother, I could wish for one of three things:
    that you were dead,
    or if alive no mother of mine,
    or that somehow you could be utterly changed at
                                        heart.

DEIANEIRA: My boy, my son, what is it that makes you
                                        hate me?

HYLLUS: Know that this day you have killed your
                                        husband,
    and my father.

DEIANEIRA: A . . . h, my son! What are you saying?
HYLLUS: That words cannot undo a fact
  when one has seen it happen.
DEIANEIRA: My child, what do you mean?
  What evidence do you have for such a horrible charge?
HYLLUS: I saw it with my own eyes—my father's catas-
                             trophe:
  I do not speak from hearsay.
DEIANEIRA: So you found him? You were with him?
                             Where?
HYLLUS: If you want to know, I will tell you the whole
                             thing.
After he came back from sacking Eurytus' city
  and was dealing with the victory plunder and the
                        offerings . . .
There is a sea-swept headland in Euboea, Cape
                        Cenaeum,
  where he was dedicating altars and a sacred grove to
                        Zeus his father.
And that is where I first saw him.
  I was overwhelmed.
He was about to slaughter
  a multiple sacrifice of beasts,
  when there arrived from home his own herald, Lichas,
  bringing your present—the deadly robe.
He put it on, as you instructed,
  then proceeded with the sacrifice of twelve perfect
                        bulls.
  These were the choicest offerings from his spoils;
  though in all he had about a hundred of all kinds
                        ready.
To begin with, poor man, he prayed serenely,
  happy with his fine costume.
But when the bloodshot flame of the holy offerings
  began to blaze, and the resinous pine wood too,
  the sweat poured from him
  and the garment clung to his body at every joint
  like carpenter's glue.
An agonizing pain bit into his bones
  as the poisonous blood, like a serpent's venom,
  began to consume him.

At which he bellowed at the unfortunate Lichas,
  who was in no way to blame for your crime,
  demanding to know the reason for his bringing the
        robe.
The poor innocent man replied
  that he had simply brought the thing as a gift from
        you,
  as instructed.
On hearing this,
  a convulsive spasm gripped his lungs
  and he seized Lichas by the foot,
  just below the ankle,
  and hurled him against a sea-beaten rock.
His head was in fragments:
  the white brains, spattered with blood, mixed with
        hair.
Everyone around cried out in dismay
  at one man's seizure
  and the obliteration of the other,
  but nobody dared to approach.
The pain plunged him to the ground
  or up into the air, shouting and screaming
  till the surrounding cliffs of Locri
  and the peaks of Euboea echoed his torture.

After a time he ceased throwing himself to the ground
  over and over as he shouted imprecations
  against you, his wretched wife
  and his alliance with Oeneus her father,
  which had wrecked his life.
At which point, out of the miasma that hung about him,
  he raised his eyes and saw me
  weeping in the middle of the crowd.
Fixing his stare on me, he called out: "Boy, come here!
  Do not run from my agony,
  even if I have to die and you die with me.
Raise me up and remove me from here,
  and if possible take me where not a soul can see me,
  or, at least if you are able,
  out of this country as fast as you can.
  Let me not die here."

After we had received these orders,
    we lodged him midships
and with some difficulty brought him to these shores
bellowing with the spasms.
In a moment you will see him,
    either alive or only just dead.

Such is the outline, Mother,
    of your schemes and acts against my father.
May avenging Justice and the Furies punish you!
If it is right to curse you, curse you I do,
    and it *is* right because right you have made it.
You have killed the greatest man on earth:
    of a man like him you will never see a rebirth.

[DEIANEIRA *creeps away*]

CHORUS: [*as she is leaving*] What makes you leave in
                                              silence?
    Do you not know that such is an admission of guilt?
HYLLUS: Let her go. And let a following breeze
    blow her far from my sight.
Why should one trump up a reason
    for respecting the name of motherhood
    in one whose conduct was not a mother's?
Good riddance and farewell!
    May she relish as much happiness as she gave my
                                                    father!

[HYLLUS *stamps off and the women of the* CHORUS *sing
an ode in which they attempt to assess the significance
of all that has happened, while prefiguring yet further
disaster*]

STROPHE I
CHORUS: See, girls, how soon the divine prediction
    Of the ancient oracle has descended upon us,
    Declaring that when the last springtime ploughing
    Of twelve months should have run its course,
    The time should spell the completion of Heracles' toils
        For Zeus's own son.

So, imminent now,
Its fulfillment is due.
For how could a man
Unable to see,
On his way to his dying,
Still be subject to servitude?

ANTISTROPHE I

For if the guile of the centaur has unleashed
Those agonies eating his flanks as the poison
Soaks and clings: the poison that comes from the
Hydra
That Thanatos, Death, begot; how can he look
On tomorrow's sun when the grasp of that serpent
holds him,

And he suffers the torture
From its deadly stings
Cunningly contrived
By the sly instructions
Of that black-haired Nessus . . .
As the convulsions boil?

STROPHE II

Unfortunate lady, she knew not a thing
Except for the threat heading for her home:
A new wedlock; she did her best
To alight on a cure: some of it hers
And some from a sinister
Source and encounter. How she regrets it now she is
ruined.

Like the most delicate dew
Her diaphanous tears
Fall and the menacing fate
Coming her way foreshadows a terrible ending.

ANTISTROPHE II

At last the floodgate of tears has broken open
As the contagion pulses through him. Never
Did his enemies ever inflict
A damage anything like this
On his magnificent frame.

O the Stygian point of the retaliatory arrow
  And the prowess that brought
A bride from Oechalia running.*
And all the while Aphrodite
In silence arranged it all—as is revealed.

FIFTH EPISODE
CHORAL DIALOGUE

NURSE: [*from within*] Oh . . No!
CHORUS: If I am not mistaken, I think I hear
  a cry of distress coming from the house.
What can it mean?
It wasn't a muted sob but a wail of anguish:
  the house has suffered another blow.

[*The* NURSE *limps in, distraught*]

Look how sadly the old woman comes to tell us:
  her eyes misted with grief!
NURSE: [*entering*] O my girls, what a catastrophe has
                                                     happened
            because of that gift given to Heracles!
CHORUS: Old woman, what is this new disaster?
NURSE: Deianeira without moving a foot
  has gone on the last of her journeys.
CHORUS: Surely, not to her death?
NURSE: You have heard it all.
CHORUS: The poor lady is dead?
NURSE: Dead, as I told you.
CHORUS: O the poor lady! How did she die? Tell us.
NURSE: Most dismally it was done.
CHORUS: Then tell us, old woman.
NURSE: She pierced herself with a double-edged sword.
CHORUS: What was the madness? What the possession
  To cut herself off with a cruel weapon?
How could she do it? Death after death
  And by the wickedest steel!
Did you see—O the futility—the convulsive act?

*The princess Iole.

NURSE: Yes, I saw it. I was standing near.

CHORUS: But done by whom? Tell us that!

NURSE: She pierced herself with her own hand.

CHORUS: You don't mean it?

NURSE: It is the truth.

CHORUS: A birth, a birth from the unwedded bride
Would summon the Furies to the house.*

NURSE: Terribly true . . . And if you had been nearby
and seen the act, you would have been full of compassion.

CHORUS: How could any woman's hand commit such an
act?

NURSE: Yes, it was terrible, let me tell it,
and you can confirm what I say.
After she had gone into the house alone,
she saw her son in the courtyard preparing a bier,
with which to go back and fetch his father.
Whereon, she hid herself where nobody could see her,
and falling before the altars she cried out
that desolation was upon them.
Fingering various objects in the house that she had used,
she burst into tears, unhappy lady.
Then she wandered through the house here and there,
and every time she saw one of her beloved servants
she looked on them and wept, lamenting her own loss.

After this, I suddenly saw her
run into the bedroom of Heracles, their nuptial
chamber.
Keeping myself out of sight, I saw her
throwing blankets on the bed of Heracles.
That done, she leapt onto the bed
and with scalding tears called out:
"Dear bed of my bridals, farewell!
On this couch you will never receive me again."
Saying which,
with a compulsive hand she undid the gold brooch
that fastens her dress above her bosom

*I take this outburst to mean that Heracles' impregnation of Iole
is a call for disaster.

and bared her left side and arm.
I ran as fast as I could
  to warn her son of what she was up to;
  but in the time it took to run there and back,
  she had driven a sword into her side
  just below the liver—the seat of life.
Her son when he saw this, cried out aghast,
  for he realized, poor boy, that he had charged her in
                                                    anger,
    having learned too late from the servants in the house
    that the centaur had tricked her to act in innocence.
Her pathetic son
  has not stopped lamenting and crying:
  covering her with kisses, lying side by side,
  moaning and repeating how he had charged her falsely
  and weeping that now
  he was bereft of both father and mother.

· That is how things stand here.
    So if anybody counts on his days to come,
    he is a fool;
    for there is no tomorrow till today is done.

[*The* NURSE *retires, while the women of the* CHORUS
*comment despairingly on what has happened in the
house, and now perhaps outside, to* HERACLES]

STROPHE I
CHORUS: What shall I bewail first?
Which sadness is the sadder?
Unhappy undecided I!

STROPHE II
One's before us in the house.
One remains a forlorn hope.
Seeing and waiting to see's the same.

STROPHE III
  How I wish a powerful wind would blow me away
Far from this place and save me dying of terror

When I behold the mighty son of Zeus
In unrelievable pain:
A spectacle unbearable.
For when I was sunk in the bitterest grieving,
Like the lamenting nightingale,
It was for what was near at hand
Not far away.

ANTISTROPHE III*

Now there comes a party of strangers from afar.
But why are they carrying him as one they love?
Carrying him tenderly in a silent march
    So sadly and so speechlessly?
I cannot tell if he is dead or asleep.

[HYLLUS *enters with an* OLD MAN, *as* HERACLES *is carried in lying supine on a bier*]

CHORAL DIALOGUE

HYLLUS: O Father—your predicament—I am utterly
                                              crushed!
How can I handle it? What can I do?
OLD MAN: My son, be quiet, do not incite
Another attack of your father's spasms.
He is alive but only just.
Check yourself and bite your tongue!
HYLLUS: You really think, old man, he is alive?
OLD MAN: Shh! Don't wake him up from the sleep he is
                                                    in!

   Don't set him off
   On the shooting pains
   That come and go, my son.
HYLLUS: But I am utterly shattered—by this tragedy.
I am out of my mind with worry.
HERACLES: [*waking*] O Zeus!

*One of the rare instances when Sophocles does not match strophe
and antistrophe in length (unless of course, the text is corrupt). Let
me remind readers that the meters of these choral pieces are those
of the original—as far as I could manage them.

Where in the world have I come to? Among what men,
Stretched out here and riddled with constant pain?
What a completely miserable state I am in! . . .
A . . . h! A spasm, a spasm has hit again.

OLD MAN: [to HYLLUS] Did I not tell you to keep your
                                    mouth shut
   And not to drive his slumber away:
   Out of his head,
   Out of his eyes?

HYLLUS: I know, but am not able
   To watch his awful pain.

HERACLES: Rock of Cenaeum on which my altars stand
   I wish I had never set eyes on you, stricken as I am.
The numberless sacrifices that I made you,
   And this is the thanks!
Yes, O Zeus:
   What destruction! What absolute ruin!
This ravening madness
   Nothing will smother!
Where is the surgeon, where the soother
   To put to sleep this virulence?
I'd be amazed to see one.
Only Zeus could lull me.
O . . . h!
Allow me to sleep, allow me to sleep,
   Allow this crumpled ruin to sleep!
Keep your hands off!
Where, O where are you putting me?
You are killing me, killing me!
You've brought on another attack.
Here comes the pain, ah, it's got me again, and you
                                          Greeks,
   Where are you from, you most unfeeling of men?
And after I almost destroyed myself for you
   Ridding you of nuisances
   In the sea, in the forests;
   And now in my crucial pain will no one come to my
                                                help
   With a merciful flame or a sword?
A . . . h!
Is there no one here who will cut off my head

And end this life of agony? A . . . h!

OLD MAN: Son of Heracles, I am quite unable to cope.
I have not the strength
   and need some of yours to help him.

HYLLUS: [*attempting to massage his father*] I am doing
                                        everything I can,
   but neither within nor without
   can I assuage his pain. . . . It's up to Zeus.

HERACLES: My boy, where are you?. . . Ah!
It's on me again, it's on me again.
Spirits of heaven, help! help!
It springs again, it springs:
It wants to kill me;
   A torture none can quell.
Pallas Athena, Pallas,* it's on me again . . . Ah, my boy,
   Show compassion for your father, draw a sword,
   None will blame you,
   And strike beneath my collarbone.
Cure the pain your godless mother gave me,
   The raving pain.
May she suffer the same collapse, the very same!
Sweet Hades, come,
   You brother of Zeus,
   Bring sleep, sleep.
Kill this suffering with a swift death.

CHORUS: My friends, I shudder to hear
   of our master's harrowing plight:
   a man like him and a plague like that!

HERACLES: Even to talk of my labors is fearsome
                                        enough:
   they were hard on my arms, hard on my back;
   but never did Zeus's wife†
   or that loathsome Eurystheus‡
   put on my shoulders such a quilt of suffering
   woven by the Furies

---

*Athena was his patron.
†Hera.
‡Heracles' cousin and hated rival, who, by the will of Zeus, imposed
on him the twelve labors.

as the daughter of Oeneus, Deianeira, has
with her intriguing face.
It finishes me.
It clings to my flanks.
It eats away to the bone.
It inhabits me and devours my lungs.
By now it has guzzled all my blood
   and my body is wrecked.
I am completely enslaved
   by its indescribable tyranny.
Not the spearsmen on the plains,
   not the earth-sprung army of giants,
   not the savagest freaks,
   not Greece nor lands beyond,
   nor any province that I came to purge,
   did this.
No, a woman did, a very feminine female,
   did it all by herself—without need of a word.

My son, be a true son to me:
   do not regard your mother's name more than mine.
Drag your mother out of the house in your own hands
   and place her in mine.
Then let me see
   if you are more appalled
   by the sight of my tortured body
   or hers when I have finished with her.
Come, my child, go through with it;
   show some pity for me—who am so pitiable:
   howling out and crying like a girl:
   something nobody can say he saw this man do before.
Even when aching with pain
   I never complained.
Now you see me revealed as a womanish thing,
   so now come close to me,
   stand by your father's side
   and gaze at the shambles I have become.
Let me display it and draw the curtain.
Look at me, all of you,
   stare hard at my wrecked body:
   see the full misery of this luckless creature:

luckless, luckless—A . . . h! It's on me again,
another throb of pulsing pain—
hot pain thrashing through my sides:
not for a moment does the torture leave me.
O prince of Hades, take me in!
Lightning of Zeus, strike me down:
    yes, lord, my father, smash me down.
O it is feeding on me again!
It blooms, it lances out!
You hands, poor hands! You back and shoulders!
And you my beloved arms,
    are you the arms that quelled the monster of Nemea,
    that lion the curse of herdsmen:
    a beast that none could come near,
    none could confront;
And the Hydra of Leraea,
    and that ferocious battalion of monsters,
    double-natured, with the fetlocks of horses:*
    lawless and insulting,
    overpowering in their potency!
And the wild boar of Erimanthus!
And Cerberus the three-headed dog
    in the depths of Hades—an unquenchable freak,
    the whelp of frightful Echidna!†
And the snake that guarded the golden apples
    in beyond the beyond!

And in my labors,
    how many other triumphs did I not have,
    none of which ended in defeat! I was strong.
But now, look at me:
    my dislocated limbs, my tattered body,
    and me—vanquished by blind pain! . . .
I, born from the noblest of mothers!
I, celebrated among the stars
    as son of Zeus!
But, but, be certain of this:
    even though I amount to nothing and cannot move,

---

*The Centaurs.
†A female monster: beautiful woman, but a serpent below the waist.

even in this deplorable state,
I shall punish her, the one responsible.
Just let her appear before me
    and be given a lesson, a manifesto that proclaims
    that, living or dying, I chastise the profane.
CHORUS: Hapless Greece,
    what sorrowing regrets do I not see
    if you lose this man!
HYLLUS: Father, since I have your permission to respond,
    listen quietly and hear me out.
Ill though you are, I make this request,
    please grant it:
    that you face me without anger and recrimination.
Otherwise you will not discover
    the mistake you are making
    in your resentment and your thirst for satisfaction.
HERACLES: Well, make it short.
I am sick and cannot apprehend
    any subtleties you may be harboring.
HYLLUS: I am here to tell you about my mother:
    how things really were,
    and how she did wrong by accident.
HERACLES: You utter rascal!
Do you dare look me in the face
    and bring up the mother that has killed your father?
HYLLUS: I do,
    because in her case it would be wrong not to speak.
HERACLES: Hardly so,
    when you think of what she has gone and done!
HYLLUS: And what she has gone and done this very day.
HERACLES: Then tell me what,
    but don't turn out to be a turncoat!
HYLLUS: I have to tell you she is dead, just dead.
HERACLES: Good news from a dismal prophet,
    but by whose hand?
HYLLUS: By her own—no one else's.
HERACLES: What a pity, she should have died by mine!
HYLLUS: Even you would change your mind if you knew
                                        the truth.
HERACLES: A curious remark, but tell me what you
                                        know!
HYLLUS: She made a mistake: far from what she wanted.

HERACLES: A fine mistake, you wretch, killing your
                                                      father!

HYLLUS: No, her mistake was to think she had a cure
   for the love match you brought home.

HERACLES: What sorcerer in Trachis could concoct a cure
                                                      for that?

HYLLUS: It was the centaur Nessus who long ago
   told her of a love charm to inflame your heart.

HERACLES: [*reeling*] Ah, dear gods, this is the end!
I am finished, finished,
   the light of day is done for me.
Yes, yes, now I understand
   my full calamity.
Go, my child,
   you have no father anymore.
Call the whole tribe of your relations.
Call Alcmena, the ill-fated,
   in vain the bride of Zeus.
let them hear before I die
   the prophecies I know.

HYLLUS: But your mother is not here.
She has gone abroad to live in Tiryns by the sea.
Some of your children she has taken with her,
   others you will find living in Thebes.
But if there is anything you want doing, Father,
   those of us who are here will see to it.

HERACLES: There *is* something, listen:
   it will prove you as a man—a fit son of mine.
Long ago my father prophesied
   that I should not die by any living hand
   but by someone who lived in Hades—someone dead.
Well, as the celestial prophecy foretold,
   the savage centaur has killed me:
   I alive and he dead.
And other prophecies confirm this—olden prophecies—
   which I wrote down
   when I was in the grove of the Selli*
   who live in the hills and whose bed is the ground.

---

*The priests of the ancient oracle at Dodona, who interpreted the
predictions of the talking oak.

It was dictated by the ancestral oak
   of multiple tongues, and said
   that at the time of this living present, now,
   I should be released from the labors that enthralled
                                   me.
I thought this meant that I should be happy at last,
   but all it meant was that I should die:
   for labor is over for the dead.
Now that all this is clearly being fulfilled,
   you must stand by me, my son,
   and not let me have to get rough with you;
   you must come to my help and work with me.
Of all laws there is no other
   higher than obedience to a father.
HYLLUS: Father, I am nervous of where you may be
                         heading,
   but I shall do your bidding.
HERACLES: First place your right hand in mine.
HYLLUS: A pledge? What makes you insist on that?
HERACLES: Give me your hand at once:
   are you going to disobey?
HYLLUS: [*holding out his right hand*] Look, you have it:
                 you are not being disobeyed!
HERACLES: Now swear by the head of Zeus my father.
HYLLUS: To do what? You must tell me that.
HERACLES: You must swear to carry out the act I ask for.
HYLLUS: All right, I swear. Zeus is my witness.
HERACLES: And in your prayer include this:
   that you will be punished if you break your oath.
HYLLUS: I'll need no punishment, for I shall do it;
   so in my prayer I swear it.
HERACLES: Very well, then, do you know Mount Oeta,
   sacred to Zeus?
HYLLUS: I do. On its summit I have often stood to
                       sacrifice.
HERACLES: You are to lift me and carry me there with
                   your own hands,
   with the help of any friends you choose.
You are to cut a heap of timber from the oak,
   that strong-rooted tree,
   and another heap of the tough wild olive.

Throw my body onto the pile
    and set fire to it with a flaring pine torch.
Let me see no tears, no lamentation.
If you really are a son of mine
    I want no mourning and no weeping.
If you refuse,
    even from the world below
    I shall haunt and curse you forever.
HYLLUS: Father, what you propose is terrible:
    will you dismantle me?
HERACLES: But it must be done.
Or find yourself another father, be mine no longer.
HYLLUS: Ah, what anguish, Father!
You are asking me to be your murderer
    and have that on my conscience.
HERACLES: On the contrary: to be my healer,
    the only panacea for my suffering.
HYLLUS: What, healing your body
    by setting it on fire?
HERACLES: All right, then; if you can't face that
    at least do the rest.
HYLLUS: I shall not refuse to carry you:
    that at least.
HERACLES: And also heaping up the pyre.
HYLLUS: But not putting a light to it.*
I'll do the rest and shall not fail you.
HERACLES: Good! But there is still a small favor I would
                                ask

    in addition to these greater ones.
HYLLUS: However great, it shall be done.
HERACLES: I suppose you know the daughter of Eurytus?
HYLLUS: I expect you mean Iole.
HERACLES: Correct . . . This is what I want you, my son.
To be true to me your father
    and true to your oath,
    when I am dead—marry her.
Don't disappoint me in this.
No other man but you must have her.
She has lain with me and only you must wed her.

*Philoctetes is usually reputed to be the one who lit the pyre.

Consent, because to fail me in a small matter
  when you have complied in a greater
  cancels your goodwill.

HYLLUS: Dear God! To be angry with a sick man is
                            wrong,
  but how can I countenance such a monstrous idea?

HERACLES: It looks to me as though you intend to ignore
                            everything I asked.

HYLLUS: But she is the unique cause of my mother's
                            death
  and of your suffering what you do.
Who on this earth could make such a choice
  unless goaded by avenging Furies?
It would be preferable, Father,
  for me to die too than to be yoked
  to my greatest enemy.

HERACLES: So he is ready to ignore
  the requests of a dying man,
  requests that ought to be honored.
Well, the curse of the gods will be on you
  if you refuse to comply with what I want.

HYLLUS: I believe you are showing
  how really sick you are!

HERACLES: Yes, my pains had abated
  and you have prompted another attack.

HYLLUS: O what a plethora of horrible decisions!

HERACLES: Only horrible because you won't obey your
                            father.

HYLLUS: But, Father, are you not teaching me to be
                            disloyal?

HERACLES: It is not disloyalty to gladden my heart.

HYLLUS: Do you seriously ask me to carry this out?

HERACLES: I do, and call the gods to witness.

HYLLUS: Then I shall do it and not say no,
  and put the responsibility of your will upon the gods.
If I am true to you, Father,
  I cannot be condemned.

HERACLES: Well done!
And now for a final kindness.
Put me on the pyre before another spasm
  nettles me and tears me apart.

But be quick and lift me.
This is my repose from suffering.
This is the end of Heracles.
HYLLUS: There is nothing now to stop this being done.
This is your command.
This is what you make me do.
HERACLES: [*To* HYLLUS *and his companions*] Hurry be-
                                    fore you arouse another attack.
And you my recalcitrant spirit
    Set a bit on my tongue as hard as stone.
Let not a whimper escape me. No.
    Let it be something I enjoy—
    This unenviable act!

[HERACLES *is lifted onto the litter as* HYLLUS *and his
company begin to move off for the trek to Mt. Oeta*]

HYLLUS: [*in a chant*] My friends,
    Lift him kindly, be full of sympathy
    For me for the things you see happening.
    Mark the callousness of the deities
    Allowing such things to be done.
They are our origins, called our parents,
    Yet they can look upon such sufferings.
What is to come, no one can tell.
What is here is painful for us,
    Disgraceful of them; and for him who suffers
    This destiny—the hardest of all.

[*Turning to the leader of the* CHORUS]

You too, young woman,
    Do not be left behind in the house,
    You have witnessed terrible dyings
    And untold calamities.
Behind it all is no one but Zeus.

[*The women of the* CHORUS *follow the cortege and in
a slow march leave the arena*]

OEDIPUS
THE KING

———

ΟΙΔΙΠΟΥΣ ΤΥΡΑΝΝΟΣ

In Aristotle's famous definition of tragedy he had in mind Sophocles' *Oedipus* as the perfect specimen. Aristotle conceived tragedy as the "imitation" (that is, representation) of a certain action of great magnitude in dramatic form embellished with poetry. In this action a person of upright character but dogged by a certain flaw heads for his downfall. The flaw is the lever for his destruction, but the irony is that it does its work, trips him up, through his finest qualities: in Oedipus, his honesty and courage.

The downfall of the House of Oedipus was foretold by the gods before Oedipus was born, but it was foretold because it was going to happen; it was not going to happen because it was foretold, and it was going to happen because Oedipus being what he was, made it happen.

Oedipus

It is true that Oedipus had no idea he had murdered his father and married his mother, so he cannot be blamed for that, but blame is not the question; the question is pollution. Knowingly or unknowingly, he did the deed and finds himself standing before humanity as a freak of fate—a polluted monster. The gods, always out to chasten hubris, allowed him to make the first mistake. His own overweening self-sufficiency propelled by his fatal flaw (temper, impatience, suspicion of those he should trust) allowed him to make the second. Each step confidently taken to lead to enlightenment becomes a step nearer to the dismantling of his humanity. This piecemeal and unhalting progression towards ruin is one of the most powerful sequences in all literature. The crowning irony is that the victim's only concern was the salvation of his people.

A look at the name Oedipus (in Greek, OIDIPOUS) is revealing, for it is stuffed with latent meanings, all of them emblematic of the themes of *Oedipus The King*. *Oida* means *I know* (with the present sense of *eido*, *I see*): which encapsulated Oedipus' compulsion to ferret out his past and see who he really is, which, when he does, impels him to punish his knowing, his seeing, by putting out his eyes.

But Oedipus was also lame: his ankles had been riveted as a baby when he was exposed on Mount Cithaeron and hung from a tree (where the shepherd discovered him). *Oideo* means *I swell up*, and *oidos* is a *swelling*, and *pous* means a *foot*. All these meanings are tucked into the name OIDIPOUS. There is no way to capture this multiple play in English. There is no way of putting into one word "Know-all-see-all-swollen-foot." The nearest I can get to it is "See-well-foot," which if you say rapidly becomes "Swell-foot." But this leaves out the *know*.

One last point about Oedipus: The Sophoclean hero goes down fighting and through acknowledging the enormity of his defeat wrests a moral victory from ruin. The total effect of this presentation on spectators is purgative and, as Aristotle points out, induces a catharsis of fear and pity.

Creon

Creon figures in all three of the Theban plays, but one must remember that a span of at least sixty years covers Sophocles' portrait of a man who may well have been, as some think, his first attempt at a portrait in *Antigone*, of Oedipus, which, though the last play of the "trilogy," was written first. The Creon shown in *Oedipus* is at his least reprehensible, dealing reasonably with an unreasonable and hysterical Oedipus. Yet even here there is a streak of his later hypocrisy and amorality in the way he is willing to shelter behind the screen of his being only third in command of the realm; and there is that sneer of superiority at the end, which betrays his sneaking satisfaction at the fate of the fallen king.

Tiresias

Tiresias fully understood the character of Oedipus, and he knew that once he began his fatal investigation nothing would halt him and the result would be horror. Therefore he does his best to persuade the king not to proceed, but faced by the latter's intransigence he lets loose a tongue-lashing of devastating power, only to find Oedipus impervious both to advice and reproof, taking them as evidence of perfidy.

Jocasta

It is difficult not to feel sympathy for Jocasta, who tries desperately to head off her husband from his questioning when she discovers that he is her son. But even before the lethal shock of that revelation when she tried to soothe his fears she fed them. Every syllable she utters out of concern and love creeps towards an unthinkably unlovely resolution.

Sophocles wrote *Oedipus* in 430 B.C., some sixteen years after his *Antigone*. It was produced at the theater of Dionysus in Athens between 427 and 426. Amazingly, this the most perfect of plays won only second prize. One can only surmise either that the judges were distracted by the beginning of Athens' death struggle with Sparta or that the two plays that went with it were of lesser quality or that simply the production in matters of actors, chorus, costumes, masks, and music was undistinguished.

CHARACTERS

OEDIPUS, king of Thebes
A PRIEST of Zeus
CREON, brother of Jocasta
CHORUS of Theban elders
TIRESIAS, a blind prophet

JOCASTA, wife of Oedipus
MESSENGER, from Corinth
OLD SHEPHERD
PALACE OFFICIAL
PALACE ATTENDANTS AND SERVANTS
CITIZENS OF THEBES
ANTIGONE
ISMENE
BOY

TIME AND SETTING

Some fifteen years previously, Oedipus, then a young man, was told by the Oracle at Delphi that he was destined to murder his father and marry his mother. Shocked, he determined never to go back to Corinth, where he was brought up by the king and queen, who he thought were his father and mother. His wanderings bring him eventually to the city of Thebes, where his real father and mother reign. However, on the way, he brawls with an old man in a carriage over right-of-way and in a fit of temper kills him. Arrived at Thebes, he finds the city in an uproar: the king, Laius, has gone on a mysterious journey and never returned, and a female monster, the Sphinx, has taken up her position on a rock outside Thebes and is strangling the inhabitants one by one for not being able to answer her riddle. Oedipus answers it, and the Sphinx throws herself from her rock. The citizens, in gratitude, make Oedipus their king, and he marries Jocasta, their widowed queen. No one knows that Jocasta is Oedipus' real mother and that the old man he killed on the road was Laius, his father. Nor do they know that these parents of his had tried to murder him as a baby (because of another dreadful oracle) and thought they had succeeded. There follow fifteen years of apparent prosperity: a sham prosperity cloaking corruption. The gods are disgusted. Thebes is struck by plague. The people of the city, led by their priests and elders, flock around the great and successful Oedipus, now in the prime of life and power. He saved them once: he can save them again. Here the play begins.

It is midmorning outside the palace of Oedipus, with Thebes in the background. There is the sound of prayer and lamentation; the air is full of incense. A procession of children, youths, and elders, all holding olive branches wreathed in white wool, are marshaled by a priest onto the palace steps and group themselves around the altar of Zeus. Oedipus comes out of the palace. He signals for silence.

PROLOGUE

OEDIPUS: My children, scions of the ancient Cadmean
line,
 what is the meaning of this thronging round my feet,
 this holding out of olive boughs all wreathed in woe?
The city droops with elegiac sound
 and hymns with palls of incense hang.
I come to see it with my eyes, no messenger's.
Yes, I whom men call Oedipus the Great.

[*He turns to the* PRIEST]

Speak, Elder, you are senior here.
Say what this pleading means,
 what frightens you, what you beseech.
Cold-blooded would I be, to be unmoved
 by petitioners so pitiful.
PRIEST: King Oedipus, the sovereign of our land,
 you see here young and old clustered round the
shrine.
Fledglings some, essaying flight,
 and some much weighted down
 (as I by age, the Presbyter of Zeus),
 and striplings some—ambassadors of youth.
In the marketplace sit others, too
 at Pallas' double altar, garlanded to pray,
 and at the shrine
 where Ismenus breathes oracles of fire.

Oh, look upon the city, see the storm
 that batters down this city's prow in waves of blood:

The crops diseased, disease among the herds.
The ineffectual womb rotting with its fruit.
A fever-demon wastes the town
    and decimates with fire, stalking hated
    through the emptied house where Cadmus dwelled.
While poverty-stricken night grows fat
    on groans and elegies in Hades' halls.
We know you are no god, omnipotent with gods.
That is not why we throw ourselves before you here,
    these little suppliants and I.
It is because on life's unequal stage
    we see you as first of men and consummate
    atoner to the powers above.
For it was you,
    coming to the Cadmus capital,
    Who disenthralled us from the Sphinx (her greedy
                                                    dues):
    that ruthless sorceress who sang.
Not primed by us, not taught by hidden lore,
    but god-inspired, we so believe,
    You raised us up again and made us sound.
So, Oedipus, you most respected king,
    we plead with you to find for us a cure:
Some answer breathed from heaven, perhaps,
    or even enlightenment from man.
For still we see the prowess of your well-proved mind,
    its tested buoyancy.

So, go, you best of men.
Raise up our city. Go, now on your guard.
Your old devotion celebrates you still
    as Defender of the State. You must not let
    your reign go down as one when men
    were resurrected once—and once relapsed.
Mend the city, make her safe.
You had good omens once. You did your work.
Be equal to your stature now.
If king of men (as king you are),
    then be it of a kingdom manned and not a desert.
Fortress and battlement are useless when
    all is nothing but a waste of men.

OEDIPUS: This quest that throngs you here, poor needy
                                                    children,
  is no new quest to me.
I know too well, you all are sick, yet sick,
  not one so sick as I.
Your pain is single, each to each, it does not breed.
Mine is treble anguish crying out
  for the city, for myself, for you.
It was no man asleep you woke—ah, no!—
But one in bitter tears and one
  perplexed in thought, found wandering.
  Who clutched the only remedy that came:
  to send the son of Menoeceus, Creon—
  my own Jocasta's brother—
  to the place Apollo haunts at Pythia
  to learn what act or covenant of mine
  could still redeem the state.

And now I wonder.
I count the days. His time is up.
He does not come. He should be here.
But when he comes—the instant he arrives—
  whatsoever he shall tell me from the god,
  that to the hilt I'll do—or I am damned.
PRIEST: Reassuring words indeed! And timely, too,
  for look, they're signaling that Creon comes.

[CREON *is seen approaching in the distance*]

OEDIPUS: His eyes are bright. O great Apollo,
  bring him here effulgent with success!
PRIEST: Yes, success it is, I think.
See the laurel chaplets thick with berries on his head!
OEDIPUS: We shall know in a moment. He can hear us
                                                    now.

[OEDIPUS *shouts to him*]

What news, royal brother?
What mandate, Son of Menoeceus, from the mouth of
                                                    the god?

[*Enter* CREON]

CREON: Favorable! I'd even say, if all goes well,
our wounds will issue into blessings.
OEDIPUS: Which means? . . . You leave me half in hope,
half buried in despair.
CREON: Do you want to hear it publicly, on the spot,
or shall we go inside?
OEDIPUS: Speak out to all. It's more for them than me,
though more my own than my own soul.
CREON: Very well, then. This is what the god has said,
The Prince Apollo openly enjoins on us
to sever from the body politic
a monstrous growth that battens there:
stop feeding that which festers.
OEDIPUS: By what purge? How diagnosed?
CREON: By banishment. Or blood for blood.
The city frets with someone's blood.
OEDIPUS: Whose? Is the unhappy man not named?
CREON: Laius, sire. Him we had as king
in days before you ruled.
OEDIPUS: So I've heard. . . . A man I never saw.
CREON: A murdered man. And now clearly is required
the just blood of his assassins.
OEDIPUS: But where in the world are they? Oh, where
can one begin
to search the long-lost traces of forgotten crime?
CREON: "Here," says the god. "Seek and you shall find.
Only that escapes which never was pursued."
OEDIPUS: Where did Laius meet his violent end?
At home? In the fields? In foreign parts?
CREON: He planned a pilgrimage, he said; and so left
home,
never to come back again the way he went.
OEDIPUS: He went alone? No companions and no
witnesses
who could furnish a report?
CREON: Dead. All done to death but one, who fled in
panic,
and he tongue-tied save on a single point.
OEDIPUS: What point? Tell it. Clues breed clues

and we must snatch at straws.

CREON: Brigands, this man insists, attacked the king:
  not one but many, and they cut him down.

OEDIPUS: No brigand would be so bold, unless . . .
  unless bought—right here—bought with bribes.

CREON: So we thought, but with Laius gone
  we were sunk in miseries and no one stirred.

OEDIPUS: What miseries could ever let you leave
                                  unsolved
  the death and downfall of a king?

CREON: Sire, it was the siren Sphinx of riddles
  who sang us from the shadowed past
  to what was sorely present.

OEDIPUS: Then I'll go back and drag that shadowed past
                                  to light.

Oh, yes, the pious Apollo and your piety
  have set on foot a duty to the dead:
  A search that you and I together will pursue.
My designs could not be suited more:
  to avenge the god and Thebes in a single blow.
Ah! Not for any far-flung friend,
  but by myself and for myself I'll break this plague.
For who knows, tomorrow this selfsame murderer
  may turn his bloody hands on me.
The cause of Laius therefore is my own.

So, rise up, children, and be off.
Take your prayer boughs too.
Summon here the counselors of Thebes,
  and muster too the Cadmus clan.
I am resolute, and shall not stop
  till with Apollo's help all-blessed we emerge,
  or else we are lost—beyond all purge.

[OEDIPUS *goes into the palace, followed by* CREON]

PRIEST: Children, rise.
The king has pledged us all our pleas
  and we have heard Apollo's voice.
Oh, may he bring salvation in his hands
  and deal a death to all disease.

[*The* PRIEST *disperses the suppliants. The* CHORUS *of Theban elders enters*]

ODE OF ENTRY

[*The first ode opens with a hymn to Apollo, the god of victory and healing (known as Paean). Its stately dactylic measure, as the* CHORUS *moves toward the altar of Zeus, is bright with hope yet weighted with awe and uncertainty. Then as the elders survey the sufferings of Thebes, the rhythm changes into one of dismay, broken by the sad lines of trochees and iambs. In the final strophe and antistrophe the elders end their prayer for help on a note of energy and determination*]

STROPHE I

What god-golden voice from the gold-studded shrine of
the Pytho
Comes to our glorious Thebes?
My spirit is tremulous, racked with its eagerness. Help
Healer of Delos—Paean!
I am fainting with fear of what fate you will fashion me
now,
Or turn in the turning of time.
Speak to me, Oracle, child everlastingly sprung
From Hope so goldenly. Come!

ANTISTROPHE I

I call on you first, Zeus's daughter, immortal Athena.
Then on your sister, earth's guardian,
Artemis ringed round with praises and throned in our
square.
Ah! And far-shooting Phoebus.
You three that are champions swift to deliver, appear!
For if ever the fire of disaster
Reared on our city, you beat its affliction away.
Defend and be near us today.

STROPHE II

Sorrows in a legion.
Sorrows none can cipher.

No shaft of wit or weapon
For a people stricken.
Shriveled soil and shrinking
Wombs in childbirth shrieking.
Soul after soul like fire
Beats, beats upward soaring
To the god of the setting sun.

ANTISTROPHE II

A decimated city
Dying. And deadly the dead.
All lying uncried for. But crying
Matrons and mothers graying
At every alter praying,
Till the chiming sorrow of dirges
Is splintered by shouts of the paean:
Rescue! O golden daughter
Of Zeus's with your smile.

STROPHE III

Muffle the wildfire Ares
Warring with copper-hot fever
Without clash of sword or shield.
Whirl him back homeward and headlong.
Plunge him down from our shores
Into Amphitrite's foaming
Lap or the unquiet grave
Of hissing Thracian seas.
For, oh, what night has spared us
He does at break of day.
Zeus, you sovereign of thunder,
Shiver him with lightning.

ANTISTROPHE III

Aureate champion Apollo,
Let us sing the song of your arrows
Shot from the bow of the sun;
While Artemis blazing with torches
Courses the Lycean mountains.
And you, O Theban Bacchus,
Wine blushed, xanthic crowned,

You smiling god of succor,
Come all torchlit flaring.
Come wheeling with your Maenads,
Fall on the god that is godless.

[OEDIPUS *has entered*]

FIRST EPISODE

OEDIPUS: You pray! Then listen:
What you pray for you can have—
  remission of these miseries and help
  if you'll hear my plan:
  a plan to stop the plague.
I speak of course as stranger to the story
  and stranger to the crime,
  being too late your latest citizen
And helpless, therefore, to track it very far
  unless you lend me clues.
Wherefore, I boldly challenge
  all you Thebans here with this:
Does any man among you know
  who killed Laius son of Labdacus?
Such a one I now command
  to tell me everything.

[*He waits for a reply*]

If self-incrimination keeps him silent,
  let him be assured
He need fear nothing worse than banishment
  and he can depart unharmed.

[*He pauses again*]

Perhaps one of you is aware
  the murderer was someone from some other land.
Let him not be shy to say it.
I shall heap rewards on him,
  besides my deepest blessing.

[No one stirs]

What, silent still?
If anyone is out to shield a guilty friend
   (or is it guilty self?),
He'd best listen to the penalties I plan.
That man, whoever that man be,
   I this country's reigning king
Shall sever from all fellowship of speech and shelter,
   sacrifice and sacrament,
Even ritual touch of water, in this realm.
Thrust out from every home,
   he'll be the very picture of that pestilence
   he brought upon our city,
As Apollo's word from Pythia has just revealed to me.
Yes, such an ally, nothing less,
   am I of both religion and the murdered man.

As to the killer, slipping off alone
   or with a band of men,
I now call down a life to fit a life
   dragged out in degradation.
And if I myself should prove myself
   to have him in my halls an intimate,
Then on myself I call down every curse I've just invoked.
See to it that every syllable I say is done.
For my sake, for the god Apollo, and for this land,
   so fruitless now and so cast off by heaven.
Why, even without a sanction so divine,
   how could you find it in you to neglect
   a monarch's death and not pursue
   this ending to the best of men?
Whose very scepter I hold in my hands as king;
His marriage bed my bed of seed,
   our children even shared with share of her
   had he been blessed with progeny—
Oh, blessed and not struck down by fate!

Such ties swear me to his side
   as if he were my father.
I shall not rest until I've tracked the hand

that slew the son of Labdacus,
the son of Polydorus, heir to Cadmus in the line
of ancient Agenor.
And those who disobey
  I'll ask the gods to curse
  with fields that never sprout
  and wombs that never flower,
  And all the horrors of this present plague and worse.
The rest of you, my loyal men of Thebes,
  who think with me, may Justice champion
  and the whole of heaven help.

CHORUS: Great king, your oath will make a perjuror of
me
  if I do not tell the truth. I swear
  I am not the killer, nor can I show you
  who the killer is.
Apollo proposed the search, it's up to him
  to point the culprit out.

OEDIPUS: Certainly, but show me a man who can force
  the hand of heaven.

CHORUS: Then, the next best thing, if I may say it ...

OEDIPUS: Next best, third best, say it—anything.

CHORUS: My lord, there lives a man who with a king's
eyes sees
  the secrets of a king: Tiresias of Apollo.
He is our source of light, our chance of learning, king.

OEDIPUS: I know. Don't think that I've been idle there.
Twice I have sent for him at Creon's bidding.
I cannot understand what keeps him so.

CHORUS: At least we can dismiss those other tall old
tales.

OEDIPUS: What tales? I must hear them all.

CHORUS: How he met his death through traveling
vagabonds.

OEDIPUS: I've heard that too. We have no witnesses,
however.

CHORUS: And he'd be a brazen man indeed who could
rest in peace
  after all your menaces.

OEDIPUS: Mere words will not stay one whom murder
never could.

CHORUS: And yet there's one to meet the challenge.
                                                    Look:
They're leading in the holy prophet,
    sole temple of incarnate truth on earth.

[*The old blind prophet* TIRESIAS *is led in by a boy*]

OEDIPUS: Come, great mystic, Tiresias—intuitive,
    didactic master of the finite and the infinite—
Though you cannot see it you must surely feel
    the overwhelming weight of all this city's woes.
You are our last refuge, Pontiff, and our help.

Apollo, if you have not heard the news,
    has sent back to us who sent to him,
    an answer saying: "No deliverance from the plague
    except you seek and find the Laius killers
    and punish such with death or banishment."
Now, sir, do not begrudge the smallest hint
    your skill from birds or any other omen can elicit.
Save yourself, the city, and save me.
Save us from this whole corruption of the dead.
We are in your hands.
What more rewarding for a man
    than stir himself to help where help he can?

[*There is an ominous pause before* TIRESIAS *answers*]

TIRESIAS: Oh, what anguish to be wise where wisdom is
                                                    a loss!
I thought I knew this well. What made me come?
OEDIPUS: What makes you come so full of gloom?
TIRESIAS: Please send me home.
Take up your load and I'll take mine.
Believe me, it is better so.
OEDIPUS: What? Refuse to speak?
Is that fair and loyal to your city?
TIRESIAS: Ah, fair speech! If yours were only so,
    I should not shy away.
OEDIPUS: By all the gods, do not deny us what you know.
We ask you, all of us, on bended knees.

TIRESIAS: All ignorant! And I refuse to link my utterance
with a downfall such as yours.

OEDIPUS: You mean, you know and will not say?
You'd rather sacrifice us all and let the city rot?

TIRESIAS: I'd rather keep you and me from harm.
Don't press me uselessly. My lips are sealed.

OEDIPUS: What, nothing? You miserable old man!
You'd drive a stone to fury. Do you still refuse?
Your flinty heart set in hopeless stubbornness?

TIRESIAS: My flinty heart! Oh, if you could only see
what lurks in yours you would not chide me so.

OEDIPUS: Hear that? What man alive, I ask,
could stand such insults to our sovereignty and state?

TIRESIAS: It will out in time. What if I hold my tongue?

OEDIPUS: Out in time! Then why not say it now?

TIRESIAS: No. I've had my say.
So choose your rage and fume away.

[TIRESIAS *begins to move off*]

OEDIPUS: Indeed I shall. I do. I vent it all on you.
Yes, you, you planned this thing,
    and I suspect you of the very murder even,
    all but the actual stroke.
And if you had your eyes
    I'd say you played that chief part too.

[TIRESIAS *turns back*]

TIRESIAS: Would you so? Then I shall charge you to
                                                abide
    by the very curse you trumpeted just now.
From this day forth keep far
    from every person here and me:
The rotting canker in the State is you.

OEDIPUS: Insolence!
And dare you think you're safe?

TIRESIAS: Yes, safe. For truth has made me strong.

OEDIPUS: What truth? Hardly learned from your pro-
                                                fession!

TIRESIAS: No. Learned from you, who force it out of me.

OEDIPUS: Force what? Say it again. I must have it
straight.

TIRESIAS: Was it not straight? You'd bait and goad me
on?

OEDIPUS: It made no sense. So speak it out again.

TIRESIAS: I say, the murderer of the man
whose murder you pursue is you.

OEDIPUS: What! A second time? This you will regret.

TIRESIAS: Shall I add to it and make you angrier still?

OEDIPUS: To your heart's content. Mouth away!

TIRESIAS: I say that you and your most dearly loved
Are wrapped together in a hideous sin, blind to the horror of it.

OEDIPUS: You think you can go on blabbering unscathed?

TIRESIAS: Unscathed, indeed, if truth is strength.

OEDIPUS: It is. But not for you, you purblind man:
in ears and mind and vision.

TIRESIAS: Poor fool! These very gibes you mouth at me
will soon be hurled by every mouth at you.

OEDIPUS: You can't hurt me, you night-hatched thing!
Me or any man who lives in light.

TIRESIAS: You're right. I'm not the one that fate casts
for your fall.
Apollo is enough. It's in his able hands.

OEDIPUS: [*remembering that it was* CREON *who urged him
to send for* TIRESIAS, *Apollo's priest*] Creon? Of course!
Was it you or he that thought up that?

TIRESIAS: Hardly Creon. You are your own worst enemy.

OEDIPUS: Oh wealth and sovereignty! Statecraft sur-
passing art!
Oh life so pinnacled on fame!
What ambushed envy dogs your trail!
And for a kingship that the State put in my hands,
all given, never asked.
So this is what he wants, Creon the loyal,
Creon so long my friend!
Stealing up to overthrow and snatch!
Suborning sorcerers, like this vamper-up of plots,
this hawking conjurer, a genius born blind
with eyes for gain. Yes, you. Tell me,
when did you ever play the prophet straight?

Or why when the bitch-dog Sphinx of riddles sang,
　　you never spoke a thing to break the spell?
And yet her riddle called for insight trained—
　　no traveler's guess—
　　which you plainly showed you did not have
　　either from theology or birds.
But I, the Oedipus who stumbled here without a hint,
　　could snuff her out by human wit,
　　not taking cues from birds.
And I'm the one you want to topple down
　　to give yourself a place by Creon's throne.
Oh! Do not be surprised if this plot of yours
　　to brand me as a scapegoat
　　turns around and brands you and him.
And were you not as doting as you seem,
　　I'd lash you with the lessons of your fraud.

[CHORUS *leader steps forward, holding up a hand in
restraint*]

CHORUS: Forgive us, Oedipus, but this is anger.
He spoke in anger too. And both beside the point.
What we want to know
　　is how best to carry out the god's designs.
TIRESIAS: Perhaps you are a king, but I reign too—
　　in words. I'll have my equal say.
I'm not your servant. No, I serve Apollo.
So don't ever mark me down as Creon's myrmidon.
I'm blind, you say; you mock at that!
I say you see and still are blind—appallingly:
Blind to your origins and to a union in your house.
Yes, ask yourself where you are from?
You'd never guess what hate is dormant in your home
　　or buried with your dear ones dead,
　　or how a mother's and a father's curse
Will one day scourge you with its double thongs
　　and whip you staggering from the land.
It shall be night where now you boast the day.

Then where shall your yelp of horror not resound,
Where round the world not ring,

echoing from Mount Cithaeron,
  when at last you see—yes, soon—
What portless port this palace and this marriage was you
                                              made,
  scudding in before a lucky breeze?
What flood of sorrows—ah! you do not dream—
  will pull you down and level off your pride
To make it match your children
  and the creature that you are.
Go on, then, hurl abuse
  at everything that I or Creon say.
No man alive shall see his life so ground away.

OEDIPUS: [*stepping forward threateningly*] Dear gods!
                                    Must I listen to this thing?
Look it dawdles! Wants to wallow in perdition!
Does not turn in panic from my home!

TIRESIAS: You called me here. I never would have come.

OEDIPUS: Nor I have ever summoned you
  if I'd known you'd go foaming at the mouth.

TIRESIAS: A born fool, of course, to you am I,
  and yet to parents you were born from, wise.

OEDIPUS: Parents? Wait! Who was I born from after all?

TIRESIAS: [*stopping and turning*] This very day will fur-
                              nish you a birthday and a death.

OEDIPUS: What a knack you have for spouting riddles!

TIRESIAS: And you, of course, for solving them!

OEDIPUS: Go on! You challenge there my strongest point.

TIRESIAS: Oh, yes! Your lucky strain. Your royal road to
                                                    ruin.

OEDIPUS: A ruin that saved the State. That's good
                                  enough for me.

TIRESIAS: [*turning his back*] I'll take my leave, then.
Your hand, boy—home.

OEDIPUS: Yes, take him home. Good riddance too!
You're nothing but a nuisance here,
  and one I can do without.

TIRESIAS: [*turning about-face*] You'll not be rid of me
  until I've spoken what I came to say.
You do not frighten me. There's not a thing
  that you can do to hurt.
I tell you this:

the man you've searched for all along
with threats and fanfares
for the murder of King Laius,
That man, I say, is here:
a stranger in our midst, they thought,
but in a moment you shall *see*
him openly displayed a Theban born,
and shattered by the honor. Blind
instead of seeing, beggar
instead of rich,
He'll grope his way in foreign parts, tapping out his way
with stick in hand.
Oh, yes, detected in his very heart of home:
his children's father and their brother,
son and husband to his mother,
bed-rival to his father and assassin.
Ponder this and go inside,
And when you think you've caught me at a lie,
then come and tell me I'm not fit to prophesy.

[TIRESIAS *lets his boy lead him away.* OEDIPUS *waits,
then stamps into the palace*]

SECOND CHORAL ODE

[*The elders, spurred on by the proclamation of* OEDIPUS,
*begin to imagine with righteous and indignant anticipa-
tion what shall be the fate of the man whose sin has
plunged Thebes into misery. The meter is swift and resolute. Then they remember the baffling threat of* TIRESIAS,
*and they catch their breath at the unthinkable possibility
that Oedipus himself may be implicated (Strophe and Antistrophe II)*]

STROPHE I

Show me the man the speaking stone from Delphi
damned
Whose hands incarnadine
Achieved the masterstroke of master murdering.
Faster than horses that beat on the wind he must fly.
The son of Zeus caparisoned in light and fire

Is on his heels.
The pack of sure-foot Fates will track him down.

ANTISTROPHE I

A Voice that coruscates from high Parnassian snows
Leaps down like light.
Apollo to the hunt will run the man to earth
Through savage woods and stony caverns.
A lone wounded bull he limps, lost and alone,
Dodging living echoes
From the mantic earth that sting and gad around him.

STROPHE II

Terrible auguries tear me and trouble me:
The seer's divining.
I cannot assent. I cannot deny.
Deserted by words,
I live on hopes—all blind for today and blind for
tomorrow.
A division between the House of Laius and Oedipus
Yesterday or today
I knew not, nor know of a quarrel
Or a reason or challenge to challenge
The fame of Oedipus,
Though I seek to avenge the curious death
Of the Labdacid king.

ANTISTROPHE II

Zeus and Apollo are wise and discern
The conditions of man.
But oh among men where is there proof
That a prophet can know
More than me, a man? Yet wisdom can surpass
Wisdom in a man. But nevertheless, I'll not
Be quick to judge
Before the proof. For once
The winged and female Sphinx
Challenged him and found him sound
And a friend of the city. So never in my mind at least
Shall he be guilty of crime.

SECOND EPISODE

[CREON *enters, distraught*]

CREON: Good citizens, I hurry here
    shocked into your presence by a monstrous charge
    laid on me by Oedipus the king.
If he thinks in all this turmoil of our times
    that any word or act of mine
    was ever done in malice, done to harm,
I'd rather end my life than live so wronged.
For this is not a trifling calumny
    but full catastrophe:
    to find myself called traitor;
    traitor to my town,
    to you, and to my friends.
CHORUS: We are convinced the taunt was made in anger,
    not coolly uttered by a mind at calm.
CREON: It was uttered, then? Said that I
    had got the seer to tell a tale of lies?
CHORUS: It was said. We cannot fathom why.
CREON: But said with steady eyes, steady mind—
    this onslaught made against my name?
CHORUS: I do not know.
I turn my eyes away from what my sovereign does.
But look! He's coming from the house himself.

[OEDIPUS *comes raging in*]

OEDIPUS: What? You again? You dare come back?
Have the face to put your foot inside my door?
You the murderer so self-proved,
    the self-condemned filcher of my throne?
In heaven's name, what cowardice or lunacy
    did you detect in me
    to give you gall to do it?
Did you think that I
    would never spot such treachery,
    such slinking jobbery,
    or that when I did I'd not be one to fight?
What madman's game is this:

To go out hunting crowns
  unbacked by friends and money,
  when crowns are only won
  by many friends and well-crammed moneybags?

CREON: Wait! Listen to my answer to your charge.
And when you've heard me, judge.

OEDIPUS: No. You're too good at talking. And I'm not
                      good at hearing
one found so laden with malevolence.

CREON: We'll deal first with that very point.

OEDIPUS: That very point, we'll leave alone:
  that you're no traitor, eh?

CREON: If you really think a stubborn mind is something
                      to be proud of,
  you're not thinking straight.

OEDIPUS: And if you really think a brother-in-law
  can get away with murder, you're not thinking at all.

CREON: All right, then—tell me what I've done.
  What's the crime I've wronged you with?

OEDIPUS: Did you or did you not urge me to send
  for that reverend frothy-mouthing seer?

CREON: I did. And I still stand by that advice.

OEDIPUS: Then how long is it since Laius . . .

CREON: Laius? I don't follow the connection.

OEDIPUS: Disappeared—died—was mysteriously dispatched?

CREON: Old calendars long past would tell us that.

OEDIPUS: And was this—this "prophet" in his practice
                      then?

CREON: He was, and just as wise, just as honored.

OEDIPUS: And did he at any time then speak of me?

CREON: No. At least never in my hearing.

OEDIPUS: And you did nothing to investigate his death?

CREON: Of course we did: a full commission, and nothing
                      learned.

OEDIPUS: But the all-seeing seer did not step forward
                      and all see?

CREON: That I cannot answer for and shall not venture
                      an opinion.

OEDIPUS: You could answer very well—at least upon a
                      certain point.

CREON: What point is that? If I know, I won't hold it
back.

OEDIPUS: Just this: were you not hand in glove with him,
he never would have thought of pinning Laïus' death
on me.

CREON: What prompted him, only you can tell.
Now *I* should like to ask, and you can do the answering.

OEDIPUS: Ask away, but don't expect to find a murderer.

CREON: Well, then, are you married to my sister?

OEDIPUS: I am. Why should I deny it?

CREON: And reign equally with her over all the realm?

OEDIPUS: I do, and do my best to grant her every wish.

CREON: And of this twosome do I make an equal third?

OEDIPUS: Exactly! Which is why you make so false a
friend.

CREON: No. Try to reason it as I must reason it.
Who would choose uneasy dreams to don a crown
when all the kingly sway
can be enjoyed without?
I could not covet kingship for itself
when I can be a king by other means.
All my ambitions now
are satisfied through you, without anxiety,
But once a king, all hedged in by constraint.
How could I suit myself with power and sovereignty as
now,
If power and sovereignty once grasped were grasped in
pain?
I am not so simple as to seize the symbol
when I can have the sweet reality:
Now smiled upon by all, saluted now,
now drawn aside by suitors to the king,
my ear their door to hope.
Why should I let this go, this ease, and reach for cares?
A mind at peace does not engender wars.
Treason never was my bent, nor I
a man who parleys with an anarchist.

Test me. Go to Delphi. Ask
if I have brought back lies for prophecies.
And do not stop,

but if you find me plotting with a fortune-teller,
take me, kill me, full-indicted
on a double, not a single, count:
not yours alone but mine.
Oh, do not judge me on a mere report, unheard!
No justice brands the good and justifies the bad.
Drive friendship out, I say, and you drive out
life itself, one's sweetest bond.
Time will teach you well. The honest man needs time,
The sinner but a single day to bare his crime.
CHORUS: He speaks well, sire. The circumspect should
care.

Swift thinking never makes sure thought.
OEDIPUS: Swift thinking must step in to parry
where swift treachery steps in to plot.
Must I keep mum until his perfect plans
are more than match for mine?
CREON: Then what is it you want—my banishment?
OEDIPUS: Banishment? Great heavens, no! I want you
dead:
A lesson to all of how much envy's worth.
CREON: So adamant! So full of disbelief!
OEDIPUS: Only a fool would believe in a rabid man.
CREON: Rabid? It's clear you're not thinking straight.
OEDIPUS: Straight enough for me.
CREON: Then why not for me as well?
OEDIPUS: What! For a treason-monger?
CREON: You make no sense.
OEDIPUS: I make decisions.
CREON: Crazed decisions!
OEDIPUS: Hear him, Thebes! My own poor Thebes!
CREON: Not just yours. My city too.
CHORUS: Princes, please!
Look. Jocasta hurries from the house:
a timely balm on both your hurts.
You must compose your quarrel.

[JOCASTA *hurries in*]

JOCASTA: You wretched men! Out on all this senseless
clatter!
Shame to wrangle over private wrongs,

with Thebes, our city, in her agonies!
Get back home, sir, you, and Creon, you
into your house.
Stop turning trifles into tragedies.

CREON: Trifles, sister! Oedipus your husband
plans to do me devilish harm, with choice of dooms:
exile from my father's land or death.

OEDIPUS: Exactly that, my wife, I've caught him in a plot,
against my very person.
So cleverly devised.

CREON: May I be stricken dead if I be guilty
in the smallest part of what you charge!

JOCASTA: For the gods' sakes, listen, Oedipus.
He's sworn by all the gods, in front of us,
for me and for us all.

CHORAL DIALOGUE

STROPHE I

CHORUS: Believe her, King, believe. Be willing to be
wise.

OEDIPUS: What! You'd have me yield?

CHORUS: He's never told you lies
before. He's sworn. Be kind.

OEDIPUS: You know for what you plead?

CHORUS: We know.

OEDIPUS: Explain.

CHORUS: Do not impeach a friend or lead
him to disgrace; his oath annulled upon a word.

OEDIPUS: It's come to that? My banishment or death
preferred
to what you want for him?

STROPHE II

CHORUS: No, by Helios, no, god of the primal sun!
Call gladless death upon me—godless, friendless—
If that be in my mind.
The dying land undoes me,
Sorrow heaped on sadness
Now to see you and him—combine in madness.

OEDIPUS: Go, then, let him go, though I go

abundantly to die,
  or flung from here and fated;
Yours not his the cry that breaks me.
He a thing that's hated.
CREON: Yes, how you hate, even in your yielding!
But passion spent, compunction follows.
Such men justly bear the tempers they created.
OEDIPUS: Get yourself gone, then! Out of my sight!

[CREON *leaves, while* OEDIPUS *continues to stand there disappointed and shaken*]

ANTISTROPHE I

CHORUS: Madam, why delay to lead him away?
JOCASTA: I stay . . . to know.
CHORUS: Hot and hasty words, suspicion and dismay . . .
JOCASTA: From both?
CHORUS: From both.
JOCASTA: What words?
CHORUS: Enough! Enough! The agony! O let it alone!
Let it sleep with all its pain.
OEDIPUS: Very well, but understand
You've numbed me to the heart by your demand.

ANTISTROPHE II

CHORUS: Sire, I've said it more than once
How insensate we'd be, what crass
And total fools to abdicate
From you who set this foundering ship,
This suffering realm, back on her course
And now again can take the helm.

[*End of choral dialogue.* JOCASTA *gently leads* OEDIPUS *aside*]

JOCASTA: In the name of all the gods, my king, inform
                   me too
  what in the world has worked you to this rage?
OEDIPUS: Willingly, my wife—so more to me than these.
It's Creon; he has played me false.

JOCASTA: What's the charge? Tell me clearly—what's the
quarrel?

OEDIPUS: He makes me murderer of Laius.

JOCASTA: His own invention or on evidence?

OEDIPUS: Ah! The fox: he sends along a mouthing seer
and keeps his own lips lily pure.

JOCASTA: Oh, then, altogether leave behind
these cares and be persuaded and consoled.
There is no art of seership known to man.
I have my proof. Yes, short and certain proof.
Once long ago there came to Laius
from—let's not suppose Apollo personally
but from his ministers—an oracle,
Which said that fate would make him meet his end
through a son, a son of his and mine.
Well, there was a murder, yes,
but done by brigands in another land, they say,
Where three highways meet,
and secondly, the son, not three days old,
Is left by Laius (through other hands, of course)
upon a trackless hillside,
his ankles riveted together.
So there! Apollo fails to make the son
his father's murderer, and the father
(Laius sick with dread) murdered by his son.
All foreseen by fate and seers, of course,
and all to be forgotten.
If the god insists on tracking down the truth,
why, then, let the god himself get on the track.

OEDIPUS: My queen, each word that strikes my ear
has shattered peace, struck at my very soul.

JOCASTA: You start! What pale memory passes now?

OEDIPUS: Laius was killed—I thought I caught the
words—
where three highways meet?

JOCASTA: So they said. That is how the story goes.

OEDIPUS: The place? Where did the mishap fall?

JOCASTA: A land called Phocis,
at a spot where the road from Delphi
meets the road from Daulia.

OEDIPUS: And the time? How many years ago?

JOCASTA: A little before you came to power here
the news was made public in the town.

OEDIPUS: O Zeus, what plaything will you make of me?

JOCASTA: Why, Oedipus, what nightmare thought has
touched you now?

OEDIPUS: Don't ask! Not yet! . . . Laius, tell me, his age?
His build?

JOCASTA: Tall, the first soft bloom of silver in his hair;
in form, not far removed from yours.

OEDIPUS: Oh, lost! Yes, surely lost!
. self-damned, I think, just now and self-deceived.

JOCASTA: Self-what, my king?
that look you give, it chills.

OEDIPUS: I am afraid—afraid the eyeless seer has seen.
But wait: one thing more . . .

JOCASTA: Yes? It frightens me, but ask. I'll try to tell.

OEDIPUS: Did he set out in simple state
or with an ample bodyguard as king?

JOCASTA: Five men in all, and one a herald.
A single chariot for the king.

OEDIPUS: It's all too clear . . .
My wife, where did you get these details from?

JOCASTA: A servant. The only man who got away.

OEDIPUS: Is he in the house by chance?

JOCASTA: No, for the moment he was back and saw
you reigning in dead Laius's place,
he begged me, pressed my hand,
to send him to the country, far from Thebes,
where he could live a shepherd's life.
And so I sent him. Though a slave,
I thought he'd more than earned this recompense.

OEDIPUS: Could we have him here without delay?

JOCASTA: Certainly. But what should make you ask?

OEDIPUS: There may be things, my wife, that I have said
best left unsaid, which makes me want him here.

JOCASTA: He shall be here. But tell me, my king,
may I not also know what it is unnerves you so?

OEDIPUS: You shall,
for I have passed into territories of fear,
such threatenings of fate,
I welcome you, my truest confidante.

*   *   *

My father was Corinthian, Polybus,
My mother Dorian, called Mérope.
I was the city's foremost man until
   a certain incident befell, a curious incident,
   though hardly worth the ferment that it put me in.
At dinner once,
   a drunkard in his cups bawled out,
   "Aha! You're not your father's son."
All that day I fretted, hardly able to contain my hurt.
But on the next, straightaway I went to ask
   my mother and my father,
   who were shocked at such a random slur.
I was relieved by their response, and yet
   the thing had hatched a scruple in my mind that grew
   so deep it made me steal away from home
   to Delphi, to the oracle, and there
   Apollo—never hinting what I came to hear—
   packs me home again, my ears ringing
   with some other things he blurted out;
   horrible disgusting things:
How mating with my mother I must spawn
   a progeny to make men shudder,
   having been my father's murderer.

Oh, I fled from there, I measured out
   the stars to put all heaven in between
   the land of Corinth and such a damned destiny.
And as I went, I stumbled on the very spot
   where this king you say has met his end.

I'll . . . I'll tell the truth to you, my wife.
As I reached this triple parting of the ways,
   a herald and a man like you described
   in a colt-drawn chariot came.
The leading groom—the old man urging him—
   tried to force me off the road. The groom
   jostled me, and I in fury
   landed him a blow.
Which when the old man sees,
   he waits till I'm abreast,

Then from his chariot cracks down on me,
   full on my head,
   a double-headed club.
He more than paid for it. For in a trice
   this hand of mine had felled him with a stick
   and rolled him from the chariot stunned.
I killed him. I killed them all.
Ah! If Laius is this unknown man,
   there's no one in this world so doomed as I.
There's no one born so god-abhorred:
   a man whom no one, citizen or stranger,
   can let into his house or even greet—
   a man to force from homes.
And who but I have done it all? Myself,
   to fix damnation on myself!
To clasp a dead man's wife with filthy hands:
   these hands by which he fell.
Not hell-born then? Not rotten to the core?·
A wretch who has to flee, yet fled cannot go home
   to see my own,
Or I will make my mother wife, my father dead:
   my father, Polybus, who reared and gave me life.
Forbid, forbid, most holy gods!
Never let that day begin.
I'd rather disappear from man than see
   myself so beggared, dyed so deep in sin.
CHORUS: King, you tell us frightening things, but wait
   until you've heard the witness speak. Have hope.
OEDIPUS: Yes, all my hope upon a herdsman now,
   and I must wait until he comes.
JOCASTA: But when he comes, what is it you want to
                     hear?
OEDIPUS: Just this: if his account is yours, I'm clear.
JOCASTA: But what was my account? What did I say?
OEDIPUS: Why, several bandits in your account,
   he claimed, cut down the king.
If he will keep to *several*, I, as only one,
   am not the killer, not the same.
But if he says it was a lone man journeying—ah, then!—
   the verdict tilts too heavily to me.

JOCASTA: Rest assured; his account was that, exactly that,
He cannot cancel what he said.
The whole town heard, not I alone.
And even if he tries to change a word,
   he still can never make—oh, surely, King!—
   the death of Laius tally with the oracle,
   which said it had to happen through a son of mine . . .
   poor babe, who never killed a thing
   but himself was killed—oh, long before!
After this, I'll never change my look from left to right
   to suit a prophecy.
OEDIPUS: I like your reasoning. And yet . . . and yet . . .
   that herdsman—have him here. Do not forget.
JOCASTA: Immediately. But let us go indoors.
All my care is you, and all my pleasure yours.

[OEDIPUS *and* JOCASTA *enter the palace*]

THIRD CHORAL ODE

[*The elders seem at first merely to be expressing a lyrical
admiration for piety and purity of heart, but before the
end of the ode we see that the reputation itself of* OEDIPUS
is at stake. JOCASTA's *blatant impiety has shocked the*
CHORUS *into realizing that if divine prophecies cannot go
unfulfilled and man's insolence unpunished, then* OEDIPUS
*himself, whoever he is, must be weighed in the balance.
It is too late to go back. A choice will have to be made.
They call desperately on Zeus*]

STROPHE I

O purity of deed and sweet intent,
Enshrine me in your grace
A minister to radiant laws
Heaven-born which have
No father but Olympus nor
Fading genesis from man.
Great is God in them
And never old
Whom no oblivion lulls.

ANTISTROPHE I

Pride engenders power, pride,
Banqueting on vanities
Mistaken and mistimed;
Scaling pinnacles to dash
A foot against Fate's stone.
But the true and patriotic man
Heaven never trips to fall.
So I for one shall never desert
The god who is our champion.

STROPHE II

But what if a brazen man parade
In word or deed
Impiety and brash disdain
Of principalities and canons?
Then dog him doom and pay him pride
Wages for his haughty greed,
His sacrilege and folly.
What shield is there for such a man
Against all heaven's arrows?
Could I celebrate such wantonness
And celebrate the dance?

ANTISTROPHE II

I shall not worship at the vent
Where oracles from earth are breathed;
Nor at Abae's shrine and not
Olympia, unless these oracles
Are justified, writ large to man.
Zeus, if king of kings you are,
Then let this trespass not go hidden
From you and your great eye undying.
The Laius prophecies are turned to lies;
They fade away with reverence gone
And honor to Apollo.

THIRD EPISODE

[JOCASTA *hurries in from the palace with a garlanded
olive branch and a burning censer in her hands*]

JOCASTA: Men of State, I have a new design:
With these garlands and with incense in my hands
   to call at all the shrines.
For rampant fancies in a legion raid
   the mind of Oedipus. He is so far from sense
   he cannot gauge the present from the past
   but pins his soul to every word of fear.
All my advice is bankrupt; I address
   myself to you, Apollo, whose Lycean shrine
   is nearest to these rites and prayers:
That you may work some way to make us clean.
For we are gone to pieces at the sight
   of him the steersman of the ship
   astray by fright.

[*While* JOCASTA *is standing in prayer a* MESSENGER
from Corinth enters]

MESSENGER: Can you tell me please, good sirs,
   where is the palace of King Oedipus,
   or better, where's the king?
CHORUS: This is his palace, sir, and he's within.
This lady is his wife and mother . . . of his children.
MESSENGER: Heaven bless her always and bless hers:
   the perfect wife blessed perfectly with him.
JOCASTA: And you sir, too, be blessed for your
                    remark . . .
But are you here to ask us news or give?
MESSENGER: To give it, madam. Happy news
   both for your house and husband.
JOCASTA: Happy news? From where?
MESSENGER: From Corinth, my lady. Oh a pleasing piece
                of news!
Or I'd think so. . . . Perhaps a little bittersweet.
JOCASTA: What's bittersweet? What's half-and-half to
                please?
MESSENGER: King-elect of Corinth is he:
So runs the order-in-council there.
JOCASTA: How so? The old man Polybus still reigns.
MESSENGER: No more. For death has sealed him in his
                grave.

JOCASTA: What? Is Oedipus' father dead?
MESSENGER: Yes, dead. It's true. On my life he's dead.

[JOCASTA *excitedly turns to servant girl*]

JOCASTA: Quick, girl—off and tell your master this!
Aha! Forecasts of the gods, where are you now?
This is the man that Oedipus was terrified to kill, so fled;
And now, without the slightest push from him, he's
                            dead.

[*Enter* OEDIPUS]

OEDIPUS: Jocasta, dearest wife,
  why have you called me from the palace here?
JOCASTA: Just listen to this man and fill your ears.
How dwindled are the grand predictions of Apollo!
OEDIPUS: Who is this? What has he come to say?
JOCASTA: A man from Corinth, come to let you know
  your father is no more. Old Polybus is dead.
OEDIPUS: What? Let me have it from your mouth, good
                            sir.
MESSENGER: Why, to give you first news first, he's gone.
Be quite assured—he's dead.
OEDIPUS: Through treason or disease?
MESSENGER: A little touch will tip the old to sleep.
OEDIPUS: He died a natural death, then? Poor old man!
MESSENGER: A natural death, by right of many years.
OEDIPUS: Aha, my wife! So we are done
  with delving into Pythian oracles,
  this jangled mongering with birds on high,
  which foretold—yes, had it all arranged—
  that I should kill my father. Ha! He's dead
  and under sods, while here I stand
  my sword still in its scabbard . . .
  or did he pine for me? And did I kill him so?
Well, he's dead, and may he rest in peace in Hades'
                           realm
  with all those prophecies—worth nothing now.
JOCASTA: Worth nothing—as I told you even then.
OEDIPUS: You told me, yes, but I was sick with fear.

JOCASTA: Forget it all. Give none of it a thought.

OEDIPUS: There's still that scruple of my mother's bed.

JOCASTA: How can a man have scruples
    when it's only Chance that's king?
There's nothing certain, nothing preordained.
We should live as carefree as we may.
Forget this silly thought of mother-marrying.
Why, many men in dreams have married mothers,
And he lives happiest who makes the least of it.

OEDIPUS: Everything you say would make good sense
    were my mother not alive—she is;
    so all your comfort cannot quiet me.

JOCASTA: At least your father's death has lightened up
                                    the scene.

OEDIPUS: It has, but now I fear a living woman.

MESSENGER: A woman, sir? Who ever could she be?

OEDIPUS: Mérope, old man, who lives with Polybus.

MESSENGER: But what's in her that she can make you
                                    fear?

OEDIPUS: A dire warning sent from heaven, my friend.

MESSENGER: Some secret too horrible to tell?

OEDIPUS: No, you may be told.
Apollo once declared that I
    would come to couple with my mother,
    and with these very hands of mine
    spill out the lifeblood of my father.
All of which has put me far and long from Corinth,
    in sweet prosperity maybe,
But what's so sweet as looking into parents' eyes?

MESSENGER: Is this the fear that drove you out of
                                    Corinth?

OEDIPUS: Exactly that, old man, and not to kill my father.

MESSENGER: Well, my king, since I came to save,
    why don't I loose you from that worry too?

OEDIPUS: Ah! If you could, I'd heap you with rewards.

MESSENGER: Ah! to be frank, that's why I came . . . to
                                    bring you home,
    and do myself some good.

OEDIPUS: No, not home. I'll not go near a parent still.

MESSENGER: My son, it's plain you don't know what
                                    you're at.

OEDIPUS: Speak out, old man. In the name of heaven—
what?

MESSENGER: Well, you've fled from home because of
this?

OEDIPUS: Yes, the fear Apollo may be proven right.

MESSENGER: And you, because of your parents, a
criminal?

OEDIPUS: Yes, old man, it's that. I'm haunted by that
dread.

MESSENGER: Then, don't you understand. you're terrified
for nothing.

OEDIPUS: Nothing? How—when I *am* their son.

MESSENGER: Because Polybus and you were worlds apart.

OEDIPUS: Worlds apart? He was my father, wasn't he?

MESSENGER: No more nor less than I who tell you this.

OEDIPUS: No more nor less than you? Than nothing,
then.

MESSENGER: Exactly so. He never gave you life, no more
than I.

OEDIPUS: Then whatever made him call me son?

MESSENGER: You were a gift. He took you from my arms.

OEDIPUS: A gift? But he loved me as his own.

MESSENGER: He had no children of his own to love.

OEDIPUS: And this gift you gave me—was I freeborn or
bought?

MESSENGER: Discovered . . . in a woody dell of
Cithaeron.

[JOCASTA *moves away. She has turned pale*]

OEDIPUS: On Theban hills? What made you wander
there?

MESSENGER: On those hills I used to graze my flock.

OEDIPUS: What! A shepherd out for hire?

MESSENGER: And on that day your savior too, my son.

OEDIPUS: My savior? Was I in pain when you took me
in your arms?

MESSENGER: The ankles of your feet could tell you that.

OEDIPUS: Ah, don't remind me of that ancient hurt!

MESSENGER: I loosed the pin that riveted your feet.

OEDIPUS: My birthmark and my brand from babyhood!

MESSENGER: Which gave you also your unlucky name.*
OEDIPUS: Was this my mother's doing or my father's?
For the gods' sakes say!

[JOCASTA *hides her face in her hands*]

MESSENGER: That, I do not know. The man who gave you
me could tell.
OEDIPUS: What, received at secondhand? Not found by
you?
MESSENGER: Not found by me, but handed over by an-
other shepherd.
OEDIPUS: What shepherd? Could you point him out?
MESSENGER: I think he was known as one of Laius's men.
OEDIPUS: You mean the king who reigned here long ago?
MESSENGER: The same. He was a herdsman of that king.
OEDIPUS: Could I see him? Is he still alive?
MESSENGER: Your own people could tell you best.

[OEDIPUS *turns to the* CHORUS]

OEDIPUS: Does any man here present know this herdsman he is talking of:
either seen him in the fields or hereabouts?
The time has come for full discovery.
CHORUS: I think he means that herdsman, sir,
you asked to see before.
Jocasta here is surest judge of that.

[*They all turn toward* JOCASTA, *who stands transfixed*]

OEDIPUS: Come, madam, do you know the man we sent
for once before?
Is he the man he means?
JOCASTA: [*wildly*] Which man? What matters who he
means? Why ask?
Forget it all. It's not worth knowing.
OEDIPUS: Forget it all? I can't stop now.
Not with all my birth clues in my hands.

*"Swollen-foot."

JOCASTA: In the name of heaven, don't proceed!
For your own life's sake, stop!
And I've been tortured long enough.
OEDIPUS: Oh, come! It won't be you that is disgraced
even if I'm proved a thrice-descended slave.

[JOCASTA *throws herself before him and clutches his knees*]

JOCASTA: Yet be persuaded, please. Do *not* proceed.
OEDIPUS: Persuaded from the truth? Pursuing it? I must.
JOCASTA: Though I'm pleading for what's best for you.
OEDIPUS: What's best for me? I'm tired of hearing that.
JOCASTA: [*rising slowly*] God help you, Oedipus! Hide it
                              from you who you are.
OEDIPUS: Will someone go and fetch the herdsman here?
We'll leave the lady to her high descent.
JOCASTA: Good-bye, my poor deluded, lost and damned!
There's nothing else that I can call you now.

[JOCASTA *rushes into the palace*]

CHORUS: Oedipus, what made the queen so wildly leave,
struck dumb? A stillness just before the storm!
OEDIPUS: Storm, then, let it burst!
Born from nothing though I be proved,
    let me find that nothing out.
And let my wife with all a woman's pride
    bridle at my paltry origin.
I do not blush to own I'm Fortune's pampered child.
She will not let me down. She is my mother.
The moons my monthly cousins watched me wax and
                                            wane.
My fealty to that family makes me move
    true to myself. My family I shall prove.

FOURTH CHORAL ODE

[*The elders, forgetting for the moment* JOCASTA's *ominous withdrawal, anticipate the joy of discovering who* OEDIPUS

really is. Ironically, they imagine themselves already cele-
brating his remarkable origins]

STROPHE

If I am a prophet with sapient eyes,
Cithaeron you, my mystical mountain,
Tomorrow before the moon's full rise,
Shall shout out your name as the nurse and the mother,
The father as well of our Oedipus.
Then shall we weave our dances around you;
You who have showered our princes with graces.
Ayay, great Apollo! May't please you, ayay!

ANTISTROPHE

Who was your mother, son? Which of the dryads
Did Pan of the mountains have? Was he your father?
Or was it Apollo who haunts the savannas?
Or perhaps Hermes on the heights of Cyllene?
Or was Dionysus god of the pinnacles
Of Helicon's hilltops where he abides
Presented with you by some Heliconian
Nymph, among whom he frequently frolics?

FOURTH EPISODE.

[*A figure, old and roughly clad, is seen approaching*]

OEDIPUS: Look, elders,
  if I may play the prophet too,
  I'd say—although I've never met the man—
  there's the herdsman we've been searching for.
He's old enough and matches this old man.
But you no doubt can better judge than I:
  you've seen the man before.
CHORUS: We know him well.
Laius never had a better servant.

[*The* SHEPHERD *enters, ill at ease.* OEDIPUS *surveys him
and turns to the* MESSENGER]

OEDIPUS: First question then to you, Corinthian:

is he the man you mean?

MESSENGER: The very man.

OEDIPUS: Come here, sir, and look me in the eyes.
Tell me straight: were you ever Laius'?

SHEPHERD: Yes, sir, born and bred, sir—never bought.

OEDIPUS: And what was your job? How were you
employed?

SHEPHERD: Chiefly as a shepherd, sir.

OEDIPUS: A shepherd where? What was your terrain?

SHEPHERD: [*hedging*] Sometimes . . . the slopes of
Cithaeron
and sometimes . . . thereabouts.

OEDIPUS: Good, then you've run across this man before?

[*The* SHEPHERD *desperately tries to avoid looking at
the* MESSENGER]

SHEPHERD: How'd he be there, sir? . . . What man do
you mean, sir?

OEDIPUS: The man in front of you. Did you ever meet
him?

SHEPHERD: Not to remember, sir . . . I couldn't rightly
say.

MESSENGER: And no wonder, sire! But let me jog his
memory.
I'm sure he won't forget the slopes of Cithaeron
where for three half-years we were neighbors,
he and I; he with two herds, I with one:
six long months, from spring to early autumn.
And when at last the winter came,
we both drove off our flocks,
I to my sheepcotes, he back to Laius' folds . . .
Am I right or am I wrong?

SHEPHERD: [*sullenly*] Aye, you're right. But it was long
ago.

MESSENGER: Now tell me this. Do you recall a certain
baby boy
you gave me once to bring up as my own?

SHEPHERD: What're you getting at? What're these questions for?

MESSENGER: Take a look, my friend. He's standing there, your baby boy.

SHEPHERD: Damn you, man! Can you not hold your tongue?

OEDIPUS: Watch your words, old man!
It's you who ought to be rebuked, not he.

SHEPHERD: Great master, please! What have I done wrong?

OEDIPUS: Not answered this man's questions on the baby boy.

SHEPHERD: But, sir, he's rambling nonsense. He doesn't know a thing.

OEDIPUS: You won't talk for pleasure?
Then perhaps you'll talk for pain.

[OEDIPUS *raises a threatening hand*]

SHEPHERD: By all the gods, sir, don't hurt a poor old man.

OEDIPUS: Here, someone twist the wretch's hands behind his back.

[A PALACE GUARD *steps forward*]

SHEPHERD: God help me, sir! What is it you must know?

OEDIPUS: The baby he's been speaking of—did you give it him or not?

SHEPHERD: I did . . . I did . . . I wish I'd died that day.

OEDIPUS: You'll die today, unless you speak the truth.

SHEPHERD: Much sooner, sir, if I speak the truth.

OEDIPUS: This man, it's clear, is playing for time.

SHEPHERD: No, not me, sir! I've already said I gave it him.

OEDIPUS: Then where's it from? Your home or someone else's?

SHEPHERD: Oh, not mine, sir! I got it from another.

OEDIPUS: Someone here in Thebes? Of what house?

SHEPHERD: By all the gods, sir, don't ask me any more!

OEDIPUS: If I have to ask again—you're dead.

SHEPHERD: Then . . . from Laius' house . . . that's where it's from.

OEDIPUS: What, a slave? Or someone of his line?

SHEPHERD: Oh, sir! Must I bring myself to say it?
OEDIPUS: And I to hear it. Yes, it must be said.
SHEPHERD: They say it was . . . actually his own.
But the queen inside could probably explain.
OEDIPUS: She, *she* gave it you?
SHEPHERD: Just that, my lord.
OEDIPUS: With what intention?
SHEPHERD: To do away with it.
OEDIPUS: The child's own mother?
SHEPHERD: To escape a prophecy too horrible.
OEDIPUS: What kind of prophecy?
SHEPHERD: A warning that he'd kill his father.
OEDIPUS: In heaven's name, what made you pass him on
                                    to this old man?
SHEPHERD: Only pity, sir.
I thought he'd take him home and far away.
Never this—oh, never kept for infamy!
For if you are the one he says you are,
Make no mistake: you are a doom-born man.

[OEDIPUS *stares in front of him, then staggers forward*]

OEDIPUS: Lost! Ah, lost! At last it's blazing clear.
Light of my days, go dark. I want to gaze no more.
My birth all sprung revealed from those it never should,
Myself entwined with those I never could.
And I the killer of those I never would.

[OEDIPUS *rushes into the palace*]

FIFTH CHORAL ODE

[*The elders, seeing that the cause of* OEDIPUS *is lost, break
into a desperate lament for the insecurity of all human
fame, so bitterly exemplified now in the fall of the once-
confident king.*]

STROPHE I

Oh, the generations of man!
His life is vanity and nothingness.
Is there one, one

Who more than tastes of, thinks of, happiness,
Which in the thinking vanishes?
Yours the text, yours the spell,
I see it in you, Oedipus:
Man's pattern of unblessedness.

ANTISTROPHE I

You who aimed so high!
Who hit life's topmost prize—success!
Who—Zeus, oh, who—
Struck and toppled down the griffin-taloned
Death knell witch, and like a saving tower
Soared above the rotting shambles here:
A sovereign won, supremely blest,
A king of mighty Thebes.

STROPHE II

Caught in the end by Time
Who always sees, where Justice sits as judge,
Your unwed wedding's done,
Begetter and begot—O son of Laius!—
Out of sight what sight might not have seen!
My sorrow heaves, my lips lament,
Which drew their breath from you and now
Must quiver and be still.

EPILOGUE

[*A* PALACE OFFICIAL *hurries out from the palace*]

OFFICIAL: Listen, lords most honorable of Thebes:
　　forget the House of Labdacus, all filial sympathy,
　　if you would stop your ears, hide your eyes,
　　not break your hearts against appalling pain.
No rivers—even Ister, even Phasis—
　　could flush away, I think, the horrors
　　hidden in these walls, where now
　　other evils, courted evils self-incurred,
Will bring to light the perfect agony of self-inflicted pain.
CHORUS: Stop. What we've seen already is unbearable.
What further agony will you load on us?
OFFICIAL: I'll tell it quickly and you can quickly hear:
　　Jocasta's gone, the queen.

CHORUS: Dead? Poor lady! How?
OFFICIAL: She killed herself.
You cannot apprehend, you who were not there,
   how horrible it was.
But I was there and what I tell you now
   is stamped upon my memory:
Oh, the struggles of that lost princess!

The moment she had burst into the palace,
   running through the doors demented,
   she made for the bridal bed,
   plunging her fingers through her hair
   and slamming shut the door behind her.
We heard her sobbing out Laius' name (so long dead),
   recalling the night his love had bred his murderer
And left a mother making cursed children with her son.
"Unhappy bed!" she wailed. "Twice wicked soil!
The father's seedbed nurtured for the mother's son!"

And then she killed herself. How, I do not know.
The final act escaped our eyes—
   all fastened now upon the raving Oedipus,
   who broke upon us, stamping up and down
   and shouting out: "A weapon, quick!
Where is the brideless bride?
Find me that double breeding ground
   where sown the mother, now has sown the son."
Some instinct of a demigod discovered her to him,
   not us near by. As if led on,
He smashes hollering through the double doors,
   breaking all its bolts, and lunges in.
And there we saw her hanging, twisted, tangled,
   from a halter.
A sight that rings from him a maddened cry.
He frees the noose and lays the wretched woman down,
   then—Oh, hideous sequel!—rips from off her dress
   the golden brooches she was wearing,
Holds them up and rams the pins right through his eyes.
"Wicked, wicked eyes!" he gasps,
   "You shall not see me nor my crime,
   not see my present shame.

Go dark for all time blind
    to what you never should have seen, and blind
    to the love this heart has cried to see."

And as this dirge went up, so did his hands
    to strike his founts of sight
    not once but many times.
And all the while his eyeballs gushed
    in bloody dew upon his beard . . .
    no, not dew, no oozing drops—a spurt
    of black-ensanguined rain like hail beat down.
A coupled punishment upon a coupled sin:
    husband and wife one flesh in their disaster—
Their happiness of long ago, true happiness,
    now turned to tears this day,
    to ruin, death, and shame;
No evil absent by whatever cursed name.
CHORUS: Poor man! What agony!
OFFICIAL: He shouts for all the barriers to be unbarred
                                and he
    displayed to all of Thebes, his father's murderer,
    his mother's . . . no, a word too foul to say . . .
    begging to be cast adrift, not rot at home
    as curser and the cursed.
His strength is gone. He needs a helping hand,
    his wound and weakness more than he can bear.
But you will see. The gates are opening. Look:
    a sight that turns all loathing into tears.

[OEDIPUS, *blinded, enters and staggers down the palace steps*]

CHORAL DIALOGUE

CHORUS: Oh, most inhuman vision!
A world of pain outsuffered and outdone.
What possession in full flush
    has swamped your brain?
What giant of evil beyond all human brawn
    pounced on you with devil's doom?
Oh, the pity and the horror!

I cannot look—and yet so much to ask,
 so much to know, so much to understand.
I cannot look for shuddering.
OEDIPUS: I am deserted, dark,
And where is sorrow stumbling?
Whence flits that voice so near?
Where, demon, will you drive me?
CHORUS: To a doom no voice can speak, no eye regard.

STROPHE I

OEDIPUS: Aah! a nightmare mist has fallen
Adamantine black on me—
Abomination closing.
Cry, cry, oh, cry again!
Those needle pains:
The pointed echoes of my sinning.
CHORUS: Such great sufferings are not strange
Where a double sorrow requires a double pang.

ANTISTROPHE I

OEDIPUS: Oh, you, my friends!
Still friends and by my side!
Still staying by the blindman!
Your form eludes, your voice is near;
That voice lights up my darkness.
CHORUS: Man of havoc, how
Could you hate your sight so?
What demon so possessed you?

STROPHE II

OEDIPUS: Friends, it was Apollo, spirit of Apollo.
He made this evil fructify.
Oh, yes, I pierced my eyes, my useless eyes, why not?
When all that's sweet had parted from my vision.
CHORUS: And so it has; is as you say.
OEDIPUS: Nothing left to see, to love,
No welcome in communion.
Friends, who are my friends,
Hurry me from here,
Hurry off the monster:
That deepest damned and god-detested man.

CHORUS: A man, alas, whose anguish fits his fate.
We could wish that we had never known you.

ANTISTROPHE II

OEDIPUS: Yes, rot that man's unlocking my feet from
                                    biting fetters.
Unloosing me from murder to lock me in a blood-love.
Had I only died then, I should not now be leaving
All I love and mine so sadly shattered.
CHORUS: Your wish is also ours.
OEDIPUS: Then I should be free,
Yes, free from parricide:
Not pointed out as wedded
To the one who weaned me.
Now I am god-abandoned,
A son of sin and sorrows
All incest-sealed
With the womb that bore me.
Oh, Oedipus, your portion!
CHORUS: But how can we say that your design was good?
To live in blindness? Better live no longer.

[End of strophic pattern]

OEDIPUS: Enough of this! Enough of your advice!
It was a good design. Don't tell me otherwise.
My best design!
What kind of eyes should I need
    to gaze upon my father's face in Hades
    or my unhappy mother's:
Those twin victims ruined by me
    for whom I should be hanged?
Or eyes that could be eyes to stare
    into my children's faces?
Joy? No no, a sight of pain
    engendered from those loins.
Or even eyes to view again citadel and tower
    and holy idoled shrine I cast away?
Most cursed I, the prince of princes here in Thebes
    and now pariah self-damned and self-arraigned:
The refuse-heap of heaven on display as son of Laius,

parading and self-dyed in sin.
What? Eyes to lift and gaze at these?
   No, no, there's none!
Rather plug my ears and choke that stream of sound,
   stuff the senses of my carcass dumb—
   glad to stifle voices with my vision,
   and sweet to lift the soul away from hurt.

Pity you, Cithaeron, that you gave me harbor,
   took me in and did not kill me straight;
   that you did not hush my birth from man.
Pity you, Polybus and Corinth,
   age-old home I called my father's:
What fair skin you housed around what foulness!
A prince of evil all revealed and son of sin.
And you three roads and dell concealed,
   you copse of oak and straitened triple ways!
   I handed you my blood to drink,
   the chalice of my father's.
What memories have you of my manners then,
   or what I did when afterwards I came here?
You batch of weddings! Birthdays breeding
   seedlings from their very seed:
Fathers, sons, and brothers flourishing in foulness
   with brides and wives and mothers
   in a monstrous coupling . . .
Unfit to tell what's too unfit to touch!
My load is mine, don't fear;
   no man could bear so much.
CHORUS: Wait! Here Creon comes to hear your pleas
   and deal with your designs.
He takes your place
   as sole custodian of the State.
OEDIPUS: Ah! What words are left for me to him?
What title to sincerity and trust
   when all my past behavior's proved so wrong?

   [*Enter* CREON]

CREON: It's not to scoff or scorn for past behavior,
                                        Oedipus,
   that I am here . . .

[*Turns to* ATTENDANTS]

You there, show some reverence for the dignity of man,
  and blush at least before Apollo's royal sun,
  which feeds the world with fire,
  to so display unveiled putrescence
  in its very picture of decay—
Assaulting earth, the heaven's rain, the light of day.
Quickly take him home. A family's ears, a family's eyes,
  alone should know a family's miseries.
OEDIPUS: For the gods' own love, you best of men
  who visit me the worst
  with clemency beyond my dreams,
  grant me one request: I ask it
  for your sake, not mine.
CREON: What favor could you want of me?
OEDIPUS: Expel me quickly, purge me far from Thebes
  to where no human voice is heard.
CREON: This I would have done at once
  but first must ask the gods' design.
OEDIPUS: The gods' design is open, all his oracle is clear:
  kill the impious one, the parricide, kill *me*.
CREON: So ran the words, but in these straits
  it's best to ask the gods again what should be done.
OEDIPUS: What! Interrogations still for a thing so down?
CREON: Yes, and even you will now believe the gods.
OEDIPUS: I do. But add to it this charge, I beg, this
                                                    prayer:
  her poor remains still in the house,
  bury them—what tomb you wish.
You must not fail your own with proper rites.
But as for me, my father's city here
  must never harbor me alive,
  so let me live among the hills,
  yes, Cithaeron, that very mountain famed as mine;
Which my father and my mother gave me while they
                                        lived to be my tomb.
There I'll be obedient to the death they planned.
For this I know, no sickness and no natural death
  will sever me from life . . . no, not me,
  preserved from death precisely for disaster.

So let my fortune follow where it will.

Now for my children, first of all my sons.
These you need not care for, Creon. They are men
   and they will always find a livelihood.
But my little girls, that stricken pair of orphans
   whose place at table never missed being set with mine,
   who ate with me, drank from my cup—ah! these
                    look after for me, guard them both.

[CREON *goes to fetch* OEDIPUS' *two little daughters,*
ANTIGONE *and* ISMENE. *Meanwhile,* OEDIPUS, *thinking
he is still there, continues to plead*]

If I could only touch them with my hands
   and weep my fill, good Creon, one last time!
Just touch them, please, you generous-hearted prince,
   and think them in my arms as when I saw.

[CREON *returns, leading* ANTIGONE *and* ISMENE *by the
hand*]

Wait! That sobbing? Don't tell me
   it's my two darlings crying!
Has Creon pitied me and sent me all my heart's desire?
Can that be true?
CREON: It is. I ordered it to stir again your old delight.
OEDIPUS: God bless you, Creon, bless your path through
                                      life,
   encompass you with surer joys than mine.
But children where, where are you? Hurry
   into these arms . . . these brother's . . . these
   father's arms—that struck out the light
   and made his face this eyeless mask.
For—oh, my little ones!—
   he did not see, he had no knowing,
When he became your father—in full view—
   the sower and the seed.

He cannot see you now but still can weep
   and ponder on those bitter days to come,

which cruel consort with the world will prove.
No public holidays, no carnivals,
    from which you will not hurry home in tears.
And then one day a marriage time will come,
    but who will marry you? Who on this earth will face
    the destiny that dogs our line?
Our record's too replete:
    "This father killed his father,
    tilled the womb again from which he sprang,
    to beget you very children from his bed of birth."
Such will be their gibes,
    so who will want to marry you?
There's none, my children, no not one,
    and life for you is all decline
    to doom and empty spinsterhood.

[*He turns to* CREON]

Listen, Son of Menoeceus,
    now their natural parents are no more,
    they have no other father left but you.
You must not see your blood go down in beggary,
    or watch them roaming husbandless.
You must not leave them to a fate like mine.
Open your heart—they're young,
    bereft of everything unless you furnish it.
Come . . . a promise, noble prince . . . your hand!

[CREON *gives his hand*]

My darling little ones, if you could only understand,
    I'd tell you, oh, so many things!
Let this suffice, a simple prayer:
Abide in modesty so may you live
    the happy life your father did not have.
CREON: These tears . . . enough! . . . Now go inside.
OEDIPUS: I must, with bitterness.
CREON: All things have their time.
OEDIPUS: You know my terms?
CREON: I'll know them when you tell me.
OEDIPUS: Then send me far away from home.

CREON: You ask what only the gods can give.
OEDIPUS: The gods? They are my enemy.
CREON: They'll answer all the swifter, then.
OEDIPUS: Ah! Do you mean it?
CREON: What I do not mean, I do not say.
OEDIPUS: Then lead me off.
CREON: Come! Let your children go.
OEDIPUS: No, no, never! Don't take them from me.
CREON: Stop this striving to be master of all.
The mastery you had in life has been your fall.

[CREON *signs to the* ATTENDANTS, *who disengage* OEDI-
PUS *from his children and lead him into the palace.*
CREON *follows and the doors are closed. The* CHORUS
groups for the exit march]

ENVOI

CHORUS: Citizens of our ancestral Thebes,
Look on this Oedipus, the mighty and once masterful:
Elucidator of the riddle,
Envied on his pedestal of fame.
You saw him fall. You saw him swept away.
So, being mortal, look on that last day
And count no man blessed in his life until
He's crossed life's bounds unstruck by ruin still.

OEDIPUS
AT COLONUS

————

ΟΙΔΙΠΟΥΣ
ΕΠΙ ΚΟΛΩΝΩΙ

This is a play about an old man by an old man. Sophocles was over ninety when he wrote it, and it must have been his 123rd play. It has all the marks of an old poet's last creative impulse. And though it does not have the dramatic tightness of *Oedipus* or *Antigone,* both of which cut to the bone with their feints and thrusts, it is no less masterly in cumulative power. The devastating blow-by-blow concisions and concussions of those plays are metamorphosed into episodes that, though lengthy and unexpected, tear one's heart out with their force and poignancy. And all the way through, the choruses and choral dialogues enhance and support the action in strong, contrasting prosody until the very end when they join mystically with the thunder to escort Oedipus in his mysterious exodus.

Above all, we are treated to language that is miraculous. After a lifetime of playwriting, with twenty or more first prizes behind him—and innumerable seconds—Sophocles has achieved supreme mastery of dramatic verse. The words are often so simple and ordinary that one wonders (as with late Shakespeare) where the magic is coming from. But it comes in a flow of swift and gentle strokes that seem to lead naturally to the farewell and demise of Oedipus—where the words move us in a way reminiscent of something out of the Old Testament, like the Book of Job.

But it is a sad time for Sophocles, and the play reflects that sadness and disillusion. He had to watch his darling Athens nearing the end of her long death struggle with Sparta. Attica had been invaded, her sacred olive trees cut down, her springing fountains left to go dry.

Colonus was a deme or village, almost a suburb of

Athens, and it is there on a small hill that the white-haired and decrepit Oedipus, dressed in rags and near exhaustion, makes his way, leaning on the arm of the faithful Antigone. It is some twenty-five years after he blinded himself. He knows that Creon, the regent of Thebes, is not his friend and will try to use him, as will his two sons who are contending for the throne. He knows, too, that his years of suffering have raised him to a holy dignity as the recognized vehicle of divine justice. His magnanimous acceptance of a fate that made him cursed has now made him blessed with a new authority. He is a talisman that others will try to capture and exploit.

Oedipus

Though old and blind, Oedipus has lost none of his fire. He is the same irascible, headstrong man that we see in *Oedipus the King*: stark, unyielding, self-assured. The lashing he gives his son Polyneices, who comes pleading for support, reduces the young man to the breaking point, and his father's curses on both of his warring sons foreshadows a gaunt and bloody future.

As for Creon, who also wants his support because an oracle has said that victory lies with those who win Oedipus to their side, he turns on him in fury and exposes him for the hypocrite he is.

Yet when it comes to speaking of Athens, Sophocles puts into the mouths of the chorus (in the presence of Oedipus) some of the tenderest sequences in all Greek tragedy.

Antigone

Antigone comes across as a gentler and softer character, though no less steadfast, than she appears to be in the play that bears her name. During all the years since her father blinded himself she has been at his side, guiding him in his dismal wanderings. She has truly sacrificed her life for him. And again, in the moving farewell to her brother Polyneices—who she knows is going to get himself killed fighting his brother, Eteocles, for the throne of Thebes—she shows how much she cares and loves. In the final scene of the play, after their father's magical walk towards oblivion, the two sisters find themselves bereft and alone in the world, though Theseus and the chorus do their best to comfort them.

Ismene

Ismene is very much the same as she appears in *Antigone*: pliant, vulnerable, fearful, but not without courage. Risking arrest, she has been slipping past the Theban sentries to bring her father news of the latest developments there—the grim struggle of her two brothers for the throne and the important revelation of the oracle that Oedipus will be the key to success for the party that can win him to its side.

Theseus

Theseus, king of Athens, is portrayed as all that is fine and noble. Though at first in awe at the discovery that he has the fabled Oedipus on his hands, he is full of sympathy and promises his support. When Creon kidnaps Antigone and Ismene and advances on Oedipus himself, Theseus arrives just in time, threatens Creon with internment in Athens, forces him to lead him to the two girls, and forthrightly lets him know what a scoundrel he is.

Polyneices

He is something of a pathetic and also a shifty character, who blithely comes to his father, not asking forgiveness for having kept him out of Thebes all those years when he had the chance of granting him sanctuary there but expecting his father to help him in his fight against his brother, Eteocles, who has usurped the throne. The answer comes like a crack of doom: it is shattering.

The play was produced posthumously in 401 B.C. by Sophocles' son Iophon, five years after his father's death.

Incidentally, how poetically right it was that Sophocles should have set his last play just outside the Athens he loved, at Colonus—where he was born!

CHARACTERS

OEDIPUS, former king of Thebes
ANTIGONE, his daughter
A COUNTRYMAN of Colonus
CHORUS of elders of Colonus
ISMENE, sister of Antigone and daughter of Oedipus
THESEUS, king of Athens
CREON, brother-in-law of Oedipus and present ruler of
Thebes
BODYGUARD of Creon
POLYNEICES, son of Oedipus
A MESSENGER
SOLDIERS AND ATTENDANTS of Theseus
SERVANT to Ismene

TIME AND SETTING

Some twenty years have passed since Oedipus blinded himself after discovering that he had murdered his father and married his mother. During much of that time he has been wandering from town to town accompanied by his daughter, Antigone. Creon, the regent of Thebes, has turned against him, as also have his two sons, who are now contending for the throne.

Oedipus is about sixty-five but looks much older. Gaunt, white-haired, dressed in rags (with a beggar's wallet) and leaning on Antigone, he slowly climbs the rocky path that leads to the edge of a wood, where the statue of a hero on a horse can be discerned among the trees. It is early afternoon in April.

PROLOGUE

OEDIPUS: So where have we come to now, Antigone, my
child,
  this blind old man and you—

what people and what town?
And who today will dole out charity
   to Oedipus the vagabond?
It's little that I ask, and I make do with less.
Patience is what I've learned from pain;
   from pain and time and my own past royalty.

But, do you see any place, dear girl, where I may sit:
   whether in public ground or sacred grove—
There sit me down
   Just until we've found out where we are.
For we are only wanderers
   and must ask advice of citizens
   and do as they direct.
ANTIGONE: [*looking at her father with concern and then gazing across the plain towards Athens*] Poor father!
                              Poor wayworn Oedipus! . . .
I can see the walls and turrets of a town,
   a long way off,
And where we stand is clearly consecrated ground
   luxuriant in laurel, olive, vine,
   and deep in the song of nightingales.

[ANTIGONE *peers into the grove*]

So rest yourself upon this boulder here:
   a rough seat, I know.
But you've come too long a way for an old man.
OEDIPUS: A blind one, too! So watch him well and help
                                          him down.
ANTIGONE: After all this time, I need no lessons there.

[*She leads him to the rock seat inside the grove and settles him there*]

OEDIPUS: Now tell me: have you the slightest inkling
                                    where we are?
ANTIGONE: Well, I know it's Athens, but this spot . . .
                              I've no idea.
OEDIPUS: Of course it's Athens. That much we know
                              from everyone we've passed.

ANTIGONE: Then shall I go and ask what this place is
called?

OEDIPUS: Do, child, if there's any sign of life.

ANTIGONE: Oh, but there must be!
In fact, I don't even have to go. I see a man approaching.

OEDIPUS: What! Coming our way? Coming here?

ANTIGONE: He's almost on us. . . . Quick, you speak,
Father—
here he is.

[*Enter a* COUNTRYMAN *of Colonus*]

OEDIPUS: Excuse me, good sir, my daughter here
whose eyes are mine as they are hers,
tells me you are passing by,
Just in time, I'm sure, to solve our doubts and let us
know . . .

COUNTRYMAN: Before you start your questioning,
come off that seat:
You're trespassing on holy ground.

OEDIPUS: Holy ground? What god is sacred here?

COUNTRYMAN: It's untouchable—not to be inhabited—
abode of most stern goddesses:
daughters of Earth and Darkness.

OEDIPUS: Then let me pray to them. What are their holy
names?

COUNTRYMAN: The All-seeing Eumenides or Kindly Ones,
we call them here.
In other places graced no doubt by other names.

OEDIPUS: Then let them welcome me, their suppliant,
for I shall never set my foot outside this haven here.

COUNTRYMAN: What do you mean?

OEDIPUS: I recognize the signs—my journey's end.

COUNTRYMAN: Well, I've no power to shift you without
a warrant.
I must go and let the city know.

OEDIPUS: Meanwhile, my friend, for the love of all the
gods,
don't disappoint a homeless wanderer, but tell me . . .

COUNTRYMAN: Ask. I have no call to disappoint.

OEDIPUS: Then where have we come to? Does this place
                          have a name?
COUNTRYMAN: I'll tell you everything I know.
This whole ground is sacred. Great Poseidon holds it.
Prometheus the Titan who bore fire is present here.
The very spot you occupy is called "The Brazen
                          Threshold,"
     the cornerstone of Athens.
That statue there, that horseman who rides above the
                          fields,
     is Colonus himself, origin and lord of all this clan,
     who gave the place its name:
Perhaps not much to sing about but, believe me,
                          stranger,
     living music to all who inhabit here.
OEDIPUS: So there are inhabitants in these parts?
COUNTRYMAN: Certainly, and called after their horseman
                          hero there.
OEDIPUS: But who governs them? Or do they rule
                          themselves?
COUNTRYMAN: A king in Athens rules over them.
OEDIPUS: A respected monarch whose word is law? Who
                          is he?
COUNTRYMAN: His name is Theseus, son of King Aegeus
                          before him.
OEDIPUS: Then could I send a message by one of you to
                          him?
COUNTRYMAN: A message, what? Asking him to come?
OEDIPUS: To say, "a little favor wins a great reward."
COUNTRYMAN: Great reward? What can a blind man
                          give?
OEDIPUS: You shall *see*—there's vision in every syllable
                          I say.
COUNTRYMAN: Listen, stranger, I am out to help.
You are obviously wellborn, though down in luck.
Stay where you are, exactly where I found you,
     while I go and tell the local people here.
Let *them* decide whether you are to stay or go.

[*The* COUNTRYMAN *hurries off*]

OEDIPUS: Daughter, has that person gone?
ANTIGONE: Gone, Father. Be at ease. Say anything you
like.
There's no one here but me.

[OEDIPUS *staggers to his knees in an attitude of prayer.*
ANTIGONE *stands watching a few paces away*]

OEDIPUS: Great mistresses of terrifying mien,
I salute you first on bended knee
in this your sanctuary.
Harden not your hearts against me or Apollo,
for even when he told my doom
he foretold me too
that after long journeys I should come
to my journey's end
at a faraway place of rest, a shelter
at the seat of you, the dreaded Holy Ones.
"There," he said,
"you will close your life of sorrows,
With blessings on the land that harbors you
and curses on the people who cast you out."
Certain signs, he said, would warn me of these things:
earthquakes, thunder, lightnings from Zeus.
I realize now
some gentle spell from you
has pulled my steps toward this grove.
How else could I have found you first
and wandered here—
I the sober and you the wineless ones—
To sit upon this holy seat not made with human hands?
Therefore, you kind divinities,
in fulfillment of Apollo's prophecies,
grant me here to reach my term at last,
my rounding off of life;
Unless you think me far too vile for that—
I a slave to sorrow far worse than any slave's.
So, hear me, good daughters of primeval Night.
And Athens, you first of cities, namesake of great Pallas,
pity this poor remnant, Oedipus,
this ghost, this carcass of what he was—a man.

ANTIGONE: Quiet, Father! Some elderly men are coming
our way,

  spying out your resting place.

OEDIPUS: Then quiet I'll be,

  while you hurry me off this path into the grove,

  until I hear just what it is they have to say.

It's always wise to be informed before we act.

[OEDIPUS *and* ANTIGONE *hurry into the trees*]

FIRST CHORAL DIALOGUE

[*Enter the* CHORUS *of elders of Colonus. They scurry about, searching among the bushes and behind the rocks, meanwhile uttering severally:*]

STROPHE I

Look for him?
  Who is it?
    Where can he lurk?
Where has he bolted?
  Oh, what a sacrilege!
Comb the ground.
  Strain your eyes.
    Search him out everywhere.
A vagabond, surely,
  some aged vagabond.
No one from here,
  would ever have pushed
Into this virgin plot of the unaffrontable maidens,
Whose very name sends shivers,
  whom we pass with averted eyes,
Whom we pray to with quavering lips.
But now a blasphemous rogue
  is hidden somewhere, they say,
And I've covered the ground on every side
But still I cannot uncover
  the cranny in which he hides.

[OEDIPUS *and* ANTIGONE *step out from the trees*]

OEDIPUS: I am the man, and my ears are my eyes,
  as they say of the blind.
CHORUS: Ah! Horrible to see, and horrible to hear!
OEDIPUS: Listen, please! I am no criminal.
CHORUS: Zeus, defend us! Who could this old man be?
OEDIPUS: No favorite of fate—I can tell you that—
  good guardians of this grove.
For who would borrow eyes to walk,
  or lean his weight on frail support?

ANTISTROPHE I

Look at his eyes!
  Great gods!
    He's blind!
Eyeless from birth?
  What a lifetime of horror!
Far be it
  from us, sir,
    to add to your sorrows,
But you trespass, you trespass;
  step no further
Into the still
  of the grassy dell
Where chaliced water from the spring, blended with honey,
Is poured in a stream of the purest offering. Go
Away from there, you woebegone stranger.
Turn back, come away,
  no matter how far you have wandered.
Can you hear us from there, you derelict outcast?
Speak if you want, and we'll listen, but not
  till you've moved from the sacred close.

[OEDIPUS *and* ANTIGONE *stand motionless*]

OEDIPUS: My daughter, what are we to do?
ANTIGONE: Do as they say, Father. We must yield and
                            listen.
OEDIPUS: Your hand, then. Come.
ANTIGONE: There, you have it.
OEDIPUS: Sirs, I am breaking cover.

You must not violate my trust.
CHORUS: Never fear, old man!
No one will drag you off from here against your will.

[OEDIPUS *takes a step forward out of the grove. End of strophic pattern but not of Choral Dialogue*]

OEDIPUS: Further?
CHORUS: Come still further.

[*He takes another step*]

OEDIPUS: Enough?
CHORUS: Lead him, girl, you understand.
ANTIGONE: I do indeed—these many years . . . Careful
now!
OEDIPUS: Oh, what it is to walk in the dark!
ANTIGONE: Come, Father, come! Let your blind steps
follow.
CHORUS: Poor harassed stranger on strange soil!
Learn to loathe what we find loathing.
Learn respect for what we reverence.
OEDIPUS: Then guide my walking, you my daughter,
Down the path of pious bidding
Where we can talk without offending.
Let's not fight with what is fated.

[*He advances onto a platform of rock at the edge of the grove*]

CHORUS: There.
You need not go beyond that ledge of rock.
OEDIPUS: This far?
CHORUS: That is far enough. Do you hear us?
OEDIPUS: May I sit?
CHORUS: Yes, sit to the side of that slab of rock.
ANTIGONE: I have you, Father. Lean on me.
OEDIPUS: Oh, what a wretched thing it is! . . .
ANTIGONE: Step by step, we together,
Old and young, weak and strong;
Lean your loving weight on mine.

OEDIPUS: Oh, how pitiable my wretchedness!

[ANTIGONE *finally settles him on the rock*]

CHORUS: You sad old man, relax at last
And tell us of your birth and home.
What prompts this weary pilgrimage?
What country are you from?
OEDIPUS: [*alarmed*] Country? None. . . . Oh, please, good
friends, do not . . .
CHORUS: Do not what, old man? What are you avoiding?
OEDIPUS: Do not . . . Oh. please—
not ask me who I am!
CHORUS: Why? What is it?
OEDIPUS: My frightening origin.
CHORUS: Tell it.
OEDIPUS: [*turning to* ANTIGONE] Dear child, must I out
with it?
CHORUS: Sir, your ancestry? Your father's name?
OEDIPUS: No, no, not that! Child, what shall I do?
ANTIGONE: Tell them, since you've gone so far already.
OEDIPUS: Then I'll say it. There's no way to cover up.
CHORUS: Both of you—you're wasting time—get on with
it.

OEDIPUS: Laius . . . Have you heard the name?
CHORUS: Dear gods! We have.
OEDIPUS: Of the line of Labdacus?
CHORUS: Great Zeus!
OEDIPUS: And Oedipus the stricken one?
CHORUS: What! That man is you?
OEDIPUS: Wait, listen—do not recoil.
CHORUS: Oh, monstrous! Monstrous!
OEDIPUS: It's hopeless now.
CHORUS: Intolerable!
OEDIPUS: Daughter, what will happen now?
CHORUS: Away with both of you! Leave our land!
OEDIPUS: But you promised! You will keep your word?
CHORUS: There is no blame attached to any
Who hits back where first he's wronged.
You deceived us, so we're playing
Trick for tricking, paying back

Treachery with trouble. Go!
Quit these precincts, quit our country,
Do not pollute our city with your tainted air.
ANTIGONE: You gentle sirs of pious intent,
If unmoved by my father's plight
And all those horrors not his fault,
To me at least be kind, who beg you.
He is my father, all I have.
I'm pleading with my eyes to yours:
Eyes not blind, but eye to eye,
Almost as if I were your daughter.
Beseeching you for a beaten man
Needing mercy. Like a god
You have us wholly in your hands.
Come, be clement past our hoping.
By all your dearest roots to life,
I implore you: child and wife,
Hearth and godhead. Bear in mind
There never was a human being
Who, god-impelled, had hope in fleeing.

[*End of Choral Dialogue*]

FIRST EPISODE

CHORUS: Daughter of Oedipus, of course we pity you,
    just as we pity him for what he suffers;
But we dare not risk divine displeasure
    and go beyond what we've said already.
OEDIPUS: Then where has fame and where has reputation
                                   gone
if this be Athens, that most pious city?
Sanctuary of the lost, savior of the needy,
    unique in both! What good are they
When you tear me from my seat of stone
    and cast me headlong from the land?
And all because you've merely heard my name!
Me, this carcass, this right hand of mine,
    you can't fear that; for what I've done is simply suffer:
Yes, suffer much more than anything I've done.
As I could prove if I but touched upon the story

of my mother and my father.
It's this that frightens you, as well I know.
Am I then a sinner born?
I, provoked to strike in self-defense?
Why, even if I'd acted with full knowledge,
   it still would not have been a crime.
As it was, where I went I went
All ignorant toward a doom too known
   to those who planned it.

Therefore, good sirs,
   since you have moved me from my seat,
   you must—by all the gods—protect me now.
Do not say you reverence heaven,
   then do nothing but ignore what heaven says.
Make no mistake,
   the gods' eyes see the just
   and the gods' eyes see the unjust too,
   and from that blazing gaze,
   never on this earth,
   will the wicked man escape by flight.
By heaven's grace, then,
   let no dishonor blot the name of Athens by abetting
            wrong.

You accepted me as suppliant and gave a pledge,
   now guard me to the end.
And when you look into my ruined eyes,
   do not look with scorn.

I am a priestly and a holy man,
   and come with blessings for your people in my hands.
And when your prince shall come,
   whoever be your prince,
Then shall everything be told and all made plain.
But in that space between do nothing mean.
CHORUS: Your words, old man, must make us think.
These solemn arguments have weight.
Let authority decide. We are content.
OEDIPUS: And where is he who wields authority?
CHORUS: In Athens, our ancestral city.
The scout who sent us here has gone for him.

OEDIPUS: What hope is there that he will come?
Why should he trouble with a blind old man?
CHORUS: Certainly he will come—once he hears your
name.

OEDIPUS: But who will tell him that?
CHORUS: The road is long, but travelers talk.
He will hear your name and he will come.
For every region of the earth has heard your name, old
man.

The instant that it hits his ears
  he will leap up from his recreation and his ease
  and hurry here.
OEDIPUS: Then may his coming bring rewards
  for myself and for his city.
Ah! Is not nobility its own reward?
ANTIGONE: Great heavens, I am speechless!
Father, I can't imagine it.
OEDIPUS: What's happening, Antigone, my child?
ANTIGONE: I see a woman coming straight towards us on
a colt,

  an Etnan thoroughbred.
She wears a broad Thessalian hat
  to shade her from the sun.
I can't be sure. Is it she or isn't it?
Is my mind wandering? It can't be she . . . surely, can it?
But it must be . . . it is.
Her eyes are flashing welcomes.
She's almost on us. She's waving now.
Of course . . . it's no one but our own Ismene.
OEDIPUS: What are you saying, child?
ANTIGONE: That your daughter—and my sister—is right
in front of me.

Wait till you hear her voice.

  [ISMENE, *attended by a single servant, advances towards*
  OEDIPUS *and* ANTIGONE]

ISMENE: Dearest Father! Sister!
The sweetest names in the world to me.
It was difficult to find you, and now
  it's difficult to see you through my tears.

OEDIPUS: Darling daughter—you?
ISMENE: Poor dear Father!
OEDIPUS: But, child, you're really here?
ISMENE: It was not easy.
OEDIPUS: Dear girl—let me feel you.
ISMENE: Let me hug you both.

[*They all embrace*]

OEDIPUS: My children! . . . My sisters!
ISMENE: The stricken ones.
OEDIPUS: Yes, she and I.
ISMENE: With me the third.
OEDIPUS: But, Daughter, what has brought you?
ISMENE: Concern for you, Father.
OEDIPUS: You mean, you missed me?
ISMENE: Yes. And I've come with news,
    trusting myself to this last loyal servant here.
OEDIPUS: But those young men, your brothers, where are
                                                    they?
ISMENE: Just where they are—in the thick of trouble.
OEDIPUS: Oh, what miserable and perfect copies
    have they grown to be of Egyptian ways!
For there the men sit at home and weave
    while their wives go out to win the daily bread,
    as you do, my daughters.
Just so your brothers, who should be
    the very ones to take this load upon them.
Instead they sit at home like girls
    and keep the house,
    leaving the two of you to face my troubles
    and make life a little easier for me.
Antigone here,
    ever since she left the nursery
    and became a woman,
    has been with me as guide and old man's nurse,
    steering me through my dreary wanderings;
    often roaming through the tangled forests,
    barefoot and hungry,
    often soaked by rain and scorched by sun,
    never regretting all she'd missed at home,

so long as her father was provided for.

And you, my daughter,
  more than once you've sallied forth
  slipping past the Theban sentinels
  to bring your father news of all the latest oracles.
You were my faithful spy
  when I was driven from the land.
But, Ismene, what new tidings do you bring your father?
What mission has summoned you from home?
You don't come empty-handed, that I know.
You've brought me something—
  something I can fear.
ISMENE: I went through fire and water, Father,
  to find out where you were and how you were
                                      surviving,
  but let that pass;
I have no desire to live it all again
  by telling you.

The trouble now is those two sons of yours—
  that's what I've come to tell you.
They were content at first to leave the throne to Creon
  and rid the city of the ancient family curse
  that has dogged our line.
But now they are possessed.
Some demon of pride, some jealousy,
  has gripped their souls
  with a manic lust for royal power.
They want to seize the reins of government.
Eteocles, our hot-brained stripling younger brother,
  has snatched the throne from his elder, Polyneices,
  and driven him from Thebes.
While Polyneices, we hear from every source,
  has fled to the vale of Argos,
  adds marriage to diplomacy and military alliances,
And swears that Argos will either
  acquit herself with triumph on the Theban plain
  or be lifted to the skies in glorious attempt.
This is no fiction but the agonizing truth.

How far the gods will go before they let some mercy
fall—
Oh, Father, fall on you!—it's impossible to tell.
OEDIPUS: Ah! Did you think that any glances of the gods
could ever be a glance to save me?
ISMENE: Yes, Father, that I hoped, exactly that.
There've been new oracles.
OEDIPUS: My child, what oracles? What have they said?
ISMENE: That soon the men of Thebes will seek you out,
dead or alive: a talisman for their salvation.
OEDIPUS: Ha! a talisman for what—one such as I?
ISMENE: In you, they say, there is a power born—a power
for them.
OEDIPUS: So, when I am nothing, then am I a man?
ISMENE: The gods now bear you up; before they cast you
down.
OEDIPUS: An old man on a pedestal, his youth in ruins!
ISMENE: Nevertheless, this you ought to know.
Creon is on his way to use you, and sooner now than
later.
OEDIPUS: To use me, Daughter? How?
ISMENE: He wants to plant you on the frontiers of
Thebes;
within their reach, of course, but not within their sight.
OEDIPUS: On the threshold, then? What use is that?
ISMENE: It saves them from a curse if your tomb be
wronged.
OEDIPUS: But bestows a blessing if it is honored.
They needed neither god nor oracle to tell them that.
ISMENE: And so they want to keep you somewhere near,
but not where you can set up as master of yourself.
OEDIPUS: And when I die, to bury me in Theban dust at
least?
ISMENE: No, dear Father, no: you spilled your father's
blood.
OEDIPUS: Then I'll not fall into their hands—no, never!
ISMENE: And *that*, one day, will spell the ruin of Thebes.
OEDIPUS: How so, my child? What way will they be hurt?
ISMENE: Scorched by the anger blazing from your tomb.*

*This refers to the day when the Theban invaders of Athens will
be routed in battle near the tomb of Oedipus.

OEDIPUS: Who told you, child, all this you're telling me?

ISMENE: Pilgrims from the very hearth of Delphi.

OEDIPUS: And Apollo really said these things of me?

ISMENE: So those men avowed on their return to Thebes.

OEDIPUS: Has either of my sons heard this?

ISMENE: Both of them alike; each taking it to heart.

OEDIPUS: Scoundrels! So they knew it! Coveted my presence less
   than they coveted a crown.

ISMENE: It hurts to hear you say it, but it's true.

OEDIPUS: Oh, you gods! Tread not down
   the blaze of coming battle between these two.
And give me power to prophesy the end
   for which they now match spear with clash on spear.

Then shall the one who now
   enjoys the scepter and the throne
   no more remain,
And he who fled the realm, not return.
I was their father,
   thrust out from fatherland in full disgrace.
They did not rescue or defend me.
No, they cared nothing:
   but watched me harried from my home,
   my banishment proclaimed.
And if you say that such was then my wish,
   a mercy granted by the city—apt and opportune—
I answer, "No!"
On that first day I wished it, yes,
   death was sweet—my soul on fire—
   even death by stoning,
   but no man was found to further that desire.
In time my madness mellowed.
I began to think my rage had plunged too far,
   my chastisement excessive for my sins.
   And then the city—city, mark you, after all that
time—
   had me thrust and hurtled out of Thebes.
Then they could have helped,
   my two boys, their father's sons—
   then they could have stirred themselves.

They could. They did not do a thing.
For lack of a little word from them
    I was cast out
      to drag away my life in wandering beggary.
Shelter, devoted care, my daily bread,
    everything within a woman's power to give,
    these I owe to my two daughters here.
Their brothers sold their father for a throne,
    exchanged him for a scepter and a realm.

No, I'll not help them win a war,
And the crown of Thebes will prove to be their bane.
That much Ismene's oracles make clear
    now that I match them with those others,
    those olden oracles Apollo made me once
    and now at last fulfills.
So let them send a Creon to search me out,
    or any other potentate from Thebes.
I shall be your city's champion and the scourge
    of all my enemies,
With you, good people, on my side,
And by the grace of the Holy Ones who here abide.
CHORUS: Certainly, Oedipus, you impel our sympathies,
    you and your two daughters here.
And now that you add the sovereign weight
    of your great name to make our city triumph
    we are more than ready to help you with advice.
OEDIPUS: Good friends, I'll carry out whatever you
                          suggest.
CHORUS: Then expiate at once those goddesses
    whose holy precincts you profaned.
OEDIPUS: By what ritual, friends? Tell me that.
CHORUS: First, from the spring of living waters fetch
    in pure washed hands the ceremonial draught.
OEDIPUS: And when I've fetched this fresh, unsullied
                          cup?
CHORUS: You'll find some chalices of delicate design.
Crown with wreaths their double handles and their
                         brims.
OEDIPUS: What kind of wreaths? Olive sprigs or flocks
                      of wool?
CHORUS: A ewe-lamb's fleece, all freshly shorn.

OEDIPUS: Good. And then . . . how do I complete the
rite?

CHORUS: Pour out your offering, with your face towards
the dawn.

OEDIPUS: Pouring from those chalices you spoke of?

CHORUS: Yes, in three libations, emptying the last.

OEDIPUS: And this last, please tell me clearly:
what should it contain?

CHORUS: Water mixed with honey. Add no wine.

OEDIPUS: And when the green-shadowed ground has
drunk this cup?

CHORUS: Lay thrice nine sprigs of olive on it
and with both hands offer up a prayer.

OEDIPUS: The prayer? That's most important. Tell me
that.

CHORUS: That these goddesses we call the Kindly Ones,
or Eumenides,
be saving kind to you, who pray to them.
Make that your prayer, or someone make it for you.
Whisper it and do not cry it out.
Then come away. Do not turn back.
This accomplished, we shall gladly stand by you;
otherwise, my friend, we are afraid.

OEDIPUS: My daughters, did you hear what these locals
said?

ANTIGONE: Father, we heard. Tell us what you want.

OEDIPUS: *I* cannot go. I am too weak and blind—
my double disability.
Will one of you two do it for me?
A single person pure of heart, I think,
can make atonement for a thousand sinners.
So do it now, but do not leave me all alone.
I am not strong enough to get along without a helping
hand.

ISMENE: Then I shall carry out the rite,
if somebody will point the way.

CHORUS: Beyond that clump of trees, young woman.
The guardian of the grove will tell you
everything you want to know.

ISMENE: To my task, then.
Antigone, you watch over Father here.

No trouble is too much for a parent anywhere.

[ISMENE *goes into the grove. The* CHORUS *turns to*
OEDIPUS]

SECOND CHORAL DIALOGUE

STROPHE I
CHORUS: Stranger, it hurts
to stir up the memory
time has let slumber,
but we must know . . .
OEDIPUS: What now?
CHORUS: The story of suffering
you have been chained to:
the fatal ordeal without a cure.
OEDIPUS: For hospitality's sake, my friends,
do not uncover my shame.
CHORUS: The tale of it echoes
all over the universe.
But the truth of it, tell us,
how much is true?
OEDIPUS: No! No!
CHORUS: We beg you tell.
OEDIPUS: Ah, the shame of it!
CHORUS: Grant us this favor
as *we* favored *you.*

ANTISTROPHE I
OEDIPUS: Friends, so many sufferings
suffered unwittingly!
God is my witness,
none of it guiltily.
CHORUS: How did it happen?
OEDIPUS: An innocent bridegroom,
a twisted wedding
yoking Thebes to disaster.
CHORUS: Is there truth in the word that you shared
the incestuous bed of a mother?
OEDIPUS: Must you, good people?
It's death to hear it.

Ah, these maidens are mine,
  but more than that . . .
CHORUS: Go on! Go on!
OEDIPUS: Two daughters, two curses . . .
CHORUS: Zeus, oh, no!
OEDIPUS: Two shoots from the birth pangs
  of a wife-mother's tree.

STROPHE II

CHORUS: What! Are you saying, your children are both . . .
OEDIPUS: Their father's offspring and his sisters.
CHORUS: Horrible!
OEDIPUS: Horror, yes horror. Wave upon wave.
CHORUS: Victim!
OEDIPUS: Yes, endlessly victim.
CHORUS: Sinner, too!
OEDIPUS: No sinner.
CHORUS: How?
OEDIPUS: I saved
  The city—I wish I had not—
  And the prize for this has broken my heart.

ANTISTROPHE II

CHORUS: Broken your heart with shedding the blood
                                    of . . . ?
OEDIPUS: What is it now? What more are you after?
CHORUS: A father . . .
OEDIPUS: Stab upon stab!
  wound upon wounding!
CHORUS: Killer!
OEDIPUS: I killed him, yes, but can plead . . .
CHORUS: What can you . . . ?
OEDIPUS: Justice.
CHORUS: How?
OEDIPUS: Let me tell you:
  The man that I murdered would have killed *me*.
  By law I am innocent, void of all malice.

[*End of Choral Dialogue.* THESEUS *and his retinue are
seen approaching. The* CHORUS *turns in his direction*]

CHORUS: But here comes our king, Theseus son of Aegeus,
bent upon your bidding.

[*Enter* THESEUS *with* SOLDIERS *and* ATTENDANTS. *He stands gazing at* OEDIPUS]

THESEUS: That story noised abroad so often in the past,
the bloody butchering of your sight,
warned me it was you, Son of Laius,
And now, hastened here by rumors,
I can see it is.
Your clothes, your mutilated face,
assure me of your name.
And I would gently ask you, tortured Oedipus,
what favor you would have of me or Athens:
You and that sad companion by your side?
Tell me.
For no tale of yours, however shocking,
could make me turn away.
I was a child of exile too,
fighting for my life in foreign lands—
and none so dangerously.
So never could I turn my back on some poor exile
such as you are now
and leave him to his fate.
For I know too well that I am only man.
The portion of your days today
could be no less than mine tomorrow.
OEDIPUS: Theseus, in so short a speech
all your birth's declared,
and my reply can be as brief.
My name, my father, and my country,
you've touched on all correctly.
There's nothing left for me to say
but tell you my desire,
and all my tale is told.
THESEUS: I wait to hear it. Please proceed to tell.
OEDIPUS: I come with a gift: this my battered body.
No priceless vision, no,
But the price of it is better than of beauty.

THESEUS: What makes it precious, this gift you bring?

OEDIPUS: In time you'll know. Not now, perhaps.

THESEUS: And when will that time of grace be known?

OEDIPUS: When I am dead and you have raised my tomb.

THESEUS: Life's last rites, you ask for that,
with all before made nothing of, forgotten!

OEDIPUS: Yes, for in that wish the rest is harvested.

THESEUS: You ask a little favor, then, compressing
everything?

OEDIPUS: Perhaps, but not so little—believe me—not so
little.

THESEUS: Does it, then, concern your sons and me?

OEDIPUS: It does, my king, they are intent to carry me
off to Thebes.

THESEUS: Which ought to please you, surely, more than
banishment?

OEDIPUS: No. For when I wanted that they would not
have it.

THESEUS: This is foolishness to sulk in time of trouble.

OEDIPUS: Wait till you've heard me out before you scold.

THESEUS: Proceed. I have no right to judge before I
know.

OEDIPUS: I am the victim, Theseus, of repeated and appalling wrong.

THESEUS: You mean the family curse that haunts your
line?

OEDIPUS: No. *That* already rings in Greece's ears.

THESEUS: But what could be worse than that—
the worst wretchedness of all?

OEDIPUS: Just this:
I am driven from my native land by my own flesh and
blood.
I can return no more. I am a parricide.

THESEUS: What, ostracized and summoned home in one?

OEDIPUS: The god has spoken. His warning makes them
want me there.

THESEUS: And what is the warning threatened by the
oracle?

OEDIPUS: A mortal wound dealt on this very field of
battle.

THESEUS: This field of battle? But Athens and Thebes
                                   are not at war.
OEDIPUS: Good son of Aegeus, gentle son,
  only to the gods is given not to age or die,
All else disrupts through all disposing time.
Earth ebbs in strength, the body ebbs in power.
Faith dies and faithlessness is born.
No constant friendship breathes
  between man and man, or city and a city.
Soon or late, the sweet will sour,
  the sour will sweet to love again.
Does fair weather hold between this Thebes and you?
Then one day shall ever teeming time
  hatch nights on teeming days,
Wherein this pledge, this harmony, this hour
  will break upon a spear,
  slashed down for a useless word.

Then shall my sleeping corpse,
  cold in sepulcher,
  warm itself with draughts of their perfervid blood,
If Zeus is Zeus and truth be truth
  from Zeus's son Apollo.
But I'm not one to bawl away a mystery,
  so let me stop where I began:
Take care to keep your word with me,
  then never shall you say of Oedipus
  you gave him sanctuary without reward;
Or, if you do, all heaven is a fraud.
CHORUS: Sire, from the first this man has sworn
  he had the power to benefact our land.
THESEUS: How could we spurn the overtures of such a
                                     friend,
  who not only rightly claims the hospitality
  of Thebes an allied city,
But comes appealing to our goddesses
  and pays no little tribute to our State and me?
I shall reverence and not repudiate his gift
  and grant him all the rights of citizen.
But more: if it please our guest to sojourn here,
  I place him in your care.

yes, Oedipus—unless you'd rather come with me—
the choice is yours,
your every wish is mine.

OEDIPUS: Great Zeus, be gentle to such gentleness!

THESEUS: Well, what is your wish? Will you come with
me?

OEDIPUS: If only that were fitting, but this very place is
where I must . . .

THESEUS: Must what? I shall not hinder you.

OEDIPUS: . . . triumph over those who banished me.

THESEUS: And as you promised, shower blessings on us
with your presence?

OEDIPUS: Only if you keep your word to me.

THESEUS: Never doubt it. I am not one to play you false.

OEDIPUS: And I'll not make you swear it like a criminal.

THESEUS: An oath would be no surer than my word.

OEDIPUS: But how will you proceed if . . .

THESEUS: What now disturbs you?

OEDIPUS: Men will come.

THESEUS: And mine will see to them.

OEDIPUS: But if you leave me . . .

THESEUS: You need not tell me what to do.

OEDIPUS: The fear in my heart compels me.

THESEUS: And there is no fear in mine.

OEDIPUS: But the threats . . . you do not know . . .

THESEUS: I know only this:
That no one is going to kidnap you against my will.
Often bluff and bluster, threat and counterthreat
can bully reason for a time,
But when the mind reseats itself
disquiet vanishes.
These people who have shouted lustily
for your abduction,
Will, I trust, run into a long and ruffled passage here.
Have confidence!
Apart from all my promises, has not Apollo
charge of you within this hallowed ground?
And when I'm gone,
my name's enough to keep you sound.

[THESEUS *leaves with his retinue. The* CHORUS *regroups*

*and faces the audience to deliver a eulogy on Colonus
and Athens*]

CHORAL ODE

STROPHE I

Stranger, here
Is the land of the horse
Earth's fairest home
This silver hill Colonus.

Here the nightingale
Spills perennial sound
Lucent through the evergreen.

Here the wine-deep ivies creep
Through the god's untrodden bower
Heavy with the laurel berry.

Here there is a sunless quiet
Riven by no storm.
Here the corybantic foot
Of Bacchus beats
Tossing with the nymphs who nursed him.

ANTISTROPHE I

The narcissus
That drinks sky's dew
Here lifts its day—
By-day-born eye:

The diadem that crowns
The curls of ancient goddesses.
The crocus casts his saffron glance

And unparched Cephisus all day
Wanders out from sleepless springs
Fingering his crystal way

Out among the gentle breasts
Of hills and dales

Swelling with fecundity.
Not seldom here the Muses sing
And Aphrodite rides with golden rein.

STROPHE II

Not in Asia
Never in Pelops
(Great Dorian island)
Was heard the like of what I sing:
A tree indomitable, self-engendered,
Challenge to the spears of armies
Lush in Athens
Sap of striplings—
Olive, the moon-green olive.
No youth in lustihood
Shall ravish her
Nor calculating age.
The sleepless eye of Zeus is on her
Athena's gaze cerulean.

ANTISTROPHE II

Add praise on praise:
Our mother city's
Prize and god-gift:
Prowess in horses, prowess in stallions
Prowess at sea. You Poseidon,
Son of Cronus, sat her high,
Rode her down
These roads displaying
How the bit and bridle
Breaks the stamping charger
How the oar blade
Sleekly stroking
Cuts the brine behind
The hundred-footed Nereids.

SECOND EPISODE

[ANTIGONE's *attention is riveted by the approach of an old man hurrying towards them with a squad of soldiers*]

ANTIGONE: Look! You much praised land, the hour has
come
for you to make your words shine forth with deeds.

OEDIPUS: [*alarmed*] Child, what now?

ANTIGONE: Creon is coming . . . And, Father, not alone.

OEDIPUS: You generous counselors, now is the time
to prove the limits of your sanctuary.

CHORUS: Take heart! Proof you'll have.
Though we be old, our country's strength is young.

[CREON *arrives at the head of his escort of guards*]

CREON: Sirs, you worthy men of Attica,
I see some apprehension in your eyes at my approach.
Do not recoil. Do not be ready with abuse.
I have not come to do you harm—
an old man against a mighty state,
mighty as ever there was in Greece.
My mission is to plead with that old man
to return with me to Theban territory.
I am no private emissary—ah, no!—
but a nation's full ambassador.
It was my lot as this man's relative
to bear the crushing load of his estate
as no man else in Thebes.

[*He turns towards* OEDIPUS]

Do you hear me, Oedipus?
Come home, you woebegotten man!
Everyone in Thebes is rightly calling for you;
I most of all, yes, I,
who'd be a brute indeed
not to weep to see an old man suffer so:
drifting endlessly, unknown, a vagabond,
a girl his single prop—and she, poor thwarted creature,
Fallen lower than I'd ever dream she'd fall,
dragging out her gloomy, squalid life of caring for you:
well ripe for weddings but unwed and waiting,
ah! for some thick-fisted yokel's snatch.
A disgrace? Indeed, we are all disgraced.

I point at you and me and all of Thebes.
Who can cover up what so emblazons forth?
You can at last. Yes, Oedipus, you can hide it now.
By all our fathers' gods, consent to come back home,
    your own ancestral city.
Say farewell to Athens, kind as she has been.
Home comes first,
    the place of your long-gone cradlehood.
OEDIPUS: You brazen hypocrite! You'd stop at nothing.
Twisting every righteous motive to your ends!
You'd trap me, would you, in your cruel coils a second
                                                    time?

Once in agony I turned against myself
    and cried aloud for banishment.
Then it did not fit your pleasure, did it,
    to fit yourself to mine?
But when my overbrimming passion had gone down
    and home's four walls were sweet,
Then you had me routed out and cast away.
Fine affection *that* for family ties!

And now again, the moment you perceive
    me being welcomed by this kindly city and her sons,
    you want to wrench me away,
    your barbed designs wrapped up in words of wool.
Who ever heard of friendliness by force?
You're like a man who spurns to grant a favor when
                                                he's asked,
    gives nothing, will not lift a finger for you,
Then when your heart's desire has passed,
    wants to push that very grace upon you,
    now a grace no longer.
Rather barren of delight, that gift, do you not think?
Yet that precisely is the gift you proffer me,
    so fair in form, so hollow in reality.
Therefore, let me shout your falsehood out to these
    and let them gaze at your duplicity.
You come to fetch me—home? Ah, no!
You come to plant me on your doorstep,

A talisman to ward away the onslaughts Attica will
launch.
That wish you'll never have, but this you will:
my curse forever on your land,
And for my sons this sole realm and heritage—
the right, and room enough, to die.
Ha! I'd say my forecast for the fate of Thebes
was more informed than yours. Oh, much!
So much the more reliable!
It stems from Zeus and from Apollo.
Yours is from a counterfeiting tongue,
double-edged and whetted to deceit.
But yours, you'll find, will reap more suffering than
success.
However, since I cannot make you see this—go!
And leave us here to lead a life of hardship as we may.
Hardship to those resigned is no dismay.
CREON: A splendid tirade!
But whom do you think it hurts, you or me?
OEDIPUS: What care I? So long as you fail as thoroughly
to dupe these people here as you've duped me.
CREON: Silly, obdurate man, whom time has not made
wise!
Must you bring even dotage to disgrace?
OEDIPUS: Such a tricky tongue! I never knew an honest
man
who could dissertate and twist speech so.
CREON: Dissertation is quite different from frothing at
the mouth.
OEDIPUS: You, of course, can dissertate and hit the bull's-
eye straight.
CREON: Not exactly straight—with such a crooked target.
OEDIPUS: Be off with you! I speak for all these people
here.
I do not want you prowling round my haven.
CREON: Then I appeal to them, these people, not to you.
You I'll deal with once I've got you in my clutches.
OEDIPUS: Got me in your clutches, eh?
With these my friends all looking on?
CREON: Just wait! I know another way to make you wince.
OEDIPUS: Another way? I'd like to see exactly how.

CREON: Certainly! You have two daughters.
One I've already seized. The other will quickly follow.
OEDIPUS: Oh, no!
CREON: Oh, yes! And you'll soon have more to groan
about.
OEDIPUS: You've got my child?
CREON: And soon will have the other.
OEDIPUS: Friends, my friends, is there nothing you can do?
You must not fail me now. Hound this horrible man away.
CHORUS: Sir, be off with you! What you have done
and what you mean to do is criminal.
CREON: [*to his guards*] Grab the girl. It's time to act.
Drag her off by force if she won't come.

[*The guards advance on* ANTIGONE]

ANTIGONE: Help! Is there no escape?
You gods! You men!
CHORUS: What are you doing, sirrah?
CREON: I shan't touch your man, but *she* is mine.
OEDIPUS: Elders, help!
CHORUS: Sir, you have no right.
CREON: I have indeed a right.
CHORUS: What right?
CREON: To take what's mine.
OEDIPUS: Men of Athens, help!

[CREON *lays hands on* ANTIGONE]

THIRD CHORAL DIALOGUE

[*The following lines form a strophe in the Greek, which
is answered later by an antistrophe when* CREON *attacks*
OEDIPUS *himself. This short choral interlude serves both
to sustain the excitement and yet to relieve the tension*]

STROPHE
CHORUS: [*approaching menacingly*] How dare you,
Stranger!
Unhand her or you run the danger
of our attack.

CREON: Stand back!
CHORUS: Not until you yield.
CREON: Then it's Thebes and Athens
on the battlefield.
OEDIPUS: Ah! My prophecy come true!
CHORUS: Let loose the girl or you . . .
CREON: Mind your own authority.
CHORUS: I'm telling you to set her free.
CREON: And I'm telling you to unbar my way.
CHORUS: Colonians, to the rescue! Help!
The State manhandled, the State itself at bay.
ANTIGONE: Friends! Friends! They're dragging me away.

[*End of strophe and of first part of Third Choral Dialogue*]

OEDIPUS: Antigone, where are you?
ANTIGONE: They're dragging me away.
OEDIPUS: Hold on to my hand, child!
ANTIGONE: I haven't the strength.
CREON: [*to his guards*] Get on with her!
OEDIPUS: This is the end of me.

[*The guards hustle* ANTIGONE *away.* CREON *pauses, then turns to* OEDIPUS *with a sneer*]

CREON: At least you won't go hobbling through your life
with those two little crutches anymore!
If that's the kind of triumph you want,
trampling over friends and fatherland—
those whose mandate I, as king,
am trying to carry out—
Then *have* that triumph
In time I think you'll learn
you are your own worst enemy, before and now:
flying into tantrums with your friends—
those damnable tempers that have ruined you.

[CREON *begins to walk away, but realizes his men have gone off with* ANTIGONE *and he is now on his own, with his way blocked by the Athenian elders*]

CHORUS: Hold there, Stranger!

CREON: Don't dare touch me!

CHORUS: Stay where you are till you restore those girls.

CREON: [*looking around and catching sight of* OEDIPUS, *who is backing into the grove*] In that case I'll present
my city with an even greater prize,
worth more than those two women.

[*He rounds on the retreating* OEDIPUS]

CHORUS: Whatever next?

CREON: Him. He's mine.

CHORUS: Braggart! You wouldn't dare.

CREON: Watch me do it!

CHORUS: Not if our sovereign king can stop you.

OEDIPUS: Villain, are you so far gone you'd even lay a
hand on *me*?

CREON: Hold your tongue!

OEDIPUS: *That* I will not.
If the hallowed spirits of this place allow,
let me give vent to one more curse.
You scum! My devastated eyes, blank so long,
saw through the eyes of this helpless girl
and now you've plucked her from me.
So, may Helios, all-seeing god of sun,
visit you and all your race
with such dotage and decay as matches mine.

CREON: Do you hear him, men of Athens?

OEDIPUS: They hear, all right. They mark you and me:
You the bully who use sheer force,
And I who can only counter with a curse.

CREON: [*advancing on* OEDIPUS] I'll stand no more of
this.

Old and single-handed though I am,
I'll take this man by the strength of my right arm.

[CREON *lays hands on* OEDIPUS *and attempts to drag
him away*]

ANTISTROPHE

[*Matching the strophe on pages 299–300 and completing the Third Choral Dialogue*]

OEDIPUS: You'll rue it.
CHORUS: Rash man!
What makes you think that you can do it?
CREON: I can.
CHORUS: Then is Athens city most degenerate.
CREON: Where right is might the little beat the great.
OEDIPUS: Hear him?
CHORUS: Rant—Zeus knows!
CREON: Perhaps Zeus knows.
You don't and can't.
CHORUS: Unbridled insolence!
CREON: Then you'll have to bear unbridled insolence.
CHORUS: Rally, people! Rulers, rally!
To the rescue—hurry,
    Before these ruffians cross our boundary.

[THESEUS *arrives at the head of a troop of men. End of antistrophe and of Third Choral Dialogue*]

THESEUS: What's all this clamor? What's going on?
Why was I called away by panic cries
    from Poseidon's altar, great sea-god of Colonus?
Explain it all,
    for I've hurried here much too quick for comfort.
OEDIPUS: Ah! welcome, gentle voice!
I am worsted by a brigand.
THESEUS: Worsted? How? Please tell me.
OEDIPUS: Creon here, this creature that you see,
    has kidnapped my two children,
    my last and darling pair.
THESEUS: Is this true?
OEDIPUS: As I tell it: the most foul truth.
THESEUS: [*to his men*] Quick, one of you to the altar
                                                place.
Break up the concourse at the sacrifice
    and have the people gallop foot and horse
    to the meeting of the roads

before the women pass:
Quick, off with you!
Before this foreign bully makes a fool of me by force.

[*A soldier is dispatched.* THESEUS *turns to* CREON]

As for him,
   if I should let my anger have full sway
   to deal with him as he deserved,
   he'd not leave my hands without a smart.
We will, however, judge him by the very laws
   to which he himself appeals.

[*Pointing at* CREON]

You, you shall not leave this country, sir,
   until those girls are back and stand before my eyes.
You insult us;
   you insult your very race and native land.
You push your way within this realm
   where right is loved and law is paramount,
   and then proceed to sweep aside authority,
   pillaging and taking prisoners at your will
   as if you thought my city was bereft of men
   or manned by slaves
   and I a nobody.
Well, it was not Thebes that brought you up to steal.
She has no predilection for a rascal brood.
Scant praise you'd have from her
   if she found you plundering me,
   plundering the gods,
   carrying off by force
   poor wretched victims come to plead.
Never could I see seize and snatch,
   entering territory of yours—
   not even if I had a more than royal right—
   unless whoever governed gave me leave for it.
I should know how a guest behaves on foreign soil.
But you, you dishonor your own city,
   so undeserving of disgrace.

Length of days has made you ripe in age
    but far from ripe in reason.
I have said it once, and I say it once again:
    restore those girls forthwith
    or you'll find your visit here prolonged by force—
    not quite according to your will.
This is no idle talk. I mean it every syllable.
CHORUS: Stranger, see what you've brought upon yourself!
By birth and race you ought to know much better.
CREON: Theseus, Son of Aegeus,
    I never thought your city was unmanned by men
    or drifting rudderless, as you suggest.
That never prompted what I did.
No, I merely took for granted
    that your people here
    were never so devoted to my family
    as to harbor one of them against my will
    and welcome here
    a parricide,
    a tainted man,
    a man discovered—oh, the filth of it!—
    both bridegroom and his own bride's son.
I took for granted that your famous Council
    on Ares' hill where Justice sits,
    would never in its wisdom let such reprobates
    roam at large within your land.
Convinced of this, I hunted down my prize.
And even then I might have let him go
    had he not heaped on me and all my clan
    the foulest imprecations.
I've stomached quite enough, I think,
    to justify reprisals.
Rage, remember, knows no age till death.
Nothing hurts the dead.
Well, do what you will.
Though right is on my side,
    what headway can I make alone?
I may be old, but I shall strain
    to counter every plan with counterplan.
OEDIPUS: Arrant monster!
On whom do you think these insults fall—

on my old head or yours?
Murder, incest, deeds of horror,
  you spew the lot at me:
  and all the lot I bore in misery,
  not through any choice of mine
  but through some scheme of heaven,
  long incensed, it seems,
  against some misdeed of our line.
Examine me apart from this
  and you will find no flaw to cavil at
  that might have drawn me so to floor
  my family and myself.

For tell me this:
  Suppose my father by some oracle was doomed to die
  by his own son's hand,
  could you justly put the blame on me—
  a babe unborn,
  not yet begotten by a father,
  not yet engendered in a mother's womb?
And if when born—as born I was to tragedy—
  I met my father in a fight and killed him,
  ignorant of what I did, to whom I did it,
  can you still condemn an unwilled act?

And my mother, your own sister, wretched man . . .
  since you're low enough to drag her in
  and force me to allude to it, I shall.
I'll not keep silent when your own lewd mouth
  has broken all the bonds of reticence. . . .
My mother, yes, she was my mother—what a fate!
I did not know. She did not know.
And to her shame she gave me children,
  children to the son whom she herself had given.

One thing I know:
  you vituperate by choice, both her and me,
  when not by choice I wedded her,
  and not by choice am speaking now.
Neither in this marriage, then,
  shall I be called to blame,

nor in the way my father died—
which you keep casting in my teeth.

Let me ask you this, one simple question:
If at this moment someone
   should step up to murder you,
   would you, godly creature that you are,
   stop and say, "Excuse me, sir, are you my father?"
Or would you deal with him there and then?
Ah! You love your life enough, I think,
   to turn on him,
   not look around to find a warrant first.

That precisely was the plight that heaven put me in.
My father's very soul, come back, would not say no.
But you, the unscrupulous wretch you are,
A man convinced that everything he says is fit to hear,
   who bawls out every secret thing,
You heap your slanders on me publicly,
   meanwhile making sure to bow and scrape
   before the name of Theseus, with flattery
   and compliments on how the state of Athens runs.
Very well, extol them to the skies, but don't forget,
   if there's any state that knows what true religion is,
   that state is this.
And yet it was here you tried to wrest
   a pleading worshiper away, an old man too,
   and have taken captive both my daughters.
Therefore I rest my case before these goddesses,
   lay siege to them in prayer,
   assail them for their help
   to fight for me, and manifest to you
   the caliber of men that guard this realm.
CHORUS: Sire, this stranger is an upright man:
   A woefully unlucky man and worthy of our aid.
THESEUS: Enough of talk!
The criminals are in full flight
   while we stand still discussing it.
CREON: I am helpless, then. What is it I must do?
THESEUS: My pleasure is
   that you yourself shall show the way

and I shall escort you
  to where the two missing girls are hidden.
But if your men have already hustled them away
  we shall spare ourselves the trouble
  and others will give chase and hunt your soldiers
                                          down,
  and none shall escape to thank their gods at home.

All right, lead off! And bear in mind,
  the looter has been looted,
  the trapper's in the trap,
  and stolen goods soon spoil.
Expect no help from your accomplice either.
Oh, yes, I'm well aware
  you did not push yourself
  to this pinnacle of daring,
  this reckless outrage,
  without some help or backing.
And I must look to it,
  not jeopardize my city for a single man.
Does this make sense?
Or do my warnings seem to you as vain
  as any scruples when you hatched your plan?
CREON: I shall not argue with you on your own terrain.
But once at home, I'll have my inspirations too.
THESEUS: Threaten away, but keep moving, please.
Oedipus, stay here in peace.
Rest happy in the pledge I give:
I'll have your daughters back, or I'll not live.
OEDIPUS: Bless you, Theseus, for your nobility;
  bless you for your loving care of me.

[CREON *is marched off by* THESEUS *and his men*]

SECOND CHORAL ODE

[*In a galloping meter, the elders excitedly follow the
chase in imagination, alluding to some of the most reli-
giously evocative centers dear to Athens, notably Apollo's
oracle at Delphi and Demeter's mystery-fraught shrine by
the sea at Eleusis. They also appeal to Pallas Athena,*

*patroness of Athens; to Poseidon, patron of horses and
ships; to Apollo, the supreme archer; and to his sister
Artemis, the supreme huntress*]

STROPHE I

Oh, to be there
  when the brigands at bay
  Turn to the clash
  of bronze on bronze
  Down by the Pythian shore
  Or the flaring sands
  of Eleusis where
  The Queens of the Night
  and their honey-voiced hymners
  Solemnly seal
  in tongues of gold
  The rites that bring blessings to man.

Ah! I think Theseus
  springs to the fight
  With presage of victory
  strong in his shout
  Soon to make safe
  two sisterly captives
  Still in our land.

ANTISTROPHE I

Or perhaps galloping
  onward they go
  To the western plains
  past rocky Oéa's
  Glens and snow-blanched sides.
Neck and neck in the race
  chariots flying
  Till Creon is worsted
  by terrible Ares
  And by Theseus'
  stalwart men.
Ah, flash of the harness,
  toss of the reins!
Thunder of chargers,

body of horsemen
Dear to Athena,
Queen of the horse,
Dear to Poseidon, ocean embracer,
fond son of Rhea.

Strophe II

The tussle is on
　Or just to begin
　A beautiful hope
tells us that soon
The two young women
are here returned,
　Cornered so cruelly
by an uncle so cruel.
Victory! Victory!
Zeus win the day!
Success in the struggle
　is what I foretell.
Oh, that my eyes—
　high over the battle—
Were the eyes of a dove
　that sails down the storm
And lifts to the passing cloud.

antistrophe II

All-seeing Zeus,
　all-ruling all,
　Let this country's
　guardians conquer.
Let them capture
　quarry and prize.
Grant, oh, grant it!
Your daughter too,
　Pallas Athena,
　Our Lady stern.
Grant it, Apollo!
Hunter who
　Beside his sister
　Artemis chases
　The light-footed moon-speckled

deer. Oh come!
Twin allies of this land and people.

[*As the strains of the Choral Ode die away, a member
of the* CHORUS *hurries back with a report*]

THIRD EPISODE

CHORUS MEMBER: Wanderer, look!
The forecast of our watchers was not false,
   for I see the girls returning under escort.
OEDIPUS: Where, where? What are you saying? . . .

[ANTIGONE *and* ISMENE *are led in by* THESEUS *and his*
SOLDIERS. ANTIGONE *runs forward*]

ANTIGONE: Father, Father!
I wish some god could give you eyes to see
   this princely man who has brought us back to you.
OEDIPUS: My child—it's you? Ah, both of you!
ANTIGONE: Both of us, saved by his strong arm:
   by Theseus and his gallant men.
OEDIPUS: Come to me, dear girls.
Let your father press you to his embrace—
   redeemed beyond all hope.
ANTIGONE: Beyond all hope! We could not ask for more.
OEDIPUS: But where—where are you?
ANTIGONE: Both here—hand in hand.
OEDIPUS: My own sweet darlings!
ANTIGONE: A father's favorites!
OEDIPUS: Dear props of my life!
ANTIGONE: And partners in pain.
OEDIPUS: My precious ones—ah, mine again!
If now I died they would not say
   he was altogether damned:
   he had his daughters with him in the end.
Press closer to me, each of you,
   don't let your father go.
Rest there from your late roaming,
   so cruel and so forlorn
   and tell me in a word what happened:

young girls need no speeches.
ANTIGONE: Father, our rescuer is here.
You should learn it all from him.
The credit is his.
There—my speech was short!
OEDIPUS: [*turning to where he thinks* THESEUS *is*] Sir, forgive me!
I cannot welcome them enough.
My children were lost. Now they are found.
And you are the one who brings this joy to me:
You rescued them, no man else besides.
The gods reward you far beyond my dreams:
    reward you and this blessed land
    where more than any other place on earth,
    among your people, I have found
    Reverence and honesty and lips that cannot lie.
These things I recognize and pay my homage to.
All that I have, I have through you and no man else.
Therefore, my king, give me your hand and let me touch
                                                    it.
And let me put a kiss upon your cheek.

[*He takes a step toward* THESEUS, *then checks himself*]

What am I saying?
What is this invitation that I make
    to handle me a man of sorrows, a temple of pollution?
No, no! Never let it be; even if you would!
Let my sufferings lodge with those tried souls
    who have drunk with me the bitter cup.
I salute you from afar.
Keep me always in your gentle care,
    as until this hour you have.
THESEUS: No, Oedipus, this is nothing strange:
    Your shower of words, your open heart, your joy.
Of course you had to greet your children first.
How could *that* fill me with dismay?
Besides, I'd rather furbish life with sparkling deeds than
                                                    words,
    as I have proved to you, good reverend sir,
    making perfect everything I pledged:

presenting you with daughters both redeemed,
and rescued from all menaces.
As to the manner of my victory,
and why should I enlarge on that?
They will tell you everything.
Meanwhile, some late news has come my way
and I should like your thoughts on it.
It hardly sounds to me important,
and yet it puzzles me.
There's nothing that a wise man should dismiss.
OEDIPUS: What is it, Son of Aegeus?
No news of anything has come to us.
THESEUS: They say a man, not from Thebes
and yet a relative of yours,
has unexpectedly appeared;
is prone in prayer before Poseidon's altar,
Where I was worshiping before I started here.
OEDIPUS: A man from where?
And what is his petition?
THESEUS: I only know he wants a word with you,
which will not cost you much.
OEDIPUS: Only a word, yet prostrate in petition?
THESEUS: Yes, he only wants to speak with you, they say,
then go his way in peace.
OEDIPUS: Who can this be, praying at the shrine?
THESEUS: Think of Argos, have you any kinsman there
who might ask a like request?
OEDIPUS: [*alarmed*] Dear friend, do not go on!
THESEUS: Why? What's the matter now?
OEDIPUS: Don't ask.
THESEUS: Don't ask you what? Explain.
OEDIPUS: Argos, you said. I know now who it is.
THESEUS: Someone I must hold at bay?
OEDIPUS: Sire, my son, my own detested son.
There's no man's voice I find so poisonous.
THESEUS: Give him a hearing at least.
If you don't like what he asks, you needn't grant it.
Where's the pain in that?
OEDIPUS: Hate, my king! Though he *is* my son.
Do not press me to give way.
THESEUS: I think you must. The man has come to plead.

You must not fail in reverence to the god.
ANTIGONE: Father, listen to me, young though I am.
Let the king's desire be honored
   and his conscience satisfied
   to give the gods their due.
And for our sakes too, let our brother come.
After all, whatever pain his words may give,
   he cannot wrench your will away.
And the sound of his voice—what damage can that do?
Besides, it's talk that best betrays the foul design.
You are his father,
   And even if his conduct plumbed the depths of
                       wickedness,
   that would never make it right for you, dear Father,
   to pay him back in kind.
So let him come!
Many a man is pricked to anger by a renegade son
   but yielding to advice more reasonable and loving,
   is coaxed from harshness back to gentleness.

Cast your thoughts on what has been,
   not what is now:
   All that your own father and mother caused you to
                       endure.
Ponder this, and the lesson that it teaches:
   catastrophic anger brings catastrophe.
Think no further
   than those two sightless sockets once your eyes.
Come, give way to us!
We should not have to plead for a cause so fair.
Can one who has just felt mercy's touch
   Then turn his back, not give as much?
OEDIPUS: Daughter, a hard-won joy you wring from me.
Well, have it as you wish.

[*He turns to* THESEUS]

But, oh, my friend, that man—if he must come—
   never let him put me in his power.
THESEUS: Enough! I've told you once, old man,
   no need to ask again;

nor shall I brag. But be sure of this:
Your life is safe while any god saves mine.

[THESEUS *departs with some of his* SOLDIERS, *leaving a contingent to guard* OEDIPUS]

THIRD CHORAL ODE

[*The elders, shaken by the wrangling and frustrations of two old men, dwell on the tragedy of life and the hopelessness of old age. The heavy trochaic and iambic beat measures out the sadness*]

STROPHE I

Where is the man who wants
More length of days?
Oh, cry it out.
There is a fool
His dawdling years
Are loaded down
His joys are flown
His extra time but trickles on
He awaits the Comforter
Who comes to all.
No wedding march
No dancing song:
A sudden vista down stark avenues
To Hades realms,
Then death at last.

ANTISTROPHE I

Not to be born has no compare
But if you are,
Then hurry hence,
For after that there is no better blessing.
When one has watched gay youth
Pack up his gallant gear
Vexations crowd without
And worries crowd within:
Envy, discord, struggles,

Shambles after battles
Till at last he too must have his turn
Of age, discredited and doddering:
Disaffected and deserted age
Confined with crabbedness
And every dismal thing.

EPODE

So are we senile—he and I:
Lashed from the north by wintry waves
Like some spume-driven cape on every side
Lashed by our agonies those constant waves
Breaking in from the setting sun
Breaking in from the dawn
Breaking in from the glare of noon
Breaking in from polar gloom.

FOURTH EPISODE

ANTIGONE: Father, I think I see our visitor approach.
He is alone. Tears are streaming from his eyes.
OEDIPUS: And who is he?
ANTIGONE: Exactly whom we thought.
It's Polyneices who has come.

[POLYNEICES *enters, advances, and stares aghast at his father and sisters*]

POLYNEICES: Oh, my sisters, I'm at a loss!
Shall I pour out tears for my own calamities
    or for this sorry sight—my decrepit father?
Just look at him:
    jettisoned with two poor girls
    in an alien land;
    arrayed in such unkempt and antique filth
    his own antiquity corrodes with it:
    his hair above his sightless eyes
    straggling out upon the breeze;
    and matching this, his beggars scrip
    with pittance for his wasted belly.

*   *   *

Ah, too late! I see it all too late.
I pronounce that this neglect of you
    brands me as the most delinquent thing on earth.
Yes, let me be the first to say it.
But, Father,
    Zeus himself sits mercy by his throne,
    so may you seat her near you too.
We can mend mistakes and not make more.

[*He pauses anxiously*]

You are silent.
Say something, Father, please.
Don't turn away from me.
Have you no reply?
Will you send me off in mute contempt?
Not even tell me what upsets you so?

[*He pauses again*]

You his daughters, my own sisters, please,
    try to move him from this dumb rigidity.
I must not be dismissed in shame
    without a word of hope
    from this blessed seat of appeal—
    the god's own sanctuary.

[OEDIPUS *turns his back.* ANTIGONE *steps towards* POLY-
NEICES *and touches his arm*]

ANTIGONE: Tell him yourself, my stricken brother,
    why it is you came.
Sometimes as words begin to flow,
    here they strike a spark of joy,
    there they fan up anger or bring a touch of tenderness,
    And anyhow, to the tongue-tied somehow give a
                                                    tongue.
POLYNEICES: Then I'll speak out, for you advise me well.
But first let me make it plain,
    the god I've called on for his help

is that very ocean god, Poseidon,
from whose suppliant shrine this country's king
has just now raised me up and let me come
with safe conduct to confer with you.
Therefore I would ask you gentlemen,
  my sisters here, and you my father,
  to respect my rights in this.

And now I'll tell you, Father, why I came.
I am driven out, banished from my native land
  because as eldest son
  I claimed my sovereign birthright to your throne.
But Eteocles, my younger brother, has cast me out:
  not by making good his claims,
  nor by proof of excellence,
  but by cajoling the city to his side.
It all seems part of the curse that dogs your line,
  and this the various oracles confirm.
So I went to Argos in the land of Doria,
  There took to wife the daughter of the king, Adrastus,
  and made a league
  of all the famous fighters of the Peloponnese
  to raise a seven-headed army aimed at Thebes
  and oust those from the realm who ousted me,
  or die in the attempt—die gloriously.

Well, then, what is my point in coming here?
To petition, Father:
  to lay our supplications at your feet,
  mine and all my allies,
  Who at this moment raise the standard of their seven
                                        spears
  and ring their seven armies round the plain of Thebes.
There's Amphiaraus, the hurricane spearsman,
  first at the spear, first at the reading of riddles.
Then the son of Oeneus: Tydeus of Aetolia.
Third comes Eteoclus, native of Argos.
Fourth, Hippomedon, sent by his father, Talaus.
Fifthly, Capaneus, swearing to mow down Thebes with
                                        fire.

Sixthly, Parthenopaeus, born in Arcadia, son of Atalanta,
   the ferocious virgin who finally wedded
   and became the mother of this stalwart boy.
And lastly, I, your son,
   or if not your son
   but the child of some appalling fate,
   then son at least in name.
I am the one who puts this fearless Argos in the field
   against the state of Thebes.

Father, will you listen to us, to all of us:
   we beg you for your daughters' and your own life's
                         sake.
Ease the harshness of your rage against me now:
   I who sally out to give this wretched brother chastise-
                         ment,
   the one who thrust me out and robbed me of my
                         home.
If there's any truth in prophecy,
   the oracles have said
   that victory lies with those
   who win you to their side.
So listen, Father,
   if you love our land
   with its springing fountains,
   its Theban deities.
Be persuaded by my prayers.
We are exiles, you and I,
   both of us are beggars.
We have to fawn on others for a home, you and I,
   both share a single destiny.
And all the time
   this creature kings it in our house.
Insufferable!
He ridicules us from his cushioned pride.
If you will only bless my scheme,
   I'll make short shrift of him and scatter him.
I'll bring you home again and reestablish you,
   and I shall be established too.
I'll make good this boast, if you make one with me.
I shall not live, if you'll not now agree.

CHORUS: Oedipus, for Theseus' sake who sent him here,
  you must not let him go without some reasonable
                                                reply.

OEDIPUS: You trustees of this realm,
  since Theseus sent him here
  and asked me to reply, I will.
Nothing less would let him hear my voice.
But now he shall be graced with it
  in accents that will bring him little joy.

[*He turns towards* POLYNEICES]

Liar!
When you held the scepter and the throne
  that your brother at the moment holds in Thebes,
  you drove me out,
  drove this your father out,
  displaced me from my city.
You are the reason for these rags—
  rags that make you cry to see,
  now that you have reached rock bottom too.
The season for condolences is past.
What I must bear must last as long as life,
  last in my thoughts of you as my destroyer.
Oh, yes, it's you that dragged me down!
You expelled me, you arranged
  that I should beg my daily bread.
But for my two girls
  I should not even be alive if left to you.
It's they who tend me, they preserve me.
They are the ones who play a man's and not a woman's
                                                part.

But you, you and your brother—bastards—
  are no sons of mine.

The eye of Fate is on you now.
Her glance is mild to what it soon shall be
  if once your armies march on Thebes.
Never shall you topple down that city.
Instead, you'll trip up headlong into blood,
  your brother too,

spattering each other.
Long ago I cursed you both,
    and now once more I summon up those curses,
    let them battle for me.
Let them teach you reverence
    for those that gave you birth.
Let them teach you what contempt is worth
    of an eyeless Father
    who had such worthless sons.

My daughters did not treat me so.
Therefore, if Justice is still seated
    side by side with Zeus
    in ancient and eternal sway,
    I consign to perdition
    your sanctimonious supplications
    and your precious throne.
So, leave my sight. Get gone and die:
    you trash—no son of mine.
Die,
    with these my curses
    ringing in your ears:
Never to flatten your motherland beneath your spear,
Never to set foot again in Argive's vales,
Instead you die,
    die by a brother's blow
    and make him dead by yours
    who drove you out.

That's my prayer for you.
I summon the pitchy gloom of Tartarus
    to gulp you down
    to a new paternal home.
I summon the holy spirits of this place.
I summon Ares the Destroyer,
    who whirled you into hatred and collision.
With these imprecations in your ears, get out.
Go publish them in Thebes.
Go tell your bellicose and trusty champions
    the will and testament
That Oedipus bequeaths to his two sons.

CHORUS: Polyneices,
　Never have your missions boded peace,
　nor do they now.
Go as quickly as you can.
POLYNEICES: How pitiful!
My pointless journey here!
My hopes in ruins!
My comrades all betrayed!
What an end
　to our proud marching out from Argos town!
And none of this dare I whisper to my allies
　to try to turn them back.
I cannot halt them in the silent march to doom.

[He turns to ANTIGONE *and* ISMENE]

But you, his little ones, my sisters,
　now you've heard our father's prayers,
　his prayers of hate, please,
　If ever they should come to bear their mortal fruit,
　and you be found in Thebes again,
　Then by all the gods,
　on that blessed chance, I beg:
　do not let my shade be damned
　but put me in the tomb with hallowed rites.
So shall you earn more praises from me dead
　than from that living father
　for all you did.
ANTIGONE: Polyneices, wait. One thing I ask.
POLYNEICES: Antigone, sweet sister, what?
ANTIGONE: Turn your army back to Argos now.
Do not destroy yourself and Thebes.
POLYNEICES: Impossible! Once seen to flinch,
　how could I put an army in the field again?
ANTIGONE: Again, my little brother?
What new madness could ever make you want to?
What can ruin of your native city gain?
POLYNEICES: Yes, but running from a younger brother,
　a laughingstock . . .
ANTIGONE: Ah, don't you see
　you'll make your father's prophecies come true:

a duel to the death—
the death of both of you?
POLYNEICES: That's what he wants. But I'll *not* give way.
ANTIGONE: Oh, I'm sick at heart!
And who will follow you once it's heard
    the future he has threatened?
POLYNEICES: It shan't be heard. I'll never say.
Good generals do not stress their weakness
    but their strength.
ANTIGONE: Your mind's made up? My poor misguided
                                                    boy!

[*She throws her arms around him*]

POLYNEICES: It is. So do not try to hold me back.
There is an avenue down which I go
    beckoned by my father's prayers
    and dark with Furies answering his call.
May Zeus reward you both
    for the obsequies you do for me
    when I am dead.
In life there's nothing left
    for you to tender me.
Now let me go. Good-bye!
You'll never gaze again into my living eye.

[*He gently releases himself from* ANTIGONE]

ANTIGONE: [*breaking down*] It breaks my heart!
POLYNEICES: Don't cry for me.
ANTIGONE: Oh, Polyneices, who would not cry to see
    you my brother hurrying to die?
POLYNEICES: If die I must, I'll die.
ANTIGONE: No, hear me—never you!
POLYNEICES: Don't press me uselessly.
ANTIGONE: Bereft of you, what is left for me?
POLYNEICES: The future is in Fortune's hands
    whether we live or die.
My prayer for both of you is this:
    Heaven keep you from every harm.
You deserve none. As all affirm.

[It would be characteristic of ISMENE, *who has re-
mained silent all this time, to have been rendered
speechless by her tears. She too now advances and
clings to her brother in a last farewell. After a moment,*
POLYNEICES *disengages himself and strides away. The
blind* OEDIPUS *has been standing by, mute as a stone]*

CHORAL ODE AND DIALOGUE

STROPHE I

CHORUS: So do we see fresh sorrows strike
    Fresh strokes of leaden doom
    From the old blind visitor
    Or is it Fate unfolding—
    Supernal in her workings which
    I dare not say can fail—
    Watched, yes, watched,
    By never-failing Time
    Shuffling fortunes from the top to bottom?

[A clap of thunder]

The sky is rift. Great Zeus, defend us!
OEDIPUS: Quick, children, oh, my children,
    send someone to bring Theseus here,
    that princely man.
ANTIGONE: Father, what should make you call him now?
OEDIPUS: That clap of thunder beating down from Zeus
    beckons me to Hades' realms.
So hurry, someone, hurry!

[Another peal of thunder, followed by lightning]

ANTISTROPHE I

CHORUS: Louder—hear it?—crashing down
    Divine report, dumb-striking sound
    Pricking up my hair with panic
    And shattering my soul.
There again! Light rips the sky
    I'm stricken to the core with fear.

Such a pregnant rush of light
  Never comes without some meaning
  Never not with monstrous issue
  Great awful sky! Great Zeus, oh, save us!

[*More thunder and lightning*]

OEDIPUS: Dear children, life is closing on me now:
  that predestined end from which there is no turning.
ANTIGONE: What makes you know? What signals do you
                                    have?

OEDIPUS: I am too well aware.
Oh, hurry to this country's king
  and fetch him here.

[*More thunder*]

STROPHE II

CHORUS: Ha! again, another crack
  shatters the air.
Come gently, you powers, oh, gently come
  if you must darken
  This earth our mother. Show us some pity,
  show us some clemency.
Though we have favored a stricken man
  hounded by destiny
  Zeus, our king, be kind!
OEDIPUS: Daughters, is he here yet?
Shall I be breathing still?
Still master of my mind?
ANTIGONE: What is so urgent on your mind to tell him?
OEDIPUS: The crowning gift I promised in return.
The blessing to repay him for all he's done.

[*More thunder and lightning*]

ANTISTROPHE II

CHORUS: Hurry, Theseus, my son, step down
  from altar and sacrifice:
  Even from worship in the deep of the grove
  at Poseidon's shrine.

Don't tarry, don't linger, oh, King, for the stranger
    brings city and people
    A grace to reward you, a sovereign blessing
    for all you have done.
Theseus, Lord, come quickly!

[*With another peal of thunder and lightning,* THESEUS
bursts in]

THESEUS: What, another summons?
Guest and people joined
    In general clamor!
Bolts from Zeus
    And catapults of hail!
All's possible when God
    Hurls down such a storm.

[*End of Choral Ode and Dialogue*]

OEDIPUS: King, how glad I am to see you come!
Some god has surely smoothed your way to us.
THESEUS: What is it now, Son of Laius?
OEDIPUS: The balance of my life is tilting.
I must not die a debtor:
    my bargain barren still
    with you and with your city.
THESEUS: What signs declare to you the end is near?
OEDIPUS: This rolling thunder rolled,
    this shuttled light.
The fulminating bolts
    of unanswerable artillery.
THESEUS: And I believe.
You never did foreshadow falsely.
Declare what we must do.

[*With great solemnity,* OEDIPUS *draws* THESEUS *aside*]

OEDIPUS: Come, listen, Son of Aegeus.
I lay before you now a city's lasting treasure.
There is a place where I must die.
And I myself unhelped shall walk before you there.

That place you must not tell to any living being:
  not where it lurks, not where the region lies,
  if you would have a shield like a thousand shields
  and a more perpetual pact than the spears of allies.

No chart of words shall mark that mystery.
Alone you'll go, alone your memory
  shall frame the spot.
For not to any person here,
  not even to my daughters so beloved,
  am I allowed to utter it.
You yourself must guard it always.
And when your life is drawing to its close,
  divulge it to your heir alone
  and he in turn to his, and so forever.

This way you will keep your city safe
  against the Dragon's seed, the men of Thebes,
  though many a state attack a peaceful home,
  though sure be the help from heaven (but exceeding
                                                    slow)
  against earth's godless men and men gone mad.
Be far from you such fate, good Son of Aegeus!
But all this you know without my telling you.

[OEDIPUS' *face lights up as if inspired. With slow, firm
steps he moves forward*]

Now to that spot. The god within me calls.
Let us go forward and linger here no more.
Come, beloved daughters, follow!
Follow this new leader guiding you:
  the father once you guided.

[ANTIGONE *and* ISMENE *attempt to assist him*]

No, no, hands off! Let me walk my way
  without a prop toward my holy hidden tomb
  where the promised earth of Attica will cover me.
This way, this way—come!

For this way Hermes beckons me,
   and Persephone, mistress of the dead.

[*He turns his blind eyes up toward the sun*]

Farewell! Farewell! You blindfold light
   once light of mine,
   last vision felt in darkness.
I walk to Hades now
   to close my life in shade.

[*Turning to* THESEUS]

Most gentle friend,
   heaven bless you, bless your land and yours.
And in prosperity remember me, the dead,
   That every grace abiding be ever on your head.

[OEDIPUS *moves slowly into the grove, followed by*
THESEUS, ANTIGONE, *and* ISMENE. *The* CHORUS *watches
until they are out of sight*]

FOURTH CHORAL ODE

[*The* CHORUS *sings a "Requiescat in pace"* addressed to
Persephone and Hades, the queen and king of the underworld, and also to the Furies. Even Cerberus, the fierce
three-headed hound that guards the portals of the dead,
is not left out of their appeal*]

STROPHE

Dare we adore the unseen queen
   And you night's children's king?
Then Aidoneus, listen, Aidoneus:
   Not in pain and lamentation
   May his death knell ring—
   This stranger passing down
   Through palisades of gloom
   Toward those prairies of the dead

*Let him rest in peace (as from the requiem mass).

His stygian home.
Much did he suffer
    much beyond deserts.
Let the finger of God's fairness
    Raise him now.

ANTISTROPHE

You goddesses or worlds deep down
    And you untamed hulk of snarling hound
    Watching, they say, the gates of hell
    For those arriving at the gaping maw
    Of Hades' pit . . . Oh, let him pass.
And Death, you son of Earth, and Tartarus
    Muzzle the cur, so Cerberus
    Shall not molest the lonely path
    Of Oedipus, who walks
    Toward those sunken
    Meadows of the dead.
O Death, bestow on him eternally
    Eternal rest.

[*After a pause, a* MESSENGER *appears at the entrance of the grove*]

FIFTH EPISODE

EXODOS

MESSENGER: Fellow citizens,
    I could cut this story short and say:
    "Oedipus is gone."
    But what was done was not done shortly,
    and my story breaks away from brevity.
CHORUS: So the man of destiny has gone?
MESSENGER: Gone. Has left this life behind.
CHORUS: But did he have a blest demise all free from
                                                pain?
MESSENGER: It was extraordinary, most marvelous.
You yourselves saw how he went:
    unled by those he loved, but walking on
    and showing us the way.
And when he'd reached that yawning orifice

where steps of brass sink rooting down,
he halted by the many branching ways
where Theseus is remembered for his famous pact
with Peiritheus to raid the underworld
and bring Persephone back. And there,
he stood at the chasm
Halfway between that basin and the slab of Thoricus,
By the old wild pear tree's hollow trunk and the mar-
ble tomb.
Then, sitting down, he undid his squalid dress,
and calling for his daughters bade them fetch
water to wash with from the spring
and some to pour in ritual for the dead.

So the women went to Demeter's hill in front of them
(that goddess of unfolding spring),
and soon had done all their father had enjoined;
Then bathed and tended him and dressed him fittingly.
And when he was content that all was done,
with nothing further he could wish,
there came a grumbling sound from Zeus' underworld.
It shook the girls with trembling, and they fell
weeping at their father's knees.
Nor would they stop, but beat their breasts and sobbed.
And when he heard this bitter burst of grief,
he took them in his arms and said:
"This day, my daughters,
you shall have no father left to you,
For all my life is done,
your double burden of me done.
It was not easy, children, *that* I know,
and yet one little word can change all pain:
That word is LOVE, and love you've had from me
more than any man can ever give.
But now you must live on, when I am gone."

So did the three of them cling to one another
calling out and crying
until at last they came to the end of tears,
and sobs gave out and all was still.

*   *   *

Then in that stillness suddenly a voice was heard,
    terrifying: their hair stood up with fear.
The voice of the god it was, calling out and calling:
    "Oedipus, Oedipus, why do we delay?
You stay too long—too long you stay."
And when he knew it was the god that called,
    he craved King Theseus to draw near,
    and when he had he said to him:
    "Dear friend, put out your hand,
    my children, put yours here.
Now swear you never will abandon them
    but wisely further all their needs
    as friendship and the time will tell."
And Theseus, noble that he is, holding back his tears,
    swore to keep his promise to his friend.

As soon as this was done,
    Oedipus, groping for his daughters with blind hands,
    said: "Sweet children, now be brave,
    as you were born to be, and leave this place.
Do not ask to see what you should not see
    or hear what you should not hear.
But go at once.
Only Theseus has the right to stay
    and see what now unfolds."

Such was his converse. We heard it all of us.
So, sobbing with the girls, we left.
But after a little while, some paces off,
    we glanced around
    and Oedipus was nowhere to be seen
    but only the king,
    holding up his hands to screen his eyes
    as if he had beheld a vision—
    one too dazzling for a mortal's sight.
Then presently we saw him hail the earth and sky
    in one great prayer.

[*The* MESSENGER *pauses*]

How Oedipus has passed, no man shall ever tell,
  no man but Theseus.
For in that hour no white-hot thunderbolt from Zeus
                             came down,
  no surge of giant sea to take him.
Some emissary maybe from heaven came;
  or was the adamantine floor of the dead
  gently reft for him with love?
The passing of the man was pangless
  with no trace of pain nor any loud regret.
It was of mortal exits the most marvelous.
But if you think that none of this makes sense,
  I am content to go on talking nonsense.
CHORUS: Where are the girls and their escort now?
MESSENGER: Not far away,
  for I hear the sound of sobbing.

[ANTIGONE *and* ISMENE, *escorted by a solemn company
of* ATTENDANTS, *slowly walk into view*]

FOURTH CHORAL DIALOGUE

[*Which lasts until the end of the play*]

STROPHE I
ANTIGONE: Cry, cry, and cry again!
Our cause is too complete:
  Two sisters and their sire
  Stained to the core.
Oh, oh, tears for the spellbound blood!
We lived his long-drawn life of pain
  Until this dazing hour
  This last suffering
  His ineffable demise.
CHORUS: What took place?
ANTIGONE: We can only guess.
CHORUS: So he is gone?
ANTIGONE: Gone as you would wish.
No bloody war,
  No deep sea caught him up,
  But he was plucked

By some unseen design:
  Rapt to the land of blind horizons.
And now a deathlike night
  Has blanketed our vision.
In distant lands, over drifting seas,
  How shall we live our bitter living?
ISMENE: I know not how.
Come, blood-dripping Death,
  And carry me down
  And lay me by my ancient father's side.
So should I miss
  The unlivable life to come.
CHORUS: Dear children, stop your tears,
  You best of daughters.
Such is our end that heaven sends us
  And Fate is our friend.

ANTISTROPHE I

ANTIGONE: Ah! What was pain was joy
  What lacked all love was love
  When I had him in my arms.
Father, my father,
  Wrapped in perpetual gloom
  In that territory of shade—
Not even there shall her
  love and mine
  Be barred from you.
CHORUS: So his work is done?
ANTIGONE: He had his wish.
CHORUS: His wish?
ANTIGONE: He wished to die on foreign soil
  He did:
  His bed beneath the mantle
  Of the gentle dark,
  His aftermath of mourning
  Rich in tears.
Oh, Father, yes,
  I cannot stanch their flow,
  It is a flood of sorrow . . .
  To die on foreign soil,
  You wanted that, but, ah,

So far away from me!
ISMENE: Poor dear sister,
  With Father gone forever
  What fate remains for you and me?
CHORUS: Dear children, think of this—
  He made a blessed end.
So cease your crying.
There's none alive
  That's free from trial.

STROPHE II

ANTIGONE: Dearest, let's go back there.
ISMENE: What ever for?
ANTIGONE: I'm gripped with sudden longing.
ISMENE: What?
ANTIGONE: To see his hidden home.
ISMENE: Whose home?
ANTIGONE: Our father's.
ISMENE: It is forbidden. And also, don't you see . . .
ANTIGONE: Why this reluctance?
ISMENE: But don't you see . . .
ANTIGONE: I do not, go on.
ISMENE: He has no tomb.
He died away from all of us.
ANTIGONE: Then take me there and kill me too.
ISMENE: And leave me helpless and deserted,
  dragging out my hopeless life alone?

ANTISTROPHE II

CHORUS: Bear up, dear girls, take heart!
ISMENE: But where, oh, where
  is there left to go?
CHORUS: There is a place . . .
ISMENE: But where?
CHORUS: Here. Nothing shall molest you here.
ISMENE: That I know.
CHORUS: Then what is on your mind?
ISMENE: We can't go home to Thebes.
CHORUS: Don't even try.
ISMENE: How terrible!
CHORUS: It always was.

ISMENE: No, worse
  than the worst before.
CHORUS: I know, a surge of sorrow
  sweeps over you.
ISMENE: Oh, where are we to turn, great Zeus?
What hope, what destiny to drive us on,
  and what the use?

[*End of strophic pattern but not of Choral Dialogue.*
  THESEUS *and his escort enter*]

THESEUS: Weep no more, sweet women.
Where death has dealt so kindly
  There is no room for sorrow
  or nemesis will follow.
ANTIGONE: Good Son of Aegeus, we beg you . . .
THESEUS: Daughters, for what favor?
ANTIGONE: Let these eyes of ours regard
  our father's place of resting.
THESEUS: That may not be.
ANTIGONE: But you are king of Athens. Why?
THESEUS: Because, dear children,
  he himself has charged me
  not to let a mortal being
  approach these hallowed precincts
  or invade with prayers and voices
  his sanctuary of quiet.
And if I keep this covenant,
  he said I keep my country
  free from every hurt.
The gods' ears heard these pledges
  And Zeus the god of treaties,
  the all-seeing god, has sealed it.
ANTIGONE: Then if his wish be this,
  enough for us. So be it.
But send us back to Thebes:
  Thebes our ancestral city.
There we must try to stem
  the bloodbath of our brothers.
THESEUS: Why, so I shall,
  and spare no pains

to gladden you and grace his tomb:
the dauntless dead so lately swept away.
CHORUS: Come, then, cease your crying
  Keep tears from overflowing
  All's ordained past all denying.

ANTIGONE

———

ΑΝΤΙΓΟΝΗ

I once got into trouble at St. John's College, Santa Fe, when, giving a talk titled "Three Formidable Women: Clytemnestra, Medea, and Antigone," I attempted to lighten the heavy pall of Greek tragedy after a full-length lecture on its remorseless doom by wondering if any of these ladies would make a suitable wife for my twenty-year-old son. Not Clytemnestra, I said: she murdered her husband. Not Medea, either: no young man could survive her fury if she caught him looking at a pair of pretty legs. As to Antigone, the effort required to match her nobility and strength would wear him down as surely as water dripping on stone.

Well, I was punished for my flippancy. A bevy of alert young females rounded on me. This was not what they expected of a visiting scholar, they said. This was not the stuff of academic learning. A telephone call was put through to St. John's sister college in Annapolis, canceling my appearance there to give a talk on Sappho.

Looking back on all this after some twenty-two years, I smile at it but stick to my guns, especially when it comes to Antigone. Her courage and intransigence are indeed marvelous when she defies Creon and ventures forth to bury her brother Polyneices.

She will forever be a symbol of the rights of the individual ranged against authoritarian power. But we must ask: has Creon no rights as well? Of course he has if the balance is to be kept between personal freedom and law and order: a balancing act indeed! There will always be the martinet, and always the martyr.

As to Haemon, Creon's son and betrothed to Antigone, he too will be a symbol: a symbol of the passionate youth who breaks with his father and chooses to die rather than live without the one he loves.

I have always regarded the opening of *Antigone* as a masterpiece of audial design. Sophocles, by the sheer power of sound, establishes in the first six lines the emotions of fear, anger, and pity that will dominate the play. The fear is for herself; the anger is against fate that has so hounded the House of Oedipus; and the pity is for her two brothers, who died fighting each other.

I have transcribed the Greek sounds into English as nearly as I can, without, of course, being able to capture the rich play of pitch against stress. One thing to beware of is the suggestion that we have no idea what ancient Greek sounded like. We do. In the last fifty years brilliant detective work has been done on the sound of classical Greek by eminent scholars, and it is safe to say that we know within 90 percent what that Greek sounded like.

I may be told that in the following transcription of Greek sounds into English I have not been careful enough in keeping to the quantities, that is, to the relative length of vowel sounds. My answer is that quantity is a theoretical value and must cede to the natural value of a vowel or word when pitted against it. This is true of Greek, Latin, French, and even English. We do not, for instance say:

The boy st&ocaron;od &omacron;n th&emacron; burn&imacron;ng d&emacron;ck

though the meter requires it; we say:

The b&omacron;y stood &ocaron;n th&emacron; burn&imacron;ng d&emacron;ck

If one reads the following transcription several times until it becomes fluent, the three dominant emotions I singled out will reveal themselves. Yes, all within the first six lines.

O&hbreve; k&omacron;in&ocaron;n &omacron;utadelf&omacron;n &Imacron;smăyn&amacron;ys kăr&amacron;
ăr &omacron;isth h&ocaron;tt&imacron; Zeus t&omacron;ne ăp &Omacron;idipou kăkone
h&ocaron;po&imacron;&ocaron;n &omacron;uki none &ebreve;t&imacron; sowez&amacron;in t&ebreve;lay
oud&ebreve;n gar &omacron;ute ălg&amacron;in&ocaron;n &omacron;ut ătays ăter
oŭt &amacron;iskr&ocaron;n &omacron;ut ătee&macron;m&ocaron;n esth h&ocaron;po&imacron;&ocaron;n &omacron;u
T&omacron;ne sone t&ebreve; kăm&omacron;ne &omacron;uk h&ocaron;pope &ebreve;go kăkone.

* * *

ᾧ κοινὸν αὐτάδελφον Ἰσμήνης κάρα,
ἆρ' οἶσθ' ὅ τι Ζεὺς τῶν ἀπ' Οἰδίπου κακῶν
ὁποῖον οὐχὶ νῷν ἔτι ζώσαιν τελεῖ;
οὐδὲν γὰρ οὔτ' ἀλγεινὸν οὔτ' ἄτης ἄτερ
οὔτ' αἰσχρὸν οὔτ' ἄτιμόν ἐσθ', ὁποῖον οὐ
τῶν σῶν τε κἀμῶν οὐκ ὄπωπ' ἐγὼ κακῶν.

Antigone

The character of Antigone is not as straightforward
and simple as it seems. Although she represents the ultimate in single-mindedness and dedication to her dead
brother, Polyneices, she is not without a certain self-
glorification in her stance against Creon. Moreover, on
the way to the living tomb in which Creon incarcerates
her she gives vent to a veritable litany of self-pity. Nevertheless, she is a genuine martyr, consumed by the mad-
dening idealism that makes martyrs such a nuisance to
authority. She is not merely willing but eager to fight
injustice to the death.

Ismene

In Ismene Sophocles creates the perfect foil to her
sister, Antigone. She is everything that Antigone is not:
soft, gentle, and preferring peace at all costs to confron-
tation. But she is also loyal and willing to sacrifice herself
if need be to support her sister. She is a character of
pathos rather than of tragedy.

Creon

Creon, for his part, on his first day as king of Thebes,
is properly concerned about the city, reeling from the
devastating turmoil of the civil war: a war caused by
Oedipus' two sons, Eteocles and Polyneices. Order must
be restored at once, even if it means jettisoning his own
niece, Antigone. He has just made an uncompromising
speech expatiating on the need for an unswerving authority if the realm is to be saved, and like all basically

weak men he must not be seen to change his mind. He lacks the statesmanship and courage to lose face if that is the right thing to do. He, rather than Antigone, becomes the protagonist of the play, and so subtle is Sophocles' handling of his character that before the end, by a twist that is almost undetectable, one finds oneself near tears—not for Antigone but for Creon.

Haemon

It is sometimes said that romantic love is a relatively modern aberration, dependent more on feeling than on suitability. Nothing could be further from the truth. There are countless stories of love in classical times: witness *Daphnis and Chloe* (the first novel), and Helen of Sparta and Paris, and Antony and Cleopatra. Witness the whole cult of Aphrodite and the fact that there were three words for "love" in Greek, one of them being *eros,* which means precisely romantic passion.

Be that as it may, there is no doubt that Haemon and Antigone were in love. When his father, Creon, shows that he is appalled and will in nowise be shifted from his determination to do away with Antigone, the young man retorts that if he cannot be united with his beloved in life, then let it be in death, and he flies off with that bitter threat.

Tiresias appears and tells Creon that if he wants to save his son he must act fast and release Antigone. When the king and his attendants hurry to the vault where Antigone has been entombed, he finds his son leaning on the dead body of Antigone, who has hanged herself. Haemon lunges at his father, then plunges the sword into himself and dies hugging his beloved. In the Messenger's words:

Corpse wrapped in love with corpse he lies,
married not in Life but Hades.

Tiresias

If one remembers that *Antigone* was written sixteen years before *Oedipus,* it is easy to see in Tiresias' speech the genesis of the warning Sophocles was later to put into his mouth when he confronts the headstrong king: a warning that Creon heeds but Oedipus does not.

Eurydice

Similarly, the portrait of Eurydice looks very like a first shot at the character of Jocasta: a caring woman driven to suicide by the enormity of the disaster before her: in Eurydice's case news of the death of her son, Haemon. Her demise and Haemon's are what finally breaks the spirit of Creon and turns the authoritative and defiant king of Thebes into a shambling wreck.

Sophocles would have been in his middle fifties when he wrote *Antigone,* with many of his 123 plays behind him. It is sometimes said to be his 32nd play in order of production. If Sophocles won first prize at the Dionysia in 438 B.C. (and it seems that he did), there is high probability that *Antigone* was one of his three plays, and it must have been written between 442 and 441.

Antigone was produced in Athens sometime after 441 B.C., and though the last play of the *Oedipus* "trilogy," it was written first—some thirty to thirty-four years before *Oedipus at Colonus* and sixteen years before *Oedipus the King.* It probably belongs to Sophocles' middle period, and he would have been about fifty-five.

CHARACTERS

ANTIGONE, daughter of Oedipus and sister of Polyneices and Eteocles
ISMENE, sister of Antigone
CHORUS of citizens of Thebes
CREON, king of Thebes and uncle of Antigone and Ismene
SENTRY
HAEMON, son of Creon and betrothed to Antigone
TIRESIAS, a blind prophet
EURYDICE, wife of Creon and mother of Haemon
FIRST MESSENGER
GUARDS

LADIES-IN-WAITING
BOY

TIME AND SETTING

After the death of Oedipus, his two sons contend for
the throne of Thebes. Polyneices, leading the Seven
Champions, attacks from Argos and batters at the seven
gates of Thebes. Eteocles defends the city, supported by
Creon, who appears to have been acting as regent. In a
great battle the two brothers meet face-to-face and kill
each other. The Argive forces retreat. It is the morning
after the battle. The dead still lie on the field, including
Polyneices and Eteocles. Creon, once again the undis-
puted master of Thebes, proclaims that Polyneices, because he died fighting against his own city, shall be left
to rot on the battlefield—the most ignominious of ends
for any Greek. Antigone, caught in a conflict of loyalties,
to her dead brother and to the State, decides to defy
Creon's edict. It is daybreak. She calls her sister out
from the palace.

PROLOGUE

ANTIGONE: Come, Ismene, my own dear sister, come!
What more do you think could Zeus require of us
    to load the curse that's on the House of Oedipus?
There is no sorrow left, no single shame,
    no pain, no tragedy,
    which does not hound us, you and me, towards our
                                                    end.
And now,
    what's this promulgation that they say
    our ruler has made to all the state?
Do you know? Have you heard?
Or are you sheltered from the news
    that deals a death blow to our dearest?
ISMENE: Our dearest, Antigone? I've heard no news
    either good or bad,
    ever since we two were stripped
    of two brothers in a single day,

Each dismissing each by each other's hand.
And since the Argive army fled last night,
   I've heard no more—either glad or sad.
ANTIGONE: That's what I thought,
   that's why I've brought you here beyond the gates
   that you may hear my news alone.
ISMENE: What mischief are you hinting at?
ANTIGONE: I think you know . . . Our two dear brothers:
   Creon is burying one to desecrate the other.
Eteocles, they say, he has dispatched with proper rites
   as one judged fit to pass in glory to the shades.
But Polyneices, killed as piteously,
   an interdict forbids that anyone should bury him
   or even mourn.
He must be left unwept, unsepulchered,
   a vulture's prize,
   sweetly scented from afar.
That's what they say our good and noble Creon plans:
   plans for you and me, yes, me;
   And now he's coming here to publish it and make it
                          plain
   to those who haven't heard.
Anyone who disobeys will pay no trifling penalty
   but die by stoning
   before the city walls.
There's your chance to prove your worth,
   or else a sad degeneracy.
ISMENE: You firebrand! Could I do a thing
   to change the situation as it is?
ANTIGONE: You could. Are you willing
   to share danger and suffering and . . .
ISMENE: Danger? What are you scheming at?
ANTIGONE: . . . take this hand of mine to bury the dead?
ISMENE: What! Bury him and flout the interdict?
ANTIGONE: He is my brother still, and yours;
   though you would have it otherwise,
   but I shall not abandon him.
ISMENE: What! Challenge Creon to his face?
ANTIGONE: He has no right to keep me from my own.
ISMENE: Sister, please, please!
Remember how our father died:

hated, in disgrace,
self-dismantled in horror of himself,
his own hand stabbing out his sight.
And how his mother-wife in one
twisted off her earthly days with cord;
And thirdly how our two brothers in a single day
each achieved for each a suicidal nemesis.
And now, we two are left.
Think how much worse our end will be than all the rest
if we defy our sovereign's edict and his power.
Remind ourselves that we are women
and as such are not made to fight with men.
For might unfortunately is right
and makes us bow to things like this and worse.
Therefore shall I beg the shades below
to judge me leniently as one who kneeled to force.
It's madness to meddle.
ANTIGONE: I will not press you anymore.
I would not want you as a partner if you asked.
Go to what you please. I go to bury him.
How beautiful to die in such pursuit!
To rest loved by him whom I have loved,
sinner of a holy sin,
With longer time to charm the dead than those who
live,
for I shall abide forever there.
So go. And please your fantasy
and call it wicked what the gods call good.
ISMENE: You know I don't do that.
I'm just not made to war against the state.
ANTIGONE: Make your apologies!
I go to raise a tomb above my dearest brother.
ISMENE: You foolhardy thing! You frighten me.
ANTIGONE: Don't fear for me. Be anxious for yourself.
ISMENE: At least tell no one what you do, but keep it
dark,
and I shall keep it secret too.
ANTIGONE: Oh, tell it, tell it, shout it out!
I'd hate your silence more than if you told the world.
ISMENE: So fiery—in a business that chills!
ANTIGONE: Perhaps, but I am doing what I must.

ISMENE: Yes, more than must. And you are doomed to
fail.
ANTIGONE: Why, then, I'll fail, but not give up before.
ISMENE: Don't plunge into such a hopeless enterprise.
ANTIGONE: Urge me so, and I shall hate you soon.
He, the dead, will justly hate you too.
Say that I'm mad, and madly let me risk
The worst that I can suffer and the best:
A death that martyrdom can render blest.
ISMENE: Go then, if you must toward your end:
Fool, wonderful fool, and loyal friend.

[ISMENE *watches* ANTIGONE *walk away, then she goes
into the palace*]

ENTRY ODE

[*The* CHORUS *in a march-dance files into the theater, singing a hymn of triumph. They celebrate the defeat of the
invading Polyneices and the victory of Thebes over Argos*]

STROPHE I
CHORUS: Sunshaft of the sun
Most resplendent sun
That ever shone on Thebes
The Seven Gates of Thebes:
Epiphany, you broke
Eye of the golden day
Marching over Dirce's streams
At dawn to drive in headlong flight
The warrior who came with shields
All fulminant as snow
In Argive stand at arms
Scattered now before the lancing sun.
LEADER: Propelled against our land
By Polyneices's claims
This screaming eagle circled round
Caparisoned with arms he swooped
His wings their shields of snow. His crest
Their helmets in the sun.

ANTISTROPHE I

CHORUS: He stooped above our towers,
   Gaped above our gates,
   His hungry spears hovered
   Then before he gorged
   And glutted on our blood
   Before Hephaestus hot
   With pitch and flame had seized
   Our crown of towers, all the din
   That Ares loves burst around
   Their rear, and panic turned
   His flank. The fight came on
   Behind their backs: a dragon-breathing foe.
LEADER: The braggart's pompous tongue
   Is hated most by Zeus,
   And seeing them advance superb
   In clank of gold, he struck their first
   Man down with fire before he yelled
   Triumph from the walls.

STROPHE II

CHORUS: Thundering down to the ground with his torch
   Knocked from his hands, this bacchanalian
   Passionate lunatic breathing out hate
   In hurricanes, fell in a flaming arc
   His brandished torch all quenched, and great
   Ares like a war horse wheeled:
   Ubiquitous his prancing strength
   Trampling in the dust
   Havoc that he dealt with several dooms.
LEADER: Seven champions dueled
   With seven at the Seven
   Gates and gave their panoplies
   To Zeus, save two, the fatal two
   Who sharing parents shared their fall,
   Brother killing brother.

ANTISTROPHE II

CHORUS: But now that this triumph, the loudest of
                       triumphs,

Oh, joy-bearing triumph! has come to our Thebes
The proud city of chariots, why
Now let us chase the memory far
Away of the wars that are blessedly past.
Come call on the gods with song and with dance
All through the night at the groves and the shrines,
And Bacchus shall lead the round—
Shouting and shaking all Thebes with his revels.

LEADER: But look who comes, the lucky
Son of Menoeceus:
The man the gods have made our king.
What new vicissitudes of state
Vex him now? Why has he sent
A herald to our summons?

[CREON *has entered from the palace, surrounded by soldiers. He addresses the* CHORUS]

FIRST EPISODE

CREON: Gentlemen, the gods have graciously
steadied our ship of state, which storms
have terribly tossed.
And now I have called you here privately
because of course I know
your loyalty to the House of Laius.
How again, when Oedipus was king,
your duty never faltered,
and when he fell you still upheld his sons.
But now that they have gone,
sharing their double end on a single day,
(mutual murder, mutual recompense!),
I nearest in line enjoy the scepter and the throne.

Now, naturally, there is no way
to tell the character and mettle of a man
until you've seen him govern.
Nevertheless, I want to make it plain:
I am the kind of man who can't and never could
abide the tongue-tied ruler who through fear
backs away from sound advice.

And I find intolerable the man who puts his country
    second to his friends.
For instance, if I saw ruin and danger
    heading for the state,
    I would speak out.
Never could I make my country's enemy my private
                                                friend,
    knowing as I do,
    she is the good ship that bears us safe.

So there you have my principles by which I govern.
In accord with them, I made the proclamation
    that you heard just now:
    Eteocles, who died in arms for Thebes,
    shall have a glorious funeral
    as befits a hero going to join the noble dead.
But his brother, Polyneices,
    he who came from exile breathing fire
    against this city of his fathers and its shrines;
    The man who came all thirsting for his country's blood
    to drag the rest of us away as slaves—
    I've sent the edict out
    that none shall bury him or even mourn.
He must be left all ghastly where he fell,
    a corpse for dogs to maul and vultures pick his bones.

You see the kind of man I am!
You'll not catch me putting traitors up on pedestals
    beside the loyal and true.
I'll honor him alone, alive or dead, who honors Thebes.
LEADER: Your disposition is quite clear,
    Son of Menoeceus, Creon,
    touching friend or enemy of this our city.
We know you have the power, too,
    to wreak your will upon the living and the dead.
CREON: Then see to it my injunctions are performed.
LEADER: Put the burden on some younger men.
CREON: No. Sentries are already posted on the corpse.
LEADER: Then what exactly do you want us to do?
CREON: Merely see there's no infringements of the law.
LEADER: No man is mad enough to welcome death.

CREON: And death it is. But greed of gain
    has often made men fools.

[*A* SENTRY, *disheveled and distraught, comes bumbling
in towards the king*]

SENTRY: King, I won't pretend I come at breakneck speed,
    all out of breath.
I kept on stopping in my tracks . . . to think . . .
    and turning back.
I held committee meetings with myself:
    "You fool," I said,
    "you're 'eading straight for the lion's mouth,"
    then, "Blockhead, what're you waiting for?
If Creon gets the news from someone else, you're done!"
So I've come scurrying at a snail's pace
    by the long shortcut,
    the "forward" voice in charge.
And 'ere I am, with a tale to tell that makes no sense,
    which any'ow I'll tell, cos I do believe
    nothing bad can 'appen that isn't on one's ticket.
CREON: Come to the point, man! What are you dithering
                           about?
SENTRY: First, sir, if I may slip in a word about meself.
It in't me that done it,
    and I dunno who darned done it, neither;
    so it in't fair to make me take the rap.
CREON: Done it? Done it? You're a great marksman—
    hit the target first time!
You must have something very odd to say.
SENTRY: It's awfully off-putting, sir, to bring bad news—
    especially to you, sir.
CREON: Then get on with it and go.
SENTRY: Right! I'll tell you straight. The body—it's bur-
                        ied like.
I mean someone's just gorne and sprinkled dust on it—
    right proper thirsty dust—and gorne . . .
    done the ritual, sir, you see.
CREON: What are you saying, man? Who would have
                         dared?

SENTRY: Don't ask me, sir!
There ain't no mark of pick or mattock,
  ground's all 'ard, unbroken,
  no wheel tracks neither:
  Not a sign of 'uman 'hands.
When the sentry of the morning watch pointed to it,
  there it was at dawn, the corpse,
  an ugly mystery that struck us dumb.
T'weren't exactly buried,
  just sprinkled with earth, ritual like
  as if someone wanted to set it free.
No marks of dog or jackal neither—not a scratch.
Then we flew at one another, guard accusing guard.
It came near to blows.
There weren't no clue to end the quarrel.
Any one of us coulda done it. See!
No evidence to disprove any one of us—not a shred.
So we dared one another to pick up red-'ot iron,
  walk through fire, and swear by all the gods
  He neither done the deed nor 'ad the slightest inkling
                                          who 'ad.
Well, one of us cut through the deadlock, saying . . .
  (We went weak as straws when we 'eard it,
  cos there weren't no denying,
  nor coming out of it in one piece neither):
  This fella there and then blurts out: "We gotta tell the
                                          king.
There ain't no way to cover up."
He convinced the lot of us, so we drew straws.
And 'oo should be the unlucky one to win the prize
  but yours truly.
So 'ere I am, unwelcome *I* can tell, and un'appy too,
  For there ain't no one likes the bringer of bad news.
LEADER: Sire, I've had misgivings from the first:
  could this be more than purely natural work?
CREON: Enough! You make me furious with such senile,
                                          doddering remarks.
It's quite insufferable.
You really think they give a damn, the gods, about this
                                          corpse?

Next you'll say they make it a priority to bury him in
state,
    and thank him for his burning down their altars,
    sacking shrines, scouting laws, and raping all the land.
Or are the gods these days considerate to criminals?
Far from it! No, from the first,
    there's been a group of grumblers in this town:
    men who can hardly abide my rule,
    who nod and whisper, chafing beneath my law,
    who are not in love with it at all.
These are the ones, I'll warrant,
    who have suborned my guards with bribes.
Ah, money! Money is a currency that's rank.
Money topples cities to the ground,
    seduces men away from happy homes,
    corrupts the honest heart to shifty ways,
    makes men crooked connoisseurs of vice.
But these plotters who have sold themselves,
    every man jack of them,
    Will end up, gentlemen,
    with much more than he's bargained for.

[*He turns on the* SENTRY]

You there! Get this straight:
    I swear by almighty Zeus whom I revere and serve,
    that either you find the man who did this burial
    and stand him here before my eyes,
    or Hades itself will be too good for you
    until you've first confessed to everything—
    yes, hanging from a cross.
That perhaps will teach you, soldier,
    where to look for profit
    and that gold can glister from an evil source.
Ah! Money never makes as many as it mars.
SENTRY: Am I allowed a word, sir? Or do I just go?
CREON: Can't you see your very voice gets on my nerves?
SENTRY: Hurts your ears, does it, sir? Or kinda your
conscience?
CREON: What business of yours is it to diagnose my pain?

SENTRY: Because I only affect your ears; the culprit, your
                                                    brain.
CREON: By God, what a born chatterer you are!
SENTRY: Maybe, but it weren't me that did the burying.
CREON: No, you just sold yourself for silver.
SENTRY: Oh, what a crying shame, when right reason
                                        reasons wrong!
CREON: A logic-chopper and a wit! But don't imagine
                                                    that
  will save your skin.
If you fail to stand the man before my face,
  you'll find that dirty money pays in hurt.

[CREON *strides into the palace*]

SENTRY: Well, let's 'ope he's found. But caught or not
  (and only chance can tell), one thing's for sure:
  you won't catch me coming back again.
It's a goddam miracle I got out of 'ere alive.

[SENTRY *runs off*]

FIRST CHORAL ODE

[*The* CHORUS *of citizens, in an intuitive foreshadowing of
both* CREON's *and* ANTIGONE's *fate, contrast the prowess
and glory of humankind with the tragedy of their downfall when they overstep the mark. There is a veiled warning to* CREON *not to exceed humane bounds, but also, by
their listing all the predominantly masculine occupations
(sailing, plowing, hunting, fishing, domesticating animals,
verbal skills, building, making laws), they are advising
women like* ANTIGONE *to beware of taking on what they
consider male roles*]

STROPHE I

Creation is a marvel and
  Man its masterpiece. He scuds
  Before the southern wind, between
  The pounding white-piling swells.
He drives his thoroughbreds through Earth

(Great goddess inexhaustible)
And overturns her with the plow
Unfolding her from year to year.

ANTISTROPHE I

The light-balanced light-headed birds
    He snares; wild beasts of every kind.
In his nets the deep-sea fish
    Are caught. Oh, mastery of man!
The free forest animal
    He herds; the roaming upland deer.
The shaggy horse he breaks to yoke
    The unflagging mountain bull.

STROPHE II

Training his agile thoughts
    volatile as air
He's civilized the world
    of words and wit and law.
With a roof against the sky,
    the javelin crystal frosts
The arrow-lancing rains;
    he's fertile in resource
Provident for all,
    healing all disease:
All but death, and death—
    death he never cures.

ANTISTROPHE II

Beyond imagining wise:
    his cleverness and skills
Through labyrinthine ways
    for good and also ill.
Distinguished in his city
    when law-abiding, pious
But when he promulgates
    unsavory ambition,
    Citiless and lost.
And then I will not share
    My hearth with him; I want
    no parcel of his thoughts.

SECOND EPISODE

[*The* SENTRY *returns, leading* ANTIGONE]

CHORUS: What visitation do I see from heaven?
And one I wish I could deny.
I am amazed. It is Antigone.
What! They bring you here in charge?
Poor Antigone, daughter of unlucky Oedipus.
Were you rash enough to cross the king?
And did they take you in your folly?
SENTRY: 'ere she is, the culprit: caught red'anded
in the very act of burying 'im.
But where is Creon?
CHORUS: Coming from the house, and just in time.

[*Enter* CREON]

CREON: Just in time for what?
SENTRY: King, it's most unwise, I find,
ever to promise not to do a thing.
Now look at me! I could 'ave sworn
I'd not come scurrying back,
After being almost skinned alive by all your flailing
threats.
Yet 'ere I am against my oath, bringing in this girl,
and all because beyond my wildest dreams,
in fact with quite a thrill,
I caught 'er at it—actually at the burying.
No drawing straws this time—I'll say not!
So grab 'er, King, she's yours.
And I'm scot-free, or I should 'ope,
quit of this 'ole goddam thing.
CREON: Tell me first when and how you found her.
SENTRY: She was burying the man. There ain't nothing
more to tell.
CREON: Are you rambling? Do you know what you are
saying?
SENTRY: Sir, I saw 'er in the act
of burying that forbidden corpse.
Is that plain and clear?

CREON: But how actually was she surprised and taken?
SENTRY: Well, it was like this.
We 'ad returned to the spot,
   our ears ringing with all your nasty threats,
   and 'ad brushed the earth from off the body
   to make it bare again
   (it was all soft and clammy),
   And were squatting there windward of the stench,
   keeping each other up to the mark
   And rounding 'ard on anybody that nodded . . .
   Watching we were, till the midday sun,
   a great blazing ball
   bashed down on us something fierce.
   When suddenly came this right twisting squall,
   sweeping across the plain,
   tearing the leaves off trees,
   buffeting 'eaven itself.
We 'ad to shut our eyes against this god-sent blight.
When at last it cleared
   there was this vision of this girl,
   Standing there she was,
   giving out little shrill-like sobs:
   'eartrending as a mother bird's
   what 'as seen its nest pillaged
   and its bairns all gone.
That's 'ow she was wailing
   and calling curses down
   on them what done it
   when she saw the body bared.
Immediately she scoops up earth—a dry 'andful like—
   and sprinkles it. Then 'olding up
   a shapely brazen urn, she pours
   three libations for the dead.
That's when we swooped and closed upon our quarry.
She didn't flinch, and when we charged 'er
   with what she'd gorne and done,
   and done before, she just admitted it.
It made me glad and sad:
   bliss to get myself out of trouble,
   distress to bring it on a friend.
When all's said and done, 'owever,

the safety of one's own sweet skin comes first.
CREON: Come, girl, you with downcast eyes,
did you, or did you not, do this deed?
ANTIGONE: I did. I deny not a thing.
CREON: You, soldier, you can go—be off wherever you
please—
Free of any serious charge.

[*The* SENTRY *stands for a moment, smiles, then
bounds away*]

Now, tell me, Antigone, a straight yes or no:
Did you know an edict had forbidden this?
ANTIGONE: Of course I knew. Was it not publicly
proclaimed?
CREON: So you chose flagrantly to disobey my law?
ANTIGONE: Naturally! Since Zeus never promulgated
such a law,
Nor will you find that Justice,
Mistress of the world below,
publishes such laws to humankind.
I never thought your mortal edicts had such force
they nullified the laws of heaven,
which unwritten, not proclaimed,
can boast a currency that everlastingly is valid,
an origin beyond the birth of man.
And I, whom no man's frown can frighten,
Am far from risking heaven's frown by flouting these.
I need no trumpeter from you to tell me I must die,
we all die anyway
And if this hurries me to death before my time,
why, such a death is gain. Yes, surely gain
to one whom life so overwhelms.
Therefore, I can go to meet my end
without a trace of pain.
But had I left the body of my mother's son unburied,
´ lying where he lay,
ah, that would hurt!
For this I feel no twinges of regret.
And if you judge me fool, perhaps it is
because a fool is judge.

LEADER: My word! The daughter is as headstrong as the
father.

Submission is a thing she's never learned.

CREON: You wait and see! The toughest will
is first to break: like hard, untempered steel
that snaps and shivers at a touch
when hot from off the forge.

And I have seen high-mettled horses curbed
by a little scrap of bit.

One who has no more authority than a common slave
can ill afford to put on airs.

And yet, this girl, already versed in disrespect
the first time she disobeyed my law,
Now adds a second insult, has done it again,
and vaunts it to my face.

Oh, she's the man, not I,
if she can flout authority and walk away unscathed.

I swear I hardly care
if she be my sister's child
or linked to me by blood more closely
than any member of my hearth and home;
She and her sister will not now escape
the utmost penalty.

I say the sister too.

I charge her as accomplice of this burial.

Call her forth.

I saw her whimpering in there just now, all gone to
pieces.

So does remorse blurt out the secret sin . . .
Although its opposite is even worse:
crime detected glorifying crime.

ANTIGONE: Is there something more you want? Or just
my life?

CREON: Not a thing, by God! It gives me what I want.

ANTIGONE: Why dawdle, then? Your conversation
is hardly something I enjoy, or ever could,
nor mine be more acceptable to you.

And yet it ought to be.

Where could I win respect and praise more validly than
this:

burial of my brother?

Not a man here would say the opposite,
   were his tongue not locked in fear.
Unfortunately, tyranny (blessed in so much else besides)
   can lay the law down any way it wants.
CREON: Your view is hardly shared by all these Thebans
                                    here.
ANTIGONE: They think as I, but trim their tongues to you.
CREON: Are you not ashamed to differ from such men?
ANTIGONE: There is no shame to reverence relatives.
CREON: And the other duelist who died—was he no
                                 relative?
ANTIGONE: He was. And of the same father and same
                                 mother.
CREON: So, slighting one, you would salute the other?
ANTIGONE: The dead man would not agree with you on
                                 this.
CREON: Surely! If you make the hero honored with the
                              blackguard.
ANTIGONE: It was his brother, not his slave, that died.
CREON: Yes, ravaging our land, while *he* fell as its
                              champion.
ANTIGONE: Hades makes no distinction in its rites and
                               honors.
CREON: The just and unjust do not urge an equal claim.
ANTIGONE: The "crime" (who knows?) may be called a
                              virtue there.
CREON: Not even death can metamorphose hate to love.
ANTIGONE: No, nor decompose my love to hate.
CREON: Curse you! Find the outlet for your love down
                              there.
No woman while I live shall govern me.

[ISMENE *is brought in under guard*]

LEADER OF CHORUS: See where Ismene comes
   Crying from the palace gates,
   Her face all flushed.
A sister's tears are breaking rains
   Upon her cheeks and from her eyes,
   Her loveliness a shadow.

CREON: [*turning viciously towards* ISMENE] Come, you
serpent, secret lurker in my home,
    who sucked my blood
    Even while I nurtured you two sister vipers at my throne—
    Speak. Confess your part in burying him.
Or do you dare deny complicity?
ISMENE: I did it too. If she'll allow my claim.
I share with her the credit and the blame.
ANTIGONE: That is not true. You do not share with me,
    nor did I grant you partnership.
ISMENE: But now that your poor ship is buffeted,
    I'm not ashamed to sail the voyage at your side.
ANTIGONE: The dead of Hades know whose act it was.
I do not take to those who take to talk.
ISMENE: Sister, do not scorn me; let me share
    your death and holy homage to the dead.
ANTIGONE: No share in work, no share in death,
    and I must consummate alone what I began.
ISMENE: Then what is left of life to me when you are gone?
ANTIGONE: Ask Creon. You and he are friends.
ISMENE: Ah! Must you jeer at me? It does not help.
ANTIGONE: You are right. It is a joyless jeering.
ISMENE: Tell me, even now: how can I help?
ANTIGONE: Save yourself. I shall not envy you.
ISMENE: Poor dear sister—let me suffer with you!
ANTIGONE: No. For you chose life, and I chose death.
ISMENE: When all my protests were of no avail.
ANTIGONE: We played our different parts, with different
                                acclaim.
ISMENE: But now we share an equal share of blame.
ANTIGONE: Look up! You live! And I died long ago,
    when I gave my life to serve the dead.
CREON: These girls, I swear, are crazed: one mad by birth,
    the other by attainment.
ISMENE: Yes, my lord, for when misfortune comes,
    he sends our reason packing out of doors.
CREON: And yours went flying fast
    when you chose damnation with the damned.
ISMENE: Yet, with her gone, what portion had I left?
CREON: Do not mention *her*. She does not still exist.
ISMENE: You would not kill your own son's bride?

CREON: Let him sow his seed in other furrows.
ISMENE: A match like theirs will *not* repeat itself.
CREON: I shudder at the jades who court our sons.
ANTIGONE: My darling Haemon, how your father heaps
                                    disgrace on you!
CREON: Damn you and damn your cursed marriage!
LEADER: You would not tear your own son's bride from
                                    him?
CREON: Let us say that Death is going to come between.
LEADER: I fear, I fear it's fixed. Her death is sealed.
CREON: Yes, let us both be quite assured of *that*.
Guards, take them away and lock them up.
No more roaming. They are women now.
The breath of Hades pressing close to kill
    Can make the bravest turn, and turn the bravest will.

[ANTIGONE *and* ISMENE *are led away.* CREON *stays*]

SECOND CHORAL ODE

[*The* CHORUS *cries out in an ode that begins by being
both a lament for the past victimization of the House of
Oedipus and an omen for the present, and then goes on
to warn all those who think they can live their lives apart
from the universal providence of Zeus*]

STROPHE I

Happy the man who has not sipped the bitter day,
    Whose house is firm against divine assault.
No planted curse creeps on and on
    Through generations like the dark and driven surge
    Booming from the bosom of the sea while Thracian
                                    gales
    Churn perpetually the ooze in waves that throw
    Down upon the headlands swept and carded by the
                                    storm
    Their thunderous mass.

ANTISTROPHE I

So do I see the house of Labdacus struck down,
    In all its generations victimized by some

Pursuing deity. Its useless dead.
Its never-ending doom. And now once more the sun
    Gone down in blood: the final hope of Oedipus
    Felled to the root, put out in smoke and Hades' dust,
    And all because of headlong folly and the reckless
                             speech
    Of a frenzied heart.

STROPHE II

O Zeus, what creature pits himself against thy power?
Not Sleep encumbrous with his subtle net
    And not the menstrual cycle
    Of the tireless moon.
Thou in ancient splendors still art young
    When worlds are old
    On Mount Olympus.
Everything past, everything present,
    And everything still to come
    Is thy domain
    No mortal thing however vast can steal
    Outside thy grasp.

ANTISTROPHE II

Hope, eternally gadding, alights on many with nothing
    But bliss, but just as blithely brings to others
    Delusions and seething ambition.
No man can tell
    What has come stealthily creeping over his life
    Until too late
    Hot ashes and pain
    Sear his feet . . . Once long ago
    A sage famously said:
    "If evil good appear
    To any, the gods are near. Unscathed he'll go,
    And then they'll bring him low."

[HAEMON *is seen approaching*]

LEADER: Here Haemon comes, your youngest son,
    Driven perhaps by pangs of grief
    For Antigone his sentenced bride:

A bitter groom, a marriage marred.
CREON: We shall see in a moment, and without the need
of seers.

THIRD EPISODE

[HAEMON *enters. The men stare warily at each other for
a few seconds*]

CREON: Son, do you come provoked against your father
for the death warrant of your would-be bride,
or still my loving son, whatever I may do?
HAEMON: Father, I am your loving son and you the wise
preceptor of my ways, whom I must follow.
No marriage I could make would ever match
the good of your abiding counsel.
CREON: Well spoken son!
Just what a right-minded son should feel:
unremitting deference to his father's will.
Such is a parent's prayer, to see grow up
a race of filial sons to deck his home:
Ready always to avenge their father's wrongs,
and of course to give his friends
the selfsame honor that the father gives.
But a man who raises a batch of worthless boys,
what has he hatched for himself but nuisances,
and jubilant sneers from the ill-disposed!

Oh, Haemon, don't lose your balance for a woman's
sake!
Don't hug a joy that's cheap and cools:
an evil woman for your bed and board.
No wound is worse than counterfeited love.
She is poison. Spit her out.
Let her go and find a mate in Hades.
Why, I've just caught her in an open act of treason—
she alone of all the city.
I *will* not break my word to Thebes. She dies.
So let her plead to Zeus
the sanctity of kindred ties.
How can I, if I nurse sedition in my house,

not foster it outside?
No. If a man can keep his home in hand,
 he proves his competence to keep the state.
But one who breaks the law and flouts authority,
 I never will allow.
Unswerving submission
 to whomsoever the state has put in charge
 is what is asked: in little things as well as great,
 in right and wrong.
And I am confident that one who thus obeys,
 will make a perfect subject or a perfect king:
 the kind of man who in the thick of flying spears
 never flinches from his post
 but stands dauntless at his comrade's side.
But as for anarchy,
 there is no greater curse than anarchy.
It topples cities down, it crumbles homes,
 it shatters allied ranks in broken flight
 that discipline kept whole:
 For discipline preserves and orders well.
Let us then defend authority
 and not be ousted by a girl.
If yield we must, then let it be to men,
 And never have it said we were worsted by a woman.
LEADER: What you say (unless my wits have run to seed)
 sounds reasonable and makes good sense.
HAEMON: Yes, Father, reason: the gods' greatest gift to
              man.
I would not dream of criticizing yours
 or saying you were wrong, even if I could.
But other men can reason rightly too.
As your son, you see, I find myself
 marking every word and act and comment of the
              crowd,
 to gauge the temper of the simple citizen,
 who dares not risk your scowl to speak his mind.
But I from the shadows hear them:
 hear a city's sympathy for this girl,
 because no woman ever faced
 so unreasonable, so cruel a death,
 for such a generous cause.

She would not leave her brother where he fell,
    for carrion birds and dogs to maul.
"Should not her name be writ in gold?" they say,
    and so the whisper grows.

You know, my father, how I prize
    your well-being and your name.
For sons and fathers crown each other's glory
    with each other's fame.
So I beg you, Father,
    don't entrench yourself in your opinion
    as if everyone else was wrong.
The kind of man who always thinks that he is right,
    that his opinions, his pronouncements,
    are the final word,
    is usually exposed as hollow as they come.
But a wise man is flexible, has much to learn
    without a loss of dignity.
See the trees in floodtime, how they bend
    along the torrent's course,
    and how their twigs and branches do not snap,
    but stubborn trees are torn up roots and all.
In sailing too, when fresh weather blows,
    a skipper who will not slacken sail, turns turtle,
    finishes his voyage beam-ends up.

So let your anger cool, and change your mind.
I may be young, but not without some sense.
Let men be wise by instinct if they can,
    but when this fails and nature won't oblige,
    be wise by good advice.
LEADER: Sire, the young man speaks good sense: worth
                                listening to.
And you, son, too, should listen. You both speak to the
                                point.
CREON: You mean that men of my years have to learn
                                to think
    by taking notes from men of his?
HAEMON: In only what is right.
It is my merit, not my years, that count.
CREON: Your merit is to foment lawlessness.

HAEMON: You know I do not plead for criminals.

CREON: So this creature is no criminal, eh?

HAEMON: The whole of Thebes says "no."

CREON: And I must let the mob dictate my policy?

HAEMON: See now who is speaking like a boy!

CREON: Do *I* rule this state, or someone else?

HAEMON: A one-man state is no state at all.

CREON: The state is his who rules it. Is that plain?

HAEMON: The state that you should rule would be a desert.

CREON: This boy is hopelessly on the woman's side.

HAEMON: I'm on your side. Are you a woman, then?

CREON: You reprobate! At open loggerheads with your father!

HAEMON: On the contrary: you at loggerheads with open justice!

CREON: My crime, of course, the discharge of my rule?

HAEMON: What rule—when you trample on the rule of heaven?

CREON: Insolent pup! A woman's lackey!

HAEMON: Lackey to nothing of which I am ashamed.

CREON: Not ashamed to be the mouthpiece for that trollop?

HAEMON: I speak for you, for me, and for the holy spirits of the dead.

CREON: The dead? Precisely—you'll never marry her alive.

HAEMON: Well, then, dead—one death beckoning to another.

CREON: So it's come to that—you threaten me?

HAEMON: One cannot threaten empty air!

CREON: My word, what wisdom! How you'll regret dispensing it!

HAEMON: If you weren't my father, I'd say your mind had gone.

CREON: You woman's slave! Don't come toadying to me!

HAEMON: Go on—make remarks and never listen to an answer!

CREON: Is that so? Then by Olympus be quite sure of this:

You shall not rant and jeer at me without reprisal.

Off with the wretched girl! I say she dies
    In front of him, before her bridegroom's eyes.
HAEMON: She shall not die—don't think it—
    in my sight or by my side.
    And you shall never see my face again.
I commit you raving to your chosen friends.

[HAEMON *rushes out*]

LEADER: Gone, Your Majesty, but gone distraught.
He is young, his rage will make him desperate.
CREON: Let him do or dream up acts as murderous as a
                                                fiend's,
    these girls, he shall not snatch from death.
LEADER: You do not mean to kill them both?
CREON: You are right. Not the one who did not meddle.
LEADER: What kind of death do you plan?
CREON: I'll take her down a path untrod by man.
I'll hide her living in a rock-hewn vault,
    With ritual food enough to clear the taint
    Of murder from the City's name.
I'll leave her pleading to her favorite god,
    Hades. He may charm her out a way to life.
Or perhaps she'll learn though late the cost
    Of homage to the dead is labor lost.

[CREON *walks away into the palace*]

THIRD CHORAL ODE

[*The* CHORUS, *apprehensive of the fate of the young lov-
ers, sings of the desperately destructive power of love.
Their words also veil a condemnation of men like* CREON,
*who overvalue the so-called masculine qualities of the
soul and fail to realize the duality of male and female
within the person*]

STROPHE I
Love, unquelled in battle
    Love, making nonsense of wealth
    Pillowed all night on the cheek of a girl

You roam the seas, pervade the wilds
And in a shepherd's hut you lie.
Shadowing immortal gods
You dog ephemeral man—
Madness your possession.

ANTISTROPHE I

Turning the wise into fools
You twist them off their course
And now you have stung us to this strife
For father fighting son . . . Oh, Love,
The bride has but to glance
With the lyrical light of her eyes
To win you a seat in the stars
And Aphrodite laughs.

[*End of Choral Ode and beginning of Choral Dialogue, which continues through Fourth Episode*]

FOURTH EPISODE

[ANTIGONE *is led in under guard*]

LEADER: And now you turn on me
Unman my loyalty
Loose my tears to see
You, Antigone,
Pass your wedding bower
Death's chamber, pass
So easily.

STROPHE I

[ANTIGONE *and the* CHORUS *chant alternately*]

ANTIGONE: See me, friends and citizens,
Look on this last walk—
The sun's light snuffed out with my dower
And Death leading me to Acheron
Alive, where all must sleep.
No wedding march, no bridal song
Cheer me on my way,

I whom Hades, lord of the dark lake, weds.
CHORUS: Yet you walk with fame, bedecked
  In praise towards the dead man's cave.
No sickness severed you
  No sword incited struck.
All mistress of your fate you move
  Alive, unique, to Hades' halls.

ANTISTROPHE I

ANTIGONE: Oh, but I have heard what happened
  To that Phrygian girl, poor foreigner
  (The child of Tantalus), who clings
  Like ivy on the heights of Sipylus
  Captures in stone, petrified,
  Where all the rains, they say, the flying snow,
  Waste her form away, which weeps
  In waterfalls. I feel her trance,
  Her lonely exodus, in mine.
CHORUS: And she a goddess born of gods
  While we are mortals born of men.
What greater glory for a woman's end
  To partner gods in death
  Who partnered them in life!

STROPHE II

ANTIGONE: Ah! Now you laugh at me.
Thebes, Thebes, by all our father's gods
  You my own proud chariot city
  Can you not wait till I am gone?
And you sweet Dirce's stream and Theban groves
  You at least be witnesses to me with love
  Who walk in dismal passage to my heavy tomb
  Unwept, unjustly judged
  Displaced from every home
  Disowned by both the living and the dead.

STROPHE III

CHORUS: Perhaps you aimed too high
  You dashed your foot on Fate
  Where Justice sits enthroned.

You fall a plummet fall
   To pay a father's sin.

ANTISTROPHE II

ANTIGONE: You touch my wounds, my memories
   Make fresh again my tears: the triple curse
   That haunts the House of Labdacus:
   The spilt and tainted blood, the horrid bed,
   My fated mother sleeping with her son
   To father me in incest . . . Parents, here I come,
   Home at last, not wed, no broken spell.
Brother, when you made
   Your blindfold match, you made
   Your death and mine—mine to come.

ANTISTROPHE III

CHORUS: Pious is as pious does
   But where might is right
   It's reckless to do wrong.
Self-propelled to death
   You go with open eyes.

EPODE

ANTIGONE: Unwept, unwedded, unloved I go
   On this last journey of all.
Eye of the blessed sun—
   I shall miss you soon.
No tears will mourn me dead.
No friend to cry.

[*End of Choral Dialogue.* CREON *has entered*]

CREON: Listen you!
Panegyrics and dirges go on forever
   if given the chance.
Dispatch her at once, I say. Seal up the tomb.
Let her choose a death at leisure—or perhaps,
   in her new home,
   An underground life forlorn.
We wash our hands of this girl—
   except to take her from the light.

ANTIGONE: Come, tomb, my wedding chamber, come!
You sealed off habitations of the grave!
My many family dead, finished, fetched
  in final muster to Persephone.
I am last to come, and lost the most of all,
  my life still in my hands.
And yet I come (I hope I come) toward a father's love,
  beloved by my mother,
    And by you, my darling brother, loved.
Yes, all of you,
  Whom these my hands have washed, prepared and
                                            sped
    with ritual to your burials.
And now, sweet Polyneices, dressing you,
  I've earned this recompense,
    though richly honored you the just will say.

No husband dead and gone, no children lisping "mother"
  ever could have forced me to withstand
    the city to its face.
By what law do I assert so much? Just this:
  A husband dead, another can be found,
  a child replaced, but once a brother's lost
  (mother and father dead and buried too)
  No other brother can be born or grows again.
That is my principle,
  which Creon stigmatized as criminal,
    my principle for honoring you, my dearest brother.

So taken, so am I led away:
  a virgin still, no nuptial song, no marriage bed,
  no children to my name.
An outcast stripped of sympathy,
  I go alive toward these sepulchers of death.
What ordinance, what law of heaven broken,
  what god left for me to cast my eyes toward,
    when sacraments must now be damned as sacrilege?
And if these things be smiled upon by heaven,
  why, when I'm dead I'll know I sinned.
But if I find the sin was theirs,
  may Justice then mete out no less to them

than what injustice now metes out to me—my doom.
LEADER: See how she goes, headlong driven
  By the capricious gusts of her own will!
CREON: Putting to disgrace her loitering guards.
Who shall be paid their just rewards.
ANTIGONE: Ah, Death comes nearer with those words!
CREON: There is no comfort I can offer
  Nor this damnation can I alter.
ANTIGONE: See me, Thebes, I am going, now going!
See me, divine ancestral Thebes!
Cast but a glance, you her princes,
  On this last and lonely royal scion,
  See what I suffer from these men
  For reverencing the rights of man.

[ANTIGONE *is led away*]

FOURTH CHORAL ODE

[*The* CHORUS, *in an attempt to comfort* ANTIGONE, *recalls
situations of fate similar to her own. First there was
Danäe, shut up by her father in a brazen tower because
an oracle had foretold that she would bear a son who
would kill him. Zeus, however, had access to her prison
and impregnated her in a shower of gold. The resulting
offspring, Perseus, did indeed later kill his grandfather
(accidentally). Next, there was Lycurgus, son of Dryas,
king of Thrace: punished by Dionysus for insulting him
and abolishing the cult of the vine in his kingdom. Lastly,
there was Phineus, who, suspicious of his two sons by his
first wife (daughter of Boreas, the north wind), prompted
his second wife to blind them in a fit of jealousy*]*

STROPHE I

Hidden from the sun
  Housed behind brass doors
  Danäe's beauty too was locked away

---

*It must be borne in mind that there are contradictory versions of
these stories in Greek mythology. Here, for instance, Sophocles'
account scrambles or conflates several others.

Her nuptial cell a tomb
And she, my child, yes, she
A royal daughter too:
The rare receptacle of Zeus's golden seed.
O Destiny, marked mysterious force!
No mound of coins
  No panoplies of war
  No ramparts keep you out
  And through the dark sea looming
  No ship escapes.

ANTISTROPHE I

The savage son of Dryas
  That Edonian king
  Was pent by Dionysus in a prison
  Clamped within a rocky cavern.
There his jeering changing,
  Changing into howling,
  Faded into echoes till he came at last
  To know the godhead whom his madness
  Baited when he tried
  To quench the god-possessed
  Flaring Bacchantes
  And offended all the Muses
  Who love the flute.

STROPHE II

Once in primitive Thrace near Salmydessus
  Where twin black doom-ridden crags
  Sever two seas, along the vicious
  Lonely shores of the Bosporus,
  War-loving Ares
  Witnessed a nightmare scene:
  The bride of Phineus, jealous, frenzied,
  Plunging the dagger of her spindle
  Into the princely eyes of his two sons . . .
  Saw their vacant scream for vengeance
  Plead in pools of socket-bloody staring.

ANTISTROPHE II

Wasting in agony, doomed so cruelly,

They lamented their mother's fatal mating
From which even her noble birth line
From Erechtheus could not save her—
And she a daughter cradled
By Boreas in the caverns
Born amid her father's tempests
Bolting like a colt from heaven
Over the uplands—child of the gods—

Even she, Antigone, they had her,
The ageless gray-grim Fates, they struck her down.

FIFTH EPISODE

[The blind prophet TIRESIAS, *led by a boy, announces his arrival in a quavering, chanting voice]*

TIRESIAS: Rulers of Thebes, here we come: one pair of
eyes for two
On a single road, and the blind man led by another.
CREON: What news, venerable Tiresias?
TIRESIAS: I shall tell you, and you must listen hard.
CREON: Have I ever failed to listen to you?
TIRESIAS: And therefore have you safely piloted the
state.
CREON: Gladly do I own my debt to you.
TIRESIAS: Then beware, you're standing once again upon
the razor's edge.
CREON: How so? Your words and aspect chill.
TIRESIAS: Listen, I'll read the signs and make them plain.
I was sitting by my ancient chair of augury,
the haunt of every kind of bird,
When suddenly a noise not heard before
assaults my ears:
A panic screeching and a pandemonium deafening
jargon:
beaks and bloody talons tearing—I could tell it—
pinions whirring,
all shocked me as a portent.
At once I kindled sacrifice to read by fire,
but Hephaestus fanned no leaping flame.

Instead, a sort of sweat distilled from off the thigh fat,
   slid in smoke upon the sputtering fire.
The gallbladders burst and spurted up.
The grease oozed down and left the thigh bones bare.
These were the signs I learned from off this boy,
   omens of a ruined sacrifice:
   he is my eyes as I am yours.

See it—how the city sickens, Creon,
   these the symptoms, yours the fanatic will that caused
                them:
    Dogs and crows all glutted carrying
    desecrated carrion to the hearths and altars—
    carrion from the poor unburied son of Oedipus.
Burnt offerings go up in stench. The gods are dumb.
The birds of omen cannot sing.
But obscene vultures flap away
   with crops all gorged on human flesh.

Think, son, think! To err is human, true,
   and only he is damned who having sinned
   will not repent, will not repair.
He is a fool, a proved and stubborn fool.
Give death his due, and do not kick a corpse.
Where is renown to kill a dead man twice?
Believe me, I advise you well.
It should be easy to accept advice
   so sweetly tuned to your good use.
CREON: Old man,
   you pot away at me like all the rest
   as if I were a bull's-eye,
   And now you aim your seer craft at me.
Well, I'm sick of being bought and sold
   by all your soothsaying tribe.
Bargain away! All the silver of Sardis,
   all the gold of India
   is not enough to buy this man a grave;
   Not even if Zeus's eagles come, and fly away
   with carrion morsels to their master's throne.
Even such a threat of such a taint
   will not win this body burial.

It takes much more than human remains
  to desecrate the majesty divine.
Old man Tiresias,
  The most reverend fall from grace when lies are sold
  Wrapped up in honeyed words—and all for gold.

TIRESIAS: Creon! Creon!
Is no one left who takes to heart that . . .

CREON: Come, let's have the platitude!

TIRESIAS: . . . That prudence is the best of all our wealth.

CREON: As folly is the worst of all our woes?

TIRESIAS: Yes, infectious folly! And you are sick with it.

CREON: I'll not exchange a fishwife's set-to with a seer.

TIRESIAS: Which is what you do when you say I sell my
                                              prophecies.

CREON: As prophets do—a money-grubbing race.

TIRESIAS: Or as kings, who grub for money in the dung.

CREON: You realize this is treason—lese majesté?

TIRESIAS: Majesty? Yes, thanks to me you are savior of
                                              Thebes.

CREON: And you are not without your conjuring tricks.
                                    But still a crook.

TIRESIAS: Go on! You will drive me to divulge something
                                    that . . .

CREON: Out with it! But not for money, please.

TIRESIAS: Unhappily for you this can't be bought.

CREON: Then don't expect to bargain with my wits.

TIRESIAS: All right, then! Take it if you can.
A corpse for a corpse the price, and flesh for flesh,
  one of your own begotten.
The sun shall not run his course for many days
  before you pay.
You plunged a child of light into the dark;
  entombed the living with the dead; the dead
  Dismissed unmourned, denied a grave—a corpse
  Unhallowed and defeated of his destiny below.
Where neither you nor gods must meddle,
  you have thrust your thumbs.
Do not be surprised that heaven—yes, and hell—
  have set the Furies loose to lie in wait for you,
  Ready with the punishments you engineered for others.

* * *

Does this sound like flattery for sale?
Yet a little while and you shall wake
   to wailing and gnashing of teeth in the House of Creon.
Lashed to a unison of rage, they'll rise,
   those other cities,
   whose mangled sons received their obsequies
   from dogs and prowling jackals—
   from some filthy vulture flapping to alight
   before their very hearths to bring them home—
   desecration reeking from its beak.

There! You asked, and I have shot my angry arrows.
I aimed at your intemperate heart. I did not miss.
Come, boy, take me home.
Let him spew his choler over younger men.
He'll learn a little modesty in time,
   a little meekness soon.

[TIRESIAS *is led out by his boy.* CREON *stands motionless, visibly shaken*]

LEADER: *There's* fire and slaughter for you, King!
The man has gone,
   but my gray hairs were long since shining black
   before he ever stirred the city to a false alarm.
CREON: I know. You point the horns of my dilemma.
It's hard to eat my words, but harder still
   to court catastrophe through overriding pride.
LEADER: Son of Menoeceus, be advised in time.
CREON: To do what? Tell me, I shall listen.
LEADER: Go free the maiden from her vault.
Then entomb the lonely body lying stark.
CREON: You really mean it—that I must yield?
LEADER: Must, King, and quickly too.
The gods, provoked, never wait to mow men down.
CREON: How it goes against the grain
   to smother all one's heart's desire!
But I cannot fight with destiny.
CHORUS: Quickly, go and do it. Don't trust to others.

CREON: Yes, I go at once.
Servants, servants—on the double!
You there, fetch the rest. Bring axes all
  and hurry to the hill.
My mind's made up. I'll not be slow
  to let her loose myself
  who locked her in the tomb.
In the end it is the ancient codes—oh, my regrets!—
  that one must keep:
  To value life then one must value law.

[CREON *and servants hurry away in all directions*]

FIFTH CHORAL ODE

[*The* CHORUS *sings a desperate hymn to Bacchus, begging
him to come and save the city of Thebes and the stricken
House of Oedipus*]

STROPHE I
Calling you by a hundred names
  Jewel and flower of Semele's wedding
  Son of Zeus and son of thunder
  Singer of sweet Italy!
Calling you in world communion
  In the bowery lap of Dio's glades
  Close by Ismenus' quicksilver stream:
  You the Bacchus haunting Thebes
  (Mother of the Bacchanals)
  Hard by the very fields where once
  The dragon's teeth were sown.

ANTISTROPHE I
Bacchus and your nymphs Bacchantes
  Dancing in the hills and valleys:
  Dots of fire and wreathing torches
  Curling smoke above the crested
  Forks (Castalia fled Apollo
  Plunging into the spring-fed pool there)
  Calling you from the slopes of Nysa
  Dripping ivy down to the seashore

Green with vineyards, while your Maenads
Storm ecstatic, shouting, "Bacchus"
On your march to Thebes.

STROPHE II

Calling you to your favorite city
    Sacred city of your mother
    (Ravished by a lightning bolt)
    Calling you to a city dying—
    People shadowed by the plague
    Calling you to leave the high-spots
    Leaping fleet-foot down to cross
    The moaning waters. Oh, come quickly,
Hurry from Parnassus.

ANTISTROPHE II

Come, you master of the dancing
    Fiery-breathing pulsing stars
    Steward of the midnight voices
    Son of Zeus, O Prince, appear!
Bring your train of Maenads raving
    Swirling round you, round you dancing
    Through the night, and shouting, "Bacchus
    Giver of all blessings, Bacchus!"
Bacchus, oh, come!

[*There is a pause, while the strains of the* CHORUS *die
away. A* MESSENGER *enters*]

EPILOGUE

MESSENGER: Men of the House of Cadmus and of Am-
                                                        phion,
    how rash it is to envy others or despair!
The luck we adulate in one today,
    tomorrow is another's tragedy.
There is no stable horoscope for man.
Take Creon:
    he, if anyone, I thought was enviable.
He saved this land from all our enemies,
    attained the pomp and circumstance of king,

his children decked like olive branches round his
throne.
And now it is undone, all finished.
And what is left is not called life but death alive.
His kingly state is nothing to him now
with gladness gone:
Vanity of vanities—the shadow of a shade.
LEADER: What fresh news do you bring of royal ruin?
MESSENGER: Death twice over, and the living guilty for
the dead.
LEADER: Who struck and who is stricken? Say.
MESSENGER: Haemon's gone. Blood spilt by his own
hand.
LEADER: By his own hand? Or by his father's?
MESSENGER: Both. Driven to it by his father's murdering.
LEADER: Oh, Prophet, your prophecy's come true!
MESSENGER: So stands the case. Make of it what you will.
LEADER: Look, I see Eurydice approach,
Creon's unhappy queen.
Is it chance or has she heard the death knell of her son?

[EURYDICE *staggers in, supported by her maids*]

EURYDICE: Yes, good citizens, all of you, I heard:
Even as I went to supplicate
the goddess Pallas with my prayers.
Just as I unloosed the bolt that locks the door,
the sound of wailing struck my ears,
the sound of family tragedy.
I was stunned—
and fell back fainting into my ladies' arms.
But tell me everything, however bad;
I am no stranger to the voice of sorrow.
MESSENGER: Dear Mistress, I was there.
I shall not try to glaze the truth;
for where is there comfort in a lie,
so soon found out? The truth is always best.
In attendance on your Lord,
I took him deep into the plain
where Polyneices lay
abandoned still—all mauled by dogs.

And there with humble hearts
   we prayed to Hecate, goddess of the Great Divide,
   to Hades too, and begged their clemency.
Then we sprinkled him with holy water,
   lopped fresh branches down
   and laid him on a funeral pyre
   to burn away his poor remains.
Lastly, we heaped a monument to him,
   a mound of his native earth, then turned away
   to unseal the vault in which there lay
   a virgin waiting on a bed of stone
   for her bridegroom—Death.

And one of us, ahead,
   heard a wail of deep despair
   echoing from that hideous place of honeymoon.
He hurried back and told the king,
   who then drew near
   and seemed to recognize those hollow sounds.
He gave a bleat of fear:
   "Oh, are my heart's forebodings true?
I cannot bear to tread this path.
My son's voice strikes my ears.
Hurry, hurry, servants, to the tomb,
   And through those stones once pried away peer down
   into that cadaverous gap
   and tell me if it's Haemon's voice.
Oh, tell me I am heavenly deceived!"

His panic sent us flying to the cave,
   and in the farthest corner we could see her
   hanging with a noose of linen round her neck,
   and leaning on her,
   hugging his cold lover lost to Hades,
   Haemon, bridegroom, broken,
   cursed the father who had robbed him,
   pouring out his tears of sorrow.

A groan agonized and loud—
   broke from Creon when he saw him.
"You poor misguided boy!" he sobbed,

staggering forward,
"What have you done? What were you thinking of?
And now, come to me, my son. Your father begs you."
But the boy glared at him with flaming eyes,
spat for answer in his face,
and drawing a double-hilted sword,
lunged but missed
as his father stepped aside and ran.
Then, the wretched lad,
convulsed with self-hatred and despair,
pressed against that sword and drove it home,
halfway up the hilt into his side.
And conscious still but failing, limply folded
Antigone close into his arms—
Choking blood in crimson jets upon her waxen face.
Corpse wrapped in love with corpse he lies,
married not in life but Hades:
Lesson to the world that inhumane designs
Wreak a havoc immeasurably inhumane.

[EURYDICE *is seen moving like a sleepwalker into the palace*]

LEADER: What does her exit mean?
The queen has gone without a word of comfort or of
sorrow.
MESSENGER: I am troubled too. And yet I hope
the reason is she shrinks from public sorrow for her
son,
And goes into the house to lead her ladies
in the family dirge.
She will not be unwise. She is discreet.
LEADER: You may be right, but I do not trust
extremes of silence or of grief.
MESSENGER: Let me go into the house and see.
Extremes of silence, as you say, are sinister.
Her heart is broken and can hide
some sinister design.

[*As the* MESSENGER *hurries into the palace through a side door, the great doors open and a procession car-*

rying the dead body of HAEMON *on a bier approaches,
with* CREON *staggering behind*]

CHORUS: Look, the king himself draws near, his load
   in a kind of muteness crying out his sorrow
   (dare we say it?) from a madness of misdoing
   started by himself and by no other.

CHORAL DIALOGUE

STROPHE I

CREON: Purblind sin of mine!
There is no absolution
   For perversity that dragged
   A son to death:
   Murdered son, father murdering.
Son, my son, cut down dead!
New life that's disappeared
   And by no youthful foolishness
   But by my folly.
CHORUS: Late, too late, your reason reasons right!
CREON: Yes, taught by bitterness.
Some god has cast his spell,
   Has hit me hard from heaven,
   Let my cruelty grow rank;
   Has slashed me down, my joys
   Trodden in the earth.
Man, man, oh, how you suffer!

[*Enter the* MESSENGER]

MESSENGER: Sire, you are laden,
   You the author loading:
   Half your sorrow in your hands,
   The other half still in your house
   Soon to be unhidden.
CREON: What half horror coming?
MESSENGER: Your queen is dead:
   Mother for her son;
   The suicidal thrust:
   Dead for whom she lived.

ANTISTROPHE I

CREON: Oh, Death, pitiless receiver!
Kill me? Will you kill me?
Your mercy dwindles, does it?
Must you bring me words
    That crush me utterly?
I was dead, and still you kill me.
Slaughter was piled high,
    Ah, then, do not tell me
    You come to pile it higher:
    A son dead, then a wife.
CHORUS: Look! Everything is open to full view.

[*The scene suddenly opens by a movement of the ek-
kuklema* to reveal* EURYDICE *lying dead, surrounded
by her attendants*]

CREON: Oh, oh! A second death blow.
Fate, my bitter cup
    Should have no second brimming,
    Yet the sight I see laid out
Compels a second sorrow:
    My son just lifted up
    A corpse, and now a corpse his mother.
MESSENGER: Her heart was shattered
    And her hand drove keen the dagger.
At the altar there she fell
    And darkness swamped her drooping eyes
    As with cries she sobbed her sorrow
    For her hero son Megareus—
    Long since nobly dead—
    And for this son her other,
    Mingling with her dying gasp
    Curses on you—killer.

STROPHE II

CREON: My heart is sick with dread.

---

*The ekkuklema was a theatrical machine that could open up the
stage to an inner scene: frequently a murder or a suicide.

Will no one lance a two-edged sword
  Through this bleeding seat of sorrow?
MESSENGER: She charged you, yes,
  With both their deaths—
  This lifeless thing
  As double filicidal killer!
CREON: Tell me, how did she go?
MESSENGER: Self-stabbed to the heart;
  Her son's death ringing
  new dirges in her head.
CREON: I killed her, I
  Can own no alibi:
  The guilt is wholly mine.
Take me quickly, servants,
  Take me quickly hence.
Let this nothing be forgotten.
CHORUS: Good advice, at last,
  If anything be good
  In so much bad.
Such evils need quick riddance.

ANTISTROPHE II

CREON: Oh, let it come! Let it break!
My last and golden day:
  The best, the last, the worst
  To rob me of tomorrow.
LEADER: Tomorrow is tomorrow
  And we must mind today.
CREON: All my prayers are that:
  The prayer of my desires.
LEADER: Your prayers are done.
Man cannot flatter Fate,
  And punishments must come.
CREON: Then lead me please away,
  A rash, weak, foolish man,
  A man of sorrows,
  Who killed you, son, so blindly
  And you my wife—so blind.
Where can I look?
Where hope for help,
  When everything I touch is lost

And death has leapt upon my life?
CHORUS: Where wisdom is, there happiness will crown
    A piety that nothing will corrode.
But high and mighty words and ways
    Are flogged to humbleness, till age,
    Beaten to its knees, at last is wise.

Afterword
Reading Sophocles

Would anyone in his senses give the single tragedy of
Oedipus *for all the works of Ion in a row?*
—Longinus, *On the Sublime*, 33

I. FORM, SUBJECT, AND PERFORMANCE

More than any other dramatist except perhaps Shakespeare, Sophocles is regarded as the quintessential trage-
dian, a touchstone of quality, and a model not only for other
dramatists but also artists and thinkers of all sorts. Just from
our own time, he has inspired writers as diverse as Anouihl,
Brecht, O'Neill, Eliot, Pound, and Sartre, as well as Freud.
Why this should be, however, is not immediately apparent.
His plays, after all, are in their form, subject matter, and
circumstances of performance utterly alien to our current
experience of theater and, one might have thought, to our
social and intellectual preoccupations as well.

Greek tragedies were unlike contemporary (and most
other) plays in that they occupied a central place in civic
observances: plays were selected for performance by the
city-state; their productions were funded by direct taxes
upon the wealthiest citizens; and they were attended not
by a select group of theatergoers but by more than fifteen
thousand Athenian citizens and visitors, who crowded into
an open-air theater built into the side of the Acropolis.[1]
These theatrical performances also had a religious and ritual context, since they took place on the feast day of Dionysus, the god of drama,[2] in a theater dedicated to him, in the
presence of his priest, and with plots that focused heavily
on religious themes and even, on occasion, on the god himself (e.g., Euripides' *Bacchae*). Communal and religious, the

performances were also competitive. Three playwrights would present four plays apiece: a trilogy of tragedies (that might or might not be connected by plot or theme) and a lighter work called a satyr play; these would vie for prizes, and of the three major tragedians—Aeschylus, Sophocles, and Euripides—it was Sophocles who won most often.

It is not just the context in which Greek tragedies were performed that seems strange to us, but also their subject matter and formal features. First, the plots were not original but were almost always drawn from traditional myths.[3] The plays we have by Sophocles, for example, focus on the heroes of the Trojan War and its aftermath (*Ajax, Philoctetes, Electra*), the royal house of Thebes (*Oedipus the King, Oedipus at Colonus, Antigone*), and the family of Heracles (*The Women of Trachis*). Next, these plays are at the furthest remove from realistic theater: they are in verse, with episodes of speech and dialogue in iambic pentameter alternating with complex lyrics sung by the chorus.[4] The characters in these plays deliver their heavily rhetorical lines wearing stylized masks. And finally, their words are accompanied by music, dance, gesture, and visual spectacle (*opsis*)—all features of the performance that have been forever lost to us, since we possess only some (and not very many) scripts and they lack stage directions.[5] So, what accounts for the enduring fascination with Sophocles? In part, this is because his works represent and negotiate contradictions and tensions in his society, and some of these at least find parallels in our own experience (see section II below). In addition to this social dimension, Sophocles' plays also construct tragic heroes whose reversal of fortune and horrific but often ennobling suffering speak to the anxieties and aspirations of ordinary human beings (section III). Finally, Sophocles' consummate artistry as a poet and a dramatist—his mastery of words, imagery, and rhythm, his taut plot construction and use of dramatic techniques like irony, and his ability to create convincing characters who not only move the plot but also move us—these artistic qualities endow his work with enduring power and beauty (section IV).

II. THE TRAGIC MOMENT

The biographical tradition recounts how, as a boy, Sophocles performed in a chorus celebrating the Greek victory over Persia at the battle of Salamis (480 BCE). By the time Sophocles died in 406 BCE, those same Greek city-states that had once been united against the Persian threat were now at war among themselves, and Athens was about to suffer its final defeat at the hands of Sparta (404 BCE). Sophocles' life, then, spans the momentous period from the Persian Wars to the Peloponnesian War. The alliance of Greek city-states that Athens had led against Persia became over time an Athenian empire, which brought wealth, confidence, and prestige to Athens, though it also sowed the seeds of arrogance, resentment, and fear that eventually led to war. This was the period during which the Athenian democracy, especially under the great statesman Pericles, freed up the creative energies of its people, when painters and sculptors refashioned the image of the human body, when magnificent architecture like the Parthenon transformed Athens into the showplace of Greece, when scientists, sophists, and philosophers were calling into question traditional religious views of the world and the place of human beings within it, when rational medicine began to locate the causes and cures of illness in the natural world rather than in the divine, and when historians like Herodotus and Thucydides inquired into the causes and lessons of human events.

Not coincidentally, this was also the moment of tragedy. The origin of the form just before this period is notoriously obscure. The word itself means "goat song" (from *tragos*, goat, and *odē*, song), and may perhaps refer to archaic performances in which dancers either competed for a goat as a prize or dressed up as goats. (We may detect a survival of this in the animal choruses of comedies like Aristophanes' *Frogs* and *Wasps*, and in the existence of satyr plays, which are named after those half-human, half-goat creatures.) Aristotle posited a different origin for tragedy, tracing it to the dithyramb, choral songs of a religious and occasionally ribald nature performed in honor of the god Dionysus (*Poetics* 1449a). Tradition held that tragedy was born when a

certain Thespis (about 535 BCE) first separated the leader
of the dithyramb from the group (the chorus) and gave him
a speaking role (as an actor).

From this (or some such) beginning, tragedy developed
quickly, with Aeschylus adding a second actor and Sophocles a third, and with Sophocles and Euripides enhancing the
dialogue and gradually reducing the linguistic and metrical
complexity of the choral passages as well as the proportion
of the play devoted to them.[6] It is a striking feature of the
genre that its full flowering occurred within a very short period of time, about seventy years.[7] This is because tragedy,
both in its dialogic form and its competitive and communal
setting, was the perfect vehicle for enacting and negotiating
the tensions and ambiguities of the Athenian democracy at
this time of intellectual, social, and political transition.

As noted above, the plots of tragedy are drawn from the
traditional myths of heroes, individuals closely associated
with kingship, the prerogatives of noble families, and archaic religious and social practices. These heroes were celebrated in the older traditions of epic and lyric poetry. But
in the newer genre of tragedy, they exemplify the values
and social structures against which the democracy had established itself but which had not yet been (and perhaps
never could be) fully displaced. Jean-Pierre Vernant has
described this tension very well:

> [T]he tragic technique exploits a polarity between
> two of its elements: on the one hand the chorus, an
> anonymous and collective being whose role is to ex-
> press, through its fears, hopes, and judgements, the
> feelings of the spectators who make up the civic
> community; on the other the individualised figure
> whose action forms the centre of the drama and who
> is seen as a hero from another age, always more or
> less alien to the ordinary condition of a citizen. . . . In
> the new framework of tragic interplay, then, the hero
> has ceased to be a model. He has become, both for
> himself and for others, a problem.[8]

Sophocles' larger-than-life characters are indeed problems—Oedipus, who rules Thebes as its benevolent *ty-*

rannos but whose overconfident and relentless pursuit of knowledge unwittingly puts at risk his city-state and eventually himself; or Ajax, who, because of his personal pride and anger at having been dishonored, threatens the legitimate leaders of the Greeks (and is punished by madness and death); or Heracles, who accomplished great feats abroad when fighting monsters and warriors, but whose return home with a concubine destabilizes the social and domestic order (and results in his death at the hands of a jealous but unwitting wife); or Philoctetes, whose magic bow is needed by the Greeks if they are to win at Troy but who resists their attempts to trick, persuade, or compel him because of the terrible suffering he has endured at their hands; or Electra, who is obsessed with hatred for her mother and has spent her life waiting for her brother, Orestes, to return and exact a deadly revenge.

This tension between heroic attitudes and behavior and their religious and aristocratic underpinnings, on the one hand, and the newer forms of legal and political thought that characterize the democratic city-state, on the other, is nowhere more clearly set forth than in Sophocles' *Antigone*. The personal clash between Antigone and the ruler Creon animates the plot of this play. But that clash enacts tensions on so many different levels. Politically, for example, Antigone argues for the burial of her brother Polyneices on the basis of kinship, whereas Creon's refusal to bury the traitor respects the interests of the state; theologically, Antigone cites in support of her case the unwritten laws of the gods, whereas Creon cites civil statutes and decrees; Antigone defers to the will of the chthonic or underworld gods, whereas Creon worships the gods of the city; Antigone appeals to nature (*physis*), whereas Creon puts his trust in law and convention (*nomos*); and the list could go on. All these conflicts reflect real tensions that were once very much alive in the community and that may even now be lurking beneath the surface.[9]

Although this reading of Sophocles focuses on the situation in Athens at the time in which his plays were produced, it may also account for the appeal that Sophocles has had for audiences and readers over the years. Tensions have always existed in the relationship that individuals have not only with their governments (regardless of the form those governments take) but also with all other collectivities that make claims to authority over us and that expect and enforce our allegiance. Theater, no less than the battlefield, ballot box, marketplace, or court, has always been an important site for working out these contesting claims.

III. TRAGIC VISION

So far we have been considering the social dimension of Sophoclean tragedy. But an equally important aspect of the genre is the way in which it promulgates a tragic vision of the individual human condition that transcends specific temporal and societal bounds.

Aristotle's hugely influential *Poetics* describes features and characteristics that, he claims, are common to all tragedies.[10] Critics over the years have disputed the exact meaning of certain passages as well as the relevance of his analysis to the interpretation of actual Greek plays. But in so far as Aristotle explicitly constructed his theory with Sophocles, and particularly *Oedipus the King*, in mind, it is worth taking seriously what he says.

Tragedy, according to Aristotle, is the imitation (*mimesis*) of a serious (*spoudaios*) action, which is complete in itself. It is distinct from epic in that it relies not on narrative but on acting; and it is distinct from history—indeed, better than history and closer to philosophy—in that it does not deal with actual events but general truths, "such things as might or could happen in accordance with probability or necessity." For Aristotle, since tragedy imitates action, the most important element of a tragedy is plot (*mythos*), and character is secondary, a by-product of the action. The character in tragedy should be someone famous or prosperous, and must experience a change or reversal (*peripeteia*) in status from prosperity to misfortune. This will be accompanied by a recognition (*anagnorisis*), a change from ignorance to knowledge, and it will result in suffering (*pathos*). This turn of events will evoke feelings of pity or fear in the audience and effect a *catharsis* of those emotions—whether we understand that word to mean emotional purgation, purification, or intellectual clarification. To that end, the tragic character must be neither completely good nor completely wicked (since the suffering of such persons would not be fearful or pitiful). Rather, the individual will be someone like ourselves and will fall because of an error (*hamartia*) that he makes. This error will derive from some aspect of character, such as the sort of violent pride (*hybris*) that denies the distinction between gods and humans.

This summary oversimplifies a very complex and, in parts, problematic text, and it would risk further oversimplification to apply Aristotle's analysis to Sophocles' plays in any mechanical way. It is striking, however, that many (though not all) of the plays do conform, at least on a very basic level, to this tragic pattern. *Oedipus the King* obviously fits the bill since it is Aristotle's test case. Rather than go through each play in detail here, the reader is invited to test the validity of Aristotle's analysis on each of the plays in this volume.

What is missing from Aristotle's analysis, however, is any sense of what lies beyond the suffering, any sense of its meaning or larger significance. To be fair, Aristotle was concerned primarily with the formal aspects of drama and their effect on the audience; and in these areas, he believed that Sophocles excelled. But Sophocles' true greatness, that which recommends him to us and to all generations, is not just formal but intellectual and even spiritual, the invention of the tragic hero.

For Aeschylus the meaning of suffering is to be found in the divine design, since he at least holds out the hope that the will of the gods, which is often painful for human beings to endure, has some larger purpose, which will be ultimately revealed to us. Euripides, on the other hand, problematizes the gods: in some plays they are reduced to an artificial plot device, the so-called deus ex machina; but his last play, the *Bacchae*, is obsessed with divinity, and its representation of the horrific violence perpetrated by the god Dionysus concludes with an indictment: "We have learned. But your sentence is too harsh. . . . Gods should be exempt from human passions" (*Bacchae* 1346–48, trans. Arrowsmith). Sophocles falls somewhere between these two positions. In his plays the will of the gods is always enigmatic, which may explain the important role that oracles play in his works, especially oracles that are misleading, misinterpreted, or ignored. The world of Sophoclean tragedy is one in which neither one's intellect nor morality can avail against the inscrutable will of the gods.

But Sophocles focuses not so much on the inevitability of the suffering that the gods inflict as on the human response to that suffering. Sophocles' characters, acting autonomously and with freedom of will, bring about their own tragic ends. And, even more important, they accept responsibility for this—as when Oedipus blinds himself, or Heracles plans his own funeral pyre, or Ajax comes to his senses and accepts his fate. For six of the seven surviving plays (*The Women of Trachis* is the exception), it is even possible to describe a tragic pattern of behavior: the hero is confronted with a dilemma and chooses not to yield or compromise; others try to change his mind through appeals to reason, threats, and sometimes force; he responds to these attempts with anger; and finally, isolated and intransigent, he goes to his doom rather than betray his true nature. Bernard Knox, who described this pattern, puts it very well:

> Sophocles creates a tragic universe in which man's heroic action, free and responsible, brings him sometimes through suffering to victory but more often to a fall which is both defeat and victory at once; the suffering and the glory are fused in an indissoluble unity. Sophocles pits against the limitations on human stature great individuals who refuse to accept those limitations, and in their failure achieve a strange success.[11]

And this is a success that even the gods can acknowledge. In *Oedipus at Colonus*, which was written when Sophocles was almost ninety years old and produced posthumously, the dramatist returns to a myth that had twice before engaged his imagination.[12] A blind old man at the end of his life, a polluted outcast, exile, and beggar, Oedipus makes his way at long last to Colonus, which happens to be the hometown of Sophocles and a suburb of Athens, the home of tragedy.

Entering the sacred and forbidden grove of the Furies, Oedipus recalls Apollo's prophecy, that he would find rest in such a shrine, and after his death, his presence would persist, as a benevolent power offering protection to the people who accepted him but a curse for those who had sent him into exile. Oedipus must persuade the chorus and the ruler of Athens, Theseus, that they should take him in. He must also overcome the plots and persuasions of Creon and his own disloyal son, Polyneices, both of whom want to bring him back to Thebes for their own purposes. Oedipus, of course, will have none of this, and Theseus generously grants the suppliant asylum. Oedipus' claim is that he is innocent, that the crimes of parricide and incest by which he had become ritually impure were committed in ignorance and as punishment for the sins of his ancestors. Beyond that, he shares the prophecy that his tomb will have the power to protect Athens when it will one day be attacked by Thebes. At the end of the play, thunder and lightning are heard, and Oedipus enters the grove. Shortly thereafter a messenger arrives to announce that Oedipus has died, alone in the grove with only Theseus to witness his apotheosis, his transformation from pariah to protector, a powerful presence who, in death, serves as an intermediary between god and man. This is, in the words of David Grene, "the final triumph of the god-doomed and god-exalted."[13] Or, to quote Bernard Knox once more:

> The gods of Sophoclean tragedy, the most remote and mysterious creation in all Greek literature, here show their respect for the hero in unmistakable terms; they gave Ajax his burial, Antigone her revenge, Electra her victory, Philoctetes his return to life—but to Oedipus, who suffered most and longest, they give, in the death he longed for, immortal life and power.[14]

Even in this, it is worth noting, Athens, the home of tragedy and of democracy, has played a decisive role: supremely confident and generous of spirit, the city takes into its midst the polluted man and thereby hopes to ensure not only his apotheosis but also its own salvation.

IV. SOPHOCLEAN ARTISTRY

We cannot talk in any meaningful way about Sophocles' development as an artist, since so few of his plays survive and since those that do come only from his middle and later years. Similarly, Sophocles may have had a theoretical interest in drama since he is said to have written a book on the chorus, but that work is no longer extant. We do not, however, need to reconstruct either his artistic development over time or his theoretical understanding of his craft in order to speak of his overall accomplishment as a dramatist and a poet.

As a dramatist, he was credited by Aristotle with several important technical innovations, such as the use of painted scenery and the introduction of the third actor (*Poetics* 1449a). Prior to Sophocles, the backdrop of the theater had been a fixed architectural facade, and this innovation, which suggests color and particularity of detail, may underscore Sophocles' interest in visual effect, which we clearly see also in his vivid language and imagery. Similarly, the introduction of a third actor (Aeschylus had also done this in his *Oresteia*, perhaps influenced by the younger playwright) is much more than a technical refinement, since it made it possible to move beyond a simple dialogue between two individuals enacting opposing points of view to a richer triangulated discourse in which a greater range of ideas and emotions could be depicted on the stage. Equally important and influential was his decision to dispense with the connected trilogy, i.e., three plays linked to one another by plot and theme. This may be the most momentous of his technical innovations since it allowed for the concentrated focus on a single problem and character, and may have led to one of Sophocles' most important theatrical legacies (which has been discussed above), the invention of the tragic hero.

Discussion of the tragic hero, however, leads to consideration of another important and related feature of his drama, the emphasis on characterization generally. As noted earlier, Aristotle regarded plot as the most important element of tragedy and character as secondary: "Without action there could be no tragedy, whereas a tragedy with-

out characterization is possible" (*Poetics* 1450a). While it
might be possible to write such a tragedy, however, it would
emphatically not be Sophoclean. In one of his most famous
passages, Aristotle quoted Sophocles' own view of himself:
"Then there is also the criticism that what the poet says
is not true. This can perhaps be answered in the words of
Sophocles when he said that he made his characters what they
ought to be, while Euripides made them what they
were" (*Poetics* 1460b). This probably does not mean that
Sophocles created ideal as opposed to realistic characters,
but rather that he depicted characters in such a way that
they would fulfill the requirements of the plot. But while
Sophocles' characters are not real persons, many of them
appear so fully realized and well rounded that Freud was
able to take them out of context and plausibly use them to
describe the psychological characteristics of individuals in
the real world.

It is also striking that Sophocles' interest in characterization did not stop with the major male figures, since he also
created some of the strongest and most intriguing women
ever to walk the stage. These include not just those who
figure prominently in their plays, like Antigone, Electra,
Jocasta, Tecmessa, and Deianeira, but also lesser figures
like Ismene in *Antigone*, Chrysothemis in *Electra*, and
Antigone and Ismene in *Oedipus at Colonus*. In fact, it is
telling that more than one critic has thought it worth noting that *Philoctetes* is unique in not having a single female
character! Finally, no discussion of characterization would
be complete without mention of the chorus. While he reduced the proportion of the play occupied by choral passages, Sophocles is also credited with enlarging the size of
the chorus from twelve to fifteen people. We may detect
behind both of these technical innovations something of
great dramaturgical importance, namely an effort to move
away from choral song as an elaborate musical interlude
between episodes and to give the chorus a larger role in
commenting on and even at times developing the plot.
Here too Aristotle weighs in with approval: "The Chorus
must be considered to be one of the actors, an element in
the play, and it should take part in the action not as in Euripides but as in Sophocles" (*Poetics* 1456a).

And when it comes to plotting, Sophocles has few peers. His plots are taut and tight; even the most complex action flows logically and of necessity from the action that precedes it and the nature of the characters that are engaged in it. He is a master of dramatic devices like antithesis (as when he juxtaposes speeches and contrasting points of view); he also makes good use of foreshadowing and irony, the latter of a particular sort whereby one character says something the full significance of which the audience understands but which the speaker or auditor in the play does not yet grasp. There are very few extraneous elements, loose ends, or gross inconsistencies. And when these do exist, they either serve a dramatic function[15] or they are extraneous to the play's time frame (e.g., as in *Oedipus the King* where we might ask why Oedipus had not earlier pursued his origins). Here too Aristotle's judgment is acute: "In the incidents of the play there should be nothing inexplicable or, if there is, it should be outside the actual play, as in the *Oedipus* of Sophocles" (*Poetics 1454b*). It is no accident that *Oedipus the King* is often regarded as the first detective story, the first example of that self-conscious genre, which privileges story and which self-consciously takes as its project to elucidate the way in which stories are built up by having a character (the detective) retrospectively reconstruct the action from clues.

Up to this point the focus of our discussion of Sophocles' artistry has been on his dramatic technique, his technical innovations in the theater, his interest in characterization, and his plot construction. But, when all is said and done, Sophocles is not just a playwright but also a poet; his art is not just dramaturgical and dramatic, but also depends in a very special way on words, imagery, and rhythms. Indeed, many of his plays even deal with problems of language—the ways in which words change or have multiple meanings depending on who uses them and who hears them.

This sort of instability is a characteristic of one form of speech that is important in Sophocles, namely prophecy. But it occurs elsewhere as well. In *Antigone,* for example, the great ode on man (pages 354–55 in this translation) seems initially to celebrate the intellectual and cultural achievements of humanity, and critics have detected in it similarities to the views of the sophist Protagoras, who held that man was the measure of all things. But the language of the very first line is loaded. As it is usually translated, the line reads: "Many are the wonders (*deina*) but nothing is more wonderful (*deinoteron*) than man." The problem is that *deina* in Greek refers to anything that inspires awe; thus the word can mean "awesome" but also "awful," "wonderful" and "terrible." And, indeed, after the ode goes through its lists of categories of human achievement, it concludes with a warning: man can cure anything—anything, that is, except death:

> Creation is a marvel and
>   Man its masterpiece....
> ...
> Training his agile thoughts
>   volatile as air
>   He's civilized the world
>   of words and wit and law.
> With a roof against the sky,
>   the javelin crystal frosts
>   The arrow-lancing rains;
>   he's fertile in resource
>   Provident for all,
>   healing all disease:
>   All but death, and death—
> death he never cures.[16]

Language and imagery here cooperate to convey this essential duality—the greatness of man but also his limitations—which is at the heart of *Antigone* and also of all Sophoclean tragedy.

If every translator is a traitor, as the saying goes, it is impossible to appreciate fully the poetic (as opposed to dramatic) qualities of Sophocles (or any other poet) by reading him in another language. But the translations by Paul Roche in this volume, while not literal, nonetheless do capture some of the poetic energy, force, and even rhythm of the original. Perhaps there is no better way to close than by quoting a selection from this translation—the famous ode from *Oedipus at Colonus* (pages 294–95) in which the chorus celebrates the landscape of Attica in one of the finest and most lyrical appreciations of nature in Greek poetry:

> Stranger, here
> Is the land of the horse
> Earth's fairest home
> This silver hill Colonus.
>
> Here the nightingale
> Spills perennial sound
> Lucent through the evergreen.
>
> Here the wine-deep ivies creep
> Through the god's untrodden bower
> Heavy with the laurel berry.
>
> Here there is a sunless quiet
> Riven by no storm.
> Here the corybantic foot
> Of Bacchus beats
> Tossing with the nymphs who nursed him.
> . . .
> Out among the gentle breasts
> Of hills and dales
> Swelling with fecundity.
> Not seldom here the Muses sing
> And Aphrodite rides with golden rein.

—Matthew S. Santirocco

Endnotes

[1] I am speaking, of course, of Athens, the home of tragedy, and of the first production of the plays. But other cities had theaters, some of which are still in use, and there were also revivals of older plays.

[2] The original festival was the City or Greater Dionysia in late March; but there were other feasts as well, such as the Lenaea, at which plays were part of the civic ceremonial.

[3] Of extant plays, only Aeschylus' *Persians* takes as its subject matter an historical event, though the defeat of Persia by the Greeks was already achieving mythic status.

[4] Aristotle *Poetics* 1449a states that the original meter of the dialogue was the trochaic tetrameter, but that it was replaced by the iambic pentameter, which more closely resembled the rhythms of speech.

[5] We know of 123 plays by Sophocles, but only seven are extant, though fragments of several others exist. The other two tragedians did not fare much better: only seven of Aeschylus' seventy plays and seventeen out of Euripides' sixty-six survive. This dismal survival rate does not reflect a negative judgment but rather the vagaries of the transmission of texts from antiquity; on this fascinating topic see L. D. Reynolds and N. G. Wilson, *Scribes and Scholars: A Guide to the Transmission of Greek and Latin Literature* (3rd edition, Oxford University Press: Oxford, 1991).

[6] While Sophocles' plays have more than three characters, they require only three actors, since one actor will play several roles.

[7]Because their styles are so different, it is commonly assumed that the list of the major tragedians—Aeschylus, Sophocles, and Euripides—represents a chronological sequence. In fact, Aeschylus (c. 525–456 BCE) was alive when Sophocles (496–406 BCE) and Euripides (485–406 BCE) began their careers, and the latter were almost exact contemporaries and died in the same year.

[8]Jean-Pierre Vernant, "The Historical Moment of Tragedy in Greece," in Jean-Pierre Vernant and Pierre Vidal-Naquet, *Tragedy and Myth in Ancient Greece* (trans. Janet Lloyd: Humanities Press, NJ, 1981), 2. The other essays in this volume are particularly relevant to this theme, as are Charles Segal, *Interpreting Greek Tragedy: Myth, Poetry, Text* (Cornell University Press: Ithaca, NY, and London, 1986), and John J. Winkler and Froma I. Zeitlin (eds.), *Nothing to Do with Dionysus: Athenian Drama in Its Social Context* (Princeton University Press: Princeton, NJ, 1990).

[9]For full discussion of this play along these lines, see my article, "Justice in Sophocles' *Antigone*," *Philosophy and Literature*, vol. 4, no. 2 (Fall 1980), 180–98.

[10]One of the most brilliant philosophers of all time, Aristotle (384–22 BCE) wrote the *Poetics* about seventy years after Sophocles. The first serious work of literary criticism, it has had an enormous influence on subsequent literary study and practice. A convenient translation is G. M. A. Grube, *Aristotle: On Poetry and Style* (Bobbs-Merrill: Indianapolis, 1956 and frequently reprinted); I quote from this translation. For a classic attempt to argue the relevance of Aristotle to the criticism of individual tragedies, see John Jones, *On Aristotle and Greek Tragedy* (Oxford University Press: New York, 1962).

[11]B. M. W. Knox, *The Heroic Temper: Studies in Sophoclean Tragedy* (University of California Press: Berkeley, 1964), 6. My account depends heavily on this view, though Knox' tragic pattern, no less than Aristotle's, needs to be tempered: see, e.g., Easterling's succinct remarks: "The term 'hero' must be used with caution, in case it leads us to adopt a formula too rigid for the fluidity of Sopho-

clean drama. The intransigent, isolated, suffering figure is clearly the most important of his symbols of mankind, but it is not the only one.... There is another respect, too, in which the image of the isolated hero is liable to mislead. This is in its associations with specifically modern, post-romantic ideas of the outsider.... Sophocles' men and women, it is true, reject the norms of ordinary behaviour ... but they do not reject society as such, and they define themselves in relation to society." (P. E. Easterling and B. M. W. Knox [eds.], *The Cambridge History of Classical Literature*, vol. 1, part 2, "Greek Drama," [Cambridge University Press: Cambridge, 1989], 62.)

[12]The three plays connected with the house of Oedipus were written at different times (*Antigone* was written first, then *Oedipus the King*, and finally *Oedipus at Colonus*). This order of composition does not, however, reflect the movement of the plot (the action of *Oedipus the King* precedes that of *Oedipus at Colonus*, and *Antigone* depicts events later still). While Sophocles jettisoned the connected trilogy in favor of the single play that was complete in itself, the fact that he returned to this myth on at least three occasions invites us to read the three plays not only separately but also together, perhaps as a sort of retrospective trilogy.

[13]D. Grene, *Reality and the Heroic Pattern* (University of Chicago Press: Chicago, 1967), 166. This classic book by a great translator of Greek tragedy studies the last plays of Ibsen, Shakespeare, and Sophocles, and the connections he sees among the *Ajax*, *Philoctetes*, and *Oedipus at Colonus* are illuminating.

[14]See Knox (above n. 11), 161–62. There may be hints of other Sophoclean characters' transformations, since Ajax and Heracles would both eventually become objects of hero cult; on Sophocles' own connection to these rituals, see Knox, 53 ff.

[15]E.g., Neoptolemus' account toward the end of the *Philoctetes* of the prophecy that he and Philoctetes would take Troy contradicts his apparent ignorance of the prophecy in the prologue. But while this inconsistency is illogical,

"there are good dramatic reasons for releasing this crucial information piecemeal and for presenting Neoptolemus at the outset as wholly dependent on Odysseus, while the deeper significance of the inconsistency seems to be that it enables the audience to share with Neoptolemus a growing awareness of the true meaning of the prophecy" (P. E. Easterling, [above n. 11], 62).

[16]I want to thank my editor Tracy Bernstein and NYU colleagues and friends, Marcelle Clements, Peter Meineck and Phillip Mitsis, for advice. For further reading, the works cited in notes 8, 9, 10, 11, and 13 provide a good start. Also, several recent collections of essays give an overview of current scholarship and contain bibliographies: P. E. Easterling (ed.), *The Cambridge Companion to Greek Tragedy* (Cambridge University Press: Cambridge, 1997); E. Segal (ed.), *Oxford Readings in Greek Tragedy* (Oxford University Press: Oxford, 1983); and J. Gregory (ed.) *A Companion to Greek Tragedy* (Blackwell: Malden, England, 2005).

Appendix:
Production and Acting

There are two main dangers in the production of a Greek play: one is to overplay the dignity; the other is not to be aware of that dignity at all. The first becomes a desperate and futile endeavor to recapture the externals of the Greek theater. It is arty and self-conscious and, in battening on period effects (we are being Greeks, boys and girls—is my mask on straight?), destroys the very humanity and timelessness it seeks to promote. The second, confusing the Greek idealization and simplification of human nature with unreality, and seeking to redress the balance, tries to turn the heroic figures of Aeschylus, Sophocles and Euripides into everyday nonentities. It attempts the prosaic, trivial, chatty, and obliterates the heights and depths of tragedy.

These are the two chief false principles. Occasionally they are blended and a third type of mistake is hatched, inheriting the artiness of one parent and the lack of restraint of the other. Professor J. T. Sheppard, the great Sophoclean scholar, well describes it in a production of *Oedipus the King* that he had the discomfort of witnessing: "[The] actors, not altogether, I suspect, of their own free will, raged and fumed and ranted, rushing hither and thither with a violence of gesticulation which, in spite of all their effort, was eclipsed and rendered insignificant by the yet more violent rushes, screams, and contortions of a quite gratuitous crowd" [Introduction to *The Oedipus Tyrannus of Sophocles*, Cambridge, 1920.]

What, then, is the enlightened producer to aim for?

Let him first of all remember that these plays were performed before enormous audiences, perhaps up to 30,000 people. Masks, costumes, spectacles, and the whole style of production (whatever its sacred origins) were designed for long-distance effect:* a purpose that no longer exists in our smaller and more intimate theater.

Secondly, this vast audience did not consist predominantly of sophisticated city dwellers but of honest-to-goodness people coming in from the country—many of them farmers and perhaps even (we cannot be certain) slaves. The point is that it was not a highbrow audience, even if it understood better than any modern audience the cultural framework of its own myths. It was not at all the kind of audience that came for culture or would tolerate any "art for art's sake." These people came to be thrilled and moved to tears. All the external apparatus of the Greek stage—song, dance, mime, masks, and spectacle—was simply a means to creating a vivid arena wherein the great human emotions could be worked out in public. In some 2,400 years these emotions have not changed. Only the external circumstances have changed. Oedipus, Jocasta, and Antigone were first of all human beings. The heart of Sophocles, which beat to their passions, was first of all a human heart—only incidentally Greek and of the fifth century B.C.

Thirdly, let both producer and actor remember that it is only through his words—by their very choice and sound—that Sophocles the poet achieves his power to move us. It is through the beauty, restraint, perfect adaptation of every tone and emphasis of the language to each situation, that he is able to sink us deeply into the pathos of his characters. Assuming that the translator has done his best to capture something of the original word-magic, let those words be heard. It is absolutely necessary that the poetry be read as poetry and not

---

*Masks not merely typed a character's predominant expression but also helped to project the actor's voice (though this second reason is now somewhat discredited).

given a prose pointing. It is absolutely necessary that the lines are not deprived of their rich embodiment of rhythm and cadence. The poet has already done the work of establishing the necessary tension and dramatic force. No amount of "acting" can be a substitute for it. Let the voice be measured but natural: never "tharsonic," that blend of stage and pulpit which some actors affect when they come to poetry. If the lines are enunciated clearly and rhythmically, if the acting follows the poetry and is not imposed upon it, then the result will tend to be great acting. It will be the transparent window through which the characters—created by the words—are sincerely seen; idealistically human yet never falsely intimate.

As to the chorus, let the producer keep in mind its purpose: to underline, develop, and if possible increase, the suspense built up by the dialogue. Certainly there can be music, mime, and dance, provided all this does not detract from the intelligibility of the words. The music should tend to build up background rather than to lead. It can be an ally to the force of the poetry if used sensitively and not as an end in itself. Woodwind and percussion instruments—flute and soft drum—would seem to be the most natural accompaniment to the Greek movement. They can be used to usher in and to usher out the main characters. The Sophoclean chorus numbered fifteen, but it can be raised to almost any number or lowered to as few as five. It is better for the chorus to speak its lines severally than to chant them in unison: though there may be occasions when a group answers a group.

The scenery should be simple and not distract the viewer's imagination by striving for realism. A drop curtain may be helpful, though the Greeks did not use one. An interval almost certainly destroys the accumulated tension. If masks are used, they should not be replicas of the Greek mask, which was much larger than life.

These, then, are the principles. There are few rules, if many possibilities. Only that production of a Greek play will be valid which puts the human emotions first and enables the spectator to feel with and for its subjects. Let producer and actor resist the two falsifying temptations: the purely mundane, which can never be heroic, and the overstylized, which can never be human.

Notes

(1) Meter

The meter throughout the dialogue of this rendering of the Theban Plays is iambic, as it is in Sophocles. If to anyone's eye it reads too unvaryingly, I can only counsel him to read it aloud, keeping to the natural stresses of the words. Dramatic speech automatically tends to create its own background of counterpoint rhythms. Indeed, the danger on the stage is not that poetry should sound monotonous but that it should not sound at all. Sophocles himself never loses his hold on an unmistakable "beat," which should not be lost in the English even though English prosody is "qualitative" rather than "quantitative." In either language it is the beauty of the measure itself that contributes to the depth, loftiness, and intensity of the drama.

In my original translation of the Oedipus Plays, published by New American Library in 1958, I wrote: "In the *Antigone* I keep to a more or less traditional blank versification, but in the other two plays I have made the attempt to tauten the metrical value of dramatic speech while at the same time rendering it more elastic and capacious. In *Oedipus the King* I have adopted a prosodical device which helps the line to follow the sense of the words more than it does in ordinary iambic pentameter. The lines lengthen and shorten as the need may be, but whether they stretch into hexameters or shrink into trimeters the overall count of a passage remains iambic pentameter. I have called it 'Compensated Pentameter.' In *Oedipus at Colonus,* to match by some kind of prosodical analogy this last and supreme mastery of Sophocles over human speech, I have done away with even compensation and embark on a completely free-wheeling iambic measure which I think (and hope) is proof against all misreading."

Since that time, I have come to the conclusion that this last solution is the best, and it is what I adhere to in this new rendition in all three plays. The "free-wheeling iambic measure" seems to me to get nearest to that amazing wedding in the Greek of formality to spontaneity and fluidity.

There is one other observation I should like to make. In the choruses and choral dialogues I have mostly returned to the traditional usage of beginning each line with a capital rather than following the present practice of using lowercase. My motive is to discourage readers (especially actors) from treating verse, even when dialogue, as ordinary expository prose. I make no apologies for this decision. We live in an age when lack of faith (or is it courage?) in the power of poetry to communicate before and beyond the point at which it enters the cerebrum drives readers to make verse look and sound like prose as soon as possible.

(2) Oedipus the King

The power of *Oedipus the King* is cumulative. It opens slowly, weightily, and rises to a flood of emotion that nothing can stop. This initial solemnity—at times almost a stiffness—I have been at pains to keep in the English. It is a formal and hieratic quality and lasts till about line 86, the first exit of OEDIPUS. However, it must not be assumed that this "grand manner" of utterance casts aside the already perceptible elements of pity, pathos, irony, fear, and suffering that come to such full fruition later.

(3) Creon

It must not be thought that the character of CREON in *Oedipus the King* corresponds exactly to the CREON in the other two plays. The Theban Plays were not written at the same time or conceived originally as a strict unity.

(4) Appearance of the Greek Script

For those who are interested, here are the first six lines of the *Antigone* written out in Greek lowercase. If they are written out in capitals (as Greek often was), they will look like the lines at the beginning of this book.

ὦ κοινὸν αὐτάδελφον Ἰσμήνης κάρα,
ἆρ' οἶσθ' ὅ τι Ζεὺς τῶν ἀπ' Οἰδίπου κακῶν
ὁποῖον οὐχὶ νῷν ἔτι ζώσαιν τελεῖ;
οὐδὲν γὰρ οὔτ' ἀλγεινὸν οὔτ' ἄτης ἄτερ
οὔτ' αἰσχρὸν οὔτ' ἄτιμόν ἐσθ', ὁποῖον οὐ
τῶν σῶν τε κἀμῶν οὐκ ὄπωπ' ἐγὼ κακῶν.

(5) Texts of the Oedipus Plays

The texts I have followed have in the main been those of Lewis Campbell (Oxford 1879) and Richard Jebb (Cambridge 1889–93). I support Campbell as against Jebb in not excising lines 904–12 of *Antigone*. These lines seem to me to throw important light on ANTIGONE's character and motives.

(6) Handling of the Chorus

In general let the director never forget that the chorus must be elevated to an art convincing in its own right. This means that the Chorus must be worth watching and listening to almost regardless of the rest of the play. Though commenting on, condensing, and recording the action of the drama, the Chorus should transcend it, lift it to a new plane of experience—the lyrical. This is accomplished only by being poetically different from the realism (naturalism) of each episode. The verses must be treated as pure poetry—that is, as a vehicle of illumination that communicates before, or at least beyond, the point at which it is understood. The important question is not so much whether the Chorus is intelligible, as whether it sweeps the audience off its feet the way music and dance can. The following suggestions on how to direct a Chorus may be helpful. They embody some of the stratagems I would employ if I were staging a Greek play.

(a) Make the size of the Chorus as large as is compatible with the size of the stage, remembering that twelve people are generally more impressive than three.

(b) Have the Chorus trained in dance and mime and let the dancing be more or less continuous through the play, though obviously more restrained during the dialogue parts of the episodes.

(c) Rarely allow the Chorus to speak directly (except, of course, where it takes part in the dialogue). Instead, have the words coming "voice-over" their movements, either by direct voice beyond the stage or prerecorded, or both: in all cases amplified and made larger than life. (The reason I am disinclined to let the Chorus speak is that I have found that performers generally appear overly self-conscious when forced to dance, sing, mime, and recite at the same time.)

(d) For this same reason, recitation in unison is difficult to bring off convincingly, and I prefer the single amplified voice. Of course, there may be occasions where voices in unison may be attempted, as well as other sonic experiments. For instance, after a first straight hearing, the words can be fragmented into various patterns of repetition, crosscutting, overlapping, truncation, and so on. They can echo liturgical prayers, litanies, chants—the English perhaps played off against the sound of classical Greek—or even turned into wounded-animal sounds. Here it would be wise to call in the assistance of an imaginative music director who knows all the tricks of electronic recording. Another inventive approach would be to have the actions of the Chorus turned into tableaux vivants during the voice-overs. These living pictures can be sometimes moving, sometimes still— frozen into certain attitudes. Remember always that the aim is to make the Chorus—both in sound and in sight—breathtaking.

(e) As to the straight recitation of the Chorus verses, they should be beaten out rhythmically, with little attempt to make them sound "natural." The design of the poetry must be allowed to appear and not turned into prose. For instance, when the sense of the words requires the end of one line to be run into the next, let the reciter create the illusion of doing this, but he must not actually do it. The ear must not be cheated of the incantatory effect of the line as a musical unit.

(f) The choice of music is crucial. There should be music throughout the play, introducing scenes, repeating themes, coming in and out of both the dialogue and the choruses. Care must be taken, however, that the words always be given first place. Never should the audience have to strain to hear the words above the music. As to instruments, I favor drum, flute, and lute (perhaps guitar and harp) as coming nearest to the Greek timbal, flageolet, and lyre.

(g) In general, let the director remember that a Greek play stands or falls by the quality of the Chorus. Too often one gets the impression that the embarrassed director, at his wits' end, wants to get the Chorus out of the way as soon as possible. Sometimes it seems the Chorus is being twisted into part of the dialogue. No, the Chorus must exist for its own sake and for the arresting beauty of its own design. Besides being aesthetically irresistible, the Chorus has the function of relieving the audience of dramatic tension (building after each episode) and introducing a new tension, which is lyric and hits below the belt—that is, below the level of the conscious mind.

Glossary of Classical Names

ABAE (ab ee): a town in the province of Phocis (northern Greece) famous for its temple and oracle of Apollo.

ACHAEA (ak ee ar): part of the Peloponnese (Peloponnesos), southern Greece. In Homer and Greek drama it became a synonym for Greece and the Greeks.

ACHELÖUS (a ke lo us): son of Oceanus and Gaea. Worshiped as a river-god throughout Greece.

ACHERON (ak er on): one of the five rivers of Hades, the river of woes, across which Charon ferried the souls of the dead. It became another word for Hades.

ACHILLES (ak kil ees): son of Peleus and Thetis. Greatest of the Greek heroes at the siege of Troy. He slew Hector in single combat and dragged him three times around the walls of Troy. He was finally killed by Paris, who wounded him in his only vulnerable part, the heel—from which his mother held him when she dipped him in the river Styx. The hero of Homer's *Iliad*.

ACROPOLIS (a krop o lis): citadel of Athens or of any Greek city.

ACTAEON (ak tee on): a hunter who spied upon Artemis while she was bathing. She turned him into a stag, and his dogs tore him to pieces. (vide painting by Titian)

ADONIS (ad o nis): a beautiful youth loved by Aphrodite. He was killed by a wild boar while hunting, and from his blood sprang an anemone. Persephone restored him to life on condition that he spend half the year with her in Hades.

AEGEAN SEA (ee gee an): an arm of the Mediterranean between Greece and Turkey, bounded on the south by Crete.

AEGEUS (ee gee us): king of Athens and father of Theseus.

AEGINA (ee jee nar): daughter of the river-god Asopus. Also island off southeast coast of Attica.

AEGIS (ee gis): the shield and breastplate of Pallas Athena, on which was depicted the head of the Gorgon Medusa, writhing with snakes. All who looked on it were turned to stone.

AEGISTHUS (ee giss th yus): son of Thyestes by his daughter Pelopia. Hated nephew of Atreus, lover of Clytemnestra and murdered with her by Orestes and Electra.

AESCULAPIUS (ees koo lay pi us): god of medicine and healing. He is represented holding the Caduceus: the wand of Hermes, a golden staff entwined with serpents. To this day it remains the symbol of medicine.

AJAX (ay jaks): the most manly and redoubtable Greek warrior at Troy after Achilles, for the possession of whose armor he quarreled with Odysseus. He offended Athena, and she drove him to madness and suicide.

ALPHAEUS (al fay us): river-god of the river running past Olympia in Arcadia. He fell in love with the nymph Arethusa, and when she fled from him to Sicily he flowed under the sea to join her.

ALTHEA (al thee ar or al thay ar): mother of Meleager (mel e aj ar). The Fates ordained that his life would last as long as a burning log thrown by them into the fire. But when he slew his mother's two brothers, she extinguished the fire, and thus his life, then killed herself.

AMALTHEA (a mal thee ar): the goat that nursed the infant Zeus in the Cretan cave. One of her horns was called "cornucopia" and was filled with whatever its owner desired. This "horn of plenty" is usually represented as a hollow horn overflowing with fruit and flowers.

AMBROSIA (am bro zi ar): the food of the gods. Nectar was their drink.

AMMON (am on): Egyptian deity identified with Zeus, whose temple in the Lybian desert was a famous oracle: consulted by Alexander the Great before his conquest of Asia.

APOLLO (ap ōll oh): also Helios, Hyperion, Phoebus; the Sun god; one of the twelve Olympians, son of Zeus and Leto, twin brother of Artemis. He was patron of the arts, medicine, music, and poetry. His oracle at Delphi was the most famous in Greece.

ARCADIA (ar kāy di ar): a pastoral region in the central Peloponnese; haunt of the god Pan and birthplace of Pan's father, Hermes. It was the symbol of quiet happiness. Hence the nostalgic expression "Et in Arcadia ego—I too once lived in Arcadia."

AREOPAGUS (ar e ōp a gus): the Hill of Ares, west of the Acropolis; it became the criminal court of Athens.

ARES (āh res or ār ees or āir ees): the Roman Mars, god of war, whose symbols were the dog and the vulture—scavengers of the battlefield; son of Zeus and Hera and one of the twelve Olympians. He had an affair with Aphrodite and was caught in the act by Hephaestus, who threw a net over the couple—to the enjoyment of all Olympus. He was despised by Apollo.

ARETHUSA (ar e thūz ar): a wood nymph who accompanied Artemis while hunting. She fled from the river-god Alphaeus and was saved from him by Artemis, who changed her into a stream in Sicily.

ARGIVES (ār gyvz): the Greeks of Argos and Argolis in the Peloponnese, but often used for all Greeks.

ARGOLIS (ār gol is): a region between Arcadia and the Aegean Sea.

ARGOS (ār gos): a city-state and the capital of Argolis.

ARTEMIS (ār te mis): the Roman Diana, also called Cynthia, Delia, Hecate, Phoebe, Selene. Daughter of Zeus and Leto, twin sister of Apollo. She was moon goddess and patroness of hunting, childbirth, chastity, and unmarried girls. Though reputedly a virgin, she fell in love with the beautiful youth Endymion as he slept naked on Mount Latmos and visited him in his dreams. He prayed to Zeus to let him sleep forever. As Hecate, Artemis was the goddess of witchcraft.

ASOPUS (ā so pus): a river-god, son of Poseidon: also a river.

ATE (ār tay): also Eris, goddess of strife and discord. When not invited to the wedding of Peleus and Thetis she rolled the Golden Apple before Hera, Aphrodite, and Pallas Athena, saying, "for the fairest," which led to the Judgment of Paris and so to the Trojan War.

ATHENA (ath ēen ar): also Athene, Pallas, the Roman Minerva, one of the twelve Olympians, born out of the head of Zeus and dressed in full armor shouting a war cry. Goddess of power and wisdom, a virgin. She is said to have introduced the olive tree and invented the plow.

ATLAS (āt las): A Titan, punished by Zeus for rebellion by having to support the whole world on his shoulders.

ATREUS (ā tree us): son of Pelops and Hippodamia, brother of Thyestes and father of Agamemnon and Menelaus. He made a dinner of Thyestes' children and served them up to him.

ATRIDES (a trī dees): the two sons of Atreus: Agamemnon and Menelaus.

ATTICA (āt i kar): a division of Greece with Athens at its center.

AULIS (ōw lis): the port in Boeotia from which the Greek armada set sail for Troy.

AURORA (o rōr ra): goddess of dawn, also called Eos.

AXIUS (āx i us): a river in the valley of Pieria near Mount Olympus.

BACCHAE (bāk ee or ai): priestesses of Dionysus, who by wine, chewing ivy leaves, and mad enthusiasm worked themselves into a frenzy at the Bacchic festivals or Bacchanals.

BACCHANT or BACCHANTES (bāk ant): also called MAENADS (mee nads or may nads): same as the above.

BACCHUS (bāk us): also called DIONYSUS and BROMIUS. Son of Zeus and Semele. God of wine, mystery, incantation, and the raw potency of nature: reared by the nymphs on Mount Nysa. Represented crowned with vine and ivy leaves.

BOEBIA (bee bi ar): a lake in Thessaly near Mount Ossa.

BOEOTIA (bee ō shar): a long stretch of territory northwest of Attica, whose chief city was Thebes. The Boeotians were proverbially regarded as dull and stupid.

BOREAS (bor ay as): god of the north wind, the Roman Aquilo. In the Persian War he helped the Athenians by destroying the ships of the "Barbarians."

BYBLUS (bĭb lus): a coastal town in Syria where Adonis had a temple.

CADMUS (kād mus): he founded Thebes by killing a dragon sacred to Ares and then on the advice of Athena sowing its teeth. Armed men sprang up from the ground and fought and killed one another until only five were left. These five then helped Cadmus to build the city of Thebes. He was the brother of Europa and the father of Agave, Autonoë, and Ino. He married Harmonia, daughter of Aphrodite.

CALCHAS (kāl kas): a seer attached to the Greek army going to Troy. He predicted that the Greek fleet could not sail without the sacrifice of Agamemnon's daughter Iphigenia, and that Troy could not be taken without the help of Achilles, nor without a ten-year siege.

CAPANEUS (kap ār nay us): one of the Seven against Thebes.

CASSANDRA (ka sān drar): a daughter of Priam and Hecuba: the most beautiful of their girls. Apollo gave her the gift of prophecy, but when she refused his advances he ordained that she would never be believed. At the fall of Troy she was dragged from the altar of Athena by Ajax and deflowered. Agamemnon brought her to Argos as his concubine. Clytemnestra slew them both.

CASTALIA (kas tāy li ar): a nymph pursued by Apollo and turned by him into a spring on Mount Parnassus near Delphi. Those who drank its waters were inspired by the poetic spirit.

CASTOR and POLYDEUCES (POLLUX) (kās ter,

polly dēw sees): twin sons of Zeus by Leda. Castor was patron of navigation, Polydeuces of boxing and wrestling.

CECROPS (sēe krops): son of Gaea and first king of Attica. He had a human torso but from the waist down was a serpent. When Athena gave Athens the olive tree he instructed his subjects to cultivate the olive and make her their patroness.

CENTAURS (sēn torz): a race half man, half horse, inhabiting the mountains of Thessaly. The greater part of them were killed by Heracles, the rest driven to Mount Pindus. Their enemies were the Lapiths, who had human bodies but the hooves of horses.

CEPHISUS (sē fe sus): the father of Narcissus; also the name of three famous rivers in Greece.

CERBERUS (sēr ber us): the three-headed dog that guarded the entrance to Hades.

CHARITES (kār it ees): the three Graces—beautiful attendants of Aphrodite.

CHARON (kāre on): a minor god in charge of the passage of souls to Hades. For a fee—a coin placed in the mouth of the dead—he would ferry souls across the rivers Acheron and Styx to the shores of Hades. Without a fee, Charon refused to take them, and they were condemned to wander for a hundred years.

CHIRON (kȳ ron): the wisest of the centaurs and tutor of Achilles.

CITHAERON (sĭth er on): a mountain range separating Boeotia from Attica and sacred to Dionysus. The scene of several tragedies.

CLYTEMNESTRA (kly tem nēs trar): queen of Sparta, wife of Agamemnon, mother of Orestes, Electra, and Iphigenia. While Agamemnon was away at Troy she took Aegisthus as a lover. When her husband came back she and Aegisthus murdered him, only to be murdered themselves by Orestes and Electra.

CORYBANTS or CORYBANTES (kori bāntz, kori bān tees): attendants of the Phrygian goddess Cybele, who followed her through the night in orgiastic revelry.

CREON (krēe on or kray on): ruler of Corinth who put Antigone to death for refusing to obey his edict forbidding the burial of her brother Polyneices, who had fought against Thebes.

CRONOS (krōwe nos): youngest of the Titans, son of Uranus (heaven) and Ge or Gaea (earth). He was father by Rhea of Hestia, Demeter, Hera, Hades, Poseidon, and Zeus. He ousted Uranus from divine supremacy and was in turn dethroned by Zeus. He is the Roman Saturn.

CYBELE (sȳ bel ee): also Rhea, the Roman Magna Mater. Titan earth goddess and wife of Cronos.

CYCLOPS (sȳ klops), also CYCLOPES (sȳ klo pees): one-eyed giants who, legend says, put together the enormous stones of Mycenae. They were shepherds and sometimes cannibals.

CYLLENE (sy lēen ee): the highest mountain in the Peloponnese.

CYPRIS (sī pris): another name for Aphrodite, born from the foam in the sea off Cyprus.

DAEDALUS (dēe dal us): a genius craftsman who designed the Labyrinth in Crete, from which to escape he fixed wings to himself and his son Icarus, who flew too near the sun, melted the wax that held his wings and crashed into the Icarian Sea (vide the famous poem by W. H. Auden).

DAEMON (dēe mon or dy mon): a spirit in command of persons and places, sometimes good and sometimes bad.

DANAE (dan ā ee): An Argive princess who was shut up in a brazen tower by her father because an oracle had said her son would one day kill his grandfather. Zeus visited her in her tower in a shower of gold, and thus impregnated she gave birth to Perseus, who years later killed his grandfather accidentally with a discus.

DANIANS (dan ȳ anz), also DANAAI (dan ȳ ee): another name for the Greeks.

DARDANUS (dār dan us): ancestor of the Trojans. He built a city near the foot of Mount Ida in Phrygia, which he called Dardania. "Dardanian" became another name for Trojan.

DAULIA (dōw li ar): an ancient town in Phocis, northern Greece.

DELOS (dēe los): the smallest of the Cyclades Islands

in the Aegean Sea. The birthplace of Apollo and Artemis. The site of a famous temple dedicated to Apollo.

DELPHI (dĕl fee or del fai): oracle and shrine of Apollo beneath Mount Parnassus in Phocis. Besides being richly endowed, it possessed more than three thousand statues. Later plundered by Nero.

DEMETER (de mēe ter): sister of Zeus and one of the twelve Olympians. Goddess of grain, harvest, fruit, flowers, and the fertility of the earth. Mother of Persephone, whom Pluto abducted while she was picking flowers in the meadows of Enna, Sicily. Demeter threatened to boycott all nature if she were not returned. Pluto restored her to earth on condition that she spend six months of the year with him in Hades. During that time the earth goes into retreat: the winter. Demeter became identified with the Roman Ceres (from which we get the word "cereal").

DIOMEDES (dy o mēe deez): one of the Greek champions in the Trojan War. He fed his horses human flesh. Heracles in his eighth labor killed him and fed him to his horses.

DIONYSUS (dy on ȳ sus): see Bacchus.

DRYADS (drȳ adz), also **DRYADES** (drȳ ad eez), also **HAMADRYADS** (hămmer drȳ adz): nymphs who dwelt in trees, the equivalent of our tree fairies. They died when their trees were cut down.

DRYAS (drȳ as): father of the Thracian king Lycurgus. He was driven mad for insulting Dionysus.

ECHO (ēk o): a nymph who pined away for love of Narcissus.

EDONIA (ee dōwe nee ar): a part of Thrace (northern Greece) where the people were celebrated for their orgiastic worship of Bacchus.

EIRENE (ie rēe nee): goddess of peace.

ELECTRA (el ēk trar): daughter of Agamemnon and Clytemnestra; sister of Orestes and married to his friend Pylades. With their help she murdered her mother.

ELEUSIS (el ū sis): a town fourteen miles west of Athens, where the Eleusian mysteries were celebrated in the temple of Demeter.

ELIS (ēe lis): a city and country of the Peloponnese

famous for its horses and for Olympia, the site of the Olympic games.

ENNOSIS (en no sis): a minor deity, the spirit of earthquakes.

EREBUS (er e bus): a region in the underworld through which souls must pass on their way to Hades.

ERECHTHEUS (e rek the us): the sixth king of Athens and father of Cecrops. He introduced the worship of Athena and other cults.

ERINYES (er in yez): the Roman Furies, dreaded daughters of Earth and Night, whose mission it was to pursue miscreants; depicted as winged crones with snakes twining in their hair and blood dripping from their eyes. They dwelt in the depths of Tartarus and punished mortals in both this world and the next, usually for disobedience towards parents, disrespect for old age, perjury, murder, violation of the laws of hospitality, and improper conduct towards suppliants.

EROS (er oes): the Roman Cupid, son of Aphrodite; also sexual love and desire, as distinct from *agape* (parental or filial love or fondness) and *philia* (the love of friendship or the liking of someone or something).

EUBOEA (u bee ar): the largest island after Crete, running alongside Boeotia.

EUMENIDES (u men i deez): the Kindly Ones, a euphemism for the Erinyes.

EURIPUS (u rip us): a narrow strait separating the island of Euboea from the coast of Boeotia.

EUROPA (u ro par): sister of Cadmus. Zeus tricked her onto his back by changing himself into a white bull, then swam to Crete, where he ravished her.

EUROTAS (u ro tas): a river in Sparta.

EURYDICE (u rid i see): see Orpheus. Another Eurydice was the wife of Creon and mother of Haemon, who was betrothed to Antigone. When she learned that her son had committed suicide she killed herself.

EURYSTHEUS (u ris thi us): king of Argos and Mycenae, cousin of Heracles and his rival. He tried to destroy Heracles by imposing on him a series of impossible tasks known as the Twelve Labors of Heracles. He was killed by Hylus, a son of Heracles.

EUXINE (yūk sine): the Black Sea. The word means "friendly."

FATES: the three daughters of Erebus and Nyx, Night—Clotho, who carried the spindle that spun the thread of life; Lachēsis, who carried the scroll that determined the length of the thread of life; and Ātropos, who carried the shears that cut the thread of life.

GAEA (jēe ar, also gee'ar): Mother Earth, the most ancient divinity, mother of Uranus (the Heavens) with whom she produced the twelve Titans: six males and six females.

GANYMEDE (gān i meed): a Trojan boy of such beauty that Zeus carried him off to Olympus on the back of an eagle. He became cupbearer of the gods.

GERYON (ger ie on): a monster with three bodies and three heads who lived in Gades (Cadiz) in Spain. Also a shepherd with a two-headed sheepdog called Orthos.

GORGONS (gōr gonz): three crones, only one of whom, Medusa, was mortal. They had snakes for hair, claws for hands, and bulging eyes that turned men to stone.

GRACES: see CHARITES.

HADES (hāy deez): Pluto, one of the twelve Olympians. Son of Cronos and Rhea, husband of Persephone. The underworld was called after him.

HARMONIA (har mōw nee ar): daughter of Ares and Aphrodite and wife of Cadmus. They produced Agave, Autonoë, and Ino.

HARPIES (här peez): filthy creatures with the bodies of vultures and the faces of women. They snatched food with their clawed feet and left a stench. The gods used them to persecute criminals.

HECATE (hēk a tee): the dark side of Artemis as moon goddess; patroness of magic and spells. Propitiated by the sacrifice of dogs, lambs, and honey.

HECTOR (hēk tor): son of Priam and Hecuba; husband of Adromache and father of Astýanax. The most valiant of the Trojan heroes but finally killed by Achilles, who was furious that he had slain his friend Patróclus.

HECUBA (hēk u bar): wife of Priam and queen of Troy. Mother of fifty sons and twelve daughters, most of whom came to a bad end. After the fall of Troy she became a slave of Odysseus, and it is said by some that in the voyage to Greece she cast herself into the sea. Vergil in the Aeneid says that she changed into a bitch.

HELEN OF TROY (hēl en): *helein* in Greek means to seduce. The most seductive and beautiful woman in Greece. Half sister of Clytemnestra. Her abduction by the dazzling Trojan prince Paris was the cause of the Trojan War. After that she was brought back in disgrace to Greece by her husband Menelaus and seems to have wheedled her way back into his affections.

HELICON (hēl i kon): a range of mountains in Boeotia that are covered in snow most of the year.

HELIOS (hēe li os): the sun-god Hyperion, and sometimes Apollo.

HELLAS (hēll as): the ancient name for Thessaly, which came to mean all Greece.

HEPHAESTUS (he fēe stus or he fāi stus): the Roman Vulcan, god of fire and the forge, son of Zeus and Hera. When he was a baby, his parents kicked him out of Olympus, and he spewed his mother's milk over the heavens (the Milky Way), and he broke a leg when he fell, making him lame. He was the smithy of the gods, with his forge under Mount Aetna in Sicily. Though unprepossessing, he became the father of Eros by Aphrodite.

HERA (hēe rar): the Roman Juno, daughter of Cronos and Rhea, wife and sister of Zeus, Queen of Heaven, patroness of women and childbirth. The most jealous of wives. She spied on Zeus's love affairs, persecuted his mistresses, was vindictive to his children.

HERACLES (hēr a kleez): the Roman Hercules, son of Zeus and Alcmena, personification of physical strength. When rendered mad by Hera, he killed his own children and those of his brother and was punished with the Twelve Labors. He died from the poison of one of his arrows, but was carried to Olympus and granted immortality.

HERMES (hēr meez): the Roman Mercury, son of Zeus and Maia. He was the messenger of the gods and is usually depicted wearing winged shoes and hat and carrying the caduceus. He conducted the shades of the dead to the lower world. Patron of travelers, traders, merchants, tricksters, and robbers.

HESPERUS (hēs per us): the Roman Vesper, brother of Atlas. In English poetry (and in Sappho) Hesperus is the evening star.

HESTIA (hēs ti ar): the Roman Vesta, goddess of the hearth and symbol of the home. A virgin, she was the oldest and most sacred of the Twelve Olympians.

HYADES (hīe a deez): the five daughters of Atlas. They wept inconsolably when their brother Hyas was killed by a wild boar. As a reward for nursing the infant Bacchus, Zeus placed them among the stars.

HYLUS (hīgh lus): a beautiful young man whom the river nymphs fell in love with. They pulled him into the water, where he drowned.

HYPERION (hie pēer ion): see Helios.

IACCHUS (ēe ak us): the solemn name for Bacchus in the Eleusian mysteries.

ICARUS (ĭk a rus): when fleeing from Minos, king of Crete, Daedalus made wings for himself and his son Icarus. The wings were fixed with wax, but Icarus flew too near the sun and the wax melted. He plunged headlong into the Icarian Sea.

IDA (ēi dar): a mountain in Asia Minor; site of the Judgment of Paris, abduction of Ganymede, and the worship of Cybele.

ILIUM (ĭll ee um): another word for Troy, especially the citadel.

INACHUS (ĭn a kus): a river in Argos.

IO (ēe owe): beloved by Zeus and hated by Hera, who turned her into a heifer and tormented her with a gadfly. She fled from land to land in a frenzy all over Europe and Asia, till at last she found rest on the banks of the Nile and returned to her original form.

IPHIGENIA (if ij en ēi ar): daughter of Agamemnon and Clytemnestra, who was sacrificed to get good winds for the sailing of the Greek armada to Troy.

IRENE (ei rēe nee): see Eirene.

ISMENUS (is mēe nus): a small river in Boeotia into which the stream Dirce flowed.

ISTER (īz ter): the river Danube flowing into the Black Sea through the land of the Scythians.

ISTHMIAN GAMES (īss th mee an): games that were held once a year on the Isthmus of Corinth.

LACONIA (lak ōwe nee ar): a country in the Peloponnese in southern Greece that comprised Sparta. The Spartans were a people of action and few words. From this we get the word "laconic."

LAERTES (lay ūr teez): father of Odysseus.

LARISSA (la riss ar): a town in Thessaly where Perseus killed his grandfather by mistake.

LATONA (la tōwe nar): also called Leto: mother of Apollo and Artemis.

LEDA (lēe dar): wife of Tyndareus king of Sparta. Zeus, in the form of a swan, seduced her (vide Yeats' famous poem), and she produced two eggs, one of which hatched into Clytemnestra and Helen, and the other into Castor and Pollux.

LETHE (lēe thee): the river of oblivion in Hades.

LOXIAS (lok see as): Apollo.

LYCAON (lie kāy on): a king of Arcadia noted for his cruelty. To test the divinity of Zeus he cut up his own son and served him to Zeus, who punished him by turning him into a wolf. *Lukos* is the Greek for "wolf." (In transcription the Greek *U* always becomes the English *Y*.)

LYCEUS (lie sēe us): a surname of Apollo, who was worshiped in Lycia, a district in southern Asia Minor whose inhabitants were renowned for their use of the bow.

LYDIA (lĭd ee ar): a part of Phrygia in Asia Minor, whose two most memorable kings were Croesus and Midas.

MAENADS (mēe nadz): the Bacchantes, orgiastic female devotees of Bacchus.

MAIA (mĭe ar): mother of Hermes by Zeus. She was the oldest and loveliest of the Pleiades, daughters of Atlas and Pleione.

MALEA (mā lay ar): there were two Maleas: one a

headland off Lesbos and one in the Peloponnese south of Laconia.

MARS (marz): the Roman name for Ares, god of war.

MARSYAS (mar see as): a satyr who challenged Apollo to a duel on the flute, the loser to be flayed alive. Marsyas lost and was.

MECISTEUS (may kis tay us): a companion of Ajax.

MEDEA (me dee ar): a beautiful witch stemming from Colchis on the Black Sea. She helped Jason to acquire the Golden Fleece, fell in love, married him, came with him to Corinth and lived happily for ten years, until Jason announced that he was going to marry the king's daughter. The fury she wreaks is among the most devastating in all literature (vide *Euripides*).

MEDUSA (me du zar): the mortal one of the three Gorgons, whose eyes had the power of killing or turning to stone. When Perseus slew Medusa he used a mirror to see her. From the drops of blood sprang the magic horse Pegasus.

MEGAREUS (meg ari us): a son of Eurydice, wife of Creon.

MENELAUS (men e lay us): brother of Agamemnon, husband of Helen, and king of Sparta. He was one of the two sons of Atreus.

MERCURY (mer ku ree): the Roman name for Hermes.

MOIRA (moy rar): goddess of Fate, sometimes identified with Anangke, Necessity.

MOIRAI (moy rie): vide the Fates.

MOLOSSIA (mol oss ee ar): a range of mountains near Dodona in northwest Greece, famous for its dogs.

MUSES: the nine daughters of Zeus and Mnemosyne (Memory); patrons of poetry, music, and all the arts.

MYCENAE (mie see nee or ai): ancient capital of Argolis in the Peloponnese, whose massive walls were built by the Cyclops. The scene of the tragedy of the House of Atreus.

MYRMIDONS (mur mee donz): a warrior people of Thessaly who followed their king Achilles in the Trojan War.

NARCISSUS (nar si sus and nar cis us): a beautiful

youth who after Echo's death fell in love with his own
image reflected in a spring.

NAUPLIA (now plee ar): an important naval station
of the Argives. It still retains its name and is an attrac-
tive town.

NEMESIS (nēm e sis): daughter of Erebus and Night;
goddess of vengeance, visiting destruction on those who
were too fortunate and displayed hubris. She became
known as the divinity who punished the criminal.

NEOPTOLEMUS (nay op tōl e mus): in Sophocles'
play *Philoctetes* he comes off as a pleasant and responsible young man. Elsewhere he is not so nice: a son of
Achilles and as brutal as his father. He slew Priam and
hurled the infant Astyanax from the walls of Troy. He
forced Andromache (Hector's wife) to be his concubine.

NEREIDS (nēer iedz): the fifty daughters of Nereus
and Doris, who rode the waves as nymphs of the sea.

NEREUS (nēer ay us): an amiable sea god who lived
in the Aegean surrounded by his fifty daughters, one of
whom was Thetis, the mother of Achilles.

NIOBE (nie o bee): daughter of Tantalus and sister of
Pelops. She taunted Leto with having only two children
(Apollo and Artemis), whereas she had ten sons and ten
daughters. Apollo and Artemis swiftly destroyed all her
children. Zeus turned the weeping mother into a stone
on Mount Sipylus in Lydia, which even in the heat of
summer was wet with tears.

NYMPHS: lesser divinities in the form of lovely virgins
who were eternally young and invested trees (Dryads and
Hamadryads), lakes and rivers (Naiads), mountains (Ore-
ads), and seas (Nereids).

NYSA (nice ar): a mountain in Thrace where nymphs
cared for the infant Bacchus.

OCEANUS (owe see ān us): the great body of water
that encircled the world.

ODYSSEUS (od iss use): the Roman Ulysses, married
to Penelope, father of Telemachus (tel ēm a kus), king
of the tiny island of Ithaca. To which it took him ten
years of wandering to get back to (hence the word "odyssey." He was the cleverest, most resourceful and most
unscrupulous of the Greek heroes at Troy.

OECHALIA (ee kar lee ar): a country and town of the Peloponnese.

OLYMPIA (o lim pee ar): a constellation of temples, workshops, gymnasiums, and stadia in northwestern Peloponnese where the Olympic games originated in 776 B.C. One of the wonders of the world there was the giant statue of Zeus fashioned in gold and ivory by Phidias, the most celebrated sculptor of the ancient world. The statue came into the possession of a Christian in the fifth century but it was destroyed by fire. The features of Zeus are thought by many to have been the model for the face of Christ as seen in early mosaics.

OLYMPUS (ol im pus): the highest mountain in Greece, located in Macedonia. It was the legendary home of the gods and goddesses.

ORESTES (or est ees): son of Agamemnon and Clytemnestra, brother of Electra. After murdering his mother, he was pursued by the Furies (that is, he went mad but was cured after visiting Apollo's shrine at Delphi and being acquitted by a court in Athens). He then succeeded to the throne of Argos.

ORPHEUS (or fuse, or fay use): son of Apollo and Calliope; master of the lyre. When Orpheus played all nature was spellbound: mountains moved, rivers strayed from their course, trees listened, animals followed. When his wife, Eurydice, was bitten by a snake and died, he went down to Hades and so charmed Pluto with his playing that he was allowed to lead her back to the light provided he did not look back. He could not resist looking back to see if she was following, so he lost her.

OSSA (oss ar): a high mountain in Thessaly where the centaurs lived.

PAEAN (pee an): Apollo and Aesculapius as gods of healing. Also, hymn of triumph addressed to Apollo.

PALLAS: surname for Athena.

PAN: son of Hermes and Drýope. The god of shepherds and flocks, living in the woods and fields of Arcadia. He sported two small horns, pointed ears, and a flat nose. He was a goat from the waist down: a mischievous randy creature who was constantly pursuing nymphs. He invented the panpipe (vide Elizabeth Barrett Browning's famous poem). In remote and desolate places, or just before a battle, he could instill sudden fear—which we call "panic."

PANDION (pān di on): king of Athens and father of Philomela and Procne. He reigned forty years and died of grief when his daughters were turned into swallows.

PARIS: also called Alexander; son of Priam and Hecuba. Though royal, he was brought up as a shepherd on Mount Ida, where he judged Aphrodite the fairest of the three goddesses—Aphrodite, Hera, and Athena. Aphrodite rewarded him by giving him Helen, who, though married, was dazzled by his Trojan good looks.

PARNASSUS (par nāss us): a mountain overlooking Delphi, sacred to the Muses, Apollo, and Dionysus.

PEGASUS (pēg a sus): the winged horse that sprang from the blood of Medusa when Perseus cut off her head. He became the symbol of poetic inspiration.

PEITHO (pīe tho): daughter of Hermes and Aphrodite; goddess of persuasion.

PELEUS (pēel use or peel' i us): an Argonaut and the father, by Thetis, of Achilles. It was at his wedding to Thetis that Eris (Discord) tossed the golden apple, saying: "For the fairest." Peleus lived to a great age.

PELOPONNESE (pel op on ēese), also PELOPONNESUS: the southern peninsula of Greece, connected with Hellas by the isthmus of Corinth. It contained the powerful city-states of Sparta and Argos.

PELOPS (pēe lopz): son of Tantalus, husband of Hippodamia, father of Atreus and Thyestes, grandfather of Agamemnon and Menelaus, he came to Elis bringing with him such riches that the whole peninsula was named after him.

PENTHEUS (pēn thay us or pen'thus): the subject of Euripides' masterpiece *The Bacchae*. Pentheus, the young king of Thebes, refused to acknowledge the divinity of Dionysus and was torn to pieces on Mount Cithaeron by his mother and two aunts, who, in their Bacchic frenzy, took him for a young lion.

PERGAMUM (pēr gam um): the citadel of Troy, also Troy itself.

PERITHEUS (peri thāy us): a hero in Attic history

who gave his name to a deme (one of the hundred townships into which Attica was divided).

PERSEPHONE (per sēf o nay): the Roman Proserpina (pros ēr pee nar, also pros er pēe nar), daughter of Zeus and Demeter, wife of Pluto, and queen of the underworld. Pluto abducted her while she was picking flowers in the meadows of Enna in Sicily.

PERSEUS (pērz use or pērz ay us): son of Zeus and Danäe, ruler of Argos and Tiryns. He cut off the head of Medusa and also rescued Andromeda from a monster, married her and was faithful—a rare occurrence in Greek mythology.

PHAEDRA (fēe dra or fay dra): wife of Theseus. She fell in love with her stepson Hippolytus. Vide Euripides' play *Hippolytus*.

PHAROS (fār os): a small island in the bay of Alexandria. Its lighthouse was one of the Seven Wonders of the World.

PHARSALUS (far sāy lus): a town in Thessaly, scene of one of the great battles of history when Caesar defeated Pompey in 48 B.C.

PHASIS (fār zis): a river in Asia Minor. A region from which the pheasant is said to come.

PHILOCTETES (fil ok tēe tees): a Greek warrior who possessed the bow that could not miss, made for him by Hephaestus. On the voyage to Troy with the Greek army Philoctetes was bitten by a snake on the island of Tenedos. The wound on his heel became gangrenous and his fellow soldiers, unable to stand the stench and his cries of pain, put him off—complete with bow and arrows—on a deserted island. Ten years later, in the tenth and stalemate year of the siege of Troy, the Greeks learned from a prophecy that they would never take Troy without Philoctetes and his bow. So they came back to the deserted island to get him and found what we would call a bitter and recalcitrant Robinson Crusoe. Sophocles turned the story into one of his most touching and beautiful plays.

PHINEUS (fīn ee us): a king of Thrace who blinded his sons for alleged treachery. The gods punished him in turn with blindness and sent the Harpies to pollute his food.

PHOCIS (fō sis): a region in central Greece in which Mount Parnassus was located and the oracle of Delphi.

PHOEBE (fēe bee): the name for Artemis as moon goddess.

PHOEBUS (fēe bus): meaning pure, bright, radiant— an epithet of Apollo.

PHRYGIA (frīg ee ar): a region in Asia Minor noted for its civilization. Its most famous town was Troy in Lydia. Its last king, Croesus ("as rich as Croesus"), was defeated by the Persians in 548 B.C. He was a patron of Aesop.

PLEIADES (plīe a deez): the seven daughters of Atlas. After their death they were placed in the heavens as constellations. But only six are visible . . . (the lost Pleiad).

PLUTO (plōo to): vide Hades.

POLYPHEMUS (polly' fēe mus): a one-eyed giant, son of Poseidon and chief of the Cyclops. He lived in a cave near Mount Etna in Sicily. Vide Euripides' play *The Cyclops*.

POLYXENA (pol īk sen ar): a daughter of Priam and Hecuba, who at the fall of Troy sacrificed herself on the tomb of Achilles.

POSEIDON (poss ēi don): the Roman Neptune: brother of Zeus and Hades, one of the twelve Olympians and god of the sea. He rode his chariot over the waves and lived in a palace deep in the ocean. He created the horse and supported the Trojans in the Trojan War.

PRIAM (prīe am): the last king of Troy and the husband of Hecuba, by whom he had fifty sons and twelve daughters, besides at least another forty-two offspring by concubines. He made Troy the richest and most beautiful city of the ancient world.

PROMETHEUS (prom ēeth i us): a god who stole fire from heaven and taught mortals its many uses. Zeus was perturbed and chained him to a rock in the Caucasus mountains where an eagle (or vulture) came every night to feed on his liver, which Zeus healed so that the eagle could begin again. Heracles eventually freed him.

Vide Aeschylus' play *Prometheus Bound* (beautifully translated by Elizabeth Barrett Browning) and Shelley's *Prometheus Unbound.*

PROTEUS (pro tēe us): a sea deity to whom Poseidon gave the gift of prophecy and also the power to assume different shapes (hence the adjective "protean").

PYLADES (pīe lad ees): cousin and bosom pal of Orestes, whom he assisted in murdering Clytemnestra and Aegisthus. He married Electra, Orestes' sister.

PYTHIA (pīth ee ar): the priestess of Apollo at Delphi. She sat at a tripod at the center of "the earth's naval," inhaling the intoxicating vapors that rose from the ground, and when in a trance delivered the answers of Apollo. These were often deceptively clever, as when a certain king asked if he should go to war and got the encouraging answer "You will destroy a great kingdom." Alas, it was his ówn! The oracle could be consulted only one month in the year, and rich presents were required for Apollo.

PYTHO (pīe tho): the ancient name for Delphi because of the python Apollo killed there.

RHADAMANTHUS (rad a mān thus): a son of Zeus and one of the three judges in Hades.

RHEA (rēe ar): mother of Zeus, Poseidon, Hades, Hera, Demeter, Hestia. "Mother of the gods," who was worshiped (often orgiastically) all over Greece. Identified with the Roman goddess Ops and the Phrygian goddess Cýbele.

SALAMIS (sāl a mis): an island three miles off the coast of Attica, where the Athenians scored a great naval victory over the Persians on October 20, 480 B.C. Xerxes, king of Persia, observed the battle from a hill and, seeing one of his allies—the Greek queen Eunice— ram a ship that was in her way, exclaimed: "See how my women have turned into men." She was in fact being pursued and rammed one of her own ships.

SARDIS (sār dis): a sophisticated city of Asia Minor that contained the palace and treasury of the Lydian kings. It is probable that Sappho went shopping there from the island of Lesbos.

SARONIC SEA (sar $\overline{\text{on}}$ ik): the Aegean Sea lying south of Attica and north of the Peloponnese.

SCAMANDER (ska $\overline{\text{man}}$ der): a river near Troy stemming from Mount Ida. Its waters gave a golden tint to human hair. Aphrodite, Hera, and Athena bathed in it before the Judgment of Paris.

SCYROS (sk$\overline{\text{ee}}$r ros): an island in the Aegean where Achilles was hidden by his mother to avoid fighting in the Trojan War. The Great War poet Rupert Brooke is bured there. "The handsomest man in England" (Lytton Strachey).

SCYTHIA (sith ee ar): an enormous tract of land reaching into Siberia. Its inhabitants were divided into several nations, nomadic and warlike. They despised money, inured themselves to hunger and fatigue, lived largely on milk and clothed themselves in the skins of cattle.

SEMELE (s$\overline{\text{em}}$ e lee): daughter of Cadmus and Harmonia. Zeus, tricked by Hera to appear in all his glory, ravished her in a bolt of lightning. The child she conceived was Dionysus, whom Zeus saved and reared in his thigh. Later, Dionysus carried her from the underworld to Olympus and she became immortal.

SILENUS (sie l$\overline{\text{ee}}$ nus): the oldest and wisest of the satyrs. With Chiron the centaur he was a tutor of Bacchus. He is depicted sometimes with the ears and legs of a goat and sometimes with the ears and legs of a horse. The Roman conception of him was of a drunken, rollicking old man crowned with flowers and riding a donkey.

SIMOIS (sim $\overline{\text{o}}$ is): a river rising in Mt. Ida and running through the battleground of Troy.

SIPYLUS (s$\overline{\text{ip}}$ i lus): see Niobe.

SISYPHUS (s$\overline{\text{izi}}$ fus): king and founder of Corinth. "The craftiest of man" (Homer) with a litany of crimes, for which he was punished in Hades by having to roll a boulder to the top of a hill and when it rolled down, to roll it up again.

SPARTA (sp$\overline{\text{ar}}$ tar): a country in the Peloponnese sometimes called Laconia. It was a military state and the age-old enemy of Athens.

SPHINX (sfinx): from the Greek "sphigo," to squeeze or throttle, hence the Strangle. The Sphinx was a monster with a lion's body and the head and breasts of a woman. She took up her station on a rock outside Thebes and strangled those who could not answer her riddle. When Oedipus solved her riddle she flung herself from her rock.

STROPHIUS (strō fee us): king of Phocis and father of Pylades.

STYX (stiks): one of the five rivers of the underworld. It flowed round Hades nine times. Charon ferried the souls of the dead across it. To swear by the Styx was the most solemn of oaths.

SYMPLEGADES (sim pleg ār dees): the Clashing Rocks through which ships had to pass to enter the Black Sea. The Argonauts managed it with the help of Phineus.

TALTHYBIUS (tal thĭb i us): the chief herald of Agamemnon, with always something horrendous to announce hate it though he might.

TANTALUS (tăn tal us): father of Pelops and Niobe, hence ancestor of the doomed house of Atreus. One of the worst of his several crimes was to kill his son Pelops and dish him up to the gods for dinner. He was punished by having to stand in water up to his chin. Food and water would come just within reach and then recede. From which we get the word "tantalize."

TARTARUS (tār tar us): the lowest region of Hades, where the most wicked went. A place as far below Hades as heaven is above the earth.

TECMESSA (tek mĕss ar): a captive Trojan princess whom Ajax married and who was deeply in love with him.

TELAMON (tēl a mon): the father of Ajax and Teucer, and swiftest runner in the Greek army.

THEBES (theebz): the capital of Boeotia, founded by Cadmus (see Amphion).

THEMIS (thĕm is): daughter of Uranus and Gaea; mother of the four seasons and the three Fates. She possessed the power of prophecy and was the first goddess to whom temples were built. As a mother-goddess, she

had a temple at Delphi that preceded the temple of
Apollo. She was the patroness of justice.

THESEUS (thee zi us): an early king of Athens and
father of Hippolytus.

THESSALY (thes a li): the largest province of Greece
until the expansion of Macedonia under Philip II (father
of Alexander the Great). Thrace, Macedonia, and Thessaly take in most of northern Greece. Mount Olympus
and Mount Ossa are both in Thessaly, which was the
home of the Lapiths and the Centaurs. It was from Thessaly that the Argonauts sailed. Its inhabitants were noted
for magic and horse breeding.

THETIS (thee tis): a sea goddess, wife of Peleus and
mother of Achilles. It was at her wedding that Eris threw
the golden apple "for the fairest," which led to the Trojan War. She rendered her son invulnerable by plunging
him into the waters of the Styx—all but the heel by
which she held him, and that was where Paris landed his
lethal arrow.

THORICUS (thor i kus): a hero in Attic history who
gave his name to one of the demes into which Attica
was divided.

THRACE (thr ai ss): an expansive region north of
the Aegean, now part of Turkey. The Thracians were
barbarous, bellicose, drank heavily, leched lustily, and
sacrificed their enemies to their gods. They were horse
breeders and superb riders.

THYESTES (thy es teez): brother of Atreus, father
of Aegisthus by his own daughter Pelopia. He seduced
his brother's wife, Aerope, and Atreus punished him by
tricking him into eating his own children. Thyestes as-
cended the throne of Mycenae, only to be dethroned by
his nephews Agamemnon and Menelaus.

THYRSUS (ther sus): a staff tipped with a pine cone
and wreathed with ivy or vine leaves. The symbol of
Dionysus.

TIRESIAS (tie ree si as): the most venerable of the
ancient seers. He was blind, twice changed his sex, and
lived to a great age.

TIRYNS (tir inz): nine miles from Mycenae, rising out
of the plain of Argolis. Its walls, twenty-five feet thick,

are said to have been put together by the Cyclops. The site of the murder of Agamemnon by Clytemnestra. Schliemann, excavating between 1876 and 1885, unearthed quantities of jewelry and the alleged death mask of Agamemnon.

TITANS (tīe tans): giant deities, the primordial children of Heaven and Earth, who were overthrown and succeeded by Zeus and the Olympian gods.

TITHONUS (ti thōwe nus): son of Laomedon, king of Troy. He was so beautiful that Eos (Dawn) fell in love with him and granted him immortality but forgot to give eternal youth, so he went on living as a decrepit old man. Some say that he shriveled up and turned into a grasshopper.

TRITON (trȳ ton): a gigantic sea god, son of Poseidon and Amphitrite. He was half man and half fish and had power over the sea.

URANUS (yu rār nus or yu raē nus): the sky and the heavens, one of the most ancient of the gods.

ZEPHIR (zēf eer): the west wind, whose sweet breath produced flowers and fruits. In his temple at Athens he was represented as a young man with wings on his shoulders and his head crowned with flowers.

ZEUS (zuce): son of Cronos and Rhea (Saturn and Ops), the Roman Jupiter or Jove. Lord of heaven and father of the gods. While still a child he vanquished the old order of gods, the Titans. Married to Hera but with uncountable love affairs, he spawned a host of offspring out of wedlock. He could change himself into many forms to gratify his passions: a shower of gold for Danäe, a swan for Leda, a white bull for Europa. His weapon was the thunderbolt, which at the slightest provocation he hurled.

Classics from
Ancient Greece

THE ILIAD
BY HOMER trans. W.H.D. Rouse
This very readable prose translation tells the tale of
Achilles, Hector, Agamemnon, Paris, Helen, and all Troy
besieged by the mighty Greeks. It is a tale of glory and
honor, of pride and pettiness, of friendship and sacrifice,
of anger and revenge. In short, it is the quintessential
western tale of men at war.

THE ODYSSEY
BY HOMER trans. W.H.D. Rouse
Kept away from his home and family for 20 years by war
and malevolent gods, Odysseus returns to find his house
in disarray. This is the story of his adventurous travels and
his battle to reclaim what is rightfully his.

THE AENEID
BY VIRGIL trans. Patric Dickinson
After the destruction of Troy by the Greeks, Aeneas leads
the Trojans to Italy where, according to Virgil, he
re-founds the city of Rome and begins a dynasty to last
1,000 years. This, Virgil's greatest triumph, was seen by
many Medieval thinkers as linking Rome's ancient past to
its Christian future.

**Available wherever books are sold or at
signetclassics.com**